Bridge of the Brocade Sash

Sacheverell Sitwell

The Bridge of the Brocade Sash

TRAVELS AND OBSERVATIONS IN JAPAN

CLEVELAND AND NEW YORK

THE WORLD PUBLISHING COMPANY

Published by TheWorld Publishing Company

2231 West 110th Street, Cleveland 2, Ohio

Library of Congress Catalog Card Number: 59-15323

FIRST EDITION

CONTENTS

ILLUSTRATIONS

COLOUR PLATES

ACKNOWLEDGMENTS

My thanks are due to Lady Alexandra Metcalfe for kind permission to reproduce photographs 9, 25, 28, 29, 32, 33 and 36; to the British Museum for numbers 1, 2, 3 and 5; to the Japan Tourist Association and the Japanese Embassy in London for numbers 22, 23, 24, 31, 35, 41, 42, 43, 44 and 46; and to the Sakamoto Photo Research Laboratory, 164 Azabu-Hommura-Cho, Minato-Ku, Tokyo, for the four colour photographs and for numbers 7, 8, 10, 11, 12, 13, 14, 15, 16, 17, 18, 19, 21, 26, 27, 30, 34, 37, 38, 39, 40, 45, 47, 48, 49 and 50.

TO
BRYHER
WITH MY LOVE
AND THANKS

INTRODUCTION

THE WRITER attempting to set down his impressions of Japan has always the feeling that over his shoulder there is someone reading what he is writing and telling him how much more beautiful and interesting China is than Japan. This could be the truth though it is difficult to believe it, but had one listened too intently one would never have got there. And having been there one can but try one's best at the subject that is in hand. I can only say for myself that I found Japan as interesting and beautiful as Italy or Spain.

What is more to the point is how rapidly Japan is changing, let us hope for the better of its teeming population. That much is being lost in the process is undeniable. All the more reason therefore for going to Japan before it is too late. For the sake of the old, though in the end it is possible that the new Japan may be not less sensational. So long as the curse of militarism does not descend once more upon them and drag them down. For that is a constant danger, with the alternative of communism. But between these two extremes, and inclining to neither, there is the hope of bringing their unique national qualities to bear fruit once more.

Of these, the most permanent are their works of art, the viewing of which was my primary object in going to Japan. And it is with this purpose in mind that so much space is devoted in this book to a description of Kyoto, a city that seemed little less beautiful than Rome or Venice. Four weeks were spent there, and we enjoyed every moment of the time. The chapters on painting and on the applied arts should perhaps be prefaced with a word of apology to the expert, and of sympathy to the general reader who may feel lost in the maze of unfamiliar names. But his plight would be worse still if left in entire ignorance of what much of this book is about. For every ten persons familiar with Hokusai and Hiroshige there may not be one individual knowing anything of Sesshû or Sôtatsu. Hence these chapters, with a further apology for the writing of a book of match-box labels as though (which is the truth) they are minor works of art. But they instance the exquisite taste and flair of the Japanese in little objects that are for daily use. Yet a further liberty taken with the reader is the reprinting of a description of a famous garden at Kyoto written by the writer before he had been there in person. The garden in question is Ryûanji, one of the most original if not *the* most original of all works of art in Japan, but I repeat my earlier account, having made a later attempt at it, and failed.

We went to Japan by the shortest possible route via the Pole for reasons of economy chiefly, and missing thereby the more usual experience of a few days in Bangkok and a visit to Angkor. But there was another and more personal reason, that my brother had been there before me, and written a description of it which I know I could not better in his book, *Escape With Me*. This at least softened an omission which I shall always feel. For two of the wonders of the Far Orient must be Angkor and the old Peking. Perhaps—and let me hope— Kyoto is the third of them, and my account of it some indication of the wonders it contains. In respect to other places it is unfortunately only too true that it is impossible to see everything. Probably the greatest lacuna in this book is an account of the holy mountain of Koyosan. But at least we saw Kyoto the more thoroughly and left few of its temples and gardens unexplored. There is a little monotony though in the constant illustrating of these same themes and it is for this reason that there are in place of them many pictures of Kimonos and pieces of lacquer or pottery. These are certainly less familiar, and may be found more interesting by the reader. There was an almost entire absence of flowers during our visit owing to the time of year. This may even have been an advantage for one saw the bare bones, as it were, of temples and gardens without their spring or autumn colouring. And not flowers only, but the fruit as well. Even the strawberries, grown in particular districts on the 'stone-wall' terrace system, and fruiting miraculously for eight months of the year, and even in mid-winter, were missing.

On the way home it was possible to spend a few days in Hawaii, and have some little visual experience of a Polynesian island, however strong the tourist infiltration. For all the hundreds and thousands who have been there, it still leaves beautiful impressions on the memory. Not least, of a long line of tents or booths as one leaves the airport and drives into the town. For each has its tenant, in form of a largely built Gaugainesque female stringing together the wreathes or *leis* of flowers. The loose gowns (*mu-mus*) worn by them are of the Tahiti, Marquesas tradition. And who could ever forget the hills and feathery palms of

Hawaii? the tropical trees, and above all the flowers? And, in particular the white ginger or *pikaki* which scents the whole air, and is even the abiding memory of Honolulu.

But all such memories and impressions would have been impossible of attainment were it not for the help and encouragement of the friend to whom this book is dedicated. The project only became material and realizable thanks to this same friend. To my cousins Isla and Jessica Sitwell I am indebted for everything that made our stay in Japan easy and pleasant. Our home was in their house in Tokyo, and neither my wife nor I can ever forget our stay with them on so many torrid days of heat and through the rigours of a bad typhoon. It was pleasant indeed to live in a Japanese household presided over by their majordomo, Okamura-san. While still in England, planning the journey, I must thank Frank Ashton-Gwatkin who lived long in Japan, for encouragement and advice given, and Soame Jenyns of the British Museum for letters of introduction. John Gunther, also, the famous author; and Faubian Bowers whom we met through him, and who is a foremost authority on the wonderful *Kabuki* theatre of Tokyo. I would also thank Miss Ena Molesworth of International Services Limited, 7 Haymarket, for arranging all the details of this journey round the world in order to visit Japaan. In Japan, itself, Colonel Figgis the military attaché to the British Embassy was an invaluable friend who obtained permission for us to hear the marvellous, ancient *Gagaku* music in the Imperial Palace, and sent us with a personal letter to the priest in charge in order to see Tôhaku's paintings in a temple at Kyoto, probably the most beautiful works of art in that city. I must express my thanks, also, to Mr Weatherby of the Charles E. Tuttle publishing company of Tokyo who are responsible for so many books on the art of Japan. I have made full use of their publications, and I hope given due acknowledgement in these pages. Among Japanese friends I would thank Mr F. Sewaki of the Showa Oil Company who took us to see the Sumô wrestling, and whose companionship we enjoyed on more than one pleasant evening. I would also like to thank Mr S. Inouye of the Showa Oil Company for sending me the pattern book of match-box labels about which I have written in chapter eleven of this book. Mr Ueno rendered us valuable services, and we spent a delightful day with him, his father and mother, and family, in their home at Kamakura. And I would thank our friend Mr F. Urata, who lives in Kyoto, for hospitality in his family home.

Among the worst problems bedevilling the writer on Japan is the question of accents. Is there, or is there not to be an accent on Kyôto? And if so, what form of accent? Kyôto, or Kyōto? After all there are accents on Compiègne, Sèvres, Armentières, Liège. Eventually, for aesthetic reasons, I determined on the circumflex, thus, Kyôto, though deciding to leave it out on names of better known towns, but follow in other matters the precedent of the excellent *Official Guide*, published by the Japan Travel Bureau, so that the accent appears in proper names, e.g. Sôtatsu, or in Sûmo. It is only unfortunate that Japan is now outside the orbit of the ordinary traveller, except from the Pacific coast of the United States. You can fly to Japan over the Pole in a matter of hours, but where expense is concerned it is now as remote as in the reign of Queen Elizabeth I. This is all the sadder because in the last year or two there has been an extraordinary revival of interest in the arts of Japan, and in all things Japanese, as witness the spate of books upon these topics. Not, I think, that the works of art export particularly well. Almost every exhibition of Japanese art is disappointing. It has to be seen *in situ* in its original setting. A personal visit is essential, and it is just this that is rapidly becoming near to impossible.

By good fortune, or directly due to American initiative, Kyoto came through the war undamaged, while nearly every other Japanese city was partially destroyed. There must be more old buildings and works of art in this one city than anywhere in the Orient, or for the matter of that in all of Asia. This gives to it a unique and increasing importance as one of the art cities of the world. The writer of these pages will always remember the happy weeks he spent there; and would in this penultimate sentence thank his wife who went with him everywhere in that tremendous, but energizing heat, and not least by her presence enabled him to emerge from the first person singular in his narrative, and at times write 'we' instead of 'I'. Finally, as often before, she has helped him read his proofs.

24th August, 1959   Sacheverell Sitwell

Chapter One

NIGHT FLIGHT
TO TOKYO

PERHAPS THERE IS NO LUXURY like falling safely and comfortably asleep in bed after the longest journey one has ever made in one's life. It belongs to the category of those other reliefs or relaxations that are a clue in themselves to human temperament and could even form two strains or divisions in the human race. The alternatives to choose between being simple enough; would one sooner come in out of the cold to be given a cup of hot soup or other warming draught, or be brought a long and cooling drink coming out of intense and tropical heat into the shade? In this wholly personal and private quandary and dichotomy my own inclination being always towards the latter, but there is no time to decide for in a moment one has fallen asleep in a blissful vacuity partaking of them both to awaken again some hours later, truly and literally, at the other side of the world.

The first sound as one opens one's eyes wondering where one can be, being the 'bleep-bleep' of some unknown insect and the call of an unknown bird, sounds never to be forgotten as first intimations of a new and strange land made audible in this moment from the garden, it being late in the evening but still light, and time to get up for dinner with our, as yet, little known cousins and hosts for it is in their house that we are staying. And soon after dinner back to bed again keeping the full pleasure of the second awakening till tomorrow morning for in fact one is entirely exhausted, if more spiritually and mentally than physically, after transit which still seems a near miracle over the North Pole to Japan.

How ominous, but without anything untoward happening, those few hours of waiting in the airport at Copenhagen 'between planes'! The apprehension of embarking for the 'big-hop' from Denmark to Alaska, of that irrevocable moment when one climbs the steps into the body of the dragon-fly and there is nothing more that one can do having surrendered all initiative. 'Dragon-fly' we call it although it cannot hover and has fixed wings, but an aeroplane is not bird-like, and all night there is the gleam or promise of flame from it as it flies above the snows. It is this that makes a journey by air a little nerve wracking although statistics prove that it is four times safer than travelling by road. And we board it and take off easily as a rocket into the skies, being served late dinner shortly after that by a blonde hostess jauntily wearing a sub-species of cocked hat, a gesture that instils confidence and may have been conceived specially for the purpose. Beds are pulled down, I try to read alternately from *Lavengro* and *The Romany Rye*, the only books in my hand-luggage, and at last drop off into a doze by which time we must be over Northern Sweden or even Spitzbergen which is, unexpectedly, the quickest route from Denmark, instead of heading straight off over the North Sea. We were told that being August most of the flight would be by daylight, and after a mere two or three hours of lying half-asleep listening to the engines, having still a reader of Jules Verne in me I am below, stationed at the porthole looking out over the wastes of ice and snow. Looking back on my childhood, I could never forgive myself if I had not been on duty. Orange juice, seeming like a draught from the tropics, and then breakfast appear around five a.m. by European time, and after that the hours mean little or nothing to one. There are black and forbidding mountains of no great height, and a while later we are over the middle of Northern Greenland if, in fact, it is land at all and not, as some geographers argue, almost solid ice some thousands of feet thick.

It is announced that we are crossing about two hundred miles south of the Pole. We must be beyond Greenland and over the Arctic for there are horrible black crevices in the ice, and I open a folder which has a map in it and wonder how far we can be from Thule, most northern of all old settlements in Greenland, where the tribe of four hundred Eskimos, when discovered, thought they were the only human beings in the world, and where there is now an enormous American airbase. The captain comes round and tells us we are never more than two hours flight from help, pointing to the new air stations and listening posts, or whatever we like to call them, marked on the map in scattered places along the desolate shores. Floating bases, also, one or two of them, upon the ice and nearer and nearer to the Russians, and in a haze of luncheons and dinners not knowing which is what, the talk turns to

Shower on the Shin-Yanagi Bridge, from
Views along the Banks of the Sumida River
by Hokusai (1806)

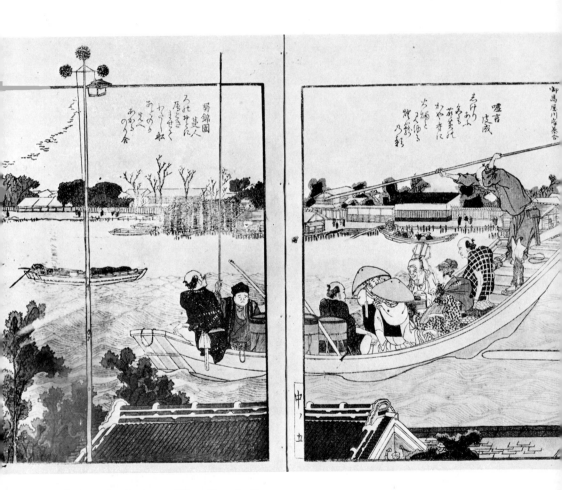

The Hanging Lantern of Kaya Temple, from
Views along the Banks of the Sumida River
by Hokusai (1806)

Anchorage which we are now approaching at some three hundred and thirty miles an hour. Friendly and hospitable are its inhabitants, he assures us, now high above the clouds though over land again, but beyond all personal contact with the known world, and at about one or two o'clock in the morning by whatever time or other we come down at Anchorage as the sun is setting.

. We go through immigration formalities which happily are not the same thing at all as emigration, and settle down for an hour or two in a waiting room at what is most decidedly an early hour of the morning. A Japanese air hostess appears out of nowhere to remind us where we are going; we drink cups of coffee, write postcards and read, desultorily, in a sort of bulletin of this week in Anchorage and other towns on the Alaskan seaboard; advertisements for roadhouses serving 'cheese-burgers' and hot dogs, and 'success stories' recounting how a young woman arrived with no capital at all and was soon owner of ten or a dozen 'piggy-wiggy' stores in this promised land. Dance halls, too, with five or seven piece bands, side by side with 'movie' advertisements and church news, views of the township which in fact looked attractive with its wooden houses and wide streets, stories of sports and fishing, and panoramas of the mountains.

Now, after only an hour or two of twilight, dawn is breaking and we are called on board again into the same seats on the identical aeroplane, but with a new crew, which includes the hostess from Nippon. We climb on a wide curve into that Arctic sky and look down on Anchorage, the only sign of human life we have seen since leaving Copenhagen. The street lights are all burning, but the population sleeping between their bouts of midnight sun. How huge and empty that sky! I remembered being told in Canada by a Gaelic-speaking writer from Nova Scotia of the skies he had seen along the Mackenzie river, and of the sudden flash and finger of light at dawn, an effect which he compared to an apocalyptic vision by El Greco. How fantastic the distance we had come! Even thus far, and no further. What months, or even years of planning must have gone into the preparation of this Polar Route! Exploratory flights were made and special meteorological stations set up to report upon the weather. It must be true that the best flying weather in the world is over the Polar regions just as the best fish come from the chill waters of the Northern seas.

It was difficult to understand just where we had come. How many

B

hundreds of miles had we been from the mouth of the Mackenzie, which is the biggest river after the Amazon in the whole of the American continent? My Nova Scotian acquaintance had told me of the great forests, the birds and wild flowers. Up there the Northern limit of the wooded country, the 'tree line' as he called it, came much nearer to the Arctic Ocean than in Alaska. Its mineral riches were untouched and inexhaustible. One day it could be as rich as Texas. By which time we are thousands of feet in the air, flying over miles of swamp and morass and with a splendid view of Mount McKinley, a giant of a mountain almost of Himalayan scale, over twenty thousand feet high, and in reality inland from Anchorage which lies at the head of a huge inlet, but appearing by some freak of aerial vision to be on an island of its own, a mountain in the sea and nothing else, but of vast bulk and looming up for some moments more, even at the tremendous speed at which we are travelling away from it towards the Aleutians.

Nothing else were we to see that morning, except clouds and occasional stretches of grey sea. Not a sight of Kodiak Island where live the biggest bears in the world, nor of that other Aleutian island—is it Kiska?—where the finest and most finished baskets are made. But, in fact, what time of day is it? Because we are nearing the International Date Line when today becomes the day after tomorrow, and already it is difficult to know whether this is the morning or the afternoon. The first lap from Copenhagen to Anchorage had been of eighteen hours, and now we are to have a further flight of twelve hours to Tokyo. We had left Anchorage at about two or three in the morning which should mean that we reach Japan at about that time in the afternoon. But of which day? Not today, at any rate, nor tomorrow, for we lose one day entirely. It vanishes as we cross the date line. 'Sunday' is written on one side of that on the map and 'Monday' on the other. And it becomes more puzzling still as we are served no fewer than four luncheons at intervals of two or three hours between each, the first of them soon after dawn, say, at four or five o'clock in the morning, and yet we are to arrive at Tokyo at about half-past ten in the morning Japanese time. In fact, I seem to remember the sun setting and rising again but cannot vouch for it for by now one is nicely conditioned, what with want of sleep, the complete abrogation and alteration of one's normal meal times, and one thing and another, not forgetting the unusual quantities of food and drink with no exercise whatever, and the simultaneous inflation and dehydration of one's whole physical and nervous system.

We are moving at enormous speed, catching up with that fragment of a day which began at Anchorage, and so far as one's by now addled intelligence can comprehend, starting on another. And after the last of that series of luncheons which surely should have been late in the afternoon, it is announced on the loudspeaker that it is now half-past nine in the morning and that we are approaching Japan. Someone says Japanese fishing boats are in sight, and sure enough a few inconspicuous black specks are to be observed thousands of feet below, and the Pacific Ocean seen for the first time in one's life has a wash of blue on it and the promise of fine weather. In about half an hour after that we lose height and come down lower, and land is to be seen from the right-hand porthole where we are sitting. We cross a strait of sea which should divide the Northern island of Japan, the Hokkaidô, from the mainland, but something is wrong there and I do not understand it for in no more time than it would take to fly a hundred and fifty miles (a half-hour) we are nearing the end of our journey, but it is more than twice that distance upon the map. I can only think that my overtired senses were playing tricks upon me, and indeed anything would have been possible at this stage.

The earth below begins to look entirely and unmistakably Japanese. It is very hilly and wooded with the peculiar feature one will get to know so well that even the tops of the hills have tall and dense trees growing upon them. Not bare hills, but hills thickly covered, or if they are low hills, terraced for cultivation. Hills that have almost the look of pincushions from the aeroplane, they are so dense with trees. Later, when one has seen more of Japan, they become prototypes for the tea-gardens with their little green rows of mounds. Is it in anticipation, that the Japanese waves seem to have their own way of curling in foam against the shores? We come down lower still and see long rows of houses, and motor-cars creeping along slowly as bumble bees upon the grass. Then, out in a wide sweep to sea again, having flown over what is obviously a peninsula, and preparing now to land. We come straight in, nearly touching the water, on to some green flats which are the airfield, and are in Japan. Out of fatigue and excitement I develop an excruciating pain and a limp in my right ankle at the very moment we step down the gangway into this new world, and down the long passages to the customs where someone has come to meet us, and up the steps to where our cousins are waiting for us, by which time it is gone entirely and forgotten, and we are in a large motor and on the road from Yokohama to the house where we are to stay.

After so long a journey one only wants to sleep, however wide awake one may feel. But one is half-asleep, none the less, and will scarcely remember unpacking shirts and handkerchiefs, or ties. More wide awake than ever as one's head touches the pillow and one falls asleep. Making little or no sense after that first awakening, as the August evening darkens and we go in to dinner from the garden. Only able to remember that we had quails to eat; quails which in some mysterious process had collided together in pairs in a way one wondered did not happen more often with aeroplanes in mid-air. The whole ground floor of the house, or at least that front of it which looked onto the garden, consisting of one very large room which formed itself up a couple of steps into dining-room, down those same steps into drawing-room, and along further into a pair of smaller rooms, with beyond that a double bedroom and sitting-room. In this latter the sliding partitions are of Japanese inspiration, and the drawers which fit so exquisitely are of native execution. In fact, they seem unable to make drawers that do not open and shut beautifully. It is the first sign on their own ground of their taste and talent. But there is little more one can take in or notice before one is in bed and asleep again.

No doubt the impact of the Far East is sharper and more complete coming to it in this fashion. There is no stopping at Bangkok, Singapore and Hong Kong upon the way. Nothing except an hour or two in a waiting room in Alaska interposes between Denmark and Japan. For the airport at Copenhagen has nothing about it to suggest that it is a gateway to the East. It is a transference almost by force, although you have paid for it and are a willing passenger, from one side of the world to the other over the sea and ice. Two thousand four hundred miles are cut off the journey, but not a human being nor a human dwelling do you see except for that 'three o'clock in the morning' interlude at Anchorage where even the immigration and customs officials are sleepy eyed, but in reassurance of where you have come from your postcards are mailed free. Therefore I would say that the shock is greater because there is nothing to mitigate its violence. Also one cannot get used in one's mind to flying over the North Pole. We cross from coast to coast of Greenland in as many minutes perhaps as there were weeks of grinding and agonizing effort by foot and sledge for the explorers of but a few years ago. It is no more difficult now than to play the gramophone when we compare that to the involved energies, massed or solo, of a Toscanini or a Horowitz, a Beecham or a Rubinstein, who made the record. Such are mechanical short cuts, some of which we have got used to while others are still subjects for wonder and almost for awe. For myself, I know I shall never understand how it is possible for Polar flights to be maintained day and night all through the winter, and no amount of explanation that the Pole revolves more slowly than the Equator because it has less space to cover and that this is why it has the best flying weather in the higher reaches of air above the Arctic storms and snows will ever convince me that it is true. But the proof lies in the performance, and as I write this, aeroplanes belonging to three air companies fly almost every day.

The trans-Polar journey is among the wonders of our age, though becoming no more of a commonplace than it is to fly higher than the summit of Mount Everest. A voice over the loudspeaker as you are somewhere near the North Pole suggests that you sit back and relax and let the others do the work. So be it. For there is in fact absolutely nothing you can do. And you have only been over Japan for a few moments before alighting after a flight of twenty-nine hours upon that green shelf of land. The transition is entire and absolute. From Denmark to Tokyo with but one stop between. The fly we brought with us from Copenhagen, and which made a minor nuisance of itself, still crawls upon the porthole pane. The incubation period is not over. You cannot be certain yet, whether, or not, you have caught that London cold. Were there a carnation in your buttonhole it would still be fresh on landing in Japan. And yet, there is no doubt of it, by the ordinary route you are ten thousand miles from home.

So far as the ambitions of a lifetime are concerned I can only say this is a wish dream fulfilled. I had wanted to come to Japan ever since I discovered Hokusai and Hiroshige for myself when I was perhaps fourteen years old. And when I was eighteen or nineteen, surely before I was twenty, I found *Masterpieces of the School of Kôrin* in its Japanese binding in the bookshop opposite the British Museum. I have museum handbooks on Japanese prints and lacquer still by me which I have owned since I was a schoolboy, just as I still have woodcuts by Hokusai which I collected in the last year of the first world war. It was at the

time when Mr Arthur Waley was translating the *Noh* plays. I have to
admit to always being more attracted by Japan than China, and this was
in obverse direction to the current of the age. I think this was because
there were great artists in Japan as late as the time of Turner and
Constable and so it did not seem so dead and remote as China. And now
the miracle was accomplished. This was Japan.

But for the moment I found it almost impossible to believe that I was
here. Would it be a land as beautiful as Spain, or Italy, or would one
hate Tokyo at first sight and want to go no further? For there are
persons who will tell you it is all hideous, that it is nothing but night
clubs and neon signs. That there is a rash of school children wherever you
look and it is one huge slum. That the *geishas* are no less than maddening
and the cherry blossom a sad deception. That the Japanese are irritating
in manner and grinning incessantly with gold teeth. And so on. But
now it was too late to turn back. And for that matter have we not
Huddersfield or Liverpool on a foggy day to explain away? Of what
use to tell the benighted foreigner he is in Shakespeare's England, with
rail or Green Line bus connection to Windsor Great Park and the Forest
of Arden? Falstaff's oak tree might seem a long way from Hull or
Birmingham, and the Tower of London a long bus ride from the
bed-sitting room. Others had told me they liked Tokyo more than any
other capital city in the world. This, perhaps, chiefly because of the
theatre. And foreigners have said the same thing of London. Which
answer was to be true? There could be sense in both opinions.

It is probable that I fell asleep that first night thinking of how I would
like Japan to be. Having drugged myself over the years with visions of
Sesshû and Sôtatsu, her great painters; inky hills and swirling rivers,
echoes of classical China but seen with his own eyes, or bands of gold
cloud, the thatched cabin and ox-drawn palanquin. Then, too, Sharaku,
master of the actor print, has a very particular place in my affections.
Had I not taken him to Spain in my imagination and set him to draw
bull-fight posters? I was prepared in my own mind to find Japan one of
the most beautiful and exciting countries in the world. It was true we
had come to it in a season when it was not in flower; in August which is
full summer and neither spring nor autumn. But to see it thus is to
reduce it to the essentials, with no adventitious aid of blossom nor of
turning leaf. Japan in winter is another alternative which must be of
utmost fascination—in the prescribed places. It must indeed be beautiful

under snow as we know from woodcuts by Hiroshige, but I am no lover of the cold. Perhaps it was all for the best that we had come to Japan in the 'off season'. To write of it flowerless and without blossom would be to see it in black and white and not in colour, and one was the less likely to form an exaggerated picture of it in one's mind.

Of a certainty I remember waking that night and putting out my hand to make sure I was not dreaming. But no; the lamp was where I remembered it to be, in two strengths if that is the way to describe it, and I switched it on and off and off and on again, just for long enough to see the sliding walls of wood and paper and the *tatami* (straw matting) upon the floor. It was three or four o'clock in the morning with no sound but, now and again, a car rushing by as it might be in nearly every living city in the world. That was nothing different. I could think of nowhere excepting Venice where this could not be. And yet of all and every civilization there has ever been this is the most unlike in everything to which we are accustomed. With good reason it is at the other side of the world from ourselves, and also from America. Not the Aztecs, nor the Mayans, neither Montezuma, nor for that matter the Inca Atahualpa, were more different in the daily surroundings of their lives. But there were neither painters nor poets, neither architects nor great actors, in pre-Columbian America. Therefore they do not come into the same category and it is of no use to compare them. But the Japanese with their strongly imitative and yet original faculty, lying at anchor as it were off China for a thousand years from the seventh to the seventeenth century and developing their own individuality and idiosyncrasies under strong influence from China, and from the seventeenth century onward to the nineteenth living and fermenting in a self-induced vacuum cut off from the rest of the world by their xenophobia and their self-sufficient pride, had inbred themselves into a human peculiarity, if logical enough in itself, to which there is no parallel. In the day of Commodore Perry when contact was restored with the rest of the world they were living, in nearly every sense of the phrase, in a world apart.

Of all of which I had as yet but little experience, putting out the light and turning on my side. For we had seen nothing up to this moment but a stretch of Yokohama, and that in circumstances such as would obtain were one to be driven in from London airport after a couple of sleepless nights. What one saw one hardly registered. But now, at last, there was

no roar of engines. Those troubles were over and we had arrived. I only
wished that the cicada or grasshopper, or whatever animal it was, would
sing again. Because, quite certainly, it was a song. Not a frog croaking,
nor the buzzing of a fly. Most decidedly, it was singing, and one had
heard that in Japan they caught crickets for their music and kept them in
a cage. It was expressed in its song that it had something to sing about, and
what could that be? How green was the greenness, and how glorious
the sun! How much I wanted to hear it again! To reassure one that the
flight was over! That the miracle had been accomplished and we were
in Japan!

And going to sleep once more all Japan opened before me. On the
morning I left London a curious thing had happened. Walking along
Shaftesbury Avenue, outside the Palace Theatre, I had passed a Buddhist
monk with shaven head wearing a saffron robe, the only time in all my
life that I had set eyes upon one. He must, in fact, have come from Siam
or Burma, or Ceylon, because we never saw his like in Japan where the
Buddhist monks wear black robes. But it was the promise of an unknown fourth part of the world, and of feelings and sentiments new to
my experience. Of the dragon kings, one to either side, guarding the
portals of the temple. And a temple, indeed, not a church, nor mosque.
Of not angels, but *boddhisattvas*, some with butterfly wings; but, one
and all of them, demons from a fiery pantomime, in murky darkness,
or by the red light of a Bengal flare.

The monk in his saffron robe seemed to be a messenger, on that day of
all days, impelled by some influence to pass me on the street. For it is no
ordinary event, even now, to start from one edge of the world for the
other. The last time I had stretched out my legs in bed had been in
London, and now this was Tokyo. The things I most wanted to see
were within reach, and no one of them more than a few hours away. If,
as was probable in the Far Orient, access to them was difficult, so much
the more exciting. It was even an enlargement for the imagination to be
shown things, not all at once, but one at a time. How could the Louvre
have its pictures all on view from floor to ceiling? Later, when we were
taken to one of the finest collections in Japan, but obviously not upon
the scale of the Louvre, precisely five objects were brought out and
shown to us.

How wonderful to be but on the same mainland as the painted
golden screens! Of the courtiers in black lacquered hats—or were the

hats starched black gauze?—but they projected at the back as though
hardly worn on the head and in fact one wondered how they stayed on
the head at all, and they wore trousers that trailed out behind as though
the courtiers were waddling backwards on their knees. Probably the
most awkward and improbable costume ever invented, and which
reminded one, inevitably, of the Japanese bantams with 'feathered
boots'. Another breed of fowl had tails so long that a man or a child
must walk behind them holding up their tail feathers like a train. I
would try to visit these in their village on one of the islands.

And now I was starting to confuse them with the monk or *bonze* in
his saffron robe. But was it, indeed, saffron? Or was it not, more truly,
cinnamon. And I began to wonder what was cinnamon and what was
saffron, but could fix on no definite shade for either of them. How like
myself to be distracted by such trivial details when I should be falling
asleep thinking of temples and gardens, at Kyoto, of Masterpieces of the
School of . . . ? But not Kôrin, at any rate, for he was but the cheap and
popular imitation of greater painters, Kôetsu and Sôtatsu, and it was
with an effort that I remembered how to spell their names. And yet?
Yet, surely Kôrin's *Wave Screen*, at Boston, is a fine painting? And
muddling it in my mind with Hokusai's *Great Wave* which Debussy
used for a music cover, and with some memory of the roar of the
aeroplane engines over the North Pole and of that weird dawn over
Alaska with the street lights of Anchorage, like a township in a
'Western' but all its inhabitants sleeping in that green interlude between
night and morning, I must have fallen asleep, myself, to be woken only
a few moments later, so it seemed by a tap on the door, by the sunlight
streaming through that, and one after another, two, three, four, little
figures of maids, bowing and bringing in breakfast, one of them carrying the coffee pot, another the milk and sugar, another a newspaper,
and another a peach, sliced thin. Coming nearer one could see their
sleek black hair and slanting eyes. So started our first morning in Japan.

Chapter Two

————————————————————————

TOKYO

Upon that first day we did little or nothing except go for a long drive, Tokyo being so huge a city that almost every experience of its streets must have that adjective to qualify it. We had arrived on a Thursday, and spent all Friday and even Saturday in recovering from the journey. London we had left behind us on Tuesday, while Wednesday had vanished entirely on the way here. Had it never dawned; or was it simply that we were told politely to call it Thursday? Or was that a fragment of Wednesday we saw over the Aleutians and telescoped, so to speak, into Thursday?

In any event Wednesday had disappeared so far as we were concerned though back in Europe things were certainly happening that day. But something of the same process affects oneself or one's metabolism upon these headlong journeys. It is of no use to pretend one is quite normal upon arrival. There has been a jolt, if nothing more than that, to one's digestion with the reversal of all the ordinary meal times and the drugged sleep or semi-consciousness which takes the place of the night's rest. It must, it does take a day or two to return to one's full senses.

Tokyo with eight and a half million inhabitants, which is more than either London or New York, and increasing at the rate of a quarter of a million a year,[1] covers an immense area in which it is difficult at first to pick out any landmarks. Nearly all its houses are one, or at the most two-storeyed, because of the dangers of fire and earthquake, and this has caused the city to spread out to an almost unmanageable extent. It is so huge that it is out of control. Many of the streets have no names, or change their names arbitrarily half-way up or down, while the numbering of the houses is based capriciously upon when each house was built. How often does not a taxi-driver having wasted valuable time cruising round and round with vacant stare, resort to the police-box where a policeman who looks no more than ten years old will ring

[1] It is calculated that by 1980 Tokyo may have a population of fifteen to twenty million, and be thirty (?) miles across.

up the shop you are trying to find and ask for the '*chome*', ward or block or district, where it lies! Incidentally, the Japanese are never so happy as when telephoning, and a seraphic smile will come over the doll-like features of the Shintô priestess as she takes up the telephone beside her in her postcard stall, answers '*moshi moshi*' (their equivalent for 'hullo hullo') and orders you a taxi on a showery day.

It is of little use, though, to start off in a taxi for luncheon or dinner in a private house. Because the probabilities are that you will get there as the meal is finishing. Sometimes it is practicable to have a sketch map drawn, and many house owners have their own printed map to give to guests. The house we were staying in is some seven miles from the Imperial Hotel, the bizarre and dwarfish creation of Frank Lloyd Wright in yellow brick, which for foreigners and also the Japanese themselves is still the social centre and magnetic pole of Tokyo. Distances are calculated from it, and whether you want to or not you find yourself making use of its amenities and meeting there. But even the long street where the Imperial Hotel stands, and where famously it withstood the earthquake, has no name. Or, if one enquired, no answer was forthcoming.

It was many a day before one could recognize landmarks on the way into the centre of Tokyo. One could tell one was on the right road, or on the wrong road, but as for directing the next turn to take that was another matter. A stone house standing back from the road, and three storeys high which is altogether exceptional, now becomes a Chinese restaurant; or the Hollywood Beauty Parlour distempered a bright pink; or, at length, and with certainty, a flower shop at a particular street corner, at long last became charted in one's memory. But to the end of my stay in Tokyo, and all in all I was nearly a month there, I could never successfully have found my way home. Upon occasion however it can work the other way; and when we were inveigled one night into a night club and insisted upon leaving early because of the long journey home it was only after losing our way many times over in a taxi that we found the night haunt was not much more than half a mile from the house were we were staying.

In the course of a few days some of the public buildings become familiar even if one would not know in what direction to make for them until they are actually in sight. For instance, the Diet Building which looks like one of the worst architectural blunders of mid-

nineteenth century Belgium; and a truncated and incomplete version of
the Eiffel Tower, if that should be qualified as a public building. Then,
there is the Meiji Shrine, to which the same strictures apply as to the
Diet, and we add to this, in parenthesis, a remark from an old guide
book of fifty years ago to the effect that 'the numerous portraits of
modern military men are depressing specimens of the painter's art'.
But the most striking feature of the centre of Tokyo is the vast enclosure
of the Imperial Palace with its wide moat and the high bank above that,
doubly effective because it hides the tawdry and ugly palaces, or halls
and portions of palaces within. But now something characteristically
Japanese obtrudes itself which is the angle at which the pine or fir trees
have been planted on the green bank. For they lean out at all angles, and
have been specially put into the soil in order to grow in this fashion,
leaning outward and not standing upright.

This much we saw on those first days, with a call in order to write our
names at the British Embassy which stands in a compound reminiscent
of our Embassy in Tehran, though of Victorian design more in
character with some military cantonment, and less suggestive of
Hanwell or Colney Hatch and their mentally detached inmates, with
at the back beds of tropical-looking coleas of flaunting colour and
enormous size. And to this point it may be wondered where the
fascination and charm of Tokyo may lie. For not having yet seen the
main streets it is not in the public buildings. They, indeed, present the
worst face of Tokyo.

But it is the swarming population and the little shops that are the
attraction. Being the middle of August most of the male inhabitants are
in their shirtsleeves but clean white shirts are worn by one and all
excepting for the occasional, scholarly-looking individual usually
carrying an umbrella, whether wet or fine, and nearly always spectacled
—horn-rimmed spectacles are almost universal—picking his steps and
often crossing dangerously in front of the traffic. Such must be persons
of conservative tendencies but cannot all be scholars. Old men, of
course, are more likely to wear their national dress, and if only they
have white beards they become, immediately, Oriental sages. It was
just after the rush hour on that stifling evening, and to be remarked how
parents and grandparents were leading children along by the hand, or
carrying them on their shoulders, the 'rush hour' in Tokyo being a
sight really to deserve that epithet for the crowded buses with young

men and women hanging onto every available inch of them, inside and out, could be carrying refugees away in front of an invading army. Many office and factory workers have to come in, two hours, or even more than that, to work every morning, and there is something more than a little appalling in the thought of this daily struggle to get to, and away from work. It is not in the temperament of the Japanese to take a siesta, and there is nowhere for them to go. They cannot rest in their offices. There are no parks or public gardens; and for this and other reasons the day begins and ends early in Japan.

The young women are carrying their babes in 'baby-holders' on their backs, a practice which looks pretty enough but cannot be good for the child. It must be one of the contributory causes for short stature. And such women as carry their children in this manner are probably wearing the *kimono* and the *obi*, and shuffling forward in their *getas* and white socks or *tabis*, feminine matters to be mentioned in more detail when we visit a big store. The first sight of a Japanese child must be always an enchantment, more particularly at the age when they are just old enough to walk, and that evening we saw many of them toddling along with a parent or grandparent. Also, nearly every night there is a festival of some sort in one or another quarter of Tokyo—the Japanese are as fond of festas as the Andalusians or the Southern Italians—and this means you will see children going along in fancy dress. Not a sign, though, of mosque or church tower; no sound of bell, nor voice of muezzin from a minaret. It is strange in all this huge town to see no structure belonging to any religion rising above the rooftops, and as you are surrounded by and constantly in danger from motor-cars, and with every evidence of refrigerators and radio sets, you might think this to be a city of atheists. Even more in other towns, Osaka, Nagoya, Kobe, than in Tokyo. Yet the festivals are largely religious in inspiration, and looking back from the road just where a little procession is forming, and they are beating drums and blowing horns, you will catch sight of a perfect joss house, as true to tradition as an opium den, but you will be past it before there is time to look.

You will also pass shops that you may despair of ever finding again. A fan shop; or one given over entirely to a display of fascinating objects with no known purpose, paper confections based on an abstraction of stork or locust or tassel of pine boughs, always with marked miniature aeroplane affinities, but rendered in red and gold and colours upon white, and all and every one of them it would seem the hallmark of one and the same individual of genius who has passed his training and formed his style in the folding of paper boats and paper hats. What can they be for? Up to this moment there is no reason at all for us to know the answer. But there are other shops no less intriguing. The groceries or general stores, and the sweetshops; and it is now that we begin to recognize the Japanese genius for packaging, a gift which is much enhanced by the beauty of their alphabet. Who else indeed could make something beautiful of a biscuit tin; and biscuits, at that, of which the substance is dried seaweed? Which remark is made in full memory of biscuit tins of long ago in England in reproduction of nothing less than Landseer's *Monarch of the Glen*,[1] but after only a day or two in Japan one comes to realize that this race are the world's masters in the littler matters of taste and that it is genuinely possible to make something beautiful out of a match box or a biscuit tin.

In pursuit of which knowledge we went on Sunday afternoon to one of the big stores. There are four of them along the famous Ginza and it is a pleasure to write down their names; Mitsukoshi, Takashimaya, Shirokiya and Matsuya, with another called Daimaru not far away, the one we entered being perhaps the second in this string of names, but the one account will hold good for all of them. Given that there is a vicarious pleasure in shopping on Sundays, the sensation is none the less extraordinary for it is another or alternate world presented before your eyes. The stores are no smaller, they may even be bigger than their equivalents in London or New York. They are certainly the size of Harrod's or Selfridge's, or of the Galeries Lafayette in Paris. They are in fact more reminiscent of the latter than of any other emporium. It is something to do with the 'hat bars' and handkerchief or scarf counters under that haunting 'nouveau art' dome with its balconies and grand stairs. But there is not the frenzied Parisian salesmanship of the French big store; and no character at all like the daemonic 'vendeuse numèro seize' of the Magazin du Printemps, next door, a typhoon and whirlwind of energy who administered galvanic shocks to every department she entered, and in the intervals of telling me about her quiet holiday in Brittany even telephoned from the lift while it was in motion up and down.

---

[1] This picture once belonged to the writer's great-grandfather, a well-known art collector in his day, and was bought by him at the then prevailing 'Picasso-price' of £30,000.

It is certainly an ingenious suggestion to go to one of the big stores in Tokyo for the first sightseeing in Japan. For besides the multitude of new objects there is hardly a familiar thing that is the same. We went down first of all to the food department in the basement. Here, in the manner of a museum exhibit, is a special grouping of blunt objects looking like—what, exactly? Boomerangs? But they are not of wood or stone, as those of the 'black fellows' in the Australian desert, or high up north in Arnhem Land where they paint themselves all over in dots and stripes, wear animal or bird masks, dance for weeks on end in a ritual more elaborate than any Wagnerian or Shakespeare festival, and cannot bother themselves to look up at an aeroplane. Not boomerangs. Or could they be Stone Age implements? Or something of the same kind as the sceptres of the Maori chieftains, but they are not made of jade? Or Indian clubs, except that these are flatter and have no handle? But they are dried bonitos, that is the answer; bonitos being sea-fish, particularly esteemed in Japan, and emblems of good luck.[1] A present of dried bonitos, therefore, is appropriate for a marriage, and these are wedding gifts.

Farther on is an enclosed cabin like that of the steersman on a ferry boat, or in the *vaporetto* on the Grand Canal, and inside it a chef and his assistant, both wearing masks, are making fritters or wafers at express speed. But they are not masks. They do not hide the eyes. They are only gags or muzzles, and their purpose is just what it would seem to be, to prevent the food being contaminated by their breath. Or it could be that both chef and assistant have got colds. Near by are the sweet stalls. Mounds that look like coloured pebbles, and others that are like petals or flowers. But they must be too sweet, or else tasteless, which is a criticism of much else eaten in Japan. The young women serving at the sweet counters wear white caps and overalls and but for their slit eyes, diminutive size and immaculate laundered whiteness, could be selling Brighton or Scarborough rock, next door to a shooting gallery, at the English seaside. To some little extent they look a race apart from the other shop assistants.

Going upstairs again to the ground floor there is the tea stall near to

[1] A Japanese seventeen-syllable poem or *hokku* goes as follows:
> Young leaves everywhere;
> The mountain cuckoo singing;
> My first bonito!

but in translation, it reads more like a Chinese poem in one of Ronald Firbank's novels.

one of the back entrances. But it is not as simple as that because this is green tea, and a particular artistry goes into its packaging. There are exquisite parcels of tea—no other word is apposite—and tins and boxes worthy of some treasure of the Indies. Next to this is an information office with printed leaflets in English giving a plan of the whole store. So up on the escalator to the top floor with an attendant on each landing like a juvenile air-hostess in pale blue cap and uniform who bows solemnly and gravely to the shoppers as they come by, the first symptom of bowing, except for the little maids, that we have seen yet in Japan. It is easier, and less tiring, to go to the top floor and come down, there being generally six or seven floors in the big stores in Tokyo, or Nagoya, or Osaka, often with a roof garden on top of all, and it being difficult for anyone with an inquisitive or speculative mind to get out of the building under an hour or two, once you are inside. Indeed, the greater part of a wet day can be spent in this way, the big stores in Japan being more interesting than the museums, where nothing of what you want to see is ever on view. You can eat your luncheon in one big store, and if it is still raining walk across the Ginza to another.

The top floor is often the furniture department, perhaps a wilderness of wardrobes, a ready made Surrealist picture only waiting for a painter. Or it may be the men's department which has all the drabness of the cheap tailors in a mining town in Midland England. With these two exceptions almost everything else is interesting while certain floors, or portions of floors, rise to extreme heights of fantasy. The china department, if it has no more than that, will show exquisite *sake* cups in eggshell porcelain, and near to them are shelves of lacquer soup bowls beautiful alike to the hand and eye. It is a little delight in itself to lift off the lacquer covers to the bowls and put them back again. And near by will be a shelf of little objects tied up with coloured cords in silken sacks or bags. They are pots by some potter or other, probably from Kyoto, and it is pandering to the Japanese passion for wrapping and un-wrapping anything and everything to have them presented in this way.

One is drawn in all directions at once by what one sees. The more expensive lacquer offers grave temptations, and foreigners are still rare in these upper regions for one is a target for mixed smiles and stares. It may be only their national habit of smiling but the shop assistants do seem still interested in their work. They are standing outside the

Onnagata (female impersonator) in *Kabuki* dress, by Sharaku (*c.* 1790)

Japanese *onnagata*

Kabuki actor in a black cloak, by
Kunisada (d. 1864)

Japanese *Kabuki* actor

machinery, still admiring it perhaps a little wearily and half-heartedly, but not yet drawn into it and tangled up in it, the machine being no less than the Moloch of twentieth-century civilization. They are still enjoying and wondering at the air-conditioning, rather as some highly sensitized race, newly 'liberated' from their Shangri-La, might take pleasure in their first few months of working in the lifts and on the platforms of London tube or New York subway. This is indeed approximately what has happened to the Japanese who missed nearly the first hundred years of our industrial age. The big store still glitters and coruscates to those employed in it. And now relayed music breaks upon the ear with sudden impact like the clearing of a throat, and we are in the middle of Beethoven's Seventh. There is a perfect craze for classical music in Japan, and it is even probable that this compulsory concert attending counts among the amenities of a shop assistant's life. Arriving at the stairway we are in the door of what looks like a white-tiled laboratory, with a familiar whiff of disinfectant coming from it. It is a dentist's parlour, almost inviting in its cleanliness, and which was to prove swift and useful on another Sunday morning when the European dentists of Tokyo had gone to church, or were playing golf. But passing it this time, and only looking in at the door, we continued down the stair reflecting that the Japanese were only in the second or third generation of servitude to the machine, and conjecturing what the dentist's room would be like, were there ever one, if preserved in one of our veteran |stores in London as a museum piece of the seventies and eighties, with primitive machine drill and early dentist's chair, by which time the music had changed and Chabrier's *España* was wafting from floor to floor.

It was to those strains, with visions of Seville, that we saw the *kimonos* at the far end and came towards them through the men's haberdashery among dummy figures of golf and tennis players, all of European feature but just slightly wrong. Next, and with chilling effect, dummies of Japanese women in Western clothes, with added height by way of compliment, and an approximation to strawberry blonde or silvered hair that is even a libel upon the models they are copying, and sad indeed to think these dummy figures are a new industry for the doll-makers of Kyoto with all their inherited taste and skill. But now the mere transit from one counter to the next is like coming out of the false into the real Japan.

c

All is at once beautiful and gay. But how to begin on the *kimonos*? For there are so many different kinds. We make a start with those of a new fashion that conforms in shape and cut to Western clothes and are quiet in pattern and unremarkable, for only a foot or two away is a colour explosion in a design of rayed suns, part-chrysanthemum, part-persimmon, in Beardsleyesque arrangement on a *kimono*, like costume drawings for his *Salomé* but translated into the most violent colours. A whole stand of this particular theme in luxuriant and tireless variation in the same gamut of tones with gold added; and then a curtain partition-ing off an exhibition of another kind of *kimono* altogether, mainly children's dresses, and here the designs are of pine branches or of butterflies, but not the pale cabbage or red admiral of our thin airs. These are huge and fanciful swallowtails like four-winged birds. Or it may be another *kimono* with a design of maple leaves and chrysan-themums in bright vermilion and yellow, bound in an *obi* with a design upon it of children's toys. Or a double hollyhock pattern in gold and silver thread with little wild white roses scattered on it, and on the *obi* of 'clear and refreshing silver', a design of roses in the same bright red. Many or most of the designs have meanings which are lost on us and are only appropriate for some particular festival or celebration. Some sorts of *kimonos* are only worn at certain seasons, and during our stay we were in time to see the summer *kimonos* put away and no longer on sale and the winter ones in place of them, including the warm, padded sort that are called *tanzen*. The men's *kimonos* are more sober in pattern, chiefly in blacks and greys.

In one and all of the big stores, if there is no time for anything else one should make for the wedding department, though one may have to look away from a dummy bridegroom in top hat, white tie and tails. But it is not so much the bride in white headdress and wedding gown all ready for the ceremony at a Shintô shrine, for that has a familiar look about it. What are astonishing are the marriage *kimonos* in her trousseau, dresses which are put away and never worn again. And it was particularly appropriate that Chabrier's *España* should be playing, too soon over and finished but still lingering on the ear, for nowhere in the Western world is there any, even the most distant approach to these dresses, but in the high combs and mantillas and moon-dotted crinolines of the *Feria* of Seville, and then it is only brought into any possible comparison by addition of the spangled suits, cyclamen cloaks, and capes embroidered with roses and carnations worn by the *toreros* as they march into the bull ring.

The most gorgeous of the other *kimonos* are always arranged around the wedding groups, and it is here we will see patterns of carp—if carp they be?—leaping up waterfalls, streams meandering among floating plum blossoms, flower cascades of dangling wistaria, or rocket flights of morning glory, which we will only see in life worn by the *maikos* in the Gion or pleasure quarter of Kyoto, again in distant parallel to Triana or the Albaicín which are the Gypsy quarters of Seville and Granada. Somewhere near to the wedding *kimonos* an earlier mystery is explained for there is a stall of wedding presents featuring those peculiar objects, half-stork or locust and half-model aeroplane, which puzzled us on one of our first afternoons. They are to bring good luck, and are perfect examples of the national genius for gift wrapping, a thing that follows naturally on their inbred love of giving and receiving presents, and that is a trait of character present in no other nation to the same degree.

On the last occasion we went to this particular store, which was early in October, the climax to all this *kimono*-viewing came in the form of a special display of *obis*, and it is now necessary to explain that the *obi* is the ceremonial sash tied in a bow at the back of the *kimono*. But its true significance is rather more than that for in *Kabuki* plays one of the only lascivious gestures permitted is the untying of the *obi*, which can have but one meaning. We may add that the extreme of lewdness in their play of convention is a derisive movement of the big toe. Inmates of the *yoshiwara* in Japanese prints wear their *obis* tied at the front instead of the back which has its particular significance. The *obi* we are examining are of the richest brocade, stiff with gold, and already tied into huge bows. It takes a long time to tie the *obis*, which together with the expense involved is one of the reasons why so few Japanese women wear *kimonos*, though this is hard to understand because the cheaper sorts only cost a few shillings. But more probably it is the adjunct of *tabis* and *getas*, cotton socks and wooden clogs, that make the national dress awkward and old-fashioned. One would like to know who are the designers of such splendid materials. They have in command what must be the largest repertory of designs in the living world, the legacy of four or five centuries, though what we now see is as nothing compared to the dresses of an earlier time. One has but to look at the clothes in Utamaro's woodcuts to be aware of this textile splendour which is something without parallel in any other land.

Red and white and gold, with green for the ubiquitous leaf or pine cone were the colours for this array of *obis*, no two of them alike. They were glittering objects, any one of which one would have liked to buy for itself. Only a day or two before this, just before we left Japan, we had seen women in Kyoto wearing red winter *kimonos* which gave a new aspect to the shopping streets and led one to think of Kyoto deep in snow. It was no less than an intoxication to take in all these patternings for the *kimono*, with only the Indian *sari* as a possible equal, is the most beautiful of all forms of women's clothing. My memory of the big stores in Tokyo, as also in Osaka and Nagoya, is to have been quite dazzled by the dresses. Coming out again into the street one had entirely forgotten it was Sunday afternoon.

But the bright lights are beckoning and it is proposed we should dine out in a Japanese restaurant, a sensation so unique that later you envy yourself your first experience of it. After discussion a famous *tempura* house was decided upon, and its card lies before me as I write this, exquisitely printed on rice paper a little bigger than a visiting card, with woodcut of a shrimp or prawn in fronds of seaweed, but printed in delicate washes so that it has the effect of a watercolour. The restaurant is off the Ginza, and on arrival you remove your shoes, of course, helped by various characters, male and female, who appear from nowhere, and are led by lilliputian *neisans* (maids) along a passage, the wooden boards of which are so immaculately clean and polished that you can scarcely believe your eyes. Whiskies or martinis that seem to belong to a rougher world altogether are served in a little sitting-room and after a few minutes you are taken along the passage again, or up some stairs, still wondering at the wooden floors and trying to look into other rooms as you go by, and so into your own dining-room where there are cushions on the floor arranged in a semi-circle round a crescent-shaped bar or counter of perforated metal only a foot or so high. A sliding partition opens behind this and the chef comes in, followed by a *neisan*, both carrying bowls of prawns and other, unknown objects that they put down on the counter, while the chef sits down, not crosslegged, but with bent knees straight in front of him in the Japanese manner, an electric ring is switched on and the feast begins. Green tea is put before you, a beverage upon which we reserve judgement till later, and in a moment or two the chef hands you a prawn wrapped in a paper napkin. In the meantime you have been given sundry bowls and saucers and a pair of wooden chopsticks that appear to cleave together from natural affection. More prawns fried in batter are handed round, and now the meal becomes more difficult because the moment has come to use your chopsticks. You must take up the prawn and dip it into the little bowl of *soy* sauce, and beside that there is a saucer of grated radish that must be brought into contact with the prawn.

The use of chopsticks now becomes obligatory for pieces of another fried fish make their appearance, all of which has been done with an incomparable neatness and deftness of hand. It is probably true that no two *tempura* houses prepare their prawns in quite the same manner. They all have their own particular recipes on which they pride themselves, chiefly a matter of the ingredients of the sauce which may have dried *bonito* stock or sweet *sake* added to the *soya*. But, as well, there are all sorts of queer little specialities; for instance, a small, pear-shaped object shining like lacquer and, at that, the work of an expert craftsman and, in fact, it is an aubergine. The bowls are of exquisite china made specially for the restaurant, and in this particular house the chopstick rests are china fish. Long before this *sake* has been circulating, drunk warm in tiny handleless cups that are the epitome of taste. Then soup, or even two different soups, appear in lacquer bowls, and rice is handed round. But we keep our discussion of the soups for another time while green tea makes another and final appearance. Our *tempura* dinner is over and we leave, taking with us a little package with a pair of the dolphin chopstick-rests inside it.[1]

The first occasion of dining in such manner is something one will always remember. At last this is the legendary Japan and it fulfils the expectation. But it is to be remarked that a *tempura* dinner is far from cheap. It is indeed as expensive as a meal in a good restaurant in Paris, maybe even more expensive considering there are no wines. But it is unthinkable, even impractical to the Japanese that you should not dine in a separate room to yourselves. There is no common dining-room. The restaurants are not built in that way, any more than Japanese hotels have public sitting-rooms. Nor, for that matter, bedrooms, as such, for you eat your dinner and have your sleeping mattresses put down in the

[1] They are neither dolphins, nor *thai* (bream), but the naturalistic rendering of some edible fish that is a stranger to our seas.

same room. It is a system which, in itself, entails expense because of the services of an individual chef and, as likely as not, three or four *neisans* who sit beside you on the floor, born to that manner of moving, and change round from guest to guest.

It is easy enough to say that the only Japanese things left in Tokyo are the *tempura* and *sukiyaki* restaurants and the *kimono* department in the big stores. One hears that from persons who have only been a day or two in Tokyo and were bewildered by its size. But, of course, its fascination is just that it has most of the mechanical aids and gadgets of our civilization and yet is entirely apart and different in fundamental ways. You have but to throw a glance at the handful of hobos or down and outs watching a wrestling match on the television screen in a shop window along the Ginza. Nothing of the Spanish or Southern Italian beggar about them, nor of the street Arabs of the Middle East. As always with their compeers of the gutter they have the look of holy men fallen from grace, but of no shrine that we have known before. One or two of them have straggling beards and this gives them a Korean look.

One cannot read a single syllable of the shop signs and in a moment everything is alien and different along the main street of Tokyo. Just in that second everything is unlike and nothing is the same. But, also, it has to be considered that in the Far East a huge city is nothing new. Kyoto with probably a million inhabitants was bigger than London in the beginning of the Napoleonic Wars. Tokyo, itself, had probably reached to larger population figures in the time of Hokusai. Therefore, the Japanese are neither unused to, nor surprised at, great cities. It is only that Tokyo with the near prospect of ten million inhabitants is getting out of hand. Speaking in a general sense, before returning to the particular, there were of course sides of Tokyo which we did not experience. Such as a dance hall with nine hundred 'hostesses' who, so someone in the aeroplane told us as we were flying to Honolulu, lined the stair for you to pick and choose from, while the management on the adage that the customer is never wrong took no offence if you were not satisfied with the girl's looks or conversation and asked for your hostess to be changed for another. All of them were '*kimono*-clad', and would obligingly accompany you next day on your shopping expeditions at a simple request to the manager. This much was to be read in an advertisement in the English language newspaper, and it is

this kind of thing which with other features gives to present day Tokyo
some of the flavour of pre-Nazi Berlin. There are also strangely
worded flourishes for Turkish baths, which are on a like scale and
equally Teutonic in scope, with individual attention in the form of
massage in a private room by 'a charming young girl in a swimsuit',
but the attraction may of course lie more in the wording than in the
accomplishment. Certainly from all accounts, and by direct evidence,
Tokyo is a pleasure town. If the hidden side of it has to some extent
come out into the open there can be little doubt that this is because of
losing the war and becoming a leave centre for the occupation forces.
If indeed, thinking of the Yoshiwara which was closed by the authorities
a month or two before our visit, such things have ever been hidden by
the Japanese. But, at its worst, it could not be a more offensive spectacle
than the nocturnal hordes along Piccadilly and Park Lane. At least, and
until recent date, the Japanese had a more elegant tradition in their
dissipations.

Shops selling the same goods in Tokyo are never near together, and
you may have to go from end to end of the town to find the shop you
want. In fact, it is a wise principle always to stop if you see something
you want for it is almost certain you will never find the place again. In
the end it is quicker and easier to do your shopping in the Nikkatsu
Arcade, under the hotel of the same name. This must be one of the most
fascinating places for window shopping anywhere in the world. Where
in the world, apart from everything else, are there such baskets or
bamboo ware? But perhaps the most unique shop in Tokyo is the paper
shop. There is nothing on a par with it, except a rather similar establishment in Kyoto. One has heard before of the beauty of Oriental papers,
and many experts have come specially to the Far East to study them.
In particular, there are, or were green papers from one or two paper
mills in China—but in this context a factory probably means a single
pair of hands—green papers prepared by a long and secret process
which must have been perfected over many generations. But on this
showing Japanese papers are no less beautiful than the Chinese. Writing
paper of exquisite sorts, some dusted with gold and silver, and worthy
of the silk-wrapped missives of Lady Murasaki, wrapping paper of a
hundred kinds, each sort in its separate drawer, drawer after drawer of
Japanese wallpapers, some of them being the ribbed silk papers, and
others printed with flowers or landscapes, and even the most delicately

printed paper napkins, together with every variety and description of paper fan. There is nothing to compare with this either in Europe or America.

But, also, there is the Korin Kaku, a name of double association, and in fact it is the palace of one of the princesses of the Japanese Imperial family, a part of which she has made over to the silk industry as a show-room for their products. Here the most lovely silks are to be seen and bought, and for its goods on display the Korin Kaku must be bracketed with Christian Dior in the Avenue Foch as one of the most beautiful shops of the modern world. Lengths of silk of enviable description in all colours and of the softest texture, with some of historical interest are on display. Among them are a silk brocade copied from a fragment pasted on the back of a mirror in the Shôsôin, the incomparable treasure house at Nara. This is a Chinese pattern of the T'ang dynasty (ninth century); while another, of which a small fragment was also found by Sir Aurel Stein in Central Asia, is of Han period and comes from the monastery at Hôryûji; and yet another from a monastery at Kyoto is taken from a design lacquered in gold and silver upon paper by the famous Kôetsu, of whom more later for he was one of the great artistic genuises of Japan. Perhaps the patterns upon these early silks are a little too light and small in design, however interesting in their Sasanian echoes they may be. Is it, or is it not, a little silly to be wearing a silk tie copied from a silk of the eighth century at the Shôsôin? Neverthe-less the silks to be seen here far surpass those of the revived silk industry at Damascus, although the raw silks are perhaps a little inferior in texture to those of Thaibok origin which are woven in Northern Siam. But, as we shall find when we come to look at them in detail, it is the textiles of the Momoyama and Genroku periods (sixteenth and seventeenth centuries) that are incomparable in boldness and beauty of design and, withal, distinctively Japanese. Perhaps, if a suggestion be permissible, it is to the silken stuffs of those later epochs that the modern industry should address itself with all its combined resources of the old and the new techniques of manufacture.

But the seasons have become elided together in the course of this discussion and summer has turned to autumn, as it did in October at the time we left Japan. Effectually, we have been little more than a day in Tokyo, having hardly been out of the house except on a couple of shopping expeditions, and becoming aware now of how hot it is.

Hotter indeed than I have ever known it in my life though when we get to Kyoto it will be hotter still. Not to be noticed so much in shops and restaurants because of the air-conditioning, but striking like a hammer blow at night and in the privacy of one's bedroom where one could wear no clothes at all, and even going into the bathroom to brush one's teeth was no mean athletic feat. Out of doors the Japanese, one and all, were living in their shirtsleeves. In such heat the vastness of the town begins to weigh on one. It came almost as a relief to find nearly nothing on view in the (Nezu) National Museum in Ueno Park which is three-quarters of an hour's drive by motor, either way, past a lake covered with magnificent lotuses so huge that, unknowing, one would take them for giant, but mysteriously beautiful cabbages of unknown Oriental strain. That is, until one saw the lotus cups, pink or white, above and distinct from the great, and faintly bluish leaves, a sight never seen before growing on this scale in nature, and the more unfamiliar because lotuses were almost the only flower while we were in Japan in August and September.

The National Museum comprises two buildings, twin to each other in the gloom and despair they inculcate; the one containing Stone and Iron Age artifacts with a first section of the clay Haniya figures found in tomb mounds, which would be exciting enough in any other setting, the second building being the repository for works of art. The huge rooms are cheerless and give the impression of having nothing in them, whatever may be on view in the glass cases. It must be one of the most depressing museums in the world, or, at any rate, in my not wholly limited experience of museums—that it contains some wonderful works of art is beyond question, equally in the matter of paintings, textiles, and ceramics. That day there were several painted screens on view, among them a famous one of fishing nets. But the paintings are set so far back in the glass cases that you can hardly see them, and the show rooms are not so much rooms as passages which one would like to traverse armed with a speedometer to mark the mileage. Never, in any museum that I have visited, have I felt so sorry for the museum custodians, the more so as these long and empty halls are not part of their inheritance and they would be happy in little rooms of lath and paper. Who can have designed these gloomy halls? Was he a native architect who had no interest at all in what he was doing? Or were the plans sent out ready made from Belgium? It may be that the very conception of a museum is alien to the Japanese temperament for it is a commonplace that they prefer to show things singly and one at a time. But it is annoying in almost every work on Japanese art to find some object illustrated from the National Museum—a painted screen, a piece of early lacquer, a fine *Noh* costume, or a pot by Ninsei or by Kenzan—to know that it is there, and that there is little or no chance of seeing it. There is, of course, the excuse of climatic conditions—in a few moments we are to experience the full force of these—and the humidity must be bad for paintings upon silk or paper, though what effect can dampness have upon lacquer, or on ceramics? Whatever the reason, and there are certainly more than enough vacant spaces upon the walls, it remains true that only a portion of the treasures it contains are ever upon view. For an instance, and this must be a case of policy, the pair of screens of *Irises* by Ogata Kôrin is only on exhibition each spring for a couple of weeks during the iris season, and yet the *Iris* screens are among the most typical, as they are surely in situation the most accessible, of this master's works.

So it comes about that in this chapter on Tokyo there is little said about works of art. No city of comparable size—and in this respect we know there is no town in the world with more inhabitants—has less to show in the sphere of architecture and of works of art. There is indeed no building worth mentioning. The Shiba temples, where several of the Shoguns were buried, were blitzed to pieces in the war, and in any case they were poor examples of the Nikkô style, picturesque perhaps in their conscious *chinoiserie*, but specimens of bad taste in a land of grace and sensibility. The Imperial Palace, which was never interesting, was destroyed nearly in entirety, and there are no shrines or temples worth the visit. What, then, can be the fascination of Tokyo for it grows upon one, and one is sorry to leave it? The answer must lie in its million upon million of inhabitants. Its little shops and side streets are the attraction. Perhaps there is no great city anywhere in the world with fewer outward signs of religion. In comparison, Chicago is a Rome of religious shrines. In Tokyo you have to look long and intently before you see a temple. You could get the impression of being in a city of eight million agnostics, which is not true though their religion may be little more to them than some of the superstitions of a state of childhood surviving in a stratum of patriotic feeling. It is only rarely that a Japanese can be induced to speak of religion, and then he is a little ashamed of being

Buddhist and hardly likes to admit to being a follower of Shintô. The two faiths are in any case inextricably intermingled. There is of course an increasing number of Christians who may be less reluctant and perhaps feel themselves more contemporary and upon a level of equality with the Western world. Never in Tokyo is there the sensation that you are in a Buddhist country, and Buddhism after all is what made Japan different in essentials from a Christian or a Muslim land.

The accent of curiosity is upon the facts of daily life which is why I have tried to describe some of the big stores in detail. It is also focused very strongly upon the theatre, the incomparable *Kabuki* theatre which could grow easily into the interest of a lifetime, and even upon something so wonderfully and typically Japanese as their wrestling matches. This, in default of an Uffizi or a Prado, and in substitution, as it were, for something as dramatic as a Spanish bull fight. Or there is the flower viewing, or the arts of flower arrangement, or even the exhibitions of dwarf trees.

But, also, the difference comes hitting at one in a hundred ways. What is the reaction on being taken to a fish bar to eat *sushi*, where a board over the counter, shaped like a target or a darts board, gives the outlines and the names of no fewer than twenty different kinds of raw fish? These are eaten in thin slices wrapped up in rice balls, the preparing of which in the bar in question is done by hand with lightning rapidity to an accompaniment of incessant roars of 'Hai! Hai!' (Yes! Yes!) as the orders are shouted in. It is part of the ritual of the raw fish bar, something equivalent to the special 'lingo' and manner of speech affected by 'gym' instructors in the Brigade of Guards, a clipping of words to go with abrupt and stylized movements. Here they 'Hai! Hai!', pounce on a fish, 'Hai!', and cut a slice from it and 'Hai! Hai!', roll it in a rice ball and 'Hai! Hai! Hai!' hand it to the customer. *Tai*, 'the number one fish' of Japan is, we need not say, a prime favourite. It masquerades in our waters as bream, is scarcely ever eaten here, and never looked on as a delicacy. But the Japanese regard thin, semi-transparent flakes of raw bream as the height of luxury. It is a taste which grows, too, on foreigners living in Japan. More than one Englishman has told me that he thought *sushi* was the most delicious of all Japanese foods, and I have even been told there is no sensation of gormandize equal to fishing for *tai* in the Inland Sea and eating them

fresh as they are hauled aboard.[1] Other fish eaten in the *sushi* bars are
raw tunny; I think, turbot or halibut, and a quantity of other fishes of
which I do not know the names. For myself, I ate *tai*, and later grew
almost to like it, and tunny and another fish, but did not try the rest.

We would conclude with *sukiyaki* which with *tempura* is the other
best known food so far as foreigners are concerned, though in the
writer's opinion much inferior to *tempura*. *Sukiyaki* being beef which is
cooked before you on a brazier with the usual *soya* and *sake* sauce, and
bean curd and, probably, onion. Japanese beef is famous; the best sorts
coming from two different centres, in one of which according to legend
the beeves are massaged to make their flesh more tender. There is in
consequence a good deal of the tiresome steak mystique which is one of
the signs everywhere of American influence. But there are also houses
for chicken *sukiyaki*. Another type of restaurant where you eat at
counters, instead of sitting on the floor as with both *tempura* and *sukiyaki*,
is an eel-bar. This is called *kabayaki*, and the Japanese who have to find
a learned authority for everything say it was developed during the
Tokugawa Period (1615-1867). And why not? Probably it was in
practice long before that time. The method of cooking *kabayaki* sounds
a little barbaric, but then eels come in for bad treatment in every
country where they are eaten; in Holland, and in Denmark where they
are skinned alive in the eel-boats in Copenhagen harbour, and on the
sea front at Brighton where a notice of 'jellied eels' is culmination to
what may have been very far from pretty in the processing. In *Kabayaki*
houses the wretched eels, dead (one hopes!) have their bones removed
and their heads cut off. Then the eel is impaled on a green bamboo
skewer and broiled on both sides, after which a sauce made chiefly from
its blood is poured over it, and it is roasted and eaten hot. Other, and
worse tales are of another type of restaurant where small fish are cooked
alive before you in a glass bowl in which the poor creatures try to hide
themselves in the weeds, and then float, dead, to the surface. But, to
end more pleasantly, there are also excellent Chinese restaurants in
Tokyo, where you sit at tables and not on the floor, and the mysteries of
lacquered duck, vintage eggs, sharks' fins, and birds' nest soup may be
studied; the rites of the Canton, Peking and Szechuan kitchens, which

---

[1] Foreigners in Japan tell one another 'horror stories' of a first course of raw fish, followed by
the appearance at table of the living fish itself with most of the flesh cut from its sides. Would a meal
of this sort in England be followed by a prosecution? One is inclined to hope so. But what of the
Colchester Oyster Feast, and all the orgies in oyster bars?

are three different schools of Chinese cooking; and even a Mongolian restaurant 'named' for Genghis Khan, where you dine in a *Kibitka* and eat lamb which, you may flatter yourself into thinking, gambolled on the plains of Tartary and was tended by a shepherd of the Golden Horde.

It was hot. Hotter and hotter, and hotter than ever. And damp, withal, and not a little ominous. The newspapers warned that a typhoon was approaching. We had already experienced one typhoon, but it was nothing much and soon blew itself away. This one was to be worse. Daily bulletins appear in the papers and the typhoons, most irritatingly, are allotted a serial number and given women's names, witticisms which must have their origin in some meteorological office where paper-backs are read in the intervals of making incautious, but 'official' weather forecasts. On the day in question we had been invited to luncheon in a house were there is the finest ceramic collection in Japan. This had been arranged rather at the last moment, and afterwards we were to meet a Japanese friend and be taken by him to a wrestling match. There was a blue and white Chinese dish of the fifteenth century as big as a chariot wheel, unchipped and in perfect condition, surely a thing unique in its kind. This stood in a corner of the room, but the other objects we were to see were carried in, one by one. There were marvellous bowls with a drip glaze upon them; one bowl, in particular, in tones of ivory and water-melon, but of the rind of the melon and not its paler flesh. Also figurines of court ladies with their black hair in high chignons and long trailing sleeves, some of them even with the shadow falling on their faces of the flowering peach under which in poetical allegory one had to think of them as standing. What a comment on mortality that these lovely figures of young women are only to be found in tombs! Then there were bowls of *blanc de chine*, incredible in delicacy of outline, conjuring up visions of the age of the great Chinese poets, bowls of the tenth and eleventh centuries, with silvered rims that age had darkened to a thin black line.

Some fifteen or twenty of such pieces we must have seen, brought one after another into the room after unwrapping from the wooden boxes in which they were stored away. But it was three o'clock and time to go and meet our friend, and so we left the house missing in this way an exhibition of treasures which continued, we were told later, until five o'clock, and departing just at the moment when the display of Chinese pieces was finishing and the show of Japanese treasures had begun. This was the more disappointing because, although no ceramic expert, one has had the opportunity of seeing Chinese pottery and porcelain on other occasions, notably at the house of Mr Eumorfopoulos in Chelsea, but Japanese pottery and porcelain are much more rarely met with. We missed in this manner a pottery ink-box by the famous Kenzan, brother of Kôrin, and perhaps pieces by Ninsei and other potters, bowls and various pieces connected with the tea ceremony, objects to which an almost inordinate value is attached in Japan, and which change hands on the rare occasions when they come into the market at prices that are about double those reached even for the finest Meissen or Nymphenburg in European sale-rooms. It is a vagary of taste that we shall have occasion to look into more closely when we visit the Seikadô Foundation in Tokyo, and try to understand what it is that the Japanese admire in a bowl by Ninsei which is one of the most famous and valuable works of art in the country.

We left the house and proceeded by taxi to our meeting place, not aware that anything out of the ordinary was happening. True, it was raining, but it had rained all day and most of the day before. Our Japanese friend was waiting for us, but just as we were about to start with him for the wrestling match, and were talking with him on the doorstep of the Imperial Hotel, our host and cousin appeared with an urgent message that warning had been given and we were to go home at once. An announcement had been made on the radio that all shops and offices were to shut and workers were to make their way home. With the incessant bickering, and worse, over Matsu and Quemoy weighing upon one's nerves it was only normal to think another war had started. But it was the typhoon approaching. We left hurriedly, calling on the way at a silk store to fetch a parcel, finding only the manager still there, and all the assistants in the act of leaving in their raincoats. During those few moments the deluge had begun, and when we came out the street was running with water and scarcely a person was to be seen. In another few moments the streets were ankle deep. The water did not stand there placidly. It was a rushing stream. A bus or two splashed along with passengers, sopping wet, holding on to it as best they could. The rain fell in heavy torrents, thicker and heavier than I have ever seen it fall. The sky was black and threatening with racing clouds. It poured more and more, and gusts of wind blew so furiously

Kintai-bashi (Bridge of the Brocade Sash), Yamaguchi Prefecture, originally built in 1673

that the few persons in the streets could only stand with their backs
turned. It was hopeless to make any headway in that tornado. The
water was up to the hubs of the wheels, and at this point we could no
longer see the way. Even the experienced driver began to lose himself.
All streets looked the same. For we were now in the long miles of low
houses with no landmarks. And still it rained and rained even in that
howling wind. But, at last, we were home.

That night we dined nervously, wondering what was coming, and
thinking of the eight million others in their flimsy houses, and of what
could be happening in other parts of Japan. Hourly bulletins were given
out on the radio, and it was announced that the main force of the
typhoon would strike Tokyo (as if it was not already doing so!) at a
precise time which they kept on postponing by an hour or so; first,
eleven o'clock, then midnight, and then half-past two. But it is the
wind which is more dangerous than the rain for not only does it uproot
trees, it tears the roofs off houses. The house where we were staying was
more substantial than most, and proof against earthquake, but it was no
comfort to be told on the wireless that this was the worst typhoon of
the century, and that more rain had fallen during the last two days than
at any time in the Meiji era, the whole modern period of Japanese
history between 1868 and now.

But the news was altering a little in tone. It was announced that the
typhoon was not to hit Tokyo, head on, fair and square, but would
probably swerve at the last moment, strike a corner of the city, and cut
a swathe inland into the ricefields and veer out to sea again, or die away
among the mountains. This particular typhoon had begun its dervish
career of whirling and spinning far out in the Pacific, it was said, near
Okinawa, so that it had crossed the narrowest neck of Japan to get here.
Water was already coming in at the windows and parts of the floor were
an inch deep in water. In the heart of the typhoon all is quiet and still,
and here we were, sitting, talking, with heaven knows what was going
on around us. I could still scarcely believe we were in Japan, brought
here over the North Pole and the Arctic ice and snow by a force two
or three times swifter than the full blast of the typhoon. Already, these
few days in Tokyo had been among the most exciting in my life, but
when I came to think of it we had seen nothing old and no works of art
except those few pieces of pottery and porcelain, and they were Chinese
and not Japanese. The real excitement was still to come, and I was

longing for Nara and Kyoto. In the meantime, the typhoon if it was to hit Tokyo, or blow itself out, was raging and howling in gusts that shook the whole house and seemed about to burst in the doors and windows. It had stopped raining, whether a good sign, or not. In the street a solitary motor went past, so people were still moving, and one slept the long night by fits and starts, waking and listening to that great gale as it struck and roared, but it had lulled and died down by the first light of morning.

Chapter Three

—•—•—•—•—•—•—•—•—•—•—•—•—•—

TOKYO (continued)

THE MORNING AFTER THE TYPHOON the sky was clear and the sun was shining. When I was a child and living on the Yorkshire coast there was much the same sensation after a winter gale had blown itself out. All would be fresh and clean as on the first day of spring, and we would go for a walk upon the sands. It would be low tide, and the waters would have run far back into the bay uncovering new archipelagos and rock pools to discover. This morning there was just that feeling. In the lands to which one was accustomed it would have seemed, and it was, in fact, a Sunday morning.

It had been settled some days before that we were to call at a nursery to order plants, lunch at Yokohama, and go on to Enoshima. Now the typhoon was over there seemed to be no reason not to keep to our plan, especially as good news had begun to come in. Just before we were ready to start, the chauffeur arrived to say he had called at his home; his family were all safe and his house was standing. Messages had arrived also for Okimura-san, the majordomo, and for the maids. All was well so far as they were concerned. But the havoc was terrible only a little distance from the house. Whole streets were flooded, roofs torn off, and hoardings bent and twisted. A pathetic sight, and giving evidence of what a terrible night it had been, was the bedding hung up to dry outside nearly every house. Many roads were blocked and huge detours had to be made. Lagoons had formed in the night, and where was once a golf links was now a placid and unheeding lake lying blue in the sunlight. It was a long way round to the nursery, where we ordered a bundle of tree peonies to be sent to England, repaired to the narrow shopping street of Yokohama, and then had our luncheon at a hotel where we overlooked the harbour.

Continuing over a hilly road with many landslides we were held up again. Now the radio in the car announced the casualties, twelve hundred killed in the whole of Japan, and a high proportion of them in this immediate neighbourhood round Yokohama. We, ourselves, passed the wrecks of several houses that had been washed away. Of course, had the typhoon struck the centre of Tokyo the destruction would have been appalling and many thousands might have died. Even so, it had been the worst typhoon of the century. The afternoon wore on, and our road came down from the hills to the sea, towards Enoshima. Once, and not long ago, this had been a sacred island, like Miyajima and Matsushima, but Enoshima is now a Coney Island or Atlantic City. Thousands of Japanese and their families come out here to spend the day from Tokyo. The shore is lined for miles on end with their bathing huts and bungalows. The island of Enoshima still has its wooded outline with some suggestion of a pagoda rising in its middle. But only a few contorted pine trees standing in Japanese poses make the shore any different from a 'blown up' photograph of Bognor. Even the hilly country on the way here had been only mildly pretty. Passing through the towns, sometimes, but only once in a hundred persons, there would be an old man looking as, one had hoped, most Japanese would look. This first day in the country had been a disappointment with the long and endless miles of slums on either side of Yokohama. The Japanese at the seaside were worse still. It might not have been so bad had we stopped to look at the fish stalls. There would be lobsters and crabs, at least, and perhaps unknown crustaceans. Was Japan to be no more than this? We had journeyed a long way in order to be reminded of things one could see in Blackpool or in Brighton. And later that same afternoon we came back towards Enoshima.

As the sun began to set we rounded a rocky bend in the road and saw a shadow in the sky over the island. It had not been there before. Then we lost sight of it, and had to go on much further and beyond the end of the beach huts to where the road petered out altogether in the sand after more and more half-hearted struggles, eventually giving it up as there was nowhere to go, and finishing near a couple of upturned fishing boats a few feet away from the open sea. It was a wide gulf or bay some miles across, and there hanging in the sky over the water was that shadow, now become a huge mountain, looming clearer as we looked at it in the light of sunset, the first grand object we had seen since coming to Japan. The huge scale of it at its distance quite took one's breath away. As we looked at it the sun was about to set behind it, and there was cloud or mist half up its slopes which now faded, leaving the huge volcano alone in the sky, except for a nearly full moon high above the darkening sea.

There was little or no snow upon Fuji and only its enormous size. No foundations of the mountain were visible. It hung or floated there. The sky was of an exaggerated clearness after the typhoon, and walking to the water's edge we watched it for a long time. There was nothing between oneself and the mountain except that desolate stretch of sea, and this added to its loneliness and mystery. It has an eternity and ubiquity of its own; always there but seldom seen, and one can understand the Japanese veneration for their snowcapped volcano. For Fuji-san holds, and must always hold, an extraordinary position in the popular imagination. It has the quality, too, of exaggerating or diminishing its own size, according to mood, as we know from Hokusai's views of it; seen like a tiny white cone or hillock from the balcony of a tea-house on the Tôkaidô; and again, casually, as the moon might rise, through the piled stacks in a timber yard with the woodmen still sawing and throwing down the logs; or down, down in the trough of waters as the long boats plunge and begin to lift under the crags and claws of spray in the hollow of the deep sea wave. Or seen, as we are seeing it now, in bulk and majesty; with the lightning flashing below it like a hieroglyph in neon lights; and in clear weather against a mackerel or rilled sky.

Vesuvius, compared to Fuji, is but a pocket volcano; and Mount Etna a white ghost above the asphodels and olive trees. A great part of Fuji's magic being that it is not always in sight. Indeed, although it can often be seen from Tokyo, for instance from the upstairs windows in the house where we were staying, and particularly on clear winter mornings or early in spring, we never saw Fuji again during our stay in Japan except for a sight of one of the lower flanks of the mountain from the window of a railway train.

If one wants to appreciate Japan one must surrender oneself entirely to its way of life which is so different from our own, to the extent, in particular, of going to stay in Japanese hotels instead of the bad and expensive imitations in Western style. This was a lesson we could hardly have learned yet, having seen so little of the country, but that first and only view of Fuji was a revelation of the real Japan. We had seen so little of it yet, and had made the most of the delights of the *sushi* and *tempura* restaurants and the big stores. But this marvellous and evocative

view of the great volcano in the clear sky after the typhoon was like a
promise of pleasures and excitements to come. For it is true that the
country round Tokyo has not much to offer. The drive to Miyanoshita
entails the inevitable progress along miles of mean houses, ending in a
thermal paradise of lush ferns and maidenhair with long rows of
souvenir stalls where there is nothing that one wants to buy.

Being no lake-lover, and knowing full well the gloom and
melancholy of the night in a lakeside hotel, whether at Como, Kil-
larney, or the Königs-See, everyone who can do so having gone home
by day, it is little consolation to carry on further still to Hakone, where
there are red *torii* standing in the water and even a promise of Mt Fuji
reflected in the lake. But at Hakone there are still remnants of the
avenue of cryptomerias that once lined the Tôkaidô, and on first seeing
these magnificent trees, so characteristic of Japan, and of which we will
admire still more splendid specimens at Ise and at Nikko, it is impossible
not to picture to oneself the trains of the *daimyôs* (great nobles) proceeding along the Tôkaidô on their way between the two capitals,
Kyoto and Tokyo (then called Yedo). For at Hakone there was a
guardhouse on the Tôkaidô where travellers were challenged and
required to show their passports. Kaempfer, the German physician who
passed this way in 1691, tells that 'all the Japanese came out of their
Norimons and Congos, and those on horseback alighted from their horses,
presenting themselves very respectfully and bareheaded to be searched'.

Kaempfer gives so fascinating an account of his journey along the
Tôkaidô that one cannot forbear to quote further from him. 'It was a
sight exceedingly curious and worthy of admiration,' he says, 'to see all
the persons, amounting sometimes to about twenty thousand men,
who compose the numerous train of a great prince or lord . . . clad in
black silk, marching in an elegant order with a decent becoming
gravity and keeping so profound a silence that not the least noise is to
be heard, save what must necessarily arise from the noise and rushing of
their habits, and the trampling of the horses and men. On the other
hand it appears ridiculous to a European to see the Pike-bearers and
Norimon-men with their shirts tucked up above their waists, exposing
their naked backs to the spectators' view. What appears still more odd
and whimsical is to see the Pages, umbrella- and hat-bearers, and all the
footmen in livery, affect a strange mimic march, or dance, when they
pass through some remarkable town or borough, or by the train of

another prince or lord. Every step they take, they draw up one foot quite to their back, in the meantime stretching out the arm on the opposite side as far as they can, and putting themselves in such a posture as if they had a mind to swim through the air. Meanwhile, the pikes, hats, umbrellas, baskets, boxes, and whatever else they carry, are tossed about in a very singular manner, answering to the motion of their bodies. The *Norimon*-men have their sleeves tied with a string, as near the shoulder as possible, and leave their arms naked. They carry the pole of the *Norimon* either upon their shoulder, or else upon the palm of their hands, holding it up above their heads. While they hold it up with one arm, they stretch out the other, putting the hand into a horizontal posture, whereby, and by their short deliberate steps and stiff knees, they affect a ridiculous air of fear and circumspection.' I had the thought of the strange sights there must have been along the Tôkaidô, and some memory of Kaempfer's phrases whirling round in my head when we went late that afternoon to a mountain where there are boiling springs coming out of the hill, and you put an egg into the water and take it out a moment later, hard boiled, and with its shell quite blackened by the fumes of this inferno in miniature upon a mountain side. It was an excitement only to have seen a fragment of the Tôkaidô, and a further promise of better things to come.

This was already beginning to fulfil itself a week or two later when we were taken to Kamakura, and had our first experience of a Japanese home. Here a large family lived in patriarchal fashion with the grandfather and grandmother; the old gentleman, himself, was an amateur potter and had one of the best potters in Japan working at a kiln in his garden, and at luncheon we were given an 'autumn soup' that looked as lovely as a flower arrangement, and was made of a particular mushroom that grew beneath the pine trees, after which the ladies were taken upstairs and asked to choose for themselves from among some beautiful *kimonos*. This was a first, but by no means the last taste of Japanese hospitality and their love of giving presents. It was a day of festival in Kamakura. There were processions and a contest of mounted archers wearing hunting dresses of the time of Yoritomo, a twelfth century hero who was first of the Shôguns and made Kamakura into the capital. Four archers took part and galloped by, shooting at the target as they came past. They were local young men who must have had considerable practice, and the hunting dresses were beautiful, particularly the wide deerskin breeches and saddle cloths and their steeple-shaped straw hats, but the effect was marred by three out of the four of them wearing spectacles. Also, there were foot soldiers or bodyguards wearing green uniforms and carrying pikes, and temple attendants in blue dresses with white characters upon them. Later, we went to the temple of Hachiman, first temple we had seen, with a huge and marvellous old tree growing out of its steps. The temple has been burnt down and rebuilt and badly needs a coat of paint, but in the galleries at the back are the litters used in the great festivals of the temple, and what appear to be the originals of the hunting dresses. A more curious object, and suggestive of an altogether new line in collecting, is Yoritomo's skull, but it is not always on view, and this is the interesting point, it is his skull 'when a youth'. The Daibutsu, or Great Buddha of Kamakura, we duly saw, but for many reasons it is difficult to be impressed by it. Too patently it is of the same category as the great bell of the Kremlin, or some giant iron cannon.

Our invitation to see the *Sumô*, postponed from the day of the typhoon, now took shape again. The Kokugikan, which is the scene for it, is a huge covered arena with a stage in its midst constructed somewhat after the fashion of a Shintô shrine. We were lucky enough to see the last day of the championship. Our Japanese friend was a box-holder and *aficionado* of twenty years standing, and knew many of the wrestlers. There were scenes of great excitement on the way into the ring, as in the purlieus of a circus among the tent ropes, or in the outer corridors of a bull ring. Dozens of trainers or attendants were rushing about in blue shirts and knickerbockers, and men and women were struggling and almost fighting at the fan stalls. Once inside the arena, it is all, or mostly boxes, that is to say, little spaces with cushions and a low wooden rail, where you sit upon the floor. And the Japanese take up so little room that the boxes are small in area and it is very cramped and crowded. It was four o'clock in the afternoon and the wrestling had begun at nine or ten. We were there for some two hours and the excitement rose to fever pitch, the number of women present and especially the shrill voices of the children showing that *Sumô* is anything but a dying art. At one time wrestlers were among the most honoured classes in the nation, and it was actors who had to go about with their faces masked. But to the public they still have something of the appeal of the matador, and like the Spanish bull fighter they are to be known in private life by their back hair combed into a pigtail on their necks. Rich men buy a share in them and they earn big money.

But what really distinguishes the *Sumô* wrestlers is their huge size. Almost before you look at the ring your attention is caught by the enormous fat boys sitting in the front rows of seats. Compared to the ordinary Japanese they are in scale as the queen bee to the common drone or worker. How this has been achieved no one seems to know for wrestling is not hereditary as are so many professions in Japan. It seems, rather, to have been attained on the principle of choosing the fat boy at a school and allowing him everything he wants to eat. We were told of wrestlers eating ten or twelve steaks a day. Yet, mysteriously, it ends in muscular strength, not flabbiness. Their girth is nearly un-believable; weights of over three hundred pounds are known, and they have been six foot six, or even six foot ten inches high. There are generally a few of them sitting together waiting their turn, but no bout lasts more than a minute or two and the next pair of contestants has to be on hand. Some are half-naked, ready for the ring, others in *kimonos*. The busts of most of them are developed in front to proportions which would surprise collectors of vital statistics, and this added to their youthful, even baby faces, gives a most peculiar impression. There was an impressive and venerable looking old gentle-man, a famous *Sumô* umpire we were told, appearing to be at least eighty years old, and dressed in a yellow silk robe and a black wizard or priest's hat which well became his thin white beard. Before we had been long in the arena two of the fattest of the fat boys rolled and bounced themselves off the platform on to his lap with what looked likely to be fatal effect, but he was sitting there serene as ever only a few moments later. This was only a part of the excitement leading to the championship.

It is the beginning of each bout that so strongly recalls Kaempfer's account of those pantomime progresses along the Tôkaidô. The umpire, and sooner than one might have thought it was the old gentleman again in the yellow silk robe, directs the wrestling of his fan. Then begins that extraordinary mimic stamping of the *Sumô* wrestlers as they lift one leg, sometimes holding it as if feeling its muscles with their hand, raise it sideways and backwards, in fact, 'drawing up one foot quite to their back,' as Kaempfer says, shaking it, as it were, sideways, and bringing it down to the floor with a resounding stamp.

This they do in competition with each other, with first one leg and then the other, repeating the exercise several times, and the spectacle was more Japanese than anything we had seen to date excepting the view of Fujiyama. It is no less than an instant introduction to the old Japan. A vaunting and boasting of strength, to prove that each wrestler could shake the earth and kick the life out of his opponent if driven nasty.

Then each pair of them goes down on their haunches opposite each other rather like a couple of fighting cocks sparring for an opening, and we notice they are naked except for a silken belt. They can continue looking into each other's faces for longer than the bout itself, obviously making use of this opportunity of increasing the excitement, but at last it is broken off and each wrestler goes to his corner of the ring, turns, and comes back, having taken a pinch from a heap of salt upon the floor, which he now tosses with ritual, but nonchalant gesture into the air. Then again each goes down upon his haunches, with the umpire close as possible, fan in hand, and the same process is repeated, pinch of salt and all, till at last one of them sees his opening and now it is the pressing and pushing of their imponderable weights. Sometimes for lighter measure one wrestler will slap the other's face to disconcert him, which always raises laughs among the public. At times one wrestler will stand perfectly still like a huge ox, till the other heaves him by his belt and gets his feet, or only one foot outside the ring. One wonders if these belt-holds injure them internally. When they fall they do really wobble and bounce upon the boards. Then, with no show of malice or temper the winner will help his opponent to his feet. *Sumô* is certainly the most good tempered of all popular sports and pastimes. Not the least curious feature of this odd entertainment being when the umpire, fan in hand, announces the winner in a stilted, high pitched voice, the result of years of practice, and the next bout is proclaimed in similar fashion by the trainers. Sometimes a result is in dispute and all the umpires meet on the platform and settle it between them.

It will be seen that *Sumô* is surrounded by much ceremony, and there is as much tradition attached to it as to a bull fight. And like that it is aristocratic in origin which is why it is still invested with a certain chivalry. Do the *Sumô* wrestlers live to be old? Do they have children who are wrestlers? The answer seems to be that they die rather young for, decidedly, they cannot be healthy, however strong, and no one knows about their children. Most of the fat boys sitting there round the ring are eighteen, nineteen, or up to twenty-five years old, and no more than that, and many of them come from country villages. They are described as being very stupid, but are chosen out and fattened up from an early age. There is a print by Sharaku, for once of a *Sumô* wrestler and not a *Kabuki* actor, and it depicts a wonder child called Daidozan Bungoro, from a village in Hokkaido, the northern island of Japan. At eight years old this prodigy was nearly four foot tall, weighed nearly a hundred and eighty pounds, and his stomach was almost four feet round. He is shown in the print snuffing a candle with a heavy wooden *gô* board held up in one hand. He wears his hair already in the approved *Sumô* style. What happened to this interesting infant in later life is not known, but he has already in his portrait the dugs and abdomen and fat face of the profession. Would he have thrown Sandor or Hackenschmidt, champions of long ago, in open combat?

But all such speculation is silenced by the mounting excitement that rises to a crescendo for the antefinal. So huge a wrestler makes his way to one of the front rows that one can hardly believe one's eyes. He sits down, towering over the others, wearing menacingly a black *kimono*. He has a heavy prognathous jaw, a face that looks as if it was carved out of some giant vegetable root, and a brow like thunder, if one had never understood before the meaning of that phrase. His frontal physique is firmer, and he appears older than the huge baby faces round him. The antefinal is over almost before one has noticed it, owing to the emotions he arouses, and now the champion, a more serious looking young man than the others and of more normal appearance, though very large, mounts upon the stage. He is Wakenona (the 'Young Flower'), about six foot tall, one would judge, and weighing about sixteen stone. Every small child in the audience, and there are hundreds of them, yells his name. And his opponent is to be none other than the gigantic thunderbrow. Both of them put every ounce of drama into the preliminaries. The manner, in particular, with which thunderbrow stoops down to pick up his fistful of salt each time, and walks forward throwing it over his shoulder is as the closing of a chapter, the ending of an age. Again and again they crouch down in front of each other, and at last spring up and are locked together as a pair of bull rhinoceroses, except that those wear plated armour of hide, and in these you see each straining, cracking muscle. Each pushes the other and is immovable, but the unbelievable happens, and by sheer force and brute strength the champion shifts an inch, and makes a last stand, and with a huge lift and heave is carried, or rather hugged across the line, and the giant with the thunderbrow has won the round—not the whole contest, but this last and final bout of it —after which we depart from the arena in a hurry in order to get out of it before the crowd begins to leave.

For dinner, although it is not much after six o'clock, we go to a Japanese restaurant, but they dine early in Japan. The restaurant is not far from the wrestling and built out over the river, though we had been a week or more in Tokyo without knowing it is on the Sumida river. Already, one was beginning to realize that the restaurants in Japan are the most beautiful in the world, a fact which is borne in upon one very convincingly in Kyoto. In that city there are ten or a dozen eating places, and probably more than that, where every object, the rooms themselves and the views from their balconies, the china and lacquer, and not least the food, can be qualified as works of art. In Tokyo there had been that outstanding experience of a *tempura* house, and we were told there were three or four more of the same calibre. This restaurant to which we resorted after the wrestling was in no way inferior to the others. Not a house that specialized in either *tempura* or *sukiyaki*, but that served all kinds of food.

The usual soups made their appearance in beautiful, covered lacquer bowls and then we were brought a strange kind of fish which had been kept warm by a layer of flat sheets of a dark substance which was sea-weed over a bed of hot black pebbles. It could have been—and probably was—a dish thought out by a penguin with humanitarian leanings. With only this shortcoming, or thing lacking, that one could not, penguin-like, swallow the pebbles too. Arm rests were provided, such as many a barbarian must have longed for at a Roman banquet, and we were beginning to show progress with our chopsticks. An English, or rather American-speaking *geisha* was present, of a sort whom our host did not approve of, for she was of an altogether different type from the *geishas* of his youth; and presently an elderly matron, but probably not more than forty years old, appeared. She was a singer with a good voice, our host said, and in her hand she held a three-stringed *samisen* which she began to tune, sitting with her knees drawn up in front of her upon the floor. She sang a song with low and wavering voice while another *geisha* danced, but the dance was mediocre and the song raucous and not pleasing.

Was one in the mood for miracles to occur? I do not know. For something happened, and it was both big and small, like something seen from either end of the telescope, or at both extremes of the scale. Once or twice I have lain awake in the middle of the night, and been in time to hear the mouse-princess arrive in the room through her entrance in the wainscoting. Everyone who has experienced this will know the little runs and scamperings and the happy nibblings and gnawings that announce her presence. And in that other and larger nocturnal world of the theatre every balletomane, and it may be the writer more especially, knows that most poetic and beautiful of all stage entrances when we see a figure flitting between the pillars of the colonnade, and in another moment Princess Aurora in her rose-pink *tutu* and sleeves and bodice of rose and silver runs out on to the stage. For something in between these extremes, but partaking of both of them, now happened.

A wall partition slid back no more noisily than that entrance through the wainscoting, and a tiny little figure came running into the room. Ran, that is to say, with little muffled steps, falling to her knees, bowing her flower-decked head and putting both hands to the floor, then ran forward again and in a moment was sitting with her knees in front of her next to me at the table. This little tiny being just arrived into our world out of Lilliput was dressed from head to foot in flowered brocade of beautiful pattern, on a ground of midnight-ice or dark wistaria blue, with long trailing sleeves reaching three-quarters of the way to the floor. She wore a huge butterfly *obi* at her waist, plain round her figure, but gorgeously patterned upon her back. Her hair was dressed with incomparable elegance, but looking through a book of illustrations of Japanese *coiffures* I am unable to decide in my mind as to whether it was the 'half-peach' or 'gingko leaf'; but not the latter, I think, for that is described as 'so informal that it is never admitted into a refined or austere family', and as being 'the favourite mode of hair arrangement with waitresses in restaurants and married women in the lower classes'. But neither is it the *Simade-mage*, described as 'most appropriate for young girls in the flower of maidenhood, and indispensable for them on the most important ceremonial occasion of their lives, the wedding-day', a style at least a hundred and fifty years old in its present form of technical perfection, and of which there were more than a dozen varieties in pre-Meiji days. So, after all, it must be the first thought of, the *Momo-ware* or 'peach cut in two', for girls from thirteen to eighteen years old, with a comb and hairpins ornamented with artificial flowers, 'still the invariable mode among very young dancing girls known in Tokyo as *hangyoku*, a style which is not only dignified, but makes one look at once pretty and sweet'.

Which it does most decidedly for it is difficult to think of any creature, human or other, prettier than this young girl. Her hands were, I am sure, the smallest I have seen on any grown being, with tapering fingers and exquisite tinted nails. Her nose was slightly aquiline and she had delicious tiny ears. She was eighteen years old, she told us, and the eldest of a family. She danced gravely and beautifully for us, a sad dance under the circle of her paper umbrella, about lovers meeting in the rain; and danced with the other *geisha*, but it was always a little sad and melancholy, while the older woman sang and played the samisen, and sang much better than before. Between dances the little creature sat between us, as before, and it was almost embarrassing to be so near the exquisite little being in one's ugly clothes. When answering a question she had a way of hiding her mouth behind her fan as though to say, 'Forgive me for breathing!', but this is Japanese good manners when an inferior is speaking to a superior, though the real answer to this would be, 'Whom to whom?' It was the first live introduction to a world of poetry and beauty which has lasted perhaps for two and a half millenniums from India to Japan, and of which there is witness in the cave paintings of Ajanta and the temple sculptures of Angkor, and from the 'moth-eyebrows' of every Celestial entertainment down the ages to the *maikos* of the Gion which is the existing pleasure quarter of Kyoto. One could not but think of this while admiring her flower-decked hair, her almond eyes which were so curious in profile, and saffron or even sandalwood skin. It is the back of the neck which is the greatest attraction to the Japanese, and their sexual stimulus, and this little being had her neck most elaborately and carefully maquillé which merged almost imperceptibly into the faint pink or carnation tones of her complexion. We had in fact spoken to our host a few days before about the *maikos* of Kyoto, and he had told us 'there was something of the same kind' in Tokyo. This evening was the fulfilment of that chance conversation. But it was getting late—late by Japanese standards of entertainment which grow inordinately expensive as the night wears on —and we must perforce go home, accompanied to the door and even into the street by the whole staff, which is to say, the *maiko*—if that is the correct name for her in Tokyo—the *samisen*-player and *geishas*, and all the waitresses and everyone working in the kitchens, and by the charming old proprietress of the restaurant. And while they all helped us out of our slippers and into our shoes, and into the taxi, all bowing low to the ground with the arms straight down in front of them, the proprietress gave us a white 'cascade' chrysanthemum in a pot 'to take home to England'.

But this white chrysanthemum is a reminder that I am now writing about early days of October in an attempt for convenience of reading to resume all our experiences of Tokyo into the beginning chapters of this book. Pages which are the result of several separate stays in the capital while the weather altered from the tropical heat of August to the first touch of autumn. The *Kabuki* season had now opened again after the summer recess and we were able to see *Kabuki* three times in Tokyo, and once in Osaka. Such excellent and painstaking accounts have now appeared in our language that it would be more than a little presumptuous to attempt to write of *Kabuki* at any length after so slender an experience. Nevertheless, so overwhelming is its impact that no poet and writer, and no lover of opera and ballet in particular, can but be impelled to leave his impressions of it.

Just the arrival at the *Kabuki-za* in Tokyo through all the traffic is an excitement. To a Londoner it is as though he found the 'penny plain and tuppence coloured' of the prints still playing in a new, air-conditioned 'Britannia' at Hoxton. It is as if the ghosts of Sadlers' Wells and Drury Lane and Covent Garden had come to life. All the characters of the spangled prints: Edmund Kean, whose acting was compared by Coleridge to 'reading Shakespeare by flashes of lightning'; Madame Sarah Lane, ancestress of the Lupino family, in the short yellow skirt of a soubrette, and with her mandoline; Sir Glorion, the Blood Red Knight; Grimaldi, most famous of clowns; Tom Ellar, the harlequin; pantaloon, and how many more, still playing in the most modern and up to date of theatres. And where? Shall we say in Shaftesbury Avenue, a mean purlieu for so many playhouses? Better still in Times Square among the flashing sky signs. For the *Kabuki-za* is more modern in its equipment than any London theatre and is 'the largest legitimate theatre anywhere'; seating an audience of 2,599 persons and with an enormously wide stage. I would say, half as wide again as the stage at Covent Garden.

We arrived during an interval, and I was only disappointed to find the souvenir stalls not selling all manner of fascinating objects bearing the family crests of famous *Kabuki* actors, as one had been told. But the portraits on the postcard and programme stalls are of absorbing interest. For here are the living actors from prints by Sharaku and Toyokuni. Many of them, moreover, have an extraordinary resemblance in their 'make-up' to our clowns. It is because of their shaved heads and the way they paint their eyes and mouths. Shaved heads, or perhaps a tuft of hair on top; or sidelocks and whiskers like some kind of fantastic mechanical toy dog. And again, painted faces like a tattooed Maori, or like a Red Indian brave in full war paint. Staring eyes, blue lines of chin and jaw, and twisted, snarling mouths. Eyebrows given great prominence as aids to acting. An extreme and pre-eminent violence to judge from the posters and the photographs, but it is time to come inside.

The *Kabuki-za* is of course air-conditioned, a state which does not obtain in London theatres though it would be as useful on foggy nights as during a rare heat wave. And everything that pictures or prints of Kabuki actors have done to lift anticipation of the performance out of the ordinary into the transcendental is eloquent in the *Kabuki* version of an entr'acte bell. It is a pair of wooden clappers or clackers that give forth sounds of a woodpecker, or some unknown but tropical woodland bird. This, at rapidly diminishing intervals as though to hurry things to their climax; and as if every clacking conveyed its own warning that this was for the last time. Iterates and reiterates and then really hurries; and slowly one whole side of the proscenium revolves as on a turntable bringing forward some six or seven seated musicians with their *samisens*, sitting gravely in their *kimonos* like so many Romans in their togas. There are beautiful curtains or drop scenes at the *Kabuki-za*; on this first occasion a scene of golden pheasants or peacocks masquerading as phoenixes. And the curtain rises; but I am not attempting any description of a play in detail. Our seats were on the left-hand side in the stalls near to the *hanamichi* or gangway from the stage to the back of the theatre. This is a great and permanent feature of *Kabuki*, and we had not been there more than a few moments before a cortège of soldiers in armour came down it including men on horseback. The *hanamichi* is an immense recruitment to the dramatic possibilities of the theatre and every use is made of it by the kabuki actors. Scenery and

dresses are of the utmost magnificence. To quote Mr Faubion Bowers:
'Some sets are huge boats that extend the entire length of the stage.
Others are three-storey palaces in which a counterpoint of action takes
place on all three levels.' Moreover, the costumes are historically
accurate for *Kabuki* is the great national repository of tradition. There
are special workshops where the materials and dresses are woven. I was
only sorry we were unable to see one of the *aragoto* plays of particular
violence and melodramatic effect, in which the actors mouth meaning-
less words which have been concocted in order to give an effect of
force and strength. Also, in such a play we might perchance have seen
actors manipulating the *shitatare*, long Court trousers that trail backwards along the ground as though the actor were walking forward
on his knees.

It seems that the great epoch of *Kabuki* is always just over and a new
one is ever beginning. The same thing has probably been said of it at all
times during its three hundred years of existence, and ever since its
golden era which was the age of *Genroku* (1688-1703), a period of
luxury and extravagance propitious for the arts, and the epoch at which
Chikamatsu the great playwright of *Kabuki* wrote his plays. 'With the
tragic death of Nakamura Kichiemon in 1954 a whole era of grand
Kabuki came to an end. The titans of *Kabuki*, Koshiro VII, Kikugoro
VI . . . and Uzaemon XIV had disappeared one by one with frightening
acceleration'. These are Mr Faubion Bowers' words. But there are
always new actors to follow them. 'The next Uzaemon will be the
seventeenth and the present Kanzaburo is the eighteenth'. And so on.
It is the 'generation number' of the actor, if he is a member of one of the
hereditary families of actors, that the audience shouts out to him in
encouragement and applause. Often it is gestures that are almost
imperceptible to a Western audience that arouse this excitement; the
dropping of a cloak from the shoulder, or the closing of a fan. Members
of the public will come to the theatre specially for such a moment, and
leave when it is over.

But the most curious feature of *Kabuki* is the playing of all female
rôles by men. That this practice has had its equivocal moments goes
without saying. But in general it is no imputation against the actor who
plays a female rôle. In the theatre programmes there are photographs
of the female impersonators or *onnagata*, as they are called, in character
and in ordinary life, where it is to be seen that they are usually spectacled

and middle aged. The Japanese even think it is only possible for one of the female impersonators to be at his best after a lifetime of experience in portraying young women. The famous Baigyoku's farewell appearance was as a nineteen-year-old girl when he himself was seventy-three. Their voices are trained from childhood, and they may learn all the graces and allurements, but it is a deception into which it is difficult for a foreigner to enter. We know that women's rôles were played by boys upon the Elizabethan stage but at least they did not continue in the same rôles until old age. The boy-actors retired when their voices broke, or they took men's rôles. There can have been, and probably there were, actors of genius among them, but it was as the natural and untaught talent of the poet and not the fruit of experience from a career that can only have lasted for a few years. This is an important difference. What a pity that a travelling company of *Kabuki* players could not have acted for a season in Elizabethan London! But the Will Hugheses of *Kabuki* are cast for excessively lachrymose rôles. They are almost continually in floods of tears. Saying good-bye to lovers; or tearfully giving away sweets to children before committing suicide. They have their own particular way of running onto the stage with downcast head and eyes, with lank hair and even their hands, we could say, are wet with tears. I hear in my head, now, their thin falsetto voices. It is exceedingly curious how in woodcuts by artists who so often portrayed the female beauties of the 'green houses', where in any case the features of the human face are given in a simple outline, the *Kabuki* are to be known and recognized at the first glance, almost as though they form another sex. This is true of actor prints by Shunso and by Toyokuni; but most of all in the prints of that unique and extraordinary genuis Sharaku, of whom more later. It is on record that these strange creatures were ordered to wear female dress in their ordinary lives and to use the women's entrances to the public baths. This did not prevent them from marrying and having children but it must have given curious aspects to their home life. It could be said indeed that the most curious, collectively, of all groups of human beings must have been the *onnagata* *Kabuki* actors and the Italian *castrati* singers of the eighteenth century, the careers of both groups being in connection with the theatre. It is certainly to be comprehended that many considerable artists of Japan spent their lives in making prints of actors. As it is today, *Kabuki* must be the most vital and living form of theatre anywhere in the world.

Champion Sumô wrestler, Tochinishiki, in his ceremonial apron

Sumô wrestlers in action

Visually, poetically, dramatically, it can have no equal; and one can sympathize with the audience including many foreigners with whom it has become a lasting passion in their lives.

But another, and last experience of an even more enthralling nature was in store for us just before we left Japan. It was the more exciting because so few other persons have had the opportunity of hearing it. Indeed it is only 'visiting dignitaries' who come as guests of the government, and members of the *Corps Diplomatique* who are invited regularly twice a year, who form the usual audience. For this is nothing other than *Gagaku* which is the music of the Imperial Household band, an auditory and visual experience which is absolutely and entirely unique for there is nothing like it in the world. The absorbing interest of this extraordinary survival from the past, or indeed from many pasts, seems only to have been realized in quite recent years, because of its inaccessible position behind the moat of the Imperial Palace in the centre of Tokyo. It was safer there than in some remote monastery in Korea or Tibet for *Gagaku* has been one of the appurtenances of the Imperial Family of Japan for more than a thousand years. The term *Gagaku*, literally translated, means 'elegant and authorized music', and when accompanied by dancing it is no longer *Gagaku*, but is called *Bugaku*. At the same time the music, only and by itself, goes by the more alliterative name of *Kangen* which means 'wind and strings'.

By good fortune, and through the kind offices of a friend, we were enabled to attend a rehearsal, and even to see one of the *Bugaku* dances performed. That the orchestral players were wearing their ordinary clothes instead of the gorgeous costumes worn when they play to an invited audience, only made the impact of the music stronger still. The rehearsal took place in the Music Building, a hall resembling a riding school, within the moat and walls of the Imperial Palace. But, for the first part of it, we were taken to a small room at the back. Some twelve to fifteen orchestral players were in attendance, though the full orchestra numbers thirty-two, and once again as so often in Japan, it is in many instances an hereditary profession going back for many centuries to be a musician in the Imperial band. The first part of the programme to be performed consisted of *Kangen* i.e. 'wind and strings', and comprised two pieces of music, *Etenraku*, described as the most popular in all the *Gagaku* repertoire, and *Bairo* a 'martial music piece'.

E

What would this *Gagaku* music be like? Would it resemble a gamelan orchestra from Bali? For we are sitting almost alone in an empty row of chairs in front of the most peculiar collection of musical instruments one has ever seen. There are several kinds of drums and gongs but, also, three instruments in particular which are entirely new to our experience, the reason for their novelty being that they are so immensely old. They are a lute with four strings called the *biwa*; and another instrument of wonderful sonority which has thirteen strings, and is rather like the inside of a harpsichord taken out of its case. Or, in fact, the *Koto* is flat and supported on a trestle, has the tone of a cymbalom or dulcimer, and is played by the fingers which have little sheaths or plectrums of horn or metal attached so that it is as if the strings are plucked or struck by the fingernails. A chord struck on the *Koto* has the resonance of a harpsichord, and in its rare moments of use has quite a thrilling effect. The third, and the most peculiar of these unusual instruments is the *sho*, a pipe-organ held in both hands, and which consists of seventeen reeds or bamboos of varying length. The *sho* gives out solid chords of ten notes, and the player blows a continuous reedy drone on it which he modulates for the inner tones. One can readily believe these three instruments, the *biwa*, *koto* and *sho* to be anything from a thousand to fifteen hundred years old. In addition there are a long flute with seven fingerholes, the Korean flute which is a shorter instrument, side drums, and kettle drums.

Then the *Gagaku* begins, and it is not in the least like a gamelan orchestra, but much stranger and more difficult. It has fewer gongs and there is more emphasis upon the wood wind. The musical effect is quite the strangest I have ever heard in my life. It takes one to an unknown world of antiquity earlier than the T'ang era in China, and even to Sanskrit India of the seventh century. But, also, some of the pieces of music are supposed to have come from Indo-China, though to one's own instinct for what that is worth they seem to have no association with the, surely, gamelan-type orchestras of the Khmer Empires and of Angkor. We are concerned with three separate kinds of music; ceremonial Court music such as withdrawal music when Court officials left the presence; music played at Buddhist ceremonies and for banquets, and brought from the mainland of Asia to Japan during the Heian period twelve hundred years ago; and music written in Japan ten centuries ago by Japanese musicians in these archaic styles. And when we add that no fewer than six scales are used in *Gagaku* it makes this peculiar music no easier to understand.

Etenraku, the first piece performed, was a most thrilling and extra-ordinary experience, entirely removed from any symbols or ideas with which one had any links at all. It was slow moving, and most portentously odd and peculiar. *Bairo*, the 'martial music piece' with considerable and marked pluckings of the *Koto* and excessively queer drones and pipings of the *sho* or pipe-organ was, it is said, often performed as a war dance by a famous warrior Minamoto-no-Yoshiiye who died in 1106, but it has more the character of a long plaint or dirge. It is one of eight pieces of music brought to Japan by Butetsu, a priest from Indo-China, some twelve hundred years ago (about AD 736), from which one is led to think that the other seven pieces by Butetsu are in the repertoire. Its name *Bairo* is said to be derived either from Virocana, the Indian 'deity of war', or from a particular ceremony at the temple in Nara at which it was first performed. But it was really 'music of war' played before going into battle and as 'a means to fore-cast the issue of the day'. When given as a dance it is performed by four warriors who carry shields and halberds and brandish drawn swords.

Next, we repaired to the big hall of the Music Building in order to watch the dancing, and the performance now turns from *Gagaku* into *Bugaku*. There is a big square stage at one end of this hall, with parapets and railings of scarlet lacquer, and at the back of this are two perfectly enormous drums. They tower up in their oval wooden frames, and are painted with a halo of flames which in fact represent the sacred fires of Siva, the Hindu god, and attach in symbol to the drum beats with which he created the world. The dance to be performed is called 'Ranryôô, Prince of Lan-ling', and is said to represent Prince Ch'ang Kung of the Pei-Ch'i dynasty (AD 550-577), in the field, a prince 'who always wore a mask whenever he went to the front'.

In effect, the dance is preluded by some terrific, shuddering thuds upon the giant drums, and the dancer appears from the left-hand side walking with a peculiar step towards the stage. This step or entrance of the dancer must be very characteristic of *Bugaku*, as we shall notice again when we see this very same dance performed on the sacred isle of Miyajima above the shallows of the Inland Sea. He wears a gorgeous orange, or rather persimmon-coloured silken robe, thickly embroidered, what appears to be a tiger or cat mask of golden metal with a dragon upon its crown, and carries a short golden stick in his hand. The movements seem to be all feline, and consist of various treadings and stampings, and gestures with the golden stick tapping his other hand. And after three or four minutes of dancing he walked from the stage with the same tread in which he came on. This piece, 'the Prince of Lan-ling', is another of the compositions of Butetsu, the Brahman monk who came to Japan from Indo-China, and used to be performed at the Court parties of *Sumô* (wrestling) and horse racing. It is to be noted that whenever any of the music is performed for dancing, as now, the stringed instruments are not employed. So we have no *biwa*, nor *koto*, neither four-stringed lute nor dulcimer or cymbalon, for their sound is thought to be too refined as a background for dancing. And once again the complication is endless. What are we to make of it when told that if this piece is given as an accompaniment to the dance, 'its musical movements of *ranjo*, *saezuri* and *ha* are played in turn. However, when the piece is performed without the dance, *ha* alone is played.' Then, too, the *koto* (or dulcimer) is played 'in the technique called *hayagaki*, with an effect which is quite stirring and active'.

But now we must go into further explanation by stating that all *Bugaku* dances are of two different schools or traditions, 'dances of the Left' and 'dances of the Right'. 'Dances of the Left' are those introduced from China, India and Indo-China, as well as those composed in Japan in similar style, otherwise described in the phrase that Left music is that of the T'ang dynasty of China and other regions in the south; while 'dances of the Right' are classical dances imported from Korea, and northern regions including Manchuria, or those in Korean style. Dancers of the Left wear generally red dresses and dancers of the Right, green, and they make their entrance on to the stage from behind the big drum, respectively, of the left or right. The Prince of Lan-ling, which we have just seen performed, is a 'dance of the Left' and the dancer, therefore, wore a red dress.

The performance was now at an end, and we were taken first of all to a waiting-room where we were given cups of green tea and introduced to the musicians who brought along their instruments for our inspection. The *sho*, or little pipe-organ, is certainly the most curious thing imaginable, upsetting, or, rather, contradicting all previous mental association with either the Pan-pipes or syrinx of the ancients of classical or Theocritan imagery; or the chamber-organ of St Cecilia at the manuals with Gothic wings upon her shoulders near to her golden hair. The *sho* suggests another and a different mythology altogether. Not the least odd anomaly of the whole complex of *Bugaku* and *Gagaku* being that the Imperial musicians rehearse this music three times a week, and for the other half of their time they are rehearsing symphonies by Mozart and Haydn.

To what extent can this music of a thousand, or even twelve hundred years ago, have come down unaltered and untouched into our time? For that is something which is almost incredible to our minds; that it should be played now as it was performed in the time of King Alfred or King Clovis, indeed a century or two before the time of Charlemagne. Would the original composers of the music, the monk Butetsu, for instance, even recognize their own compositions as performed in Tokyo in 1958? But we must remember the unique, hereditary status of the musicians. Perhaps we would be more certain in our belief were we to see them playing in their Court dress; in the baggy silk trousers, soft shoes of felt, long sleeves, and the thin black hats of gauze that proclaim them as Imperial Court Musicians. It is difficult to believe that the little men standing around in their ordinary drab suits, holding, admittedly, very strange instruments in their hands, have just been playing music of a thousand years ago.

But there is a great deal of evidence of its authenticity. The *taikos*, or great drums of the *Bugaku* stage, appear exactly as now in Sôtatsu's screen-painting of the Court dance, a picture which we hope to look at in more detail later on, and Sôtatsu was a painter who was 'active early in the seventeenth century'. We must take it on trust that 'there are transcriptions in music notes by contemporary students, preserved after long centuries in the Imperial Court, and in the libraries of some Buddhist temples'. Another piece of the *Gagaku* music is Chôgeshi, described as a composition by Hakuga, 'a well-known virtuoso player of *hichiriki*', a kind of primitive oboe, and of the *biwa* (four-stringed lute), who lived in the reign of the Emperor Daigo (AD 897–930), written for 'withdrawal music', and now played as finale or music for the departure of the audience at the end of a programme of *Bugaku*, and usually played for this purpose with a quicker tempo, the name of which sounds almost contemporary to our Western ears for it is called *Bugaku-buki*. In all, the present repertoire of the Imperial musicians consists of more than seventy pieces, an extraordinarily large number, for during the long ages all but one or two of these unbelievably ancient tunes in ordinary circumstances would have been forgotten.

We ended the visit by being taken along to a kind of wardrobe room with long tables in front of the windows on which a number of books were lying open. They were coloured drawings of the dancers' dresses, all easily distinguished as to whether they were of the 'left' or 'right' by their colour which was, accordingly, red or green. These drawings form a very full documentation and seemed to be late seventeenth century in date. They would certainly repay many days or weeks of study. Then cupboards which lined the wall were opened and we were allowed to see the dresses. There were, in particular, some beautiful green dresses in Korean style, but it is obvious that all the dresses must be renewed from time to time. They must have their own workshops where repairs are done, and some male official in charge who corresponds to a wardrobe mistress. The dancer was there, still in costume, holding his mask in his hand. It is one of several masks which are classed as national treasures, and dates from the sixteenth century. This man who was one of the chief dancers told us that their repertoire, as distinct from that of the orchestral pieces alone, consisted of fifty dances of each kind, of the 'left' and 'right', and that there are twelve to sixteen dancers in the troupe.

Gagaku music, and the accompanying *Bugaku*, are certainly the most remarkable survival out of the ancient and classical past into present day Japan, and indeed one of the most curious and unlooked-for survivals to be found anywhere in the world today. These, and the contents of the *Shôsôin* at Nara. But *Gagaku*, over and above its magical and strange sound, has an important message to give to modern music which is to increase the number of instruments in the orchestra. Here a whole new battery of instruments is waiting, and they open the way from an old into a new world of music. It would seem more than likely that this will be the new direction of music, and one can but hope such possibilities will fall into good hands. For there is a marvellous poetic content, and a world of poetry to itself, in this ancient music. No one could listen to the timbres of such a composition as *Agon* by the veteran Stravinsky and not wish this master had such new, but old instruments at his disposal.

How to describe *Gagaku* I do not know, but it seemed to me the strangest of all aesthetic experiences, and I can only think of that strangeness in other terms, as, for instance, of coming face to face with the Mayan bas-reliefs of feathered caciques and astronomers in the jungles of Honduras and Yucatán, sculptures which are entirely outside the norm of ordinary aesthetic experience, and finding them still in the living world of the Indians who carved them. It is as strange as that. It is as though everything to do with the creators of this ancient music is different from the world we know. The images they associated with music must have been as different as the food they ate. It is as though, not the song of a bird, of thrush or nightingale, but the chirping of a cricket or a frog croaking must be their equivalent in aural image to moonlit night or the dawn of a summer day. *Etenraku*, the first piece played to us, and which is described as 'perhaps the most popular of all *Gagaku* pieces', has lately been scored for a Western orchestra by an American composer, Mr Henry Eichheim, who learned it from a well-known Japanese musicologist, and it has been performed in the United States, 'arousing keen interest among American music lovers'. Mr Lincoln Kirstein, moreover, has taken *Gagaku* music and dancing to the United States in the spring of 1959 where it was given for the first time in a thousand years outside Japan, but in the form of orchestral interludes during a programme of ballet. I would, personally, doubt the wisdom of this importation even with the beautiful costumes, for the music will sound almost too strange in a Western Theatre.[1] *Gagaku* and *Bugaku*, apart from the Music Department of the Imperial Household, are only performed in 'a very few shrines and temples', so that it was a remarkable proof of its authenticity to hear the very same *Prince of Lan-ling* performed in identical manner at Miyajima.

After attending the rehearsal of this extraordinary music there was little more to do in Tokyo. Except that this could never be true of a town of eight million inhabitants where a new *Kabuki* programme is put on the first day of every month. But at least we had done everything we wanted to do, and had now a longing to start off for Kyoto and be among works of art, having, in fact, up to this moment seen little or nothing of what we had come to Japan to see. On the other hand Tokyo was beginning to assert itself as the biggest human population in the modern world. Some of the possibilities of this enormous Asian city began to show themselves on the day I saw for the second time the same beggar, but, incredibly, in another part of the town. He

[1] It may be added that there are Japanese (Columbia) recordings of *Gagaku* music but they are monotonous and disappointing and do not 'come across' nearly as well as a Balinese gamelan.

had a thin black beard which is unusual for a Japanese, and makes it more probable that he was Korean, while his rags and ascetic leanness gave him the look of a renegade priest escaped from some mountain hermitage into the Barcelona slums. This character from another 'blue period' was the same man I had seen watching *Sumô* on the television screen in a shop window along the Ginza. But this was a different part of the town altogether and the chances were more than eight million to one against my ever seeing him again. Our eyes met and obviously he remembered me. It makes me wonder what image comes before him while I write this sentence. Then he turned away and I could see him walking, but that is not the right word for it, strolling, ambling, at half the pace of the passers by, with all of time in front of him, while they were busy every moment of the day. The last I saw of him, I could see the back of his head, and his bare elbows showing through his ragged sleeves, the perpetual and ghostly jay-walker of the Ginza, too quick to get run over in the traffic but too slow to be caught up into life. In fact, like others of more intellectual attainments he is a little outside life, and recognizes another in the same category, however different, when he sees him.

There is every drama of life in this huge town and it has all shades of meaning. A night haunt which presents a memory of towering 'hair do's' under a low ceiling. Like one of Fuseli's nightmares which he drew on paper, the sight of the curious beings in their huge wigs who come out and sit down at the tables in full rig of *obi* and *kimono*. A night haunt of the *onnagata* of *Kabuki*; or of those with inclination only in one direction, and therefore like some kind of lock-up or sponging-house of the spirit. The poor creatures are talking in their falsetto voices, and no doubt their nightmare loves are changing and evolving, but never to a happy ending. The little room is full of them, and more and equivocal rooms are upstairs. One wonders if any survive at all out of this pool of Malebolge, or if all are condemned for ever to stir the dark and foetid waters. Under their thick white paint, as thick as that upon the face of the Great Khanum, or chief wife of Timur, which appeared to Clavijo 'to be entirely covered with white lead or some such cosmetic, the effect being to make it look as though she was wearing a paper mask', they are probably bank clerks or shop assistants. For not all are the *onnagata* of *Kabuki*. Some are but playing at it, and wearing the clothes of the *onnagata* under cover of darkness. Only to see them in their giant 'hair do's' in travesty or perversion upon Utamaro's inhabitants of the Green Mansions is something one can never forget, and it should certainly have come before the eyes of the poet of *Âmes Damnées*. Serpent-like, as we were leaving, one of them came in, not wearing one of the huge wigs, who was quite indistinguishable from a young girl.

Upon one of our last evenings, entertainment of a less precarious nature took the form of visiting some of the bars in streets leading off the Ginza. There are a number of these and we entered three or four of them. Our visits must have been pre-arranged because the moment we came in at the door we were surrounded by young women. Four or five of them came and sat down at our table, most, if not all, of them, remarkably pretty, with one in particular wearing a scarlet *kimono* who was pointed out as being of Polynesian type. She had somewhat of the same looks as the young girls we were to see later in Honolulu, who are of mixed Hawaiian, Japanese and Hindu-Indian blood, as seductive of appearance as the *capresses* of Guadaloupe and Martinique with nectarine or coppery skins as described in Lafcadio Hearn's *West Indian Diary*, the more alluring for having nothing of the African negress in them, and probably among the most attractive hybrids of the human race. It is not easy to define the status of these young women. They are professional entertainers and yet they are not *geishas*. They are there to talk to and amuse the clients, and persuade them into ordering drinks. Hours of attendance are from five o'clock until midnight, and the future of any individual young woman depends upon her not succumbing to the long hours and joining her clients in incessant whiskies. We were told that some of them earn as much as thirty to forty pounds a week. Most are dressed in Western clothes and hardly any of them wear *kimonos*. Only a few of them speak a word or two of any other language, but certainly they are charming companions for an hour or two of the evening. One is left to draw one's own conclusion as to what further embroilments lie beyond that. But it is evidence as to the multiplicity or even superfluity of females in this enormous population that as many as twenty-five to thirty young women are on the lists of this one establishment.[1]

[1] 'Excellent *tempura* shop located in the centre of the famous Tsukiji *geisha* district, where nightly you can see *geisha* being carried quietly to customers in high-wheeled *Jinrikishas*. No *geishas* at this *tempura* house, but the unique *geisha* delivery service is quite a sight.' Quoted from *Today's Tokyo*, a weekly bulletin, 20 September, 1958.

Perhaps these bars of the Ginza district in Tokyo preserve some of the pleasanter aspects of the Green Mansions of old. Later that evening we visited another of them where the proprietress, a former film star, gave us a copy of a novel she had written, inscribed with her signature in black felt pencil, a beautiful piece of calligraphy. Like the others they were small premises full of people, with everyone talking and laughing. One must guess that this form of entertainment in Japan will never die. It is entirely in the Japanese tradition. For how many centuries have the equivalent of many hundreds of pounds been spent in training young women to be attractive companions and professional entertainers! And on leaving, and for our special benefit, a young girl of nineteen and still a novice, danced for us on a little cleared space of floor. She danced the *Gion Kouta*, a *geisha* song which takes on a special significance to anyone with a perceptive ear for after a few days in Japan you hear it everywhere. It is the song of the *Gion* or pleasure quarter of Kyoto, but at the time one did not even know what the song is called. One could only think what pleasant hours a young man could spend in conversation with the young women, and perhaps wonder whither it would lead him. And with that little nostalgic tune in our ears which we were so often to hear again until our time comes to say farewell to it far away in the south, upon the further bank of the 'brocade bridge' or *Kintai-bashi*, we leave Tokyo. Like all huge cities it is a place of mysteries. It could take all of a lifetime to understand even the most simple of them, but we leave because everything that in our hearts we have come to Japan to see begins tomorrow. All indeed is almost time wasted until you reach Kyoto.

- -

Chapter Four

KYOTO

IT HAD BEEN AN EXCITING and fervently hot morning. So hot that packing was a torment and a penance, and as we were going away for three weeks or a month there was a lot of packing to be done. On the previous evening it had been worse still when two electric fans whirring together and playing from side to side only seemed to whip up and heat the alternating draughts of air. When we were in Kyoto it was to be hotter than I have ever known it anywhere in my life, but that can be according to temperament the most inspiring of all times for working. Circumstances, therefore, were more than usually propitious.

That first time of going by train in Japan must be always somewhat of an adventure. The main station in Tokyo is so huge and large and the service almost alarmingly efficient. The 'red cap' takes you at once by the souvenir stalls, part seaside holiday, part pilgrimage shrine, down long white tiled underground corridors, and up on to the platform to the marked space where your compartment will be halted. It is our first journey and we are to travel in luxury on the observation car. Our luggage is piled at one end of the coach, and we are given arm-chairs in a club car which has a palm standing in one corner and a vase of lilies in another. Rich-looking business men in linen or silk suits are curled up on the other arm-chairs with their shoes off, and the attendants hand round magazines and thrillers from a bookcase. Looking over my shoulder I was sorry to see that one of the most glossy of the magazines was a golfing paper, and sorrier still to see bags of golf clubs among the luggage. But such is old and family prejudice which should have been dispelled when my neighbour took some cashew nuts and what appeared to be sugared persimmons from a lacquer box in his bag and began to eat them.

Luncheon was announced and we went along the train to the dining-car through the second class, in which we were often to travel on other journeys, past row after row of passengers, most of them male, sitting with their shoes off in clean white shirts, the majority wearing horn spectacles, and many of them listening in to the radio with the aid of earplugs thoughtfully provided on the backs of all the seats. The meal was being served by a gang of air hostesses to judge from their neat uniforms and forage caps, and on being brought the menu we decided on a 'prunier' dinner which consisted of a slice of salmon and some fried prawns. Alternatives were a chicken luncheon, which was more expensive, and what looked to be excellent beef, with *bentôs*, which are the little Japanese luncheon-boxes in which it is so easy to become interested, on sale as well.

We had now been travelling an hour. It was half-past one, and we were due in Kyoto at half-past seven, in about another six hours. The train emerged out of some tunnels with views of the sea down to the left, and at about this point the journey became an entire enchantment. I have never enjoyed a journey more in my life. We were to travel by the same train again on five or six occasions and I found it more fascinating every time. There were mountains covered with mist on the right, and it is about here that Fuji is often seen, though as mentioned elsewhere on the day after the typhoon, we were never to see more than a glimpse of the flank of the mountain from a train window. Presently we were going through lagoons with water on both sides of us, and huge cantilever bridges in the distance, so many of them that it looked as though it could not be necessary and must be a Japanese hobby. At the same time there were isolated houses on long spits of land that reminded me of the old customs house you still pass when going from the mainland at Mestre across the lagoons to Venice. It must have been a familiar sight to tens of thousands of travellers before the railway was built, and no wonder I thought of it because by whatever means, arrival at Venice is still the most exciting journey in the world.

This transit down the middle of Japan was no less thrilling though this main island of Honshu is of so curious a configuration that it is nowhere much more than a hundred miles wide, and long before we get to Kyoto will be scarcely half that width. It is a journey in length and not in breadth. The hills are still mist covered, but one has heard so often that in Japan misty days are thought to be masculine while a fine clear day is despised as feminine. But the mists in Japan have their own particular way of clinging to the hills. The gold clouds of the masters are at once explained the moment you see a sunrise or a sunset, while the monochrome painters are before you at almost every moment of the day. But now we are passing magnificent woods and looking into wooded valleys. They are forests of pine and fir trees getting apparently thicker as they climb towards the hilltops. They are altogether different and of another mythology from our woods, or from any other woods one has ever seen. Not woods of the faun or satyr; neither the oaks of Herne the Hunter, nor Claudian woods of ilex near to a broken column and a blue Mediterranean bay; neither the steep fir woods of Altdorfer, nor the green limes and elms of France. Their only point of identity with our woods is that they could be the haunt of pheasants, but it must be a native breed of greener and more fiery coloured pheasants.

All this from windows on the left-hand side, and now on the right are paddy fields with the rice growing as high as lilies-of-the-valley and nearing ripeness, and peasants at work, men and women alike, in peasant dresses of blue, and huge straw hats the shape of inverted lampshades. For scarecrows they have sometimes a face painted on a kite, tethered low down, in fact a hobbled kite, but, mostly, long glittering ribbons of metallic ruby-red or silver, turning and flashing in the sun, and tied to stakes. Every now and again a river or water-course has one solitary white stork, and at times a whole group of them, standing on the bank or fishing in the shadows. The houses are now peasants' cabins and have high thatched roofs. They have not changed at all since Sôtatsu made them the theme for one of his famous fan paintings. That is to say, they are the same now as three hundred years ago, and we may be certain, centuries before that, even if they now have the radio and are on the telephone. Where there is a considerable number of the cottages there will be a temple, often on a little hillock in the middle of a grove of trees. And a few moments later we may be passing a power station, or some modern factory.

In the meantime another group of air hostesses perambulates the train, always in pairs, selling iced coffee, or iced orangeade, and through the loudspeaker come long announcements always including the syllables 'allemass' at nearly every other word. The train rushes through a big station where we had been promised we could buy mouth-organs on the platform, rushes through, without stopping; and about then, or soon after, we pass a large temple quite near the line on the left-hand side with a lifesize figure of a white elephant standing in front of it, but although I looked for it on subsequent journeys the white elephant eluded me and I never saw it again.

No cattle to be seen anywhere, and the famous beeves must be kept indoors and be hand-fed somewhere near to the thatched cottages. It was to be noticed, too, that many of the village temples with *torii* at their gates stood in bamboo groves, but we were never near enough to catch more than a glimpse of their swaying stems and feathery tops. The bamboo glades are among the great beauties of Japan. They open new vistas and have their own imagery of association which will make appeal the moment there is opportunity of coming closer to them. But it can be said already that the first time of seeing a glade of bamboos growing on its native soil is as that moment of coming to a vineyard with the grapes on it, or seeing an orange grove. There were indeed terraces of orange trees in a few places, and another and beautiful fruit just ripening was the persimmon.

But most characteristic of all were the tea plantations, a thing entirely new to me, which brought home to me that I was in Japan. Perhaps I had thought beforehand that the tea shrub was a tallish bush, or even a small tree. Probably through having read announcements that the best crop of Ceylon or Assam tea was the 'tips' or 'tops' of the plant; and from remembering a fantastic story that at a sale of the Dowager Empress of China's collection of teas the biggest price had been fetched by a variety which grew so high on the tree that it could not be reached by human hand and had to be picked by a posse of trained monkeys. The tea shrub, which is related to the camellia, grows to a taller height everywhere else but in Japan; and in any case the tea plantations seen from the train window do not look so much like dwarf camellias, as miniature azaleas, not in flower. But from this distance, flashing by, every terrace or little row of tea plants could be an individual nursery devoted to growing box-bushes in identical shape for some particular purpose. The little terraces are in fact separately owned by peasant proprietors and owners, the Japanese being the most specialized and individual race in the world, coming even before the French in this respect. Their tea shrubs are about the size of cushions, or, I say, miniature azaleas, but not the prostrate sort which cling to the ground, for the essential of a tea plant is that it should be vigorous and rounded. They are grown everywhere, whenever there is a space of ground, as though the huge population of tea drinkers must be satisfied.

This is indeed the race who would spend months on a tiny lacquer box, carving and inlaying a *netsuke* which would fit into the palm of a hand, or growing a couple of rows of shrubs which soon become as beautiful in poetic imagery as the rows of beehives on the lake isle of Inisfree. And in a moment more we may be passing the huge bluish leaves and white lilies of a lotus pool.

It was exciting and indeed nearly incredible to be passing through Nagoya when the train stopped for a few moments somewhere round half-past five. I had longed to go to Nagoya, and to how many other towns in Japan, for so long and never thought it could come true. To be luxuriously rushing past, without even bothering to get out, only made the prospect of coming back later to Nagoya more enjoyable still. Soon afterwards it began to get dark, even at the end of August, so that those wonderful hours of looking out of the window were over and done with. Also, one became acutely conscious that the air-conditioning in the train had now brought about a condition of intense and glacial cold. It was becoming cold enough to catch pneumonia; and I was thinking of going into the locked compartment where the luggage was kept in order to take out a sweater when it was discovered that we were arriving half an hour earlier than we had understood and were due in fact in Kyoto in a few moments. This most punctual of trains, which goes on to Osaka and Kobe, came into the station with not a second to spare, and our luggage was thrown out in a trice for even in this great town with a million and a quarter inhabitants the express stops no longer than two minutes. There we were met in the station, as big as and much cleaner than any London terminus, and driven through the tropically hot night to the hotel, where again there was trouble with the air-conditioning in the bedroom, which was out of order and made a 'chug-chug' noise all night long like a tramp steamer beating up the Channel so that one slept uneasily with the rhythm of Masefield's poem pounding in one's head. Also, it was so hot that one could only lie on the bed on one's back without even a sheet over one, not daring to turn to either side.

What a difference in the morning! It was wonderful to wake up in this lovely town. There was a drop of a few feet from our window, and then a steep wooded hill rose straight up till it filled half the skyline, wooded, as always, right up to its summit with some trees like ilexes or holm oaks near by, changing to cryptomerias as they began to climb the hill. We looked out on to this wooded hill, morning and evening for more than three weeks, and got to love it. Far away down to the right were the roofs of a part of Kyoto but hardly a sound came up from there. Instead, we were in midst of unknown and fascinating sounds of bird and insect. Not all were noisy. On the windowsill, and hiding in the ivy or virginia creeper, was a strange creature two or three inches long, hardly distinguishable from the leaves and bits of twigs which were its background. It must have been the chrysalis of some butterfly, probably a swallowtail, and not only was it the colour of the browner of the leaves, it had upon it several and distinct bits of snapped off twig the shape and size of broken matches. Only occasionally it made a lazy movement of its hawser-legs, or worked its jaws; but, oddest of all, it had fastened itself to the wire cable of the air-conditioner, as if of preference, and seemed to suffer no inconvenience from the shaking and rattling of that lame machine.

But there came a metallic whirring of unbelievable force and happiness, as though enjoying every whirr of it, and winding itself up to whir and whir again, like a metallic spring or coil wound up and let go. And hovering, whirring, darting off, and whirring and hovering again. I have never heard such insect, or animal exuberance. It was exulting and shouting in the heat, except that it is nothing vocal. There is never such exaltation in the motor of an aeroplane. It revvs up and up and roars because it has to. It never shrieks in its metal of its own accord. But this is a thing that has hurled itself into the heat to whirr and make its noise. And having done so, hovers, and darts off to whirr again. It is a cricket, and no wonder they catch them in Japan and try to induce them to sing in wooden cages. Certain woods or stretches of land are famous for crickets, and their singing is admired more than the song of birds. But there were, as well, fascinating and luscious croakings of frogs as though they, also, were in enjoyment of the hot days; and the only unpleasantness was a skirmish, now and again, with huge black-beetles which came out of the walls of the bedroom, and frequented especially the bathroom. They ran with horrid speed, and not being able to kill them myself, I had to ring the lift-bell and have it done for me. It seems that they are only a nuisance in buildings that are semi-Western in style like our hotel, and that in a real Japanese hotel there are no holes for them to come out of the walls, and in consequence there are no beetles.

Street vendor in Tokyo

Porcelain jar 'Yoshino–Yama', by Ninsei. (Early eighteenth century. Exact dates unknown). *See pages 184-5.*

Porcelain jar 'Yama-Dera', by Ninsei

Porcelain jar 'Wakamatsu', by Ninsei

Soon we established a régime in our lives, to have our luncheon in the hotel, and whenever possible dine in the town. But this has its hesitancies, with the result that on several of our first evenings we found ourselves eating a horribly nasty and expensive dinner at so called Western-style restaurants in the town. Moreover, you dine much too early, such places are often shut by half-past eight, and it costs as much as any dinner in London or Paris. It needs a little resolution to make up one's mind always to 'eat Japanese'. And it is a mistake not to do so because Kyoto, as we have said, has some of the most beautiful dining places in the world. Those must reveal themselves as we proceed, but before we go any further we have now to consider the status of Kyoto as one of the wonders of the Far Orient. Several persons well acquainted with both told me they preferred Kyoto to Peking. I do not think this answer can have been true while Peking was still its ancient self, until some thirty years ago, that is to say. The marvellous, if pantomime spectacle of its street life must have coloured what is now an ant-like population, all uniformly clothed and indoctrinated, and Peking cannot be so beautiful as formerly. Peking apart, it may be true to say there is little or nothing left in China. Temples and palaces are destroyed, and Chinese works of art are in Formosa and Japan, and in the USA. What did once exist in China is no criterion for, one way or another, it is no longer there. The lover of actualities will perforce choose Kyoto even though its great buildings are of wood, not stone.

Then, too, its wonders instead of being confined in anonymity in the Forbidden City are scattered about in every quarter of the town, and we can go to see gardens knowing the name of the garden architect, and to admire paintings knowing the name of the painter. Sightseeing of this nature has not been practicable in China for two or three centuries. In Kyoto you can sightsee just as in Venice or Florence. You can visit a couple of temples and gardens in the morning, and a couple more in the afternoon or evening, and go on doing this for three weeks or a month without ever seeing the same things twice over, and this is true of only one other city in the world, and that is Rome. In comparison, such cities as Toledo or Siena are at the end of their resources in a single week.

Again, what is unique in Kyoto with its huge population is that, except in the hotel, you never see a Western face. But neither are they so unused to foreigners that they turn round to stare. With great towns

F

like Osaka that has two million people, and Kobe with one million, so near, they are a sophisticated population inured to train and tram and film and sky sign, taking those in fact for granted and pressing on towards the Welfare State with its insurance benefits and old age pensions. The monuments of Kyoto, far exceeding in number and variety those of, shall we say, Oxford or Cambridge, are all one-storeyed and therefore cover an area comparable almost to that of Paris or Washington. You may easily drive for half, or even three-quarters of an hour, in order to reach some temple which is still within the city limits. No particular quarter of the town has been spoiled by modern 'improvement', and having survived the war during which mercifully it was not bombed, it seems probable that national pride will keep its beauties intact as far as possible. If this happens, within not much more than a decade from now Kyoto may be the least spoiled great city left in Asia.

The quantity of its old temples is quite overwhelming. They must outnumber the Roman churches and the mosques of Istanbul. Many of them, as well, contain a number of smaller temples and gardens within their walls. So that when you go to visit a particular shrine, Daisen-in, for instance, or Nanzenji, there will be three or four, or more, temples and gardens to be seen, subsidiary to the main one, but all known by their own names. Sometimes it can take a morning or an afternoon to see a complex of temples. One of the difficulties in Kyoto is the tracking down of the lesser sights for there is scarcely ever a porter or custodian, and passers by know nothing at all. Once only, on the hottest of hot days, we met a *bonze* (monk) with shaven head, and in a black toga, who directed us to his monastery compound in between the shutting and opening of his fan. Somehow I had never anticipated a monk with a fan, but this should be nothing unusual in a land where the umpires in wrestling matches carry lacquered fans with long silk tassels, and where the warriors in their lobster-armour carried fans.[1]

Of course the reverse side to this eulogy of Kyoto would be that one soon tires of rock gardens and wooden houses and temples that are little bigger than a Maori hut. It is true that there is some basic element in Japanese building that betrays a kinship with the Polynesians. Of

[1] War fans were iron-ribbed, and were used by the military commanders to direct their forces and emphasize their orders. With regard to the monk with the fan, the monks of the Mieido temple in Kyoto are supposed to excel in their manufacture, so that fan shops all over Japan are often called 'Mieido'.

their own nature the Japanese are more inclined to build like Maoris than like Chinamen. Not, we are inferring, the paper houses in their towns which again are entirely national and idiomatic, but the thatched cottages of the countryside. Those could be without much stretching of the imagination, peasants' cabins in Fiji or Samoa. Wherever, as in certain Melanesian islands, or in Sumatra and Celebes, the inhabitants have erected large communal or club houses for themselves, the dimensions of most, if not all Japanese dwellings are likely to be far exceeded. Then, too, the cult for simplicity associated with the great tea-masters and garden designers of the seventeenth century, such as the famous Kobori Enshû, had the effect of still further diminishing the scale until a building destined for the tea ceremony would take on the proportions of a rustic summer-house and, at that, a low hut designed for a few persons who crawled into it through an aperture like a dog-door and sat on mats upon the floor. All this by one of the anomalies ever present in Japanese art history being contemporary to the sumptuary splendours of so true a palace as Nijô Castle with its painted rooms worthy of a Doge of Venice.

The revelations of Kyoto are its wooden temples and its rock gardens. After seeing but one or two of the gardens it becomes evident that this is an art form so highly developed over a long period of time that it puts another meaning and a new scale of values upon Italian gardens. Those are masterpieces of the Mediterranean world but the Orient can rival them. How do the mountain rocks in the 'dry' garden of Daisen-in, where water is but simulated, compare with the Isolotto or stone island of the Bóboli at Florence; or the spatial rocks of Ryûanji to the fauncaryatids of Caprarola? Even the avenues of Beloeil and Versailles, long green tunnels, begin to lead nowhere once we have walked the meandering paths of Katsura and Shûgakuin. Some of the most lovely gardens in the world are in Kyoto. They are small in scale, of course, but all is in proportion, and this is neither true of Italian grandeur, nor Bourbon conceit. The Japanese gardens are the great works of little masters. But they have the perfection of form of the little masters and their flawless execution.

In such a plethora for there are about a hundred gardens in Kyoto, it is difficult to know where to begin. We could start at Ryûanji which is the most sensational of all, or go to see the larger lakes at Kinkakuji, the 'Golden Pavilion', or at the Imperial villa of Shûgakuin. It is even a little practical to get used already to the strange names for it cannot be anything but confusing to have a Kinkakuji and a Ginkakuji, the one a 'Golden', and the other a 'Silver Pavilion'; but which is which? When it is a matter of Nishi Honganji or Higashi Honganji; Chichakuin or Shûgakuin; Daikakuji or Daitokuji; Nanzenji or Ninnaji; the names are growing harder still, to the point almost where it becomes impossible. But they are of course, in fact, no more difficult and confusing in the memory than English or any other names. One has to try and attach something seen to the name itself, as though that meant it. Then Ryûanji becomes not improbable as a synonym for a lot of rocks set out in raked sand; but is the tinkle of a gold coin or ornament a 'Ginka' or a 'Kinka' sound? For Kinkakuji is the 'Golden Pavilion', and Ginkakuji which is a 'moonlight' garden is the 'Silver Pavilion', as we shall soon discover.

Ancient or idyllic calm is the supreme lesson of these gardens, where it can be seen as nowhere else in the world now the classical gardens of China are all gone, and for an experience of its thaumaturgic and poetic powers I would suggest going to see the 'Moss Garden' or Saihôji before embarking upon the more famous gardens of Kyoto. It is a first tasting which should on no account be missed. The idyllic calm of Saihôji is a poetic blessing one would like to remember all the rest of one's life.

The 'Moss Garden' or Saihôji, also known by the endearing name of Kokedera, is some distance out of Kyoto through what in any other city would be a suburb, but one is loth to call it that. It lies to the north-east, and must be some six or seven miles from the centre of the town. The 'Moss Garden' is by no means the most famous of Kyoto gardens, and only those making a long stay here are likely to see it. I think there can be no doubt it is one of the beautiful gardens of the world, with all the more reason for seeing it because it is not so well known. If this be our first experience of Kyoto there is the probability of going to it by way of the scarlet *torii* at the entrance to the Heian Shrine, at a corner beyond which, should this be so, there is an intriguing detail to be noticed, namely, a ladies' hairdresser with dummies of all the different forms of Japanese coiffure in the window. Further on, we may pass the cyclopaean walls and golden roofs of Nijô Castle, still in the modern part of Kyoto, but soon we are in purlieus that are untouched and unspoilt.

This was something one had come a long way to see. It is the real

Japan, in no way vitiated by the passing lorry of doll-size with its steering wheel shaped like the handlebars of a bicycle. We are in a street of low shops like a village high street, and are now passing the most charming little houses each with its bamboo fence of differing design. Probably Kyoto is the centre for this art of garden fencing, a subject upon which whole books have been written. They give an entire individuality to the exterior of the smallest house, as though each householder must be an aesthete of exquisite taste. We see a little flagged path leading to the door, and pairs of slippers of varying size neatly laid out inside the doorstep. Each house is diminutive, and they are neither huts nor houses but more properly garden villas, even if the garden is no bigger than the sunken area in a London street. Suddenly we know how hot it is at the sight of old men, who must be the aesthetes of whom we are talking, wearing nothing more than white cotton breeches, with bare feet and bare yellow chests, and naked children. Even the old men are glistening with sweat, and we know they live at this time of year, in August, nearly naked in their little rooms of lath and paper, fanning themselves, and sitting on the matting.

This road to the 'Moss Garden' is a marvellous introduction to the Far East if you have never been here before. It made me think how lucky I have been in my life; to have known long ago that road from Naples through the courtyard of Portici with its stone cypresses just as Fragonard sketched them for the Abbé de Saint-Non, with all the slum houses, Pulcinella-haunted, with their backs turned to the view, *carricolos* careering along at full gallop with pheasant feathers tied to the horses' heads, and smouldering Vesuvius near by; and to have breathed at least the air of Mexico, for I was only there for five days, Mexico having been touchstone and intoxicant to my youthful fancy, but I saw at any rate four or five of her longed-for golden churches and their altars, and beautiful Taxco, but now there is no time for more because, miraculously, this is Kyoto, and the 'Moss Temple' or Kokedera, incredibly, is but a few hundred yards ahead.

At last, after a dream-like transit past those enchanted garden houses we must stop and get out to walk, oblivious of the heat, down a long path, and turn at a right angle to buy our tickets which, in this land of minute objects beautifully carried through, are quite a delight in themselves owing to their delicate printing in colours, as are so many other tickets of admission to temples in Kyoto. There follows another longish walk, only to add to our anticipation, and we are in front of a low building though I never made out whether, or not, this is the pavilion or tea-ceremony house that has a unique earthen ceiling, seen nowhere else in Japan. But this gives the character of the place, and that the lake has seven earthen bridges, Kokedera being a temple of the Zen sect, wherefore all is utmost simplicity except what tends to the imagination.

Already, the heaving and billowing mosses are hummocking and bowing themselves, and inviting you to tread upon them. This moss-element is something new and never experienced before. One looks at the way the trees and rocks come out of the moss precisely as if out of a new element, a dusting from Betelgeuse, or fine powder from galaxies beyond the Milky Way. Or the garden with its primitive stones could date from a primaeval period when another vegetation clothed the ground. What is the history of Kokedera? Can it really have been designed by the Zen priest, Musô-Kokushi (1275-1351)? But he is not as mysterious as all that for another temple garden, Tenryûji, is attributed to him. One would say, since Plantagenet times, Kokedera must have altered or been changed. But now we come to the lake with its earthen bridges leading to the islands, and fifteen stones set in the water, representing, as we like it, Chinese treasure ships touching at a Japanese harbour in the evening, or a line of small boats lying at anchor for the night. It is late in the day, either way, and towards evening. And then we notice the extraordinary and venerable-looking stones of the garden, and can really believe that they date from the time of Musô-Kokushi and were seats of meditation for the early sages. One rock, which in the fourteenth century was found in the morning mysteriously hung around with sacred straw festoons or garlands, 'is worshipped as a deity up to the present'; and one can believe, too, that after Musô Kokushi's death his successor lived here, and showed the garden 'with its abstruse atmosphere to high priests who came from China'.

There are 'more than twenty' and, some say, even fifty varieties of moss growing in this garden.[1] Even to an untrained eye, mosses of russet colouring an inch or two high, shaggy, satyry-beard-like of texture, alternate with velvet-pile mosses as springy as the mattresses onto which acrobats tumble and bounce up when they leap down from the trapeze. Having doubted it at first, one would be willing to believe

---

[1] There is, or was, an old garden at Nikko planted with over a hundred varieties of mosses, no doubt in emulation of Kokedera at Kyoto. When at Nikko I enquired for it, but could not find it.

now that the 'Moss Garden' is older, older far than the time of Musô Kokushi and dates back to the first sages. But the mosses? Are they here by accident, or design? The same puzzle occurs as with the *Gagaku*. Would the composers of that ancient music ever recognize their tunes? Are they altered beyond recognition, and have they taken on a different meaning? Or has *Gagaku* really come down untouched by time? For the whole moss-element in this garden could be of accidental growth. It could be the swarming of the mosses. Or a moss garden may have been the intention, but in six centuries the mosses have rioted and got the upper hand. Now it is too late to know the answer. Even the waters of the lake are stained green with algae, and there are lichens on the tree trunks. A white gean grew on one of the islands, and wistaria, iris and azaleas are in flower in their proper seasons. I think it was better to see the 'Moss Garden' when nothing was flowering except a lotus or two in their bluish, water-lily leaves, and the moss-element like a green Sahara spread its velvet dunes and hummocks.

It may be this is the first time one has seen the great stones of the classical Chinese garden but at Kokedera they are so invaded by the mosses that this is not the place either to write of them, or admire them. Then, too, up some precipitous steps at the back there is a 'dry' cascade and pool which, also, may be new to our experience, and here the mosses do indeed make a mimicry of water. But the 'dry' gardens of this wonderful new garden world can wait for more dramatic instances, and in particular at Daisen-in, for now there is another revelation, a bamboo-glade in all its feathery and rustling, swaying beauty. It is to be known in that first moment of seeing it that this is one of the beauties of their classical gardens, and one can perceive why in China there was a school of bamboo-painters who were all *literati*. There are hundreds of varieties of bamboos, differing in their leaves and in the jointings of their stems, and in Kyushu the southern island of Japan there are even bamboos with square stems and a kind which has black stems. But in the 'Moss Garden' they were just bamboos, and it was worth while coming all the way to Japan to see them.

After this unique experience one can waste no more time before hurrying to Ginkakuji, the 'Silver Pavilion', which is probably all things considered the most beautiful garden in Japan. It is on the green hillside only a little way out of the town. Already, the idyllic and peaceful beauties of Kokedera have shown that these gardens are comparable to the most famous of Italian gardens even if their poetry is entirely different. The green shades and ilex shadows are not satyr-haunted. Here are no goat-gods, and neither statues, nor fountains. In their place we have to accustom our minds to 'dry' cascades and pools, rocks of curious shapes, moon or snow viewing, and green retreats for the sages. Together with other anomalies that we may experience for the first time at Ginkakuji. But the entrance to this marvellous garden is not unreminiscent of the ilexes of Italian gardens. One could fancy oneself in this hot moment to be walking the long paths of the Bóboli in Florence.

For the way takes a right turn between high hedges of clipped trees which have the authentic ilex glitter even if they are not ilexes. And at the next corner we are in the garden of the 'Silver Pavilion' with something exceedingly curious only a few feet away. It is a conical hill or mound of white sand, exactly as though poured out of a mould, or child's pail at the seaside, and some five or six feet high. Its surface has hardened into a sort of crust. Near by is a 'sea' of white sand raked into a design of waves. We are back again with the same problem as with the mosses of Kokedera or the music of *Gagaku*. For the 'Silver Pavilion' and its garden were made by Yoshimasa, one of the Ashikaga Shoguns, in 1479, the layout being attributed to one of the greatest of garden architects in Japan, the fifteenth-century monk, Sô-ami. How long have those heaps of sand been there? Have they really stood here since the fifteenth century? For now they are a beautiful feature in the garden, and the legend is that they were used for moon-viewing. But, really, they were piles of sand kept in readiness for strewing the paths in case an Imperial visitor arrived, and in theory a sand heap should be able to keep its shape for five hundred years. But, more truly, it is a kind of ghost story, and an example of how such stories have their beginning, the point being that the mounds of sand were useful and beautiful for their white shapes, like snow.

Now we see the 'Silver Pavilion', itself, a building in two storeys, and intended to be admired by moonlight for which purpose it was to have been coated with thin silver leaf. The interior is so simple as to be uninteresting; and the same comment holds true of another pavilion with a tiny room in it which is the model of all rooms used for the tea ceremony. The Shôgun Yoshimasa, who was the perfect aesthete, used to sit here for hours drinking tea, writing poems, and judging incense. It must be said in no spirit of disrespect to so beautiful a work as this garden of the 'Silver Pavilion', that what an old book says of such pavilion rooms is true, that 'they are marked by elegant and striking simplicity, are devoid of every comfort, but quite satisfy the Japanese, who spend hours squatting in them or lying flat on their stomachs, with heels in the air'.

Now the exquisite trained shapes of the trees begins to grow upon one, and as we walk round the lake we see that the shore and the artificial islands are bordered with great stones. If one could be here for long enough these stones might become more interesting and less monotonous than the statues in our gardens. They have been chosen for their curious shapes with an infinity of care, many of them being presents from various daimyôs to the Shogun. They are rocks taken from river beds and collected for their shape and texture. It was a cult from classical China, and this explains the curious and gnarled forms which have so fantastic an effect in Chinese paintings of gardens. But in China this cult was carried further than in Japan, and they collected calcareous dolomites, ten or fifteen feet high, worn away and eroded until they were hardly rocks any more. Before now one has wondered what the strange shapes could be, but they are garden rocks dredged up from the bed of one particular lake in China.

The bridges to the islands are not earthen, as at Kokedera. They are formed of pairs of monoliths, or even from one huge stone in slight curve like a stone sword. Round and round the view opens as you walk round the lake, mostly with that white mound of sand like a kind of moon platform in the foreground somewhere. The Pavilion, we know, was to have been silvered, and now we begin to see resemblances between this garden and Kokedera, upon which it is said to have been modelled by order of the Shogun, but as though this was done before the mosses took control at Kokedera, so that it is an interpretation in another medium and meant in any event for moonlight. The moon rising over the wooded hill was the famed beauty of this garden and, as one authority points out, invites the eye to lift up to the skyline, garden views in Japan being often, as here, upward instead of downward as in our gardens. The Pavilion was to have been silvered for that magical moment of the moon coming over the hill, when the ghosts of white sand would become night ornaments of the garden.

Kinkakuji, the 'Golden Pavilion', should be seen while its moonlight companion is still in mind, the two being some way apart though in the same, northern quarter of the town. But this contrasting of Ginka and Kinkakuji must take into account that the latter is a hundred years older, and built in 1394 by the grandfather of the Shogun who was so fervent an amateur of moonlight. Moreover, the 'Golden Pavilion', or Kinkakuji, was completely destroyed by a religious or political fanatic— or was he a too zealous or over jealous aesthete?—who set fire to it and burnt it down, deliberately, in 1950. It is a curious story which has been made the subject of a drama by a well-known playwright. Now, in fact only three years ago, the Pavilion has been remade, that is to say, copied in exact facsimile, something which does not convey any of the same implications as in Europe. Indeed, the Shintô shrines, as we shall see, are rebuilt on principle every twenty years, which is not difficult for they are wooden buildings. Copying the 'Golden Pavilion', and gilding it, was no large or overwhelming project for, though three storeys high, it has only the dimensions of a large summer-house. This, too, was obviously the haunt of aesthetes and its second floor, one is told, and expects to hear, was intended for poetry and incense parties.

There is a beautiful reflection or doubling of the 'Golden Pavilion' with all its gold leaf in the lake waters. Even so, one comes away from Kinkakuji more than a little disappointed. The lake covering several acres is one of the largest in Kyoto, but not impressive in that respect to anyone knowing the lakes in private parks in England. It is true though that the landscape gardeners who laid out the lakes in question were working away from the formality of Italian gardens and the canals of Le Nôtre towards what they imagined to be ancient Chinese proto-types, and this is also precisely what the Japanese garden architects of six centuries ago were doing. So that Repton or 'Capability' Brown would have greatly admired the lake of the 'Golden Pavilion'. One large island floats upon the lake, and there are a number of monolith or cyclopaean islets made from large single rocks, giving to the waters of the lake a thickly populated appearance. What after all is the extra-ordinary feature of such gardens is that they were the resort of aesthetes and dilettantes at about the time when Edward I was building the Welsh Castles. Even with a little juggling of the dates, the 'Golden' and 'Silver Pavilions' are in eloquent contrast to Conway and Caernarvon. In place of Henry de Elreton, military architect to the Plantagenet, we have Mûso-Kokushi once again, or so it is said, for some authorities see the hand of the priest-architect of the 'Moss Garden' in a moss and rock garden at the back of Kinkakuji. Taking a last look at it, the 'Golden Pavilion' floats upon the waters which are almost solid with water-lilies, the rocky islands are intoxicating to the child's mind which longs to move from one to the other as though they are stepping stones, and what are beautiful and admirable in this beautiful country are the shapes and outlines of the trees.

We have now in the course of what need be no more than a single day had a true taste of Japan, and seen the works of two great garden architects, both of them Zen priests, Mûso-Kokushi and Sô-ami. This Buddhist sect, dating from the thirteenth century, with its strong emphasis on contemplation, and its injunction to seek salvation by divine emptiness and meditation, had a particular propensity for making gardens. Gardens which are not palace gardens in Kyoto, and those are in a minority, are Zen gardens. One will never forget this impression of temples with gardens round them. Their proportions are so cleverly worked out that one forgets how small they are. The 'Silver Pavilion' garden is about the size of the Tudor garden at Hampton Court, or not much bigger than a large old kitchen garden, but it is as full of incident as the gardens of Versailles. Yet it is not too crowded and lies light upon the mind. Again, the lesson of these gardens is classical tranquillity— but that in another sense from ours—and idyllic calm. So many of the gardens are as little oases of tranquillity in the middle of a great town. Kyoto has had a huge population for many hundreds of years. It seems a big city now, and it must have appeared much bigger then.

If we have been here no longer than a day we are already succumbing to the fascination of the shops. Probably our first landmark will be one of the bridges over the Kamogawa, and it is on its western river bank that the interest of Kyoto begins apart from its temples and gardens. The curving street just over the river is where so many restaurants are built over the water. Here, too, are the small shops on both sides of the river. Many an hour can be spent walking about here, but the best shops are in the main street, Kawara-machi. As they stay open until at least nine or ten o'clock at night we often used to walk there in the late evening. It would be exceedingly hot, although one was becoming used to it, and the shopowners would be throwing pails of water on to the pavement in order to cool it and keep down the dust. Quite a number of *kimonos* are about though not nearly so many as one would wish to see. There are cinemas with lurid posters of Clark Gable purring down

at you from the hoardings like a tom-cat; and next door, narrow
saloons filled with four rows, no less, of what must be gambling
machines, and an all male clientele hazarding their *yen* while tinned
music blares forth from the door. Within a step or two there may be
crickets for sale in wooden cages the size of match-boxes. The eating-
houses have glass cases at their door filled with shelf after shelf of
sample dishes like waxwork, but they are done in plastic. One wonders
if one could point to this or that, and have it brought to one. Or are
they all made in the same factory—a hideous thought to be employed
there!—and bear no relation to the day's menu? I think that must be
the answer for the weird combinations of fish and sugary cakes and
seaweed, all in aniline dyes, must be beyond the ability of all but the
most brilliant of cook-technicians.

Two main streets meet at a crossing, near the opening of an arcade,
and here is a shop with a quantity of fascinating bales or bundles, one
cannot make out what they are, but they are melon-shaped and made
of rope or straw and prove, eventually, to be *sake*, though I never
discovered how the *sake* was contained within the bundle—that indeed
being not at all the correct term for it for they are the neatest parcels
ever seen. Over the way, and almost the first shop in the arcade, is the
best sweet shop in Kyoto. Exquisite is the only word for this, but not, it
is sad to say, delicious. The shapes and textures of the sweets, in the
form of leaves and flowers and fishes, and their colours, are beyond
praise; as, also, the cleanliness. The Japanese, as we will find in their
restaurants, like to have their kitchens visible to all and open to
inspection. Here the sweets are made in the shop under what we can
only call hygienic, hospital conditions. Curiously, for they eat chocolate
as much as any other nation elsewhere, in sweet shops such as this
where the traditional Japanese sweets are made, chocolate does not enter
into their calculations, and there is no sign of it at all. The sweets must
date from before Commodore Perry and his 'black ships' cast anchor
off Japan. The wrapping papers are quite beautiful. Altogether, this
shop would not be out of place among the sweet shops of the Rue St
Honoré. How often while I was in Japan did I not think what French
and Japanese shopkeepers working together might produce in fields of
packaging and making their goods look attractive and appetizing! Not
only their sweet shops, of course, but in all manner of other lines as well.
I thought the best thing in this particular shop must be a paste or

preserve made of persimmons but the other sweets which are so beautiful to look at are, alas!, too sugary and tasteless for our palates.[1]

Whichever way you go from here there is sure to be a doll shop within a few moments. These are of a fascination amounting to entrancement, even for someone who like the writer has never been interested in dolls before. Kyoto has been famous for its dolls for centuries, and the making of them is hereditary in many families. The German physician, Engelbert Kaempfer, writing in 1690, strikes just the right note when he is describing the trade and manufactures of Kyoto, and says 'There are but few houses in all the chief streets where there is not something made or sold', concluding his remarks with: 'And after the best fashion, all sorts of toys, puppets moving their heads of themselves, and numberless other things too many to be here mentioned.' There are eight or nine big doll shops in this main street, and its cross road, and many smaller ones in side streets in the town. You pass one doll shop, and obviously it is the best in Kyoto, but there will be a better one next door, or across the road.

How am I to describe the charm and fascination of the doll shops? Every one of them an enticement into an unknown world where everything, as Kaempfer says 'is after the best fashion', but a 'fashion' strange and unfamiliar as the kingdom of the birds, a civilization in duodecimo, as it might be, the kingdom of the humming-birds. With nearly four weeks to spend in Kyoto there will be time to look into it more closely, however swiftly time is on the wing, but here is a first sketch. There is generally a show case in the door with some of the smallest and most lilliputian objects ever seen upon the shelves. A fan the size of a postage stamp but painted with pine branches; a palanquin as used in processions, but more correctly, if not quite, a pagoda upon wheels; tiny drums and *samisens*, the strings and battery for a fairy orchestra; and little paper parasols and umbrellas, miniatures of those of the *maikos* of Kyoto, and that are as indispensable to them in their dances as are castanets to the Gypsy dancers of Seville.

In the window will be the bigger dolls, but not the biggest of all. Perhaps one or two of the sitting figures of *daimyôs*, or great lords, for in their mimicry of the 'best fashion' the doll makers have never forgotten

---

[1] Below are names of some Japanese cakes, in translation: night time plums, bush warbler rice cake, cherry rice cake, camellia rice cake, eight-fold bridge, tea way, chestnut drizzling shower, snow of Koshi province, and sleet rice cake. The accent, as in Japanese woodcuts, is on showers of rain.

that nobles and courtiers had their capital in Kyoto for upwards of a thousand years. They are dolls in Court dress sitting with their knees in front of them—as Japanese, every inch of them, and they are perhaps six inches high, as the *geisha* in her *kimono* and *obi*, kneeling or tripping about on mittened feet, or the goldfish with fantail, bulbous head and goggle eyes, of the sort that are called 'lion heads' in Japan—and as voluminous of garment as Anne of Denmark in her hooped skirt or farthingale, or the Empress Eugénie in her crinoline.

Inside the doll shop there will be glass cases all round the walls. And after a day or two, and visits to two or three of the doll shops, certain figures become familiar. They are to be seen in many shops and must be the stock in trade. A witch-like character like some kind of demon warrior with masses of red hair, such being considered barbarian and diabolic in this land of saffron skins. And another figure hardly less alarming of aspect but with torrents of white hair. Both of them are characters from *Kabuki* plays, which one might have guessed earlier for this particular shop in Kawara-machi is called Kabukiya. Most of the dolls here are probably taken from *Kabuki*, and a *Kabuki* poster hangs near the door. A detail of utmost fascination is the collection of little rows of flowered brocades used for the dolls' dresses in the far corner of one of the glass cases. What glorious stuffs and colours, and what a tribute to the silk weavers of Kyoto! They are worthy of a *surimono* by Hokusai, one of his woodcuts specially printed in all the luxury of gold and metallic colours and embossed *gauffrage*. Quite a number of his *surimonos* are of still-life subjects such as this. Or there are enchanting children's play balls made of skeins of coloured silks with tassels, objects which 'grown ups' want to buy, at first sight, and hang up in their rooms at home. On several evenings we came quite late to the *Kabukiya* as it was putting up its shutters, and could hardly drag ourselves away.

Other shops, and I think the *Kabukiya*, too, have the extraordinary dolls with the enormous heads. They are called *gosho-ningyôs* for we had best begin to be accustomed to the strange names. They are baby boys, always, usually wearing no clothes at all, or only a sash or loin-cloth like the *Sumô* wrestlers. They are either bald, or have black hair, worn like the hair of a Japanese small boy, only in exaggeration. They have all the plump character of a baby only in giant form, as tending towards the three or four hundred pounder 'fat boys' of *Sumô* wrestling. But sometimes, too, the *gosho-ningyôs* are dressed up in baby version of the clothes worn in *Noh* plays. Of course it is to be understood that none of these dolls are play dolls. They are not meant for children to pull to pieces and destroy. The *gosho-ningyôs* have a peculiar quality in themselves as though living in a *chinoiserie* world of their own. The literature on Japanese dolls is illustrated with grotesque and fanciful, early eighteenth-century specimens of this race of giant babes. Not only must they have some connection with the *Sumô* 'fat boys' but, also, and in reverse, as it were, *gosho-ningyô* dolls imported from Japan by way of the Dutch merchants at Dejima must have influenced the porcelain figures called 'Malabars' that were made in the Meissen kilns, figures with big heads and wearing gigantic hats, only the name 'Malabars' being, in itself, an indication of their ignorance as to where the dolls came from. It was only, alas! after we had left Kyoto that I was told there is a temple called Reiganzi which is practically the dolls' temple, and that many fine specimens of *gosho-ningyô* are to be seen there. Now that companies of actors, and operas and ballets, can exchange visits to theatres all over the world, how much one wishes a visit to the dolls' temple in Kyoto could have been arranged for the children, and adults, who made the spangled London actor prints of a hundred years ago, and also bought toy-theatres from Redington's or Pollock's Juvenile and Theatrical Tinsel Warehouse down in Hoxton!

But, of course, the most popular dolls in the Kyoto doll shops are those of *maikos* or *geishas*, and there are always some beautiful figures upon the shelves. They are made with particular care, the faces and necks of the more expensive ones which can cost anything from forty to sixty pounds being treated with a special composition in order to give them the correct, youthful, if artificial complexion, and each hair of their elaborate coiffure being separately applied. There seem to be two main types of *maiko* or *geisha* dolls, *Fujimusume* and *Musume Dôjôji*, which are taken from classical dances in *Kabuki*. The first is a girl with a spray of trailing wistaria over her shoulder, and a flowering branch of what I take to be flowering pomegranate, but it is probably something quite different; and she wears a most elaborate dress of which the outer garment has a pattern of wistaria. Her inner dress may be of orange-red, for in Japan they either disregard, or go all out for colour clashes, and she may wear a yellow sash: but what is entirely distinctive of her is her hat, a circular hat which could be of black lacquer, ribbed like a melon, and tied under her chin with red silk ribbons, while there are more clusters of wistaria in her hair. The other type may vary a good deal in colour of dress, but in principle it is a *maiko* dancing with a parasol. She will be wearing flowered brocade, high *getas* or pattens, and a gilded, drooping *obi* hanging to her knees. Her parasol opens and shuts like a real parasol, and must be inserted between finger and thumb of her porcelain hand.

One has the longing to know more about these exquisite creations. How large is the repertoire of dolls, and how many are there in all? Are the silk stuffs in miniature only intended for one doll, and no other? Certain shops must be famous for their special dolls. The art is particularized, we are told, down to craftsmen who only make the dolls' heads, or accessories of dress, or artificial eyes. For how long have they been making them? All the dolls in the shops are of course trade dolls, but again there are craftsmen of a superior order who either produce figures too nearly resembling modern 'art-marionettes', or are at work rather in the spirit of our own craftsmen who are 'reviving 'clavichords and recorders. Nevertheless some of their work is beautiful to judge from photographs, especially in the *gosho-ningyô*, *Sumô*-baby line. The bane of the less good doll shops is the 'cute' American night-club, and 'telephone tea-cosy' horror. Most beautiful of all must be the dolls belonging to private families and connected with the Boys' and the Girls' Festival, some of them dating back to the eighteenth century, or even earlier. All the little objects to do with the festivals; tiny litters, bullock-carts, little lacquer chests, miniature, living orange and cherry trees, special sweets in the form of fish, shell-fish and vegetables, rice cakes and *sake*, miniature furniture covered with gold or silver leaf, or gold lacquered, could, one can easily see, become obsessive. It is a mini-cult which has been carried further here than anywhere else in the world. Each, and every evening, it was a wrench and a harassment to walk away from a doll shop in Kyoto. How many great doll masters there must have been over the centuries in this old city! One would like to spend a week of one's life, if no more than that, in admiring their masterworks! Or only one night; or even a part of one night!

If only to look into the mirror of Court life and watch the ancient and extraordinary dresses! Court ladies in twelve or even fourteen *kimonos*, worn one over the other like edged petals of different colours, are talking in high bird-like voices. They are as big as life, not very big,

Pottery bowl with design of snow on pine branches, by Kenzan (1663-1743)

Pottery bowl 'Matsu-Jawan', by Kenzan

Porcelain bowl used for tea ceremony, with knotted 'noshi' design, by Ninsei

Porcelain vase with ornamental design, by Ninsei

Set of six triangular pottery cups with design of plum blossom, by Kenzan

that is to say, and have the Heian eyebrows, 'moth-eyebrows' like the two halves of a thick moustache, in the 'best fashion' of so many hundreds of years ago. There are figures from *Noh* plays wearing masks, or imitating the puppets of *Bunraku*. There is a *daimyô* wearing the *shitatare*, the long trailing trousers that we longed to see; and as in a hand-glass all the beauties of the Green Mansions. All, all are coming to life. If only we could stay for a few moments longer! But a young girl turns the lights out, and the *Kabukiya* is shutting for the night. The mimic life of the doll shop closes down and we are out on the dampened pavement among the jostling crowd.

G

———————————————————————

Chapter Five

KYOTO (continued)

BUT WE RETURN TO OUR sightseeing in order to visit two gardens, the pick of the art in Japan, and which are so entirely different from anything to which our Western eyes are accustomed that they could be upon another planet. Not only that, but they are in entire antithesis to each other as though in illustration of two opposing schools of philosophy. They were in fact built within a decade of each other in monasteries belonging to two different schools of Zen Buddhism. More extraordinary exhibitions of economy and imagination could not be found; and it may be allowed to someone who has long admired and loved Italian gardens; Isola Bella like a flower-hung galleon, Armida's galleon at anchor in the lake; the green box-garden of the Escurial; Versailles and its trees and flashing waters; the *serres chaudes* and terraces of Potsdam; Schönbrunn and its hornbeam alleys; together with the clipped hedges, yew obelisks, roses, pinks, auriculas, of our own old gardens, to express astonishment and admiration for the genius that designed them. Both gardens, while in absolute contrast to each other, are probably the work of the same man, the monk Sô-ami, an aesthetic genius of the fifteenth century, of whom little is known except that he was painter, poet, calligraphist, and tea-master.

Both gardens are within the town limits of Kyoto. The first to be described is Daisen-in of Daitokuji, a Buddhist temple, or rather group of temples, for it has many gardens. If this is the first time we have seen one of the garden monasteries of Kyoto there is the unforgettable impression of a huge walled compound with maybe a dozen or more temples in it. Daisen-in is only a part, and a small part of huge Daitokuji. A map lying before me as I write this gives no fewer than twenty-one named temples in its enclosure. You can go by car right into the compound, driving up the flagged paths between the cryptomerias, and almost inevitably losing the way. We saw Daisen-in several times, and on every occasion the abbot, for each of the temples has its abbot even if there is only an aged housekeeper to attend on him, and no other monk, was busily engaged in pounding and stirring a huge cauldron that contained some sort of paste or porridge made out of nuts, and I would say, slightly fermented. It took the place of the liqueurs distilled in more convivial lands, and while it had the aspect and some of the drawbacks of a Christmas pudding, this 'exclusive preparation' was a speciality of Daisen-in and was to furnish the principal diet, we gathered, for some months to come. It looked meagre fare, and brought with it the impression of how cold it must be here in winter.

The garden of Daisen-in occupies an 'L' shape, round two sides of the temple drawing-room, and between its arms a wooden platform has been put down so that the two arms of the 'L' may be better seen. It will be obvious from this arrangement that there is more than one intentional axis or perspective or, in fact, there are quite different views of the mountains according to where we stand. For the Daisen-in is no other than a reproduction of a Sung landscape,[1] as it could be, the rocky gorges of the Bohea hills. This wonderful masterpiece of the imagination, for it calls for no other word, is an ancient scroll painting unrolled, in all weathers, for five hundred years. It has been created with only moss and rocks, and the two arms of the 'L' are not more than twenty or thirty feet in length. There are a hedge and trees behind it, for a background. But the intention is a landscape, in sepia or monochrome, of towering mountains. We see rocks and waterfalls, and river gorges. But not a drop of water. All lies in the suggestion.

This has been achieved by the choosing and rejecting out of many hundreds or even thousands of individual rocks and stones. Their assembly must have been the work of years. Not one is ordinary. They portray every type of crag or mountain. Some like the rocks of Meteora are split and fissured from top to bottom. Others are worn smooth by water. There are some that are like lava cliffs. Others drop perpendicularly like a fearful precipice. There are distant mountain ranges reared up, for no reason, out of the plain. But, most remarkable of all, are the flat-topped rocks portraying glacial action. They are the most primitive of mountain shapes, as though instinct, for it could not be knowledge, had told this truth to the scientific mind.

Having assembled his material, this most subtle of geniuses set to work with his prehistoric forms. It is an uninhabited wilderness of

[1] Sung dynasty of China (960–1260).

rocks and falling waters. Gigantic spires rise in the distance, and the dry
river flows out from between two mountains. They are, in fact, tall
pointed rocks set close together, and of abnormal shape. It is to be
remembered that such mountains are of no occurrence in Occidental
art. They are the invention of Zen Buddhism. The ink landscapes of the
Sung painters, in mere sepia, had for their aim the suggestion of
permanence through the most transitory and impermanent of means,
through an impressionism which was merely haphazard to the untrained eye. The river breaks forth from between the mountains and
flows down, waterless, between the rocks. The flat mountains of the
ice-cap are on either hand, and it runs in a deep valley. At the back, the
Himalaya of the holy hermits lifts up and up into the clouds.

Half-way down this little space, which is so huge in effect, a long flat
stone thrown right across divides the landscape, for it is that and not a
garden as we know it, into two levels. This stone could be a mountain
barrier, or a line of limestone cliffs. Below, the river spreads out into a
lake. But a rock, at either side, of a texture or formation that exactly
resembles falling water, suggests that the whole river flows over,
bodily, in a low, broad cascade and pours down into the lake. And the
water seems to run off under the porch of the temple, where another
rock, marked with the same vertical of falling water, ends the landscape.

But, as we know, this is not all the gardens of Daisen-in. Indeed the
greater part of a day could be spent in looking at them. Or longer than
that, to judge from the Japanese to be seen there, sitting in their socks,
staring in ecstasy and scarcely moving. Certainly, according to the map,
we missed many gardens in this monastery owing to the difficulty of
enquiring, and there may be as many as twenty, all told. There is a sand
garden consisting only of raked sand, that we never reached, and
another in 'Chinese style' with a high bridge; but we saw another small
garden attributed to Sô-ami, in two portions, a moss garden and a dry
garden. The main temple garden, or Kojo of Daitokuji, we were
shown by the abbot, a person of great natural dignity and charm, who
said, enchantingly, 'I'm a lucky boy', his only words of English, when
congratulated on the beautiful surroundings in which he lived.
Counting little pieces of garden, and what are called passage gardens,
beautifully designed and arranged, but not much bigger than a billiard
table, I think I counted seven or eight just in his one compound alone.
I have never seen more elaborately clipped and trimmed trees, probably

the abbot's handiwork for he is exceedingly proud of his gardens. The main garden is a famous masterpiece in the 'flat sand' style. The sand is raked into designs, and the trees and shrubs with their rounded, clipped shapes suggest hills. Also, several taller but shaped trees are allowed for background, and can be seen higher than the enclosing wall and against the sky. Hereabouts, though we missed it, too, is a small moss garden to suggest the green waves of the sea, with the top of a hill above a clipped hedge to give the effect of an island above the water. But Daisen-in, and the main temple garden which is attributed to the famous tea-master Kobori Enshû (1579-1647), are the chief sights of Daitokuji, a wonderful old monastery which besides containing many works of art which are hardly ever shown, has in the Kohôan which is one of its principal buildings no fewer than seven ceremonial tea rooms designed by Kobori Enshû, but these have, most decidedly, appeal to Japanese more than Occidental tastes. I have never had an impression in my life quite like this of being surrounded every way you look by the little gardens of a Zen monastery. It is the blossoming of a civilization which though so different in every way was as much in flower as the Florence of Filippino Lippi and Botticelli. But it is the Daisen-in that is the masterpiece of Daitokuji.

We come now to an artistic creation that is more extraordinary still. And having had it in mind for many years, and thinking I would never have the luck to see it, despairing of doing better I am reprinting an account I wrote of it in 1945, thirteen years before I saw it. The reader will condone with me when we reach Nanzenji, another temple in Kyoto, in order to admire the paintings of tigers by Kanô Tan-yû, a painter who had never seen a living tiger. This extraordinary work of art is the garden of Ryûanji, the greatest of the works of Sô-ami, if, indeed, he did design it, for that is not entirely certain. Should it be true, though, that the same hand was responsible for the mountain gorges of the Daisen-in and for Ryûanji as well, then we are in the presence of an aesthetic genius and one of the most original of creative minds that there has ever been. The date of Ryûanji is about 1500, and perhaps it could be called the most modern work, of any of the arts, in all antiquity. Modern, too, in the latest and most recent sense, meaning that its importance is in the immediate future that lies ahead.

Ryûanji is a small space of white sand, covering an area about the size and shape of a tennis court. This is raked into straight lines. Placed in this sand there are five groups, of fifteen stones in all. There is nothing else at all.

The stones are not, even, remarkable in themselves. They are not to be compared to the hand-picked monoliths of Daisen-in. Moss grows round the bases of the stones, and that is all. There is no other vegetation. There are no flowers. It is bordered on two sides by buildings, and on two sides by walls. At the back, but not originally, there are some trees. Since there are no flowers the garden never alters, and does not change with the seasons. It is, in fact, stronger than nature, for flowers are impermanent and transitory. But the eye and mind never tire of it. For its simplicity has mysterious importance. It is impossible ever to forget it. The little rectangle is as full of movement as Piccadilly Circus, or the Piazza of St Mark's. But the energy is of another sort. For it is not human movement. It is more as though we were looking upon some familiar corner of the skies and our eyes find again, if the clouds allow of it, the Plough or Bear, a constellation that never changes and holds a message meaning everything or nothing.

But Ryûanji is a Zen temple garden and its purpose is to lead to contemplation. We must realize that its calculated simplicity is equivalent to that object with shining surface upon which the mesmerist would have us fix our eyes in order to induce the trance. In light of that, it becomes an old, old instrument for magic. And it is no more than an old box with nothing inside it. But remark the shapeless stones upon the sand! It does not matter that a modern wall confines this little space upon two sides, and that ordinary trees are in the background. For you may look out from any window, in all centuries, upon the starry night. And, for a moment, these stones could be displaced and rolled away. Have they not, in fact, been disturbed during five hundred years? They are not, even, so peculiar in shape that small movement would make much difference. If an absolute precision in their placing were essential, then the effect would be altered or ruined by the shifting of an inch. And it seems to be no better than an old games board with the pawns tumbled into their corners by an earthquake or the trembling of a hand.

But another change comes over it. If there has been an alteration it is only that the stones have sunk a little into the sand, in subsidence, and that the moss and lichen have gathered around them. The stones that were chosen were not remarkable for this very reason that their positions would undergo changes, in the course of ages, and that this must be allowed for, and must not affect the general plan. The law which governs their placing is that of the survival of ordinary lives or objects that do not attract attention to themselves. Are they pretending to be haphazard? Is it enough that they should lie at different places on the sand? The farthest, most isolated of the rocks, out in the middle, or at one end, seem to lay at interminable distances on the raked sands. But they are connected together by some inner harmony. It is a constellation and the stars are in its orbit. They obey its rhythms. But the sand is kept raked, each day, and that makes it to be as though, by this, it is preparing for performance. That the performance, even, will be a little different each time. That it is fresh and living, and continually renewed. That the drama is unpredictable and may have another ending. That, no two occasions together, is it alike. That it depends upon the actors and the audience. The initiates and the uninitiated. And it can change in every aspect and become magnified.

Would it be possible to build up such drama from the loose boulders on some mountain side? From the huge stones of the glacier rolled down on the moraine? But we know those are chance accidents; that such is a drama in suspension, waiting for the next act, which has been pending for a million years. Their drama is of a moment and an aeon. And it consists in that climax which can never come. But this is calculated. It is not chaotic. It has created its own laws. The brain that conceived of this has outplayed mere nature. Or would any other arrangement of the groups of stones possess this magic? Did he consider every move; or was it done by inspiration? Or does it portend nothing at all and have no meaning? For there are moods in which no message is apparent from five groups, of fifteen stones in all lying in thin sand. It is of no importance, and any other arrangement of the stones would have done as well. But the mood changes. In a moment it can become a chart of the heavens. We are looking down upon planetary space, of which this is the model, or we are to imagine that we are so aloof and far removed from it that we can stay here for eternity looking down on its gyrations.

For a moment it can appear like some disaster of the utmost magnitude, like a world or system split into its fragments. But the farthest portions are upon the tether. They are affected by the same law of gravity that governs all, and cannot escape from it. Or the rocks are the tops of mountains coming up above the clouds. No! no! for we see their whole configuration. They are entire lands or continents, not mountain peaks. They are too big for human interest, as it could be the earth seen from so far away that it bears no evidence of human habitation. And the thought of this lifts us out of the world and above all consideration of humanity. We are in an emptiness inhabited only by the primal forces. The walled space would suggest that we are looking down on a portion of the universe enclosed by the ruled lines of the mathematicians, within which we may watch the movements of the orbs. But they are shaped like dolmens or megaliths. They have not the polished roundness of the celestial spheres. They do not revolve, endlessly, in outer space. They are not refulgent with strange or borrowed lights. There is not the milky efflorescence, like a path through the meadows, but we are told that it is a million nebulae.

There can, even, come a time when the drabness of the surrounding wall stands for dullness and drabness of quotidian life, and can explain how splendours and miseries are found side by side. Or that things terrestrial and celestial both have existence. That the fact of the one is no detraction from the other. That we pass as easily from life to death. That explicable and inexplicable are near together. That finite and infinite are the same, for, in fact, this open space which seems endless and eternal is bounded by walls, and has a wooden platform on two sides from which to view it. The stones, each time you look at them anew, take on another meaning. If the one group bears no message, then there are method and harmony in the components. The three groups, at the far end, have an importance which no islands have on any map. And the fifth group, away at the other side, is in relation to them. This is not a still-life, of nothing at all, of objects that are indeterminate. Neither have they been moved together so that they only share the rhythm of their propinquity and nothing more. But, in fact, the groups of stones mean nothing in themselves. One group only, individually, is nothing but misshapen stone. It has not, even, fortuitous likeness to some other thing. It is only a rock grown older by five centuries since it was put in place, and that has lost all sharpness of angle so that it is no more an object that has just reached its destination, that preserves the freshness of its new position. And it appears, now to be a divination board, where the future is foretold according to aspects and conjunctions of the planets. This is some fixed part of a system, the nucleus or main rhythm of its parts, and the casting of horoscopes is done according to its indications, that is to say, from the favourable or threatening lights upon it and from the substance of its shadows taking those, as ever, to constitute the ghostly world of unseen influence, which is to say, as we see it ourselves, different each time and never twice the same.

The raking of the sands compares, we could say, to the hand that rubs away the breath upon the mirror. Or it is the sweeping of the street before the procession passes. The suit of cards put down, and the pack reshuffled for another game to play. It is impossible not to realize that the secret lies in the dressing of the pawns or statues for their special purposes. The seasonal growth and decay of nature are abolished, and the stage is set for more enduring things. But the sand is not swept clean and sprinkled anew to hide the bloodstains. This is not an arena, not an amphitheatre. The rough shape of the stones does not suggest statues of the living or the dead. Nor the idols of any religion at all. So that it is not a place of sacrifice or religious ceremony. Not a field of decision or of indecision in obedience to the omens. For the shadows are not so transitory. But the combinations are within the laws of mathematics. The fifteen stones, seen in their different angles, take on the significance of a scale of music. They are the notes and semitones and quarter notes, but their multiple possibilities could be computed. There must be a set number, however endless, of their conjunctions. Within these limits it is comparable to a language of so many million words or more. We begin to think of these five groups of stones, never varying in their number, but in their shades of meaning, as forming some portentous theme in music. The significance is musical. But the meaning is a mystery. The key to the secret lies in the music. And in form it is a palindrome, a theme or sentence that can be read both ways. It is of no moment from which you see it, even if you could climb to the other side and look down upon it from the wall. That is because the rectangle of white sand circumscribes the action, while we are audience upon its edges. It is a magic glass put down to magnify what lies beneath it. Here are the primal law and order. It is a theme or rhythm imposed by the eternal forces. Something of which the architect was the recipient, not the author. It may have come to him quickly, without long reflection. Like the invention, therefore, of a theme or melody. Not, however, to the meditative mind, that works by quick decision after much preparation. One move, and one move only, of the pawns after a long silence. Or it can come by choosing the one out of the multitude. How are we to know? For it is quite impersonal. And yet, alone of its kind and never to be forgotten.

Is it just arbitrary; or would not the moving of a stone, by so much as a hair's breath, impair its meaning? But, in truth, it is both too big and too little for such criticism. According to what it means to you, whether much or little. In this, again, it is akin to music. For it is so conceived that, were it surrounded on all four sides by tenement buildings or by tram-lines it would be no different. So long as its sacred area is inviolate; so long as the sand can be new raked whenever necessary. In this respect it could be compared to some theme in music that can be carried in the head, and to which environment brings no difference. But constructed so carefully that it returns upon itself; that it has no exit; that there is no easy entrance to its meaning; that the form is that of a riddle or an epigram, holding the primal secret that it cannot explain, and which must be sufficient in itself. Like the theme from which a fugue is built, and in fact it has the property of music that no precise meaning can be applied to it, that it is personal and individual, and that you may alter your interpretation of it according to your mood. So you never come to the end of it. The developments are endless, although each could bear a number, but it would be a number in a hundred million. But if the number, however huge, is finite, then there are law and order and we may conceive of these endless possibilities as being directed and not arbitrary. Every theme is a solution already numbered, and it is only the discrepancy between its solitary existence, to be explained apparently by the descent of genius or inspiration, and the multitudinous host of other multiples or tracks of numbers, that makes the mystery. The astronomers claim, even, to have seen to the end of our universe, and that there is an outer space beyond it which we must conceive to be the empty anarchy. Or it may be the outer pull of other influences, forces and potencies that we shall never know, that are, in fact, beyond our comprehension, while all within this is obedient to our laws. This is as far nature reigns, up to those limits, not beyond them. We are to apply or not, divine powers to this, according to our fancy, but certainly the powers of good and evil are at work within them. Is it quite arbitrary, or predetermined? That is the mystery. Or may there not be a body or texture of probability, an influence alike of past and future, upon the present, that shapes it and gives direction to it? How else are we to explain the highest works of art, the facts of history, or the fortunes and misfortunes of the individual person? How else are we to account for the mystery of the greatest music? For it existed, in exact facsimile, before. It was always there, in theory. And, if that be true, then equally, all other conjectures have been covered. They, all, have had their previous existence, whether dormant, or already befallen in some other instance. The only solution to the mystery must be that, out of such endless number, the individual keeps the choice of detail, but that, in all respects, his action is not free. That it depends on circumstances that are within his control whether such and such a train of numbers is probable to his fate. That, therefore, the path of numbers may be, in some sort, the reflection of his attributes, moral and physical, and of the degree of his affinity to the superior or supernormal influences. This is the secret of the fifteen stones lying in the thin sand. They show the relation of the human being to the laws of nature. They take us deep into the mystery, only to show that it is more mysterious still.

What are we to call Ryûanji? For it is not a garden in the ordinary meaning of the word. Nor an abstract painting done in rocks and sand. Nor the magician's divination board. We would call it, more, a theme or rhythm that is like the subject of a fugue, a formula that inspires energy and transports the mind, by means of imagination, into the higher spheres. But the simplicity of its method makes it to be among the most original conceptions of the human intellect. It may seem to individual persons, according to their temperament, universal or absurd. Some may see nothing in it but the affectation of the Oriental aesthete. Others may be inclined to exaggerate the precision and accuracy of its parts, according to which, many subtle implications may have become lost or obliterated in the course of time. But we have seen that, in a sense, this has been designed especially so as not to be subject to such changes. The stones were, even, chosen particularly for their ordinary shape, while the device of placing them in sand was in order to make sure of their diurnal dressing and that they should not suffer the changes of the recurring seasons. It is a wonderful conception to create from the immortal rocks and mortal sands. This cult of great stones or monoliths on the part of the aesthetes of Japan is to be connected, in all probability, with the veneration of the Chinese scholars for their primitive cauldrons and sacrificial vessels of green bronze, relics of early history and regarded by them as the greatest works of art. Saurian shapes, of sinister and uncertain purpose; but, even to our Western appreciation, which is only in its beginnings, they are the relics of an age of giants and dinosaurs. By this, and by something of the Surrealist discovery of *objets trouvés*, chance shapes of wood or stone conveying a fortuitous hint or parody of something else, or of nothing at all but their own mystery and strangeness, is the cult of the stone and monolith to be explained.

Having now seen Ryûanji with my own eyes I find I have little to add to my unseen impression of it, except that in the monastery records it does not appear to be at all certain that Sô-ami was its designer, according to the latest information. Whoever he may have been, it is one of the most original works of art in the world, and if I am asked, 'How original?', I would say as original as Sharaku's actor prints, which are another wonder of Japan, or as Stravinsky's *Sacre du Printemps*.

But it is time now for the evening meal after this long day, and I can never forget our first dinner in a Japanese restaurant in Kyoto: at one of the restaurants with open balconies built over the river bed. It has stepping-stones dampened with water at the entrance, and many palms or bamboos growing in the court as you come in from the narrow street. We take off our shoes, are given slippers that are much too small, and led by a posse of *neisans* upstairs, where we recline on one of the balconies while dinner is preparing. To both sides there are balconies belonging to other restaurants, perhaps ten or a dozen of them in a row. This bed of the Kamogawa has been important for many centuries in the pleasure life of Kyoto. A painted screen in the Seikadô Foundation in Tokyo gives a picture of the mountebanks and jugglers, the dancers and performing bears, and an unfortunate creature looking like a huge porcupine which is imprisoned in a stockade, and is being tormented by a pack of dogs, and all and sundry, right here in this river bed. There are hundreds of figures on the screen and one can pore over it for a long time, having to crouch down to the floor in order to catch the details of all the striped and patterned dresses, and form some idea of what is going on at so many booths and raree shows in this crowded evening scene three hundred years ago.

It is a *tempura* house, and when we come in from the balcony the cook is already squatting in his place behind the horseshoe table. Never has one seen so immaculately clean a white gown. He has the look of a

Celestial and white-gowned conjurer. It is a clown or juggler's gown he wears, and the quick moves of his hands are those of an expert performing a card trick. His shaved head gives him the look of a monk and yet, disconcertingly, he seems to produce objects from his sleeves. Conjured up out of nowhere a little dish is set down before me which for the space of a moment I mistake for a piece of china. I think it to be a little still life in *blanc de Chine*, beautifully modelled, but it is a quail's egg, and more were to follow. There is a high consumption of these quails' eggs in Japan though no one could tell me where they come from. My guess is from the Northern Island or Hokkaido; but whether from quail farms, or some large marsh area, I do not know.

The next surprise was lily bulbs, tasting rather like Chinese water chestnuts. Then came something, sweet but mysterious, wrapped in a sheath of green bamboo leaf. There followed one or two of those objects seemingly in black or dark purple lacquer, which we had already encountered in Tokyo, and which are either artichokes or aubergines. I thought that as craftsman or lacquerer his technique was even more finished than that of his colleague in the capital. The prawns, too, tasted a little different, no doubt owing to a secret sauce. In all he was a remarkable technician, part-Cinquevalli or some past master in jugglery and conjuring, part-priest or monk. On more than one other day, walking past the restaurant, I saw this prestidigious character standing in the street, talking, and on another occasion bargaining for vegetables, but he never recognized me from which I deduce that, improbable as it may seem to ourselves, to the eyes of a Japanese all foreigners look the same.

We never returned to this restaurant but only because there are so many others to go to. The evenings of ten days, or perhaps a fortnight, could be spent in dining at different restaurants just along this same street. On the same bank of the river, but above the Sanjô-dôri bridge, in the farther row of eating houses, there is Hiuntei, a famous Chinese restaurant, where one can enlarge one's experience of exotic foods. It is not possible to exaggerate the delights of dining on the river in Kyoto. The restaurants have such beautiful dining-rooms; the little *sake* cups are such lovely and fragile works of art. Often the tables are of red lacquer and there are beautiful flower arrangements. There is a fascination in being in the heart and centre of this thousand year old Oriental city with its unique civilization, which in all essentials is so unlike our own. There are probably eight or ten separate dining-rooms in each of the restaurants, and from the next room through the sliding partitions, or from a balcony built out over the river only a few feet away, will come laughter and sounds of singing and dancing. We see the brocaded dresses of the *geishas* and hear their muffled footsteps, and as we come away, late though it is (after nine o'clock), other guests arrive.

Something which it is absolutely essential to do in order to savour the beauty of Kyoto's surroundings is to go out into the country, and our first trip of this nature was to see the garden at the Shûgakuin Imperial Villa, pronounced something like 'Sugar Queen'. Special permission has to be requested for this but it is easily obtained. It is out to the north-east of the city at the foot of Mount Hiei. The road had been taken up, and we had to get out and walk for some distance which had the advantage that we were able to go slowly by some cottages with high pitched roofs of thatch, the exact counterpart of those on Sôtatsu's fan screen which had been exhibited but a month or two before in London. This particular fan from the screen is often reproduced as something typical of Japan, and the screen is one of the treasures of the Sambôin monastery, the other side of Kyoto. When we saw Sambôin a few days later I thought it the most beautiful temple and garden in Japan. But now we are nearing Shûgakuin with Sambôin still to look forward to, and Shûgakuin is still very much an Imperial Villa, in the sense that it is so well kept up with all its hedges clipped and thick gravel on the paths. No sooner had we arrived than it began raining, but with the Japanese rain that soaks while you are, yourself, dripping with sweat so that you are never dry, perhaps for hours on end, and yet never catch cold. There are really three gardens at Shûgakuin which cover a very large area of ground. An Emperor lived here early in the seventeenth century who like almost everyone else was poet, painter, calligrapher and garden amateur, but he was satisfied with accommodation of simple summer-house description, and the various little pavilions seen through a veil of rain are not interesting except for one, where there are paintings of the processional cars that can still be seen in Kyoto every July in the Gion Festival. These cars, called *yama* and *hoko*, are palanquins carried on poles, or else ornamental towers on wheels, and models of them are to be seen in every toy shop in the town. But now while it is really drenching, and a superb rainbow bridges the sky, we come out into rice fields where peasants are working in their inverted lampshade hats, giving an almost ghostly illusion as though they are not really there in this artificial landscape, and we come up higher along an English park drive with clipped rhododendrons or azaleas to a large and most ingeniously designed lake. It must be the biggest lake in any of the Kyoto gardens, with at least two islands, and a panorama which unfolds as you walk along until you see the islands joined together by a Chinese bridge. This, however, is an act of wilful *chinoiserie* dating from when the villa was put under repair for a later Emperor in 1824.

Nothing less than several months on end of intensive hard work would enable one to see everything in Kyoto that is worth a visit, and it has already been mentioned that we missed the dolls' temple or Reiganji, as, also, that other temple Mieidô where the monks are famous makers of fans. And near Shûgakuin, where we have just spent a hot midday walking in the rain, there is another temple garden which completely eluded us both times we were near it. This is Manjûin, and no amount of enquiry with the name clearly written down in Japanese characters, even when we must have been within a few hundred yards of it, met with the smallest response. Obviously it is a temple with a nickname like the 'Moss Temple' or Saihôji which is known as Kokedera. Everyone, though, will remember asking for some street just round the corner in London or Paris and being met with incredulous stares. In and around Kyoto there are real difficulties because often there is no road and you have to walk a quarter of a mile or more down a path or lane to your objective. It was a pity to have missed Manjûin because it has a garden attributed to Kobori Enshû, or his pupils, a sand garden shaped like a lake with winding banks with an island in the middle planted with clipped shrubs, and a view of stone lanterns and pagodas in the distance against the wooded hills. Just one small garden such as this can be a revelation of beauty on a summer afternoon while the cricket is not so much singing as whirring like a wound up, and released steel spring.

If in the mood for a large garden after Shugakûin this is the moment for the Heian Shrine. Never, as long as I live, will I forget how hot it was on the morning we saw the Heian Shrine, but I say this loving the heat almost as much as cricket or grasshopper and drawing, I think, the same kind of pleasure from it. Being a Shintô shrine, and built to commemorate Kyoto's eleven hundredth year as a city, the vermilion temple buildings are practically new. But this is the special attraction of

Shintô temples in Japan, though a point to be kept in reserve until we
reach some, perhaps less imposing but more beautiful shrine, for at the
moment there is the ordeal of walking across a gravelled space the size
of a parade ground between the scarlet lacquer pavilions in almost
dangerous heat. In order to reach the modern garden at the back which
is the most ambitious thing of its kind in Kyoto with a very large lake
laid out like the lakes of the Heian period for boating parties, or, in fact,
it is like the lakes of *The Tale of Genji* of a thousand years ago, with an
immensely long pavilion-bridge in scarlet lacquer, in Chinese style. I
could not help comparing it in mind with the Palladian bridges in the
parks at Wilton and Prior Park and Stowe built, too, just at the period
when landscape gardening was coming into fashion in England. The
azaleas must be a marvellous sight here in spring, and over and above
all the cherry trees. This is the finest collection of *sakura* in Kyoto, the
trees being above sixty years old, and at their best. There are dozens of
gardens famous for cherry viewing, and even individual trees which
the Japanese will make a pilgrimage to see. But the huge old trees with
branches trained along bamboo trellises are past their prime. This is the
youngest and newest of the cherry gardens, and one can scarcely walk
round the lake for the boughs of weeping cherry just at eye level and
dangling against one's face. Also, there were the husks of irises by the
lake side in between the stones, and having already seen so many
gardens by great landscape architects of the epoch when this old
Oriental city was itself in flower this was in reminder that, notwith-
standing, we had seen little else but rocks and sand. Despite their
inventions of 'dry' gardens and 'sand' gardens it is as a city of flower
festivals that Kyoto is famous, this old town that has been well
described as 'a felicitous blending of Moscow and Seville'.

Another group of temples to explore is Myôshinji which lies out in
the same quarter of the town as the 'Golden Pavilion' and the rock and
sand gardens of Ryûanji. And if each of these experiences brings its own
discovery with it this may be the first complex of temples in Kyoto in
which we see good paintings. So far they have been slow and obdurate
in appearing. But, also, the temples are becoming temples in themselves, and not merely the hut or pavilion accompaniment to gardens.
At Myôshinji much has been rebuilt after a fire, and there are the long
covered passages with squeaking floors which remain one of the temple
memories of Kyoto. Their heavy timbers tell one the intention is not

Pottery plate with design of flowing water, by Kenzan

Lacquered wood eighteenth-century ink-stone box, by Kôrin (1658–1716)

Visiting cards of the *maikos* of Kyoto

only for shade in walking from one building to another but, also, for winter protection against snow which must lie thick upon pine bough and tilted roof. As for the squeaking, which tends to monotony, the Japanese with their mania for specialized information will not allow it to be a 'nightingale floor', and leave it at that, but have to remark it is so constructed that 'at every step the boards emit a sound resembling that of *uguishu*, Japanese bush warbler'. It was on one of the endless wooden corridors of Myôshinji, which one cannot conceive all to be necessary, but perhaps they play the part of the tunnels, bridges, signal-boxes, of a child's toy railway, that we met a young priest or student who took us round. He spoke good English, an exceedingly rare accomplishment in Japan, and was an admirer of Hemingway and a student of English literature which with Japanese students means but one name, T. S. Eliot. Could it mean anything at all to this young man at Myôshinji who was in training to be a schoolmaster; any more than to that other ex-student 'managing' the night-life when we went on a silly excursion one Sunday evening in the hotel bus; or to the hotel manager, a former student, at Miyajima? The results of this species of poetical open cast mining are meagre enough on the barren lands of England. What point can it have at all in Japan? They would be much happier reading Herrick. Just at the time we were in Kyoto there was a music festival at Karuizawa at which it transpired that the young Japanese composers were imitating Schönberg and Webern. Jackson Pollock and Riopelle are no doubt the idols of the young painters. From all of which extremities of situation as with the Trans-Polar route, it is both a long, and at the same time the shortest way back to Japan, according to the temperament and talents of the individual.

There are said to be more works of art at Myôshinji than in any temple in Kyoto but all, or most of them, are stored away, including many landscape *fusuma* by Kanô Motonobu, though there are conflicting accounts as to their number. We saw various rather sketchily painted screens by other artists, and Myôshinji is evidently a monastery where the works of art must be taken upon trust. But the gardens, or bits of gardens, are almost numberless; an uninspired imitation of the rocks and sands of Ryûanji, just serving to show the original is a work of genius, but, also, several raked sand and clipped azalea gardens not much bigger than large rugs or carpets, including one said to be the work of Motonobu. One leaves Myôshinji a little disappointed not to

H

have had introductions to see the paintings, and within a few minutes can be at Ninnaji, another and a more rewarding monastery. These, also, are huge precincts, even if the buildings are chiefly the size of huts, and there were at one time as many as sixty sub-temples in the enclosure. An early Emperor became the first abbot of Ninnaji, and it always had an Imperial prince for its abbot for a thousand years until 1868. It must be a marvellous sight in the spring, for this is one of the most famous cherry viewing sites in Kyoto with enormous old cherry trees pensioned out, as it were, upon bamboo trellises and stakes, double cherries with enormous blossoms, and even it is said of a variety to be seen nowhere else. They are indeed most wonderfully impressive with their stout, thick trunks, the understructure of the fireworks, like the skeleton of the tableau or set piece of firework seen by day. But the inner part of Ninnaji has a beautiful and most typical Japanese garden by Kobori Enshû with a stone bridge and clipped azalea bushes pretending to be stones, perhaps one of the prettiest of Kyoto gardens after the 'Silver Pavilion', and intended for the recreation of its Prince-Abbot.

At another temple in this neighbourhood, Kôryuji, there is one of the most curious of the Kyotan festivals. It takes place on the night of the 12th October when a man dressed in white, impersonating the Buddhist god Madara, riding on a bull, comes into the temple yard followed by a quartet of men in devils' masks. He rides three times round the temple compound, and then there is a religious ceremony and the chanting of a prayer in archaic language which no one can understand. This Oxfestival with its echoes of the Tibetan devil dance must be of great antiquity and could be as much as a thousand years old. It would seem to go back to pagan times, and to a classical antiquity which is entirely alien to our own, even if we like to attach the present to the past and think that the jewelled Madonnas of the Semana Santa in Seville are borne in procession from chapels that are on the sites of pagan temples, and that the Virgen de Gran Poder or La Macarena had the goddess Diana as direct ancestress. This man in white riding a bull into the temple precincts has the same ring to it as the festival at the Shimogamo and Kamigamo Shrines, near by, a double festival at both Shintô shrines, one after the other, held on the 15th May and called the Aoi Festival. In the early morning of that day a man dressed like an Imperial messenger, with his suite in ancient Court dress, assemble at the old Imperial Palace, and parade through the main streets with horsemen and halberdiers in attendance, and a sacred ox-drawn chariot covered with hollyhock (Aoi) leaves, arriving at the Shimogamo Shrine towards evening. The priests perform a ceremony, and then they go to the Kamigamo Shrine where there is another service before they return to the palace.[1] This is not Kyoto of the snows, with frost blossoming on every copper eave and cryptomeria leaf, not Kyoto of the same latitude as Moscow, but Kyoto when it is in the same temperature, or hotter still, than Seville, and the cherry viewing and the sacred chariots covered with hollyhocks are not wholly inappropriate to the cloisters of orange trees of Córdoba and Seville.

How hot it was getting! Hotter and hotter still in these last days of August or the beginning of September while certain of the public rooms of the hotel, and the bar in particular, were cold as icebergs owing to air-conditioning. Nearly every day the big dining-room was taken over for some public function or other, and we had to eat our inevitable hamburger in a little room next to the 'cooler' and only a foot or two from the cold. But these banquets, fashion shows, and so forth, were at least interesting because of the number of Japanese attending them, wearing their national dress. On one occasion, the large lobby was crowded with some thirty to forty ladies all dressed in *kimonos*, and talking with animation. What is more, they were all about the same age, and all of them good looking. Many of them were smoking, which I thought curious, and at a certain moment all produced lipsticks and powder-boxes and began to make up their faces. They were waitresses brought over from Osaka and Kobe and the banquet they were to serve was about to begin. We had been long enough in the hotel by now to tell one lilliputian lift-girl from another, and to know that such is the superfluity of population there were nearly always six to eight salesmen in the souvenir shop on the way into the dining-room. Cloisonné of an appalling hideousness was on sale, and also dreadful porcelain with embossed gold upon it. But there were beautiful dolls, rows of necklaces of cultured pearls, and nice objects in basketwork or bamboo. And at the end of the lobby, against the far wall, there was a showcase of miniature helmets in Japanese armour.

Those were objects of really beautiful workmanship. There were a dozen of them, with a larger one, life-size, belonging to, and mounted

[1] There is, also, a historic horse race at Kamigamo on 5th May, to ensure a good harvest, when twenty horsemen, dressed in ancient Court costume, pray at the shrine, and then race on a course within the temple precincts.

on, a splendid black lacquer box with violet cords. From looking at them every day I got to know the black stags' antlers of Honda Tadakatsu, for they were all copied from the helmets of famous heroes; another helm with the sickle moon for device, and another with two blades like the half of an electric fan, or early aeroplane propeller. They were so perfectly finished in detail, the brocade head-flaps so good in pattern, the sun-rays of Hideyoshi's helm so portentous, the 'monkey-face' Taikô of plebeian origin, who fought in Korea and dreamed of conquering China. In the end we had to pay a visit to this craftsman and it was a most fascinating experience. He lived in an outlying part of the town, in a little house like any other little house, behind a bamboo curtain, but once this had parted its long strings you were in his show-room and he could be seen in a tiny room at the back hammering away, half-naked, sitting cross-legged on the matting. He appeared to have no one to help him, and to do all the work alone. Round the first room in showcases were his helmets, in miniature and life-size, and a whole suit of armour. But the most interesting object was something I had almost imagined for myself, but had never seen. This was a helmet fashioned entirely out of the claws and breast-plates, if that is the right word for them, of prawns and lobsters. For Japanese armour is always of crustacean appearance; it is 'lobster armour',[1] so that this little *chef d'oeuvre* of craftsmanship was in the nature of a brilliant caricature, in fact, a self-caricature of the armourer.

There was, I have said, a figure in great harness (full armour) but this armourer's speciality is evidently helmets, or *Kabuto*, of which there were some extraordinary specimens. One in the form of a fish's tail, another made of feathers, several of deer's antlers or buffalo horns and, most far fetched of all, an immensely tall and elongated black lacquered paper hat, probably a courtier's hat worn as the crest upon a helm, but it looked like an antipodean hybrid of necromancer, dunce, and Misericordia. For myself I would have liked the black hat which had so extreme a significance to it, and the shrimp or prawn helm more than anything else in the showroom. But there was the armour of

[1] At Shimonoseki which is at the farthest southern point of Honshu, the main island of Japan, are caught the *Heike* or *Taira* crabs, one of the most striking instances of mimicry in nature, described by Mr Julian Huxley as the only case of nature consciously, or unconsciously imitating man. There was a great naval battle at Shimonoseki in 1185 when the Taira clan was exterminated, and a species of crab caught along this stretch of coast do bear on their shells some markings resembling a human face, even if it is not true that 'the fury or agony of the death struggle can still be discerned in the faces and upon the backs of the crabs'.

Japanese heroes of all dates from the eleventh century until the seventeenth, which was the period of the fantastic *Kabuto* or helmet crests,
of which another specimen was now held up for our admiration in the
form of a pair of fern fronds bent into the shape of antlers. The colour
in Japanese armour depends upon the lacing; there is scarlet, or white
laced armour, or purple lacing, like as many clans of coloured lobsters,
but specialization, as always, is carried further still into silk braid of
'rotted leaf colour', or deutzia blossom, or wistaria, or, of course, and
almost tritely, cherry or pink plum blossom, and then, again, fern, or
water plantain, or, more beautifully, jay's feather, it must be the blue
wing feather, lacing. There is even a special mystique about the
kuwagata (antlers) which are often etched with dragons and clouds,
and inlaid with gold; the body of a 'great harness' would be ornamented
with bamboos and sparrows; the shoulder blades with tigers and
bamboos; or another 'great harness' with chrysanthemum blossoms.
All this without even a mention of their swords which are more of a
religion than a mystique, and form an entire subject to themselves.
What a densely inhabited world of the imagination this craftsman
worked in! One supposed he must go round from shrine to shrine
taking sketches of the old suits of armour, for they are preserved
mostly in temples though many were destroyed during the war,
Japanese armour being the more interesting because nothing has been
said or written about it for so many years. One would like to know
how much of his piece work is done for him by other craftsmen. Who
makes the silk lacing (*odosige*) for his suits of armour? Does he forge his
own *kuwagata* (antlers), and so forth? A visit to this artist and craftsman
was like watching one of the old lacquerers at work who would ply his
craft in just such tiny premises, probably with no one else to help him.
It was only a pity we were unable to see one of the potters of Kiyomizu
at work at his kiln.

And now for a drive into the country for that is something we have
not seen except for the unreal-looking rice fields in the middle of the
gardens of Shûgakuin. There are such beautiful excursions for an
afternoon or evening that we plan to end our two other chapters on
Kyoto with a country drive. On this first occasion it is to the north-east
of the city, and beyond Shûgakuin, to the foot of Mount Hiei; and here
I have to say that owing to our refusal to be bothered by a guide, and
insistence upon finding things by ourselves, we never knew of the new

motor road to the top of the mountain which had only been opened a
few weeks before. We missed seeing what must be a marvellous view,
and the monastery at the summit though not much can be left of that
after its destruction by Nobunaga in 1571, which ended in 'the
extermination of every occupant of the hundreds of monasteries that
had studded the mountain and its thirteen valleys', and the death of
thousands of the warlike monks. Also, preferring to spend every
available hour in Kyoto, or near it, we never went on to Lake Biwa. It
is not so much that Lake Biwa is a little larger than the Lake of Geneva,
occupying far too large an area of Central Japan, as that, had we gone as
far as the Miidera Temple on its shores we would have seen the Otsu-e
prints still sold there, a sort of *images d'Épinal* which is one of the oldest
folk arts in Japan. They were sold to travellers, and are the parallel
'made by farmers and simple artisans' to the more professional Ukiyô-e
woodcuts of Tokyo. And there is a temple on the lake shore where Lady
Murasaki wrote *The Tale of Genji*.

Instead, we were going to Jakkôin Temple, a little tiny convent in
the hills towards Mount Hiei. A most exquisite scarlet wild flower was
growing in clumps or clusters above the paddy fields, some sort of
liliaceous plant, though not a lily, and no one knew its name. When we
stopped the car in order to pick some of the flowers the chauffeur
would not let us, and we understood from his gestures that the flower
was poisonous, or, at least, inflamed one's hands. This is apparently
true, though a Japanese friend told us his daughter used a concoction of
the plant to paint her nails. It is sad to think this scarlet wild flower,
and the white or pink lotus, were practically the only flowering plants
while we were in Japan from August to October. We saw Japan in
black and white and not in colour. But already we were climbing
higher than the paddy fields, and driving along the narrowest of lanes
with not one familiar plant, not even the simplest and humblest, in
sight. Each single leaf and blade was different. There were o'er arching
trees, as along a lane at home, but one could not even name the trees.
Noises of water in every direction, running water in little conduits by
the road, and plants of fern-like nature as we got deeper into the hills.
Eventually, when the road could go no further we walked up some
steep steps to Jakkôin. It is a nunnery where a twelfth-century Empress
came to live in the green solitude, and hidden in the winter snows,
after her son had been killed in that naval battle near Shimonoseki,

whereafter the Taira crabs pursued their curious line in nature, and a more perfect and humble seclusion than Jakkôin could not be found. It is of tiny size with a little lovely garden of a pond and clipped azaleas, which one need not believe to be of the twelfth century, all under repair that day with workmen everywhere, and while we looked into the lilliputian temple a small figure in a black gown with shaved head which made her look like a boy ten or twelve years old, came up the wooden steps. She was the abbess, and the innocent creature said prayers for us with curious, never heard before, intonation of 'Boudda', 'Boudda', and gave us a poem inscribed on a tiny scroll in her own handwriting. There appeared to be but one other nun in the nunnery with her, and then she showed us the minuscule rooms of the convent, paper apartments only metaphorically bigger than card houses, with paintings, one of them clearly from the hand of Jakuchiu, the painter of cocks and hens. It was difficult to leave this holy being, and when I think of her I still hear her childish voice.

We had not far to go from here to Sanzen-in, another temple garden that we wished to see. But before this, or, indeed at its door, is an idyllic village, one of two that are famous in this respect, Yase and Ohara, and the village where we are standing under a tall avenue of *gingkos*, is Ohara. There were, as well, many maples which, on the day we saw them, were beginning to turn. We had come through Yase, and not thought much of it, but Ohara is one of those beautiful places that stay in the memory. The women of the two villages are to be seen all over Kyoto as flower sellers and porters, and there are dolls in the Ohara costume in all the doll shop windows. Their dress is blue and white, or, at least, it seems generally to be dark blue with a white criss-cross pattern on it, and in distinction to other peasant women in Japan they wear handkerchiefs on their heads where they balance their flower baskets or whatever they are selling. Because of this they have the walk of an Italian amphora-bearing peasant woman coming from the fountain, and a part of their tradition is that for generations they have provided nurses for princes and princesses of the Imperial family. They could be flower girls and nursemaids from the Roman hill towns, were it not for slanting eyes and for their *obis* and white *tabis*, and here under the *gingko* avenue it was not unlike some village near Viterbo, perhaps Bagnaia which is at the gates of Villa Lante, most beautiful of all Italian gardens. Ohara is right at the entrance to Sanzen-in, but just as at a villa or monastery in Italy a big flight of stone steps, moss grown, climbs up in midst of their dappled shade, and shadow was never so dappled as the *gingko* shade. Which was the way into the temple? Through the wooden postern at top of the stairway; or down at the far end of the avenue where were stairs up into another building? Although high in the hills it was too hot to risk guessing the right way in, and failing, and we had to ask at one of the stalls set up in the shade, where were two exceedingly pretty Ohara girls talking to others who were going past with bundles of firewood on their heads. All of them seemed taller and prettier than their compatriots.[1]

So we clambered the stone steps, lichened as any in Italy, up out of the *gingko* shade, passing under the boughs of a cherry tree that must be a beautiful sight in blossom. We went up long passages into the monastery. Its main hall is an old wooden building of lovely timber, grey with age, with shingled roof of mouse-fur thatch, and on the bank to one side of of it a quantity of maples with, here and there, just one leaf turning. The garden, too, has a little of Italian formality about it with the straight stems of cryptomerias instead of cypresses. It is deep in the wooded hillside, a forest garden like Kokedera. With the same feeling that here are no 'lily-silvered vales' of our pagan antiquity, no 'love-whisp'ring woods and lute-resounding waves', but that their gods of nature are of another order as different from ours as if they came from the other face of the moon. The smooth mounds of clipped azaleas, closely cropped as though they were nibbled, and with no respect for the azalea flowers, might suggest that this is no garden made by human hands, but work of an intelligent animal that builds and dams and makes ponds, even some kind of beaver. Here, at Sanzen-in, as at the 'Silver Pavilion', the moon may come over the wooded hill and this is a garden that should be seen by moonlight; or, if not that, in autumn when the maples turn. The fiery tinting of the leaf above the mossed ground must be a marvellous sight. Now, in early autumn, it was green; green as the stalk and leaf of a lily-of-the-valley. Coming away from Sanzen-in on that idyllic afternoon one wanted not to talk in order to remember everything.

---

[1] Another temple in this neighbourhood is Kurama-dera, half-way up a mountain, where on the 20th June every year there is a curious ceremony when two priests of the temple 'cut the raw bamboo trunks with a sword in a breath'. Fresh bamboo shoots are much looked forward to by the gourmets of Kyoto, and the best come to the markets of Kyoto from the bamboo groves of Mukomachi, near Osaka. In autumn, the gourmets look forward to mushrooms from the pine groves round Kyoto, but they must be torn lengthwise, and never touched with a knife.

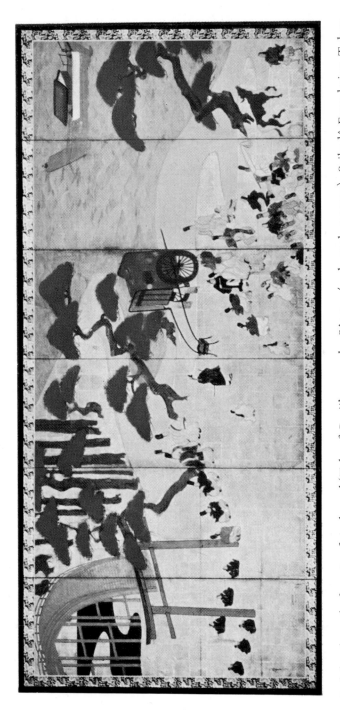

Left-hand panel of a pair of six-leaved 'Tale of Genji' screens by Sōtatsu (early 17th century). Seikadō Foundation, Tokyo

Chapter Six

<hr/>

NARA

IN KYOTO IT IS DIFFICULT to believe that Osaka, with two million inhabitants and the blight of Birmingham or Chicago upon it, is only thirty-eight minutes away by electric train. Nara is at about the same distance but in another direction. It is an hour away by road, but the difference between Kyoto and Nara in terms of European cities is that between Florence and Siena.

There are many to whom Nara will be the most beautiful city in Japan. Its charm and beauty are that its temples and works of art are of an antiquity to which few, if any European cities can aspire. The temples of Nara and their wooden sculptures are of the eighth and ninth centuries, five hundred years before the Sienese paintings and the churches of Siena. Of Byzantine date, but with a freedom and a flowing line that were never the purpose in Byzantine mosaic. As a city, in spite of having a population that has doubled its size in a few years, Nara is largely unspoilt and not even obscured by fogs from its huge neighbours, Kobe and Osaka.

Nara lies to the south of Kyoto, passing by Uji and Sambôin, after which the road is uneventful until you see pagodas and temple roofs in a great wood of trees. This is Nara, which seems to consist of nothing but temples, for you are hardly aware of the town. But it is because of the deer park surrounding the temples, twelve hundred and fifty acres in extent, and about the size of deer parks in England such as Petworth or Badminton. We went straight to the hotel, which is good and comfortable, and then set off for the Great Temple or Tôdaiji.

Now the point of going to Nara in the middle of a stay at Kyoto is to break that chain of wonderful experiences and go back to what was in many ways the golden age. We must conceive of the temples of Angkor as being works of a golden age, just as we have to think of the inhabitants of the island of Bali as living in something equivalent to a golden age contemporary to ourselves. Nara, where the arts are concerned, was the first or vernal flowering of Japan, and nothing in any human ambience ever surpasses the first blossoming. It, also, gives the impression that their every energy went into it, and that Japan was then a poor and small kingdom. The temples of Nara are, of course, fruits of a first conversion for Buddhism had only arrived in Japan a generation or two earlier, and was still redolent of Korea and China and the holy places of India whence it had come.

This last, but first country of origin calls out aloud at Tôdaiji. One comes to it through the deer park, being probably interrupted and importuned by deer upon the way, and in midst of a great concourse of persons all making for the temple. We go through the Nandaimon, or Great South Gate, a huge wooden affair with double roof, or as it were, two roofs superimposed one on top of the other for no apparent reason but to give importance. This gateway was rebuilt, probably on the original lines in about the year 1200, and in the covered porches at its two sides are a pair of enormous wooden statues of demons. They look like pantomime demons, stamping and gesticulating, one of them with tight shut mouth inhaling or holding power, the other with mouth open breathing it out. Their intention can be no other than to frighten, and this gives no pleasant impression. They have horrible, rippling torsos and great ugly hands, and are making grimaces. But they are very big and very old. In fact, in this land not given to superlatives in size they are, it seems, the tallest wooden sculptures in existence anywhere. Twenty-seven feet in height, carved and assembled out of blocks of wood, and are works of the famous Unkei (*c.*1175-1210) —a late date for Nara—and his pupils. They are a pair of Kongô Rikishi, Warrior Guardians or Thunderbolt Bearers.

We are now in a quadrangle which is glaring white and almost incandescent in the midday heat, and immediately in front is Tôdaiji, which is overwhelming in bulk. It is the largest wooden structure in the world, and does really loom gigantic. Here again, it has a double roof but it looks necessary because of the higher inner core of the temple; and withal it is so hot, so gloriously if tiringly reverberant with sun, that one climbs the steps on to the platform and dives into the dark. Within is all that one had ever hoped a pagan temple could be. But the abiding impression is Indian; and I am not perhaps far wrong in thinking that, albeit in a very different way, there are some points of similarity in feeling between Tôdaiji and the abbey church of the Gerónimos or Belém, on the Tagus. In both places the link being that the builders had heard all about India, but not been there. The Portuguese of the fifteenth century had felt the poetical mystery exhaling from India as had the Japanese of the eighth century—and, also, the builders of the temples of Angkor for they are in the same 'movement'. But the altogether astonishing feature of Tôdaiji is its date for it was entirely rebuilt in 1708, and it must be this knowledge which is not difficult to come by that prevents any writer from saying it is the most beautiful temple in Nara and—dare one say it?—not much less impressive than Hôryûji. First built as long ago as AD 745, Tôdaiji was burned down in 1180, and again in 1567. Odder still, in the last rebuilding of 1708, its proportion was altered; it is the same height as originally, but only two-thirds the size. But another account quotes 1629 as the date of its rebuilding, and probably that is the date at which it was given altered dimensions.

The interior of Tôdaiji is enormous and dark and cavernous like a huge cave to hold the statue of Buddha which, contrary to the general opinion, I found to be a much more moving and beautiful sculpture than the great, outdoor Buddha of Kamakura. It is a bronze statue cast in the eighth century, and belonging therefore to the great age in Nara; a Buddha floating on a bed of lotuses, with enigmatic, thaumaturgic smile. The other sculptures are of different intention and eloquent again of demon pantomime. One wonders, naïvely, how men and women could worship deities that get so angry and impatient with them. In the cavernous gloom the other images fume with rage, or menace you with threatening gestures. At any instant a trap door may open and a statue go down in a puff of smoke and burst of flame. This theatrical impression, but always of the old pantomime, is stronger still as one walks round the back of the Buddha and it is exactly like going backstage in an old opera house. Curiously, it is not of the *Kabuki* theatre that it is reminiscent, but of the old London pantomime. A hundred years ago there were always scenes in Peking—an imaginary Peking!—in *Aladdin* or *The Forty Thieves*, and the interior of Tôdaiji is the perfect 'heathen' temple of the scene-painter's imagination. One expects to find harlequin or pantaloon in a dark corner waiting to go on. One looks among the props to find the resin-box.

Coming out of the cool temple, there is time now for the huge octagonal bronze lantern standing just in front of it below the steps, with openwork panels in the curious Nara *art nouveau* manner of the eighth century. For this astonishing object dates from then, and the flute-playing and floating Boddhisattvas are as old as that against their trellised background. And now, looking at the plan of Tôdaiji, some confusion arises owing to its sub-temples, and it would have been wiser to call the main temple where we have just been the Daibutsuden, or Hall of the Great Buddha, for it is only a part, if the main part of Tôdaiji. The sub-temples are the 'February' and 'March' temples, Nigatsudô and Sangatsudô.[1] The 'February' temple is a little further and higher than the great bronze bell of Tôdaiji, of Kremlin scale, in a wooden pavilion or belfry all to itself, but the interests of the little wooden temple that is hung with hundreds of metal lanterns, are in a sense strictly negative for its two images of Kan-non are so sacred that they are never shown, and even their measurements are unknown.

The 'March' temple or Sangatsudô is more generous of its treasures. A little building, not much bigger than a cricket pavilion but, it would seem, the oldest and least restored of Tôdaiji's structures, it has wonderful sculptures of the school of Nara. The main altar has a great 'dry lacquer' or painted wooden Kan-non, with a jewelled diadem entirely reminiscent of those in Catholic churches; and also statues of demigods of thunderbolt brand, 'in terrific divine wrath against evil', one of them, at least, being considered too sacred to be continually on view, and so its sealed shrine is only opened once a year, as with the relics in many Catholic churches. But there are other, more noble, painted wooden figures of Kongô Rikishi or Warrior Guardians which have the entire aspect of armed warriors and, at that, great soldiers or nobles of a thousand years ago. There are yet more Naran sculptures in Kaidan-in, another sub-temple of Tôdaiji, but this time of clay, four armoured warriors of fierce, but gentlemanly, and not pantomime expression. One, at least, of them is on duty, patient and reasoning, and neither howling with rage, nor trampling down a foe and crowing victory with one foot on the fallen demon's head.

The early sculptors of Nara seem to have had an equal mastery in bronze or wood or clay. There are moments when it seems to be the greatest school of sculptors there has ever been, uniting the strength and grace of Donatello to that extraordinary emphasis and importance that the great and anonymous African sculptors can give just to the head of a

[1] The 'March' temple or Sangatsudô is, also, called the Hokkedô.

human being, whether it be one of the heads from Ife, or a bronze from Benin. Better still, most of the Naran sculptures are still in their temples and *in situ*, in the places where they were designed to stand. It would be entirely possible to go only to Nara, and nowhere else in Japan, and come away satisfied. For there is an extraordinary amount of sculpture of the great period, and one must go on from Tôdaiji to Tofukuji temple which with attendant pagoda is nearly on the edge of Sarusawa Pond, a lake about the size of the Round Pond in Kensington Gardens, alive with carp, but with live turtles swimming in it instead of toy-boats. Among the sculptures here which have survived numerous fires is a lifesize statue of Ashura, a benevolent spirit, with three faces and three pairs of arms, an Indian complexity of features, but it is extraordinarily youthful and beautiful and it could teach Picasso a lesson in the simultaneous vision of a human being from three sides at once. How gracefully this problem has been managed by the unknown sculptor! The statue has one body, but three lovely, youthful faces; and in one impersonation the figure of Ashura, a benevolent spirit 'who achieves victory over the enemies of Buddhism not only by strength but also by charm' (Professor Yukio Yashiro), stands with hands clasped in front of him in an attitude of prayer while his secondary or ghost-self places one long thin hand of his other being upon his shoulder as though his ghost-self was dancing and himself was partner. And there is yet his third self with uplifted pair of arms, and youthful, benign expression.

So many are the Naran sculptures that in writing of them there is no other course but to name the most beautiful of those others not already mentioned. These would seem to be two portrait statues of priests, one of a blind Chinese priest at the Tôshôdaiji temple, and the other at Tôdaiji (the similarity of the temple names is very confusing, but Tôshôdaiji is in the plain of Nara, outside and below the town); and a seated wooden statue of a hooded Shintô goddess, with all its original colouring, which is at Yakashiji temple (this is acclaimed as the most beautiful as well as the oldest specimen of Shintô sculpture but, in truth, it nearly resembles a child's doll, one of the sort which are weighted and always, therefore, fall upright if they are tumbled). It should be added that there is no certainty of seeing the sculptures in the temples of Nara for some of them are still considered so sacred that they are kept secret, and seldom if ever shown. The sculptures in the museum at Nara offered an interesting comparison to anyone with memories of the museum of sculpture at the Colegio de Santa Cruz in Valladolid, where are the processional figures or *pasos* of Gregorio Hernández and his school (1566-1636), not forgetting the polychrome figures by Martínez Montañés of the Semana Santa in Seville. The two schools of sculpture at opposite ends of the world are separated, it is strange to think, by a thousand years in time. But the realistic portrait statues of Nara are Spanish in their direct depth of feeling, and the flowering of the school of Nara into decorative forms, as in the panels of the octagonal bronze lantern in front of the steps of Tôdaiji has not a little of the Baroque feeling that is in the air of southern towns like Valencia and Murcia, only it is of another world and a thousand years ago.

It is at Nara, and not at Kyoto, that one begins to appreciate pagodas. I have to admit that in Kyoto pagodas such as that at Toji, which is the tallest in Japan, were quite remarkably unimpressive, and seemed altogether lacking in religious significance. Inevitably, one's thoughts returned to the pagoda by Sir William Chambers in Kew Gardens, and by obvious stages, thence, to Choiseul's pagoda at Chanteloup, near Chénonceaux. By the time one's mind had wandered as far as the pagoda in the lake at Alton Towers, in Staffordshire, a pagoda was a garden, or even a table ornament, and we are nearly arrived at Brighton Pavilion. To these stray thoughts the five-storeyed pagoda of Kôfukuji at the pond's edge is a strong corrective for it is the most conspicuous landmark in the whole of Nara. It is of the fifteenth century but is an exact copy of its predecessor of seven hundred years before. And if this is not enough to persuade one of the beauty of a pagoda in its proper setting there is another, this time a three-storeyed pagoda, just near the pond.[1] Also in the same vein of architectural feeling is the octagonal hall of Kôfukuji, a most picturesque object with its uptilted eaves even if doubts now again are beginning to set in. But this octagonal pavilion— and is it anything more than that?—dates from 1216, the distant year when Henry III came to the throne of England. Another, and beautiful pagoda of Nara is that of Yakushiji, in five storeys, and stated by the authorities to be authentically in seventh-century style. And yet?—And yet it could so easily be standing in a garden, which is what, in fact, it is doing in the garden, or rather, park city of Nara, that is one immense

[1] Mr Yukio Yashiro remarks that not long after the Meiji Restoration the Governor of Nara offered the five-storey pagoda of Kôfukuji for sale as old wood, at the price of fifteen *yen* (about thirty shillings). *Two Thousand Years of Japanese Art*—Oxford, Bruno Cassirer Ltd, 1958, page 259.

deer-haunted park though without a solitary instance of the landscape gardens that are the feature of Kyoto.[1]

And now at Nara there is to be a new sensation and the taste of something we have never known before. For the Buddhist temples are more striking in their similarity than their dissimilarity from Catholic churches. The monks (*bonzes*) with their shaved skulls, the priests in their vestments, the abbots, even the nuns, and particularly the begging monks and nuns, are familiar symptoms; and so are the altars, and the statues in their haloes. The chanting, and droning as of bees buzzing their wings, we know already, and the gilded lotuses for altar flowers. Perhaps the only strange note will be at Nishi Honganji in Kyoto where we will see sliding screens painted with peacocks and golden pheasants, and a pair of stages for *Noh* plays. With these, and a few other exceptions, all is familiar and the wooden cathedrals of Kyoto, for certain of the temples are decidedly upon that scale, could have separated themselves not so many centuries ago from the Vatican. Or, what is probably the truth of the matter, the Early Church in many of its practices and ceremonies appears to have some resemblance to Buddhism because both helped themselves to the common fund of liturgical uses set up by Mithraism, and other Indian or Middle Eastern religions. Now we are to see something entirely different which is a Shintô shrine.

Kasuga Shrine is in the deer park of Nara, and no better indication of its character can be given than that legend says it was founded by a Shintô god who rode up through the forest on a white deer, a god who was ancestor and tutelary deity to the famous and powerful Fujiwara family. The Shintô god and his wife chose the site, and then invited two other gods to come and join them. Or, more prosaically, a member of the Fujiwara who was Minister-of-the-Left, founded it as the family shrine in AD 768. It is a long ascent up to Kasuga, past one *torii* and on to another where you have to get out and walk, and if this is a first experience of a sacred grove in Japan it is something always to remember. For the deer park of the temples lower down in the town now becomes a forest of tall cryptomerias, though not so gigantic as

[1] The most beautiful of all pagodas in Japan may be that of Murôji, about a dozen miles from Nara. It is in five storeys, built of wood, and painted vermilion, as though lacquered, but with white cornices and black eaves. In the background, as with the pagoda at Nikko, are tall cryptomerias. A structure of complicated 'tie-in' beams, but for beauty and ingenuity not to be compared to an East-Anglian 'angel'-ceiling, as at March or Salle. A pagoda, at its best, is more of Maori or Polynesian standard, and of 'willow-pattern' connotation. Is it, for instance, more important architecturally, than the Eleanor Cross at Geddington? The true answer to this must be the negative.

those of Nikko and at the Shrines of Ise. They are, of course, non-deciduous and must look most wonderful under snow. We have nothing like this in the West for it is of no use to compare the fir trees of the Black Forest. Such a comparison gives no idea at all of a cryptomeria, which is much huger in height and girth, and more nearly related to the giant sequoias or redwoods of California. But the sacred groves of Kasuga, or of Ise, have something of the tallest of Italian cypresses as at Villa d'Este, and somewhat of the forest or *désert* of the Grande Chartreuse, in Dauphiné. At Kasuga, in April and May, the crypto-merias have wistaria festooning their boughs, to judge from the cables and lianas upon the trees, and it must riot here in as uninhibited a fashion as the bindweed in an English kitchen garden. In this torrid, torpid noontime, when it is so hot that the inclined slope and the steps up under the trees are as tiring as a feat of mountaineering, the cryptomerias seem more like an avenue of tethered animals and to have the furry-smelling presence of live beings. All along, on both sides of the path, there are monotonous hundreds of stone or bronze lanterns, lamps which look as though they were never lit, but it seems that this is done occasionally, and even, unromantically, can be arranged for on payment at the hotel desk.

At last, and it has been a long time in coming, there are the first signs of the shrine, and climbing up on the left-hand side we find our-selves in a court, all wooden, and painted a bright vermilion. It is now that the particular fascination and charm of the Shintô shrine strikes upon one, this being that, at least in theory, it is taken down and rebuilt every twenty years. It is an entirely novel conception of architecture with an only parallel in the feverish demolition and rebuilding of the office-skyscrapers in New York. But in this, as so often, it is an instance of the oldest approaching nearer than anything else to the new, for this is the primal or basic form of Japanese temple before ever Buddhism appeared, and no expert can put an approximate date to the emergence of this type of wooden building. It is a style which stabilized itself, or became static, some time between the sixth and the tenth century AD.

We are in a long covered passage or corridor, painted vermilion, if I remember right, and leading uphill. This, too, is hung with lanterns; and at the back, in and between the galleries, are those enormous cryptomeria trees. The shrine, itself, is quite a small building; and at this moment a priest comes down towards us with quick, youthful

Doll shop in Kyoto

Japanese dolls

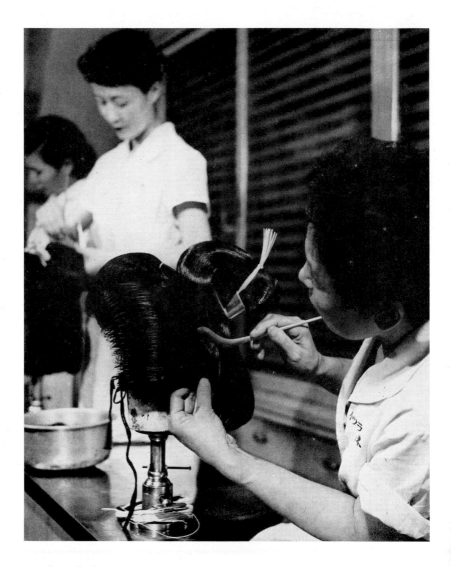

Hairdresser's shop

step, wearing a cloak of watery green silk, like a surplice of green-blue
silk over a white gown or *kimono*. He appears to be taller than most of
his race, probably only because of his priestly robes, and wears one of
those hats of black gauze which we have only seen before in the figures
upon sliding screens. He holds some sort of wand or sceptre of dark
wood in his hand, which reminded me of the sceptres of dark green
jade carried by Maori chieftains in their war-cloaks of dogs'
hair. A marvellous experience to pass a priest belonging to an unknown
religion, new, that is to say to one's own experience! His dress was so
exactly what it should have been.

Almost immediately after that we saw our first Shintô priestess
which came as a lovely surprise for one had heard of the virgin
priestesses but not thought much about them. Or for that matter ever
before seen living priestesses of any kind. For they are not at all the
same as Buddhist nuns or *amas*. They are young and generally good
looking and wear a beautiful and distinctive dress. In fact they are
young girls fourteen to twenty years old; seldom if ever older. At
that age they leave the shrine and marry; and it is to be noticed that in
all the many Shintô temples we were to see there was never a priestess,
if, indeed, that is the correct term for them, older than that age, or, so
far as one could see, any older woman in charge of them. Their dress,
which we much admired, is a wide red divided skirt, of red silk of
beautiful colour, cut so that it appears as if they are wearing trousers; a
white shift or undergarment, and over that a semi-transparent, gauzy
cape or mantle. At other shrines, but only rarely, their divided skirts
were of green silk. We were told that their gauzy mantles bore the
Kasuga crest of wistaria, taken no doubt from the wild wistaria rampant
on the cryptomerias if, in fact, it is wild wistaria and not a 'garden
escape', but in the excitement of our first Shintô shrine I forgot to look
for it upon their dresses. Their function is really that of dancing girls,
and the sacred dances they perform are called *Kagura* but we keep our
account of their dancing until we reach the Shrines of Ise. The name for
the priestesses is *Miko* which means a maiden serving the gods; and it
would seem that the maidens of Kasuga Shrine are particularly renowned, or thought to be 'outstanding' compared to those attached to
other shrines for there is a special name for them and they are called
Mikanko. We did not see the sacred dancing hall at Kasuga; but there
was one of the *Mikanko*, and a very pretty one, with the dark smooth

I

looks of a Gypsy or barge-girl, busying herself and much in evidence at the ticket stall. We dallied and delayed, hoping she would stand up, when we would see whether she was wearing trousers or a divided skirt, but that moment never came. But by making an excuse of looking at the postcards in her stall we could see her long sleek hair 'gathered' into a long tress hanging down her back, and the ends of it put into a little folder of clean white paper. Further investigation seemed ill-mannered and so we moved away.

The *Miko* maidens, perhaps that is a better name for them than virgin priestesses, are much in demand at Shintô marriage ceremonies, but it is with extreme difficulty that an educated Japanese can be brought to talk of his religious beliefs. You are married in a Shintô shrine, but that is about all until the time comes to be cremated, and the ceremony for that is more often held in a Buddhist temple. A certain proportion of the uneducated Japanese, and probably it is larger than one might imagine, are still believers, but it does not follow that all of the tens of thousands who go on pilgrimage are performing it for any other reason than the pleasures of a holiday. Like Italians and Spaniards they are '*festa*-minded'. Almost everything conceivable has been made into a Shintô god or goddess, gods and goddesses of the seas, the winds, the mountains, of industries, of rice, of silkworms, and the population of the Shintô pantheon is an estimated fourteen thousand. What one would like to know, taking it as proved fact that their shrines are of extreme and primitive simplicity in design and shape, is the extent to which the priest's vestments and the sacred dances are faked or genuine. For Shintô was largely revived in the eighteenth century as leading principle in the national movement which eventually dislodged the Shogun and restored the Mikado. Much study was done on ancient records of a thousand years before by historians, and by philologists or political theorists like Moto-ori Norinaga (1730-1801), one of the pioneers of 'The Way of the Gods' who gave to it some of the special and particular emphasis which was to carry it in a direction closely parallel to national fascism, tendencies which ended in national catastrophe and eventual disestablishment under the American Occupation in 1945. Of the sacred dances as performed at the Shrines of Ise, and they were beautiful and moving, I would say they had been touched up and 'produced' by someone of exquisite taste in the not distant past.

The Shrines of Ise we were to see on an unforgettable day of rain and thunder; and after Kasuga and Ise the chief Shintô shrine in Japan is that of Izumo where a guide book of sixty years ago describes the services as 'conducted by priests gorgeously arrayed in white and purple robes figured with gold', not, be it noted, the turquoise-blue silk robes worn by Shintô priests today. The chief priest was then supposed to be eighty-second descendant in a direct line from a Shintô god, and in fact like some of the Tibetan lamas, a living god. This Shrine of Izumo is on the other coast of Japan, facing Korea, and at a point on that coast about opposite to Okayama, the town which could be indicated as being half-way along the Inland Sea.[1] The nearest town to it is Matsue, on an inland lagoon, about nine hours by train from Osaka, in a remote and little visited part of the main island, the unspoilt character of which not so long ago in terms of years is expressed in *Terry's Guide* (1920) where it recommends an inn, advising 'an apartment overlooking the river because of the sustained entertainment offered by the many bizarre craft plying to and fro', and praising the 'excellent food, cooked well and appetizingly', and set out in blue and white porcelain (from Kaga province) 'of such dainty and charming design that one is tempted to start out at once and ransack (in vain) the city shops'. Lafcadio Hearn lived for some time in Matsue, and in *Glimpses of Unfamiliar Japan* describes how, only in 1891, he was the first foreigner ever to enter Izumo Shrine. He was received by the chief priest and living god, and tells of the continuous, surf-like roar of clapped hands as the host of pilgrims to the Shrine invoked the spirits of the Shintô gods. It only remains to add that Izumo Shrine, never seen by Western eyes until less than seventy years ago, has the usual, wonderful park-like setting of the Japanese shrines, and is approached down a long avenue of cryptomeria trees, a thousand years old, with sacred groves to right and left.

But any mention of millennia where Nara is concerned, even on topics stemming from it as of this other leading Shintô shrine, Kasuga once seen and enjoyed, brings one's mind back to the Shôsôin which is in many respects the most interesting thing in all Japan. There is certainly nothing like it in the Western world, unless we suppose all the treasures in all the cathedrals in all Europe put together and combined in one, and then it would fail in its purpose because the

[1] On the same coast, at no great distance, is the famous beauty spot of Ama-no-hashidate, at whose bar or sand-spit, two miles long and covered with pine trees, the Japanese prefer to look standing with their backs to it and their heads between their legs.

objects would be all, or nearly all of them sacred, and none of them profane. The unique character of the contents of the Shôsôin being that they are the entire personal belongings of an Emperor of the eighth century. When he died, his widow gave them to Tôdaiji temple at Nara, and they are housed in an unobtrusive log-cabin standing upon stilts, which should perhaps have been mentioned with the other buildings at Tôdaiji, the 'February' and 'March' temples and the Kaidan-in, but for its immeasurably greater historical and aesthetic importance which puts it into a class apart, as, we might say, all the contents of Tutankhamen's tomb, or all of Pompeii and Herculaneum in one log-cabin. Ever since the eighth century the Shôsôin has been kept, locked and inviolate, under Imperial seal. Even the dates of its airings and openings are known and recorded. The earliest of these was in 787, at about the equivalent lapse of time since its first sealing up that separates us today from the closing of the Prince-Consort's rooms at Osborne when he died. The Shôsôin was opened again in 793, 811, 856; 'repaired' after a long spell of darkness in 1193; and after one or two more openings, in 1261 a retired Emperor entered it and took away a robe but was commanded in a dream to return it to its resting place, which he did, obviously terrified; even in mid-thirteenth century, at its hoary age. Even now the contents are not all catalogued. It can only be opened by Imperial messenger and the same ceremony attends each re-sealing. Unfortunately, the Shôsôin is absolutely inaccessible to any member of the public, whatever his credentials, except during its annual opening which is for about a fortnight at the end of October or beginning of November. Then the contents can be seen, although the interior of the Shôsôin is described as being so dark that it is necessary to take round an electric torch, with the result that one is completely exhausted with eyes ready to drop out of one's head after an hour or two of peering into its ancient darkness. But the contents of this treasure house are familiar from illustration, and fully documented, and it is there that they can best be studied. The marvellous textiles of Chinese, and more distant Persian and Sasanian provenance; carved masks in quantity; mirrors of various metals with engraved backs; game-boards; theatrical robes; weapons; and, particularly, musical instruments, great Korean harps or *Kotos*, many types of flute, some of spotted bamboo, lacquered black, with figures in gold and silver; plectrums of ivory, dyed scarlet, with flowers and birds in white, or of sandalwood with figures in silver; all these relics of an age which in the West would be within a generation or two of the death of Mahomet, and a human life or two earlier than the time of Charlemagne, make of the contents of the Shôsôin something which is hardly credible as having come down, intact and uninjured, to our day. But all we could do was to walk round outside the Shôsôin and wonder at it, for this fantastic repository of ancient works of art is no more imposing, I have to say this, than the log-cabin in a painting by the Canadian Krieghoff, or in a Currier and Ives print.

In the plain below Nara there are other monasteries, and a nunnery, which we did not see. The nunnery is Hokkeji where there was always an Imperial princess for abbess. In this temple is a wooden statue of Kannon, according to tradition by an Indian sculptor who came to the nunnery and was so captivated by the beauty and saintliness of the Empress who lived there as a nun that he wanted to carve her image, but could come no nearer to accomplishing this than by copying her reflection in the lotus pool. The statue is later than her time, and the dates do not fit, but so beautiful is this image in 'a large, dark hall, attended with great devotion by the nuns', that Professor Yukio Yashiro, nurtured on Botticelli and the Florentine painters, finds the temptation almost irresistible and is willing to believe the tradition without too close enquiry. As though in proof of the legend, her statue stands upon a lotus, holds a lotus in a vase in her hand, and has a halo or *mandorla* of lotus leaves springing from the ends of wires. Tôshôdaiji, the temple with the wooden statue of the blind Chinese priest, is near by, but I was unable to discover whether the statue is now on view, or still considered so sacred that it is kept in a sealed chest and not allowed to be seen. The Lecture Hall or Kôdô of this temple is indicated by the same eminent authority, just quoted, as 'perhaps the finest ancient wooden building in the Far East'.

The other monastery is Yakushiji, near by, with a trio or trinity of bronze figures. They must indeed be marvellous statues of the seventh century, with a thaumaturgic or healing Buddha in the middle, of benign and calming aspect. It would seem more than probable that this bronze Buddha, which unfortunately I have not seen, may be the most beautiful bronze sculpture in the world. It is late seventh century in date, and even in a photograph can be judged to be an extraordinary translation of human emotions into cast metal. The seraphic wisdom and tranquillity of Buddha's features, the beauty of his gestures with his hands, the flow of his garment, and the overflowing of the skirts of that to form a sort of flounce of drapery on which he sits, cross-legged, could have been achieved by none other than a great genius among sculptors. In their original condition, a thousand years ago, this trio of bronze figures were gilded which must have accentuated their Indian appearance. The side statues look to be even more Indian of feature, except for their eyes and eyebrows which are Chinese, and all in all these sculptures have a fluidity and technical assurance together with a holiness of spirit and a poetical beauty which are truly marvellous when we think of their development from the wax model into metal. It will be obvious that some of the most spiritual and beautiful sculptures in existence are in these decaying temples of the plain. At Yakushiji there is, also, a much admired pagoda of the same period, of the eighth century, but in paired storeys so that its three storeys present six rows of eaves. But its ingenuity of design, and of the criss-cross tying in of its beams and brackets—above all its great age—should not blind us in assessing it as a work of art, and the question will remain as to whether a pagoda can rank higher than the wooden 'stave' churches of Norway which are of about the same date. The wooden and bronze sculptures of Nara are another matter. They are great and consummate works of art, but a pagoda is—and stays—a pagoda, and a tier or tower of painted storeys below the cryptomeria boughs.

Alas! that we came no nearer than a goldfish hatchery to the temples of the plain. For, maddeningly, at Koriyama, just at the doors of Yakushiji, and only three or four miles from Nara, is the most famous goldfish garden in Japan. We passed it on the way to Hôryûji, having looked at a tank of them in the hall of the hotel at Nara; a few of the goggle-eyed variety on patrol among the weeds, and looking like fish-caricatures of old and disagreeable Pekinese dogs; the lion-headed kind; and others surprisingly silvery, with what appeared to be wings instead of fins or tails. But we were on our way to Hôryûji; and it was only a pity we had no time to go to Hasedera which lies out in another direction from Nara, but is not far away. For Hasedera has a mountain temple that is famous for its peonies[1]—making one wonder why no

---

[1] For flower amateurs, the *Official Guide to Japan*, published by the Japan Travel Bureau, an invaluable authority, names another famous peony garden situated at Sukagawa, which is about 130 miles north of Tokyo, ôn the railway to Sendai. There are a thousand tree peonies in the garden, several hundreds of which are two hundred years old. *The Official Guide*, which is nothing if not detailed, gives thirty-eight 'noted cherry resorts', thirteen famous cherry trees, and twelve apricot resorts, with one garden of old dwarf apricot trees.

church anywhere in England, or Europe for that matter is renowned for its hollyhocks or sweet peas! A mountain temple built out on a wooden platform with scaffolding like Kiyomizu, with pretty shops and inns leading up to it, and long zigzag, covered galleries climbing to the temple, with the peony beds on either side; while Hasedera is, as well, scarcely less famous for its azaleas and cherries. A little farther on is Danzan Shrine at foot of Mount Tônomine, with a pagoda of thirteen storeys and 'a troupe of young girls and musicians in readiness to perform the *Kagura* dance', as at Kasuga Shrine in Nara.

Murôji temple, and its vermilion-painted pagoda among the cryptomerias lies in the hills, not far away. Better still, Yoshino is quite near, where the cherries are planted on the hillside in four groves of trees, a thousand at a time, blooming in succession one after the other. It is the finest display of cherries in Japan. And sated with that, if ever, one could repair in another direction from Nara, to Tsukigase for the pink and white blossom along the river bank, except that a more recent authority says they are not plums but apricots, originally planted not for their blossom but for a red dye made from the fruit, and now that the dye is no longer in demand jelly is made from the apricots.

But such paradisial mornings and afternoons must give place to Hôryûji, about twenty minutes away from Nara, and in many opinions the most beautiful, and certainly the oldest Buddhist temple still in use. There are those to whom Hôryûji is as wonderful a work of art as Chartres cathedral, as beautiful as the Parthenon, and as impressive as the temples of Angkor; one of the wonders, in fact, of the living world, and difficult to look at with other than either prejudiced, or indifferent eyes. It is not long after leaving Nara that one sees the tilted roofs of a group of temples among trees and against some low hills. Within a few moments one is in front of the double-roofed gateway, and in the temple enclosure near to the pagoda. It is the oldest, and perhaps the most solid and impressive of all pagodas in Nara and in the temples of the plain. As to its sacred purpose it is a matter of doubt how much this can ever be achieved in pagoda shape. The doors of its lower floor are open, so that at least this is a pagoda which has some uses, and one can see into the clay grottoes with their little figures that resemble those of the *presepio* in some old church in Naples.

The immensely old wooden buildings standing inside the temple enclosure of Hôryûji are none of them characterized by great size, and were not intended for a great concourse of persons. They are of modest dimension but give an overwhelming impression of age. But, unfortunately, a major tragedy befell the *Kondô* or main hall of the temple only as recently as 1949.[1] For the paintings upon its walls were badly damaged in a fire, and what is left of them has been scientifically removed as though by surgical operation. The only loss compared to this would be were the cave paintings of Ajanta to perish by a single act of God, and not by slow deterioration from old age and damp. Fortunately the destruction at Hôryûji is not complete for good colour reproductions of the paintings were made not long before the fire. There is no large series of frescoes left in China of this age and on this scale. But although the language of the paintings was, so to speak, Chinese, to the point that it is endlessly in dispute as to whether they were in fact painted by Chinamen or Japanese, the tradition is Indian, and this although in all probability no one in Hôryûji had ever seen a living Indian. They are, or were, T'ang wall paintings done by Japanese under Indian influences, felt by them, but where they had never been.

It is of course disappointing, and it could not be otherwise, that the *Kondô* or main hall is a reconstruction. Again, the smallness of scale strikes one more than any other one thing at Hôryûji, except its age. The extent of roofed area to the whole temple enclosure is very small indeed, no bigger than in a Maori village. On the other hand, as in no Polynesian settlement in whatever island, there are wonderful sculptures at Hôryûji, most beautiful of all being the figure of Kannon, in camphor wood, cut from one single block, and more than six feet tall, once gilded, and wearing an immensely tall crown of floral pattern, much resembling the high tortoiseshell combs worn by Spanish women with their mantillas. This figure which must be more than twelve hundred years old has been kept so carefully over the centuries that the sharp flow of its line is that of a statue cast in metal, and one could mistake its wood for bronze.[2] This statue, however, is not in the *Kondô* with its three tiers of roofs, but in the equally old (not rebuilt) and famous *Yumedono* or 'Hall of Dreams', of Hôryûji, an octagonal structure which it could be said, irreverently, is the shape and size of a bandstand. A number of other sculptures including another wooden figure of Kannon, even

[1] The *Kondô* of Hôryûji has been rebuilt after the fire so that it is now, speaking largely, a new building upon the old lines.

[2] This statue of Kannon is only exhibited for a few weeks in the year, in the spring and in the autumn.

taller, and almost as beautiful as the foregoing, together with a quantity
of carved wooden masks and old weapons and armour, are in various
buildings at Hôryûji, the kiosks and pavilions of which are nearly as
confusing in plan as those of the Old Seraglio at Istanbul. There is for
instance a nunnery called Chûgûji, in another compound, at the back
of the octagonal 'Hall of Dreams', which we did not see. A kind of
covered cloister runs all round the main compound, and walking in it
leaves a beautiful impression of this oldest temple in Japan, if only
because of its entire harmony with the wooded hills that rise in the
background. That Hôryûji even after the fire has some of the greatest
works of art in Japan must be undisputed, but if only because of the
Kyotan gardens, I cannot agree that it is as beautiful as Sambôin, or
many another temple in or near Kyoto. Nor do I think that it is reasonable to compare it to churches such as Chartres or Vézelay, or to the
earlier and plainer mosques which are the wonders of the Moslem
world. No collection of pagodas and pavilions can enter into serious
competition with those greater soarings of the human spirit. After a
visit to Nara and its sculptures one returns to Kyoto in anticipation
with one half of its temples and gardens still to be seen.

Chapter Seven

KYOTO (continued)

HAVING BEEN THREE WEEKS IN Kyoto one had become acclimatized enough by now to hear its inhabitants speaking of it with affection as 'Kyot' not Kyoto. A Japanese friend, who lived in Kyoto but worked in Osaka, was perhaps the first to make us understand this. But what a beautiful old city it is! How could one ever forget being in an Oriental city with a million and a quarter population where there cannot be as many as a hundred European inhabitants of all races! An unfailing interest was walking in the narrow streets. But even in the main streets with all the cars and traffic lights there are the big stores to explore, and things seen nowhere else as, for instance, the huge paper rosettes, but, no! they are immense cartwheels of paper flowers, on poles, in all colours, which are a sign that some new business is opening, and that we were told all the neighbouring shopkeepers subscribe to. But, of course, the narrower streets are more interesting; rows of what must be bath-houses, lacquer shops, silk bag shops and a paper shop almost the equal of that in Tokyo, with exquisite slabs of Indian ink marked with gold characters for sale. One most curious contraption was a handbarrow carrying something the shape and size of a barrel-organ, with a thing steaming and boiling inside it, though it was no engine, and which gave a little shrill whistle at every few yards. It was some sort of a machine for roasting chestnuts, except that they were not chestnuts, and the old man who dragged it along had the look of an astrologer with his straggling beard and thin, parchment face. Walking away from him, the short hissing whistles wheezed away into the distance, and then died. A few days later, walking by the river and thinking by some process of telepathy what his machine could have been, it came on to rain and as I sheltered in a door there were a dozen or more of the things drawn up, unattended, in a yard just opposite, as if it was their parking place. Each one of them, I then noticed, had a number plate and they must be something known and recognized in Kyoto, but I never discovered what it was.

There were narrow lanes consisting of nothing but little bars. What do they drink there, for one or two Japanese friends in Kyoto had never tasted whisky? Yet the bars are certainly not intended for the tea-ceremony. Nearly every one of the wooden houses had a little court set with stepping stones and a bamboo or two grown more for the noise of the leaves than for their shade. Then we would come sadly to the end of the narrow streets, and turning the corner just by the electric railway halt (to remind us who and what we are), close to the theatre where the Cherry Dance or *Miyako Odori* is performed by the *geishas* in April and May against painted cherry blossom scenery which must be, at one and the same time, meretricious and very pretty, we turned into a street only a few steps from the main bridge, and what did we see? A tall man walking towards us in a grey monk's robe, wearing a bulbous waste-paper basket, rather the shape of a guardsman's bearskin, upon his head. He was a begging monk, now somewhat of a rarity in Kyoto for all the time we were in Kyoto we only saw one other. We turned and hurried after him to bring him to a standstill, and ask him to let his photograph be taken. This he agreed to, apparently with pleasure, but all Japanese love to have their picture taken. It must rank next to, or after, their love of telephoning. This sergeant-major of a monk held himself proudly before the camera, looking through the interstices of his straw head-mask, really intended to make him keep his eyes upon the ground; and refusing a small present, walked on as though to question and inspect the sentries. Formerly, there were many more of the begging monks but nearly all are gone now. The sight of one of them does give an impression of the Middle Ages, of the Middle Ages in general, and not only in Japan; though one should be aware of the anomaly in this, as, for instance, in thinking what a survival from the past it is that there should be a Grand Lama in Tibet, and realizing in the next moment that there is still a Pope in Rome. In Italy, and not only in Italy, there are still Discalced Franciscans and begging nuns in plenty.

But there is much in Japan that is entirely unique and can be seen nowhere else, and in Kyoto this is of application to the works of art. One of them is Katsura Rikyû, or Katsura Detached Palace, which is of deep contemporary importance to our own time. Perhaps it is the most modern of all old buildings anywhere in the world. Such mid-twentieth century structures as Mies van der Rohe's glass towers on Lake Side Drive in Chicago, or the bronze Seagram building on

Madison Avenue, it would be little exaggeration to say, trace their tradition and ancestry to Katsura more than to past models in Italy or Greece. Or, if unconscious of their origin, they are moving in the same direction, for the architect in question has never visited Japan. It may be difficult to reconcile these theories to the concept of a modern sky-scraper, and to agree that a structure like Katsura that shows many of the elements of a primitive dwelling house as that is still found in the South Sea Islands should be the prototype for advanced buildings of our own day. Nevertheless it is true, and the truth is mathematical as well as spiritual. For the proportion, and therefore the architectural discipline of the Japanese house is based upon the *tatami*, their unit of matting, which is of positive racial affinity to the Polynesian Islands, while in the metal and glass skyscrapers of Mies van der Rohe the architectural unit is the gridiron formed by the units or panes of steel and glass. Also, the extreme precision, the close fitting of their sliding doors, has its parallel in the dead line accuracy of every rivet in its frame of steel in Chicago or New York. It is true to say that these giant buildings of modern times look more to Katsura than to the Parthenon, and that Florentine and Venetian palaces have given place to little pavilions connected with the tea-ceremony in Kyoto.

Having said this, I have to admit to being somewhat disappointed by Katsura, though not by the garden. Its pavilions in all their purity and over exquisite refinement have an unescapable affinity to the South Seas. Katsura which is still Imperial property so that a special permit must be obtained in order to see it, is some three or four miles from the centre of Kyoto, and out to the south-west of the town. Its history is that Hideyoshi ordered it to be made for the grandson of an Emperor, a prince who was an aesthete, and Katsura is famous to this day for cherry blossom and autumn moonlight. The aesthetician in charge was the famous tea-master and garden architect Kobori Enshû (1579-1647), who was allowed *carte blanche* and never questioned as to expense, though he can have had little or no personal contact with Hideyoshi who is said to have given him these promises for Hideyoshi died before Kobori Enshû was twenty years old. Katsura must have grown slowly and gradually which we may believe when we know there are no fewer than seven houses in it, simple though those may be with rush ceilings and walls of bamboo and paper. None the less they are the ultimate and last word in Japanese aestheticism and inmost citadel of the tea-ceremony.[1] In the more substantial buildings, that are still little more than pavilions, walls and floors are exquisitely worked in *hinoki* wood. The 'new' building which in its very lack of sensationalism is the most sensational of all the structures at Katsura, has its floor raised above the ground and the wooden posts which carry it stand upon bits of stone. The water that drips off the roof falls on a bed of gravel, which itself becomes a decorative feature as it follows the advancing and receding angles of the building. The sliding partitions were open and one could look into the rooms which were of entire and utter simplicity, and floored with the finest matting. The roofs are thatched, mouse-fur fashion, with a thatch of reeds. 'Precious' interior details, which one cannot properly see, are the door fastenings on the sliding doors which take the form of bamboo baskets filled with daffodils, the flowers of the narcissi done in silver and the leaves and stalk in gold. Yet the whole main group of buildings at Katsura with the trees and lawns and mosses in front of them are of an overrefined Pacific feeling, of Oceanian origins, and could have the 'Maoris' whom Gaugain painted for their proper inhabitants. At Katsura, too, perhaps more than anywhere else in Japan, and just because it is so exquisite and finished in detail, one should not forget that the whole proportion, and every angle and aspect of view, are of another eye level from ours, that is to say, of a race who do not sit on chairs but squat upon the floor.

At Katsura the garden is surely a masterpiece, and Kobori Enshû should be a famous name among garden lovers all over the world. This is the moment to reiterate that the 'Silver Pavilion', and the 'Moss Garden', the 'Dry' garden of Daisen-in, and the rocks and sand of Ryûanji, are the most beautiful gardens that we have seen so far. Of these, Ryûanji is an original and epoch-making work of art; Daisen-in is to be admired as a landscape of the imagination carried out in stones and sand; the 'Moss Garden' is a meeting place of the sages; and it is difficult to choose between the 'Silver Pavilion' and Katsura as the most typically beautiful of Japanese gardens. Each of them is as lovely as any garden in the world. The lake at Katsura must be the most minutely planned and considered of all ornamental waters. It is edged with a series of bizarre and wonderful rock shapes, masterpieces of the *objet trouvé*, that reveal Kobori Enshû as a past master in the art of rock

[1] The greatest of the tea-masters was Sen-no-Rikyû (1521-1591), and his precepts were the great influence with Kobori Enshû. Rikyû also designed gardens, e.g. Chisakuin Temple Garden at Kyoto.

arrangement. Japanese connoisseurs claim to be able to tell his rock siting from that of other garden architects, so individual is his style. The garden at Katsura has monolith bridges that give the sensation of walking across water on a sword-blade, and artificial islands that are studied externally and internally, from the island itself, that is to say, but also from the mainland. There are artificial stretches of beach with smooth round pebbles, a long and interesting promontory supposed to recall the famous sandspit of Amanohashidate, and groups of rare palms (cyads) which one begins to associate in mind with the tiger paintings (of imaginary tigers) by Kanô Sanraku, for young palms of this variety burst, rocket-like, out of his foregrounds. The winding path leads from shore to island, and from pavilion to tea-house; and one can look through a sliding partition at a room with a rush cornice which is walled only with squares of blue and white paper, and is entirely satisfying. It was only a pity we could not walk round the rooms for those are studied to open out on the landscape through their sliding panels. Garden and pavilions are works of art that work both ways. Harmonies reign here that do not inhabit the elongated house of cards that is Versailles. At Katsura there is no striving for magnificence. But its rocks and winding paths, and vistas of isle and water, have a lively restfulness.

After Katsura one may want to see something that is upon a bigger scale, and for this it is necessary to go no farther than the monastery of Nishi Honganji which is in the middle of the town. It is no less than a wooden cathedral, or two cathedrals, for it has the *Hondô* or main hall, 'constructed of rare and carefully chosen woods from the sacred forest of Kôyasan', and it connects with covered wooden galleries with the Amida Hall. This pair constitutes the largest and most splendid wooden structures in Japan after one has seen Hôryûji, and the yet more marvellous Daibutsu, breathing of ancient India, in the park at Nara. The *Hondô*, as it stands now, is not more than two hundred years old, but has the air of much greater antiquity, and walking, shoeless, on its polished floor one can become familiar with the abracadabra of Buddhist worship, the incense, the golden lotuses, and continue down the long covered passage to its twin building where a conspicuous object is a sliding screen painted with a peacock and peahen on a golden ground, perched on a white blossoming peach tree. Yet it is true that these huge wooden buildings are a little empty of interest, and one hurries back in order to penetrate into the halls behind them where are the works of art. But here we were in for a disappointment. At the time of our visit repairs on a great scale were in progress. There was scaffolding in the *Shoin* or 'Stork Chamber', perhaps the most splendid of all painted rooms in Japan, which was brought here from Hideyoshi's palace at Fushimi, outside the town. Sacking hung over most of the painted screens, and the floor was deep in dust. Owing to these restorations we missed seeing some fifteen to twenty rooms painted with bamboos and sparrows, monkeys and flower cars, wild geese upon a gold leaf ground, willow trees and silver pheasants, gold and white chrysanthemums, white peacocks under double blossom cherry trees, or even a little room painted with musk cats and fern palms, in fact the whole or nearly all of the repertory of Japanese decorative art. What we did not see were passages with cedar wood panels painted on the grain of the wood with monkeys.

Almost at the side of the 'Stork Chamber' is a famous garden of the sixteenth century called 'The Valley of the Tiger'. It is composed entirely of enormous rocks simulating a rocky river, but with no water, and the peaks of high jagged mountains in the distance. A huge monolith bridge crosses it, cut out of one stone. The valley is green with ferns and mosses and with sago palms. It is a hot, steaming river gorge of the tropics, it could be in Borneo or Burma, confined in imagination to a mile or two, not classic and illimitable in the celestial sense, as in the Daisen-in, and all carried out in a space not larger than a tennis court, but in a sad state of dilapidation when we saw it owing to the dust caused by repairs. Yet a more 'tigerish' landscape than where the living tigers roam. We also saw, at some distance past the splendid main gateway, a depressing tea house brought here from another of Hideyoshi's palaces. This in three storeys, with rooms with 'dog doors', and overlooking a sad lake and garden. It was more encouraging to look once more at the Storll Chamber which was the Abbot's audience hall, even in its sackcloth, and to note that there was a *Noh* stage at one end. There are, indeed, two *Noh* stages in the monastery of Nishi Honganji. The other great wooden cathedral of Kyoto is the Higashi Honganji which was almost entirely rebuilt about sixty years ago. Here, too, there is a *Noh* stage, but not many paintings or works of art. Both cathedrals belong to branches of a Buddhist sect of which the priests are not celibate and are allowed to marry. The abbot of Higashi Honganji is a hereditary office in the Otani family, and when we were in Kyoto there was much excitement in the newspapers because the abbot, a young and very rich man, had broken off his engagement. Here, also, there is a garden by Kobori Enshû called Shôseien, or Kikokutu,[1] with a biggish lake, but we heard of it too late, and did not see it. The effect of the wooden cathedrals, for they are authentically upon the cathedral scale, is much enhanced if one has seen a forest of growing cryptomeria trees, as at Nikko, or in the sacred wood of Ise. The scores of wooden columns forty foot high were once living pillars through which the winds sang, and which had their live animal scent as one walked below them. Wood is more musical than stone in its response to heat and cold, and it is scented. The columns of both wooden cathedrals, Nishi Honganji and Higashi Honganji, should take one in imagination to the sacred woods of Koyasan.

A day or two after the *Noh* stages were shown to us in Nishi Honganji, for there are a pair of them, there was opportunity to see a live *Noh* play. The performance which had already been in progress for some hours on our arrival had become a slow monotonous chant intoned by some dozen or more singers robed in black *kimonos* and squatting on the floor. An endless recitative without instrumental accompaniment, and one singer or other now and again raising his voice to a falsetto monologue. So it went on for three-quarters of an hour which gave time to look at the stage and at the audience. There must be a word in the language for a passionate and loving admiration for wood textures and wood surfaces and it prevails perhaps more in Japan than in any land in the world. This one can tell from the cheapest chest of drawers. It is a talent for carpentry which rises to genius in the temples of Nara, or at Kiyomizu. But it is, also, very much a part of the *Noh* plays for the stage is made of cypress wood polished only with the natural oil of the wood. It is built like an open pavilion with thatched roof of reeds like a *Shintô* shrine, all this in the middle of a modern air-conditioned theatre. The dimensions are worked out in minutest detail; the stage proper being invariably so many feet square, and having a pillar at each corner to guide the actors when they are playing female parts and, therefore, wearing masks. The stage is entered by a covered passage from the left, with always three small pine trees planted in the gravel below it. Many of the audience sitting near us were following the chanting, word by word, as with students and music lovers in the

[1] Because it had a hedge of Kikoku (trifoliate orange) round it.

First writing lesson

Garden at Shûgakuin, Kyoto (17th century)

upper rows of seats at Covent Garden. Nearly all of them were wearing
their national dress which is so neat and becoming that one could not
tell what social strata they belonged to. At a guess one would say they
were, one and all, the wives or daughters of university professors.

But now the chanting is over, rapturously enjoyed, and the play
begins. The actors take up their places, and the ghost heroine played by
an actor in a mask, makes his entrance from the left, walking all down
the passage with that curious stilted walk of the *Bugaku* dancer, in its
turn copied from or influenced by the *Noh* drama. The play was by
Ze-ami (died 1443) who with his father Kan-ami, both of them famous
actors, wrote most of the old repertoire,[1] but even with the Japanese
it is a very specialized taste, and if one does not understand the language
it is next to impossible to follow the action which is stylized and poetic
to a degree that does not tally with anything at all in the Western
world. After only one viewing of a *Noh* play it would be presumptuous
to express any decided opinion upon it, but in spite of its poetical
subtleties which must appear upon closer acquaintance, I know for
myself that I would always prefer *Kabuki*.

On the afternoon following our visit to the *Noh* play we embarked on
a conventional excursion of another sort, shooting the Hozu rapids. In
order to do this we had to drive some miles out of the town to an inn
where flat-bottomed boats are waiting. Three boatmen came with us,
and the youngest of them who acted as steersman bore the most
disconcerting likeness to an old friend, and enemy, the late painter and
writer, Wyndham Lewis. Again and again as we shot down the narrows,
seeming to slide off the rocks in the last second only to plunge down
into a seething mill race of waters, I saw the caricatural resemblance and
could not but think of that genius *manqué* and marvellous talker as he
was when I first knew him. I first heard the magic names of Kôetsu
and of Sôtatsu from him, though I suspect he knew little more of that
greatest of Japanese painters, or of Kôrin, than having read of them all
in Fenollosa.[2] And while shooting the rapids I pictured him to myself
arriving at the Court of the Shogun at some year in the time of Ieyasu
or Hideyoshi. He loved intrigue and to live on the fringe of violence,
but how curious to be thinking of him in this remote place owing to
this chance resemblance! Far away we certainly were, except for a

---

[1] There are more than a hundred plays by Ze-ami.

[2] *Epochs of Chinese and Japanese Art*, by Ernest Fenollosa, 1912.

K

railway line that kept on vanishing into tunnels at different levels above
our heads, and coming out again. A train apparently full of school
children, but they were really horn-spectacled adults, came puffing
slowly up the gradient in the opposite direction, and one would have
thought from their interest and excitement at the train windows that
we were going over Niagara Falls, no less, in a barrel. Again, not a
single plant growing by the water was to be known or recognized
though we were told that the hills are beautiful in their proper seasons
with maples or wild azaleas.

Even the birds darting over the water were different; one of them
which was pied black and white being presumably a kingfisher. It was
exciting enough but, also, a little boring and presently we came to a
long tea-house, or an open-air restaurant, and were nearing Arashiyama.
Immediately, it became interesting. The wooded hills began to dwindle
in height, and there could not be more than one or two more windings
of the river, the waters of which had now quietened and were flowing,
deep and placid. At last we came out from those wooded banks into the
open, but just at the last decline of the trees where only their shadow
lay along the water we passed a couple of pleasure boats, not flat-
bottomed punts like ours, for these were gay with awnings and the
sound of voices came from them. Young men and women were singing
in the boats, and we saw the women's dresses and knew they must be
geishas on their way to the long tea-house we had passed. There was
singing, too, from both banks of the river, and we found ourselves,
suddenly, out of the rapids and in a pleasure quarter. Arashiyama is one
long row of inns and restaurants along the river bank, and maple and
cherry trees with their more delicate leaves stand out against the dark
pines in the background. It is a village from which one takes back an
echo of music and enjoyment upon the water, and the way home to
Kyoto is idyllic in the evening light, passing a big lake that is all there is
left of a pleasure palace that stood there in Heian times, more than a
thousand years ago, and one longs to have seen the boating-parties
and the beauties of that long dead age afloat upon the water.

Deciding it was time we saw a pagoda in Kyoto from close to, having
only caught sight of their many-tiered silhouettes against the cryptomerias and approached no nearer than that, we now set off for Toji
where is the highest pagoda in Japan. It is down in a south-west district
of Kyoto, not far from Nishi and Higashi Honganji, in what the guide

book itself calls 'a somewhat frowsy neighbourhood'. There had been a downpour of rain and we had to splash our way through pools of water, to the left, always to the left from the entrance gate, towards the pagoda which grew darker and dimmer and dirtier the nearer we came to it through the puddles, and also had the property of growing taller as one looked up at it till it seemed to be more than its hundred and eighty feet high. But the pagoda of Toji is famous in legend for its elastic proclivities for at one time it was a leaning pagoda, and is said to have righted itself in a night. It is a five-storey pagoda and was rebuilt in the seventeenth century. I could not see that it was either particularly beautiful or venerable but to a European pagodas are of incurable association with a number of things that have nothing to do with religion. If it is the tallest in Japan one could only remember having seen cryptomerias in the sacred woods which were as tall as that, and recall that there are redwoods growing on the Pacific slopes of North America, that are twice as high, in fact they would reach up to the golden ball and cross on top of Saint Paul's Cathedral. This pagoda of Toji is ill-placed. There are no green hills behind it and it looks dingy and unhappy. The storehouse of Toji is supposed to hold more works of art than any other temple in Kyoto, including many from China, but it would be an affair of weeks or months to get permission to see them, and one comes away a little dissatisfied from the least picturesque temple in Kyoto.

From here it is not far to Shimabara which is one of the old pleasure quarters of the town. The houses are old and wooden and it is one of the more treeless parts of Kyoto. First of all we set out for Honkokuji, a temple near Nishi Honganji, which is described as having several gardens, but the large area that it used to cover has been broken up by new roads and buildings so that many outlying parts of it are no longer within its compound, and we drove around for half an hour or more making vain enquiries. Eventually, in the backyard of one little wooden house which could have been one of a hundred other wooden houses and seemed to have no connection at all with Honkokuji, we discovered what we were searching for only hardly anything was left of it. An extremely intellectual-looking young man, who was probably nothing of the kind, roused himself from sleep on his mattress in a little cell near the door, and came half-naked to the bamboo fence. In this perpetual excitement of seeing new things every day one was forgetting how hot it was. He seemed to be the only inhabitant of this house (or temple?) called Shinnyô-in, and took us to a verandah at the back looking on to the wreck of what was formerly the unique example of a 'pebble garden', one of the most far-fetched *minutiae* of garden craft, more resembling the garden of a bower-bird than anything arranged by human hands. It is a 'dry' river bed with water simulated by hundreds or even thousands of river stones, laid down by hand, one over the other so as to overlap like fish scales, and all heading one way to imitate the river current. The technical trick or *coup de main* comes, or rather came, in mid-stream where the waters separate and flow two ways, all of which is faithfully portrayed in the pebbles. The great name of Kôetsu has been associated with this high-tension little affair,[1] for in fact it was all disturbed and shaken to pieces with the pebbles lying in heaps having lost their direction. What had happened to it? Had someone lost his patience with it? There are stories of even more nervously exhausting gardens. One made entirely of pine needles, for instance, which has to be brushed or dressed at least twice a day. The young intellectual seemed to infer that disaster had overtaken the garden not long ago, and that it was to be restored. Who was the culprit? But, in any case, this was a question that we could not ask.

And now we began to ask for the Sumida *geisha* house which is in the middle of the Shimabara quarter, having already sent a telephone message and been told we could be shown over it at four o'clock. It was a little like finding that one of the *mauvais lieux* which Toulouse-Lautrec frequented, and where he lived eventually, was still active, and asking the receptionist of our hotel to ring up the manageress and say we wished to see over the establishment. We had been told that if we went there by night they might ask for a lot of money from us. So, early in the afternoon, we set off when the streets were rather empty as everyone who could stayed indoors because of the heat, and we were coming along an almost deserted road of wooden houses when an extraordinary apparition came out of a doorway some way ahead and walked in front of us down the street. Not walking, so much as teetering with an odd stilted walk, in a *kimono* of most gorgeous colours like great splashes of flowers, but we were too far behind to catch the pattern. We could only see her huge *obi* flashing with gold and towering

[1] Kôetsu is, also, credited with the design of a garden at Hompôji temple, near Daisen-in, where he was priest. It was a sand garden, but is now grassed over, thereby losing its effect of circular movement which was centred round a pool, perhaps intended to portray a whirlpool.

bee-black, lustrous 'hairdo'. But the young woman, walking on high
pattens or chioppines as did the Venetian courtesans in the time of
Titian and Aretino, turned a corner and was gone.

Almost at once after this we reached the Sumida house in high
expectations after what we had just seen. The interior was large and
cavernous, covered in but rather like the yard of an old coaching inn,
and an old kitchen hag was the only female in sight. An old man like
an ostler led us upstairs into some big rooms which looked empty and
almost too old for party giving. The Sumida house must date from the
seventeenth century to judge from its lacquer and paintings, and there
were smaller rooms suggestive of more private parties, one of them with
the marks of several sword cuts on the panelling which must be witness
to a wild evening, ending more likely than not in death for someone.
The old man who showed us round only pointed to the marks, and
said the one word 'samurai' in explanation. It was only when we came
away some moments later that we realized the apparition we had seen
in the street outside was one of the *maikos* of the Shimabara. This was
the first we had seen, and we saw no more until we went into the Gion
quarter.

A treat was in store the morning we went to Nijô Castle, which
really is a palace and perhaps deserves that name more than any other
existing building in Japan. Often we had passed its cyclopaen castle
walls, white corner-turrets with tilted roofs, and very 'Japanese' pine
trees, while going to other parts of the town, but we had never set foot
inside it. It is the palace of Ieyasu, first of the Shoguns of the Tokugawa
family, and dates from just after 1600, but from 1634 for two hundred
years no Shogun came to Kyoto so that Nijô Castle, or what is left of it,
gives an untouched picture of its time, curtailed by many fires which
destroyed huge portions of it, and not helped at all by the years after the
Meiji Restoration when it was used as Prefectural Office or Town Hall
of Kyoto. For the study of Japanese paintings of its epoch Nijô Castle is
indeed a kind of Doge's Palace, but instead of huge paintings by
Tintoretto or Veronese there is the entire range of Japanese decorative
painting in its golden age. White herons, cherry blossom and long-tailed
birds, sparrows asleep in a bamboo grove with snow upon them, snow-
covered fir trees on a gold ground, or in stricter detail, 'wild geese and
brown-eared bulbuls', form the subjects.

After entering the castle precincts through the cyclopaean walls one comes to the Karamon, a gate of ceremony brought here like the 'Stork Chamber' at Nishi Honganji from Hideyoshi's palace at Fushimi. It is in 'Chinese' style, that is to say, in the kind of *chinoiserie* the Japanese invented for themselves, which is almost as fanciful as 'Chippendale' *chinoiserie*, and in which the temples of Nikkô were built. The Karamon is compound of gilt metal and woodcarving, and has storks and paeonies and butterflies for theme, with striped tigers and 'lion-dogs' for accompaniment. Passing through this gateway which is so unlike anything we associate with castle architecture in the West, and which is in a different style from other buildings in Kyoto, and is in fact in Nikkô style, we face two or more flights of reed-thatched, copper-eaved, long buildings outlined in gold, containing a multitude of glorious painted rooms, leading one into another.

The halls in which the Shoguns gave audience to the *daimyos* have paintings of intimidating character, with huge eagles on lichened pine trees, or tigers and bamboos. 'Nightingale floors' are everywhere in Nijô Castle, but are explained here as being designed to give warning of approaching footsteps. The door fittings are more gorgeous versions of the simple baskets of daffodils at Katsura, and even take the form of the folding papers used for wrapping up presents, and in particular those strands of dried seaweed which are served up at banquets on important occasions. Long corridors lead from one wing of the castle into the other, where are the Shogun's private apartments from which the menacing eagles and huge pine trees are absent. Here the painted screens are slighter and more delicate, and the atmosphere more feminine. A few of the rooms have superb, carved and pierced wooden panels or *rammas* along their cornices, with themes that are different on both sides, peacocks, perhaps, on one side among pine twigs, and full blown paeonies on the other, painted and gilded, and due to the famous Hidari Jingorô, a carver who worked, also, at Nishi Honganji and at Nikkô. These apartments at Nijô Castle, and the 'Stork Chamber' at Nishi Houganji which we saw in dust and sackcloth, literally, for the scaffoldings were hung with sacking, are, we say, upon a Venetian scale of splendour and quite overwhelming in their magnificence. The garden of huge rocks at Nijô Castle, intended as a tribute to Hideyoshi's military glory, which I had long looked forward to seeing, I found disappointing and took away the impression that many of the rocks must have been tumbled about, perhaps in an earthquake. But

the apartments are wonderful, and not even Isfahan in the reign of
Shah Abbas, or the Court of Tamerlane at Samarcand, can have
presented a more marvellous spectacle to the eyes than when Nijô
Castle was the seat of the Tokugawa Shogun and his court.

After Nijô and Nishi Honganji one needs to take time off to think.
For of a sudden everything is upon a bigger scale. A new impression of
this old capital of Japan comes to take its place beside the picture of the
Zen monasteries set down with gardens round them in every direction,
and carrying with them the implication that a garden is a better place
for meditation than an anchorite's cell. The 'Stork Chamber' with the
Noh stage opening off it for dances, and the 'Valley of the Tiger
Garden' beside it, produce an altogether exceptional impression of
sumptuary magnificence. Nearly all Oriental palaces, and particularly
those of the Moslem world, not excluding the Alhambra of Granada,
convey a sense of boredom and frustration after the first impression has
worn off. It is not enough to say this is only because of the abstract and
geometric ornament of 'Arabian' architecture but, in fact, this profusion
of flowering or blossoming forms at Nijô Castle and at Nishi Honganji
gives a vernal excitement that the half-orange domes of the Moors and
their filigree and stalactite motifs can never impart. We are once more
in a land of actors and painters, with a theatre that mirrors the far-
fetched conventions of a thousand years of aesthetic experience. To
come down to detail, no one who has seen the Imperial robes of the
Manchu Emperors with their monotony of cloud and dragon patterns
could maintain the Forbidden City to have been a more thrilling
aesthetic excitement than the court of the Shogun with the marvellous
dresses of which there is still tangible evidence, and against this golden
background of the sliding screens.

But the other and simpler side of life in Kyoto, so far removed from
what their own aesthetes think to be the vulgar splendours of the
Shoguns, appeared again a day or two later when we went to Tenryûji.
Crossing one of the bridges, a whole stretch of the river bank was bright
with long strips of silk or cotton laid out to dry, while men and women
wading into the river to their knees were holding other strips in the
current to set or fix their colours. Tenryûji lies out beyond Katsura,
near Arashiyama, the lovely village where you disembark after shooting
the Hozu rapids. It was a delight to see it again, even with the Coca
Cola notices, and in a side street there was a sight I would not have

missed for anything, a begging nun, an *ama* being somewhat of a rarity compared to a monk or *bonze*. We were walking along, admiring the houses with their bamboo fences in different designs, when we heard certain little flutings, I thought probably a *minah* bird, and looking round saw a white-clad figure standing outside a house a few feet behind us. One could not see if it was a man or woman and thought, at first, it must be holding the bird on its hand, or in a little cage. But there were no more flutings, and I saw it was a woman and knew her to be a nun. She, too, like the begging monk we had seen, wore a curious, basket-shaped straw hat, hiding her face, but it was less of a waste-paper basket and more feminine of shape. Her bamboo pipe was in her hand, and at least we had seen a flute-playing nun.

We had passed near by Kôryûji, the temple of the Bull Festival—a man 'clad all in white', riding on a bull, and impersonating a Buddhist god (see page 115)—and close to Seiryôji, where there is a Torchlight Festival on 15th March, three great bonfires are lit in the temple precincts in order to divine the season's rice crop, and another three-day festival is held in April when the villagers wear masks and old costumes, and dance and beat drums and ring the bells—and are not far from Nison-in, a temple which is famous for its maple trees in autumn. There are more popular festivals than in Italy or Spain, but the spirit is different, and there is nothing in Europe really comparable unless it is the Feria in Valencia or Seville with its *jeux floraux* (*jochs florals* in the Valencian dialect), battles of flowers, processions, less the bull fights. Again and again in Kyoto one is reminded of Seville, but Seville with a population of a million and a quarter, and three thousand temples, reputedly, but nearly a thousand shrines is the sober truth.

Tenryûji has been rebuilt after a number of fires but it does not seem to have been spoilt by that. In any case one comes to Tenryûji in order to see its garden which like the 'Moss Garden', near by, is said, incredibly, to have been designed by the priest Musô Kokushi (1275-1351). That is to say, it is credible at the 'Moss Garden' which looks old enough to date back to the time of Gautama Buddha, himself, in the seventh century BC, but at Tenryûji let us be content with thinking that the lake, whether or not in its present shape, may be due to the hand of that fourteenth-century priest, who was the first abbot of the temple. It is among the largest lakes in any of the Kyoto gardens. I shall always remember the beautiful heat on the day we saw Tenryûji and the twang and whirring of the grasshoppers like wound up springs of metal, wound up and let go. On the distant waters towards the far bank were masses of water-lily leaves, but the beauty of Tenryûji is not so much any particular feature of the garden as the wooded hill rising behind it, a hanging wood from which it was impossible to take one's eyes away, and which must vary in marvellous manner from hour to hour of the day. How beautiful it must look by moonlight! Three or four generations of trees must have succeeded each other since Musô Kokushi dug the lake, but one can conceive of no more poetical linking of woods and water. The hand of a great artist and poet is to be felt here, and in the marvellous sage-haunted 'Moss Garden' or Kokedera.

As in so many of the monasteries there are long wooden galleries at Tenryûji, leading uphill, in this instance, to a temple or tea-house, it is often difficult to distinguish between them, in front of which stands a tremendous *sakura* (cherry tree), its farther branches tied down, if you think of it in that way, or else supported upon bamboo stakes and palisades. But it does really seem to be moored there, to be anchored, or tied to mooring posts, as though it might sail away, perhaps on a night of full moon over the hanging wood, and away! Coming down again, down the long wooden gallery to the lake, there was a sound we had not heard before rising out of the water, more musical than that whirr and twang of the grasshoppers. This must have been the singing frogs for which Arashiyama, just behind the wooded hill, is well known. The Japanese buy them and keep them in little cages, and call them 'river deer', and 'when contented', they utter a sweet but piercing short note or whistle, 'like the sound made on a silver flute'. If there was ever a musician of genius among the begging nuns, one would have her play her bamboo pipe in the moonlight by the lake side in competition with the singing frogs.

In order to round off this wonderful early September afternoon we went on to Daikakuji, a temple towards the hills which has some beautiful paintings. There are the usual stone flagged walks leading to it under the cryptomeria trees which in this great heat had an almost animal fragrance seeping down from their branches. At Daikakuji the wooden outside passages that lead round the buildings are as complicated as a garden maze or child's puzzle, and you may have to retrace your steps all over from the beginning if only in order to enter the *hondô* or main hall. There are two series of sliding screens painted by

Kanô Sanraku, one of paeonies and the other of red plum blossoms, and a sort of dado or lower part of a sliding screen which you have to go down on your knees to look at. It is by the famous Kôrin, but this great decorative painter and designer was in whimsical mood at Daikakuji, and only did a few rapid and vapid sketches of 'bunny rabbits'. 'A small precious masterpiece' is exaggerated praise for these few washes by his hand. There is no garden, but to one side of the temple is a large artificial lake of Heian times, of a thousand years ago, where one of the early Emperors had his summer palace, its banks now planted with cherry trees, and we drove back past another lake of Heian days, through the unforgettable and lovely evening to Kyoto.

Chapter Eight

----------◆-◆-◆-◆-◆-◆-◆-◆-◆-◆-◆-◆-◆-◆-◆-◆----------

KYOTO (continued)

To BEGIN THIS LAST OF four chapters on Kyoto with an account of going for the first time to Kiyomizu is to give oneself the pleasurable sensation of starting all over again from the beginning, as though just arrived in the heat of last night out of the ice-cold, air-conditioned train from Tokyo into this wonderful, cryptomeria bough'd and branch'd, pagoda'd, bronze-bell-booming, old city. For in fact we went to Kiyomizu on our first morning, and it was only the first of several visits. The longer one is in Kyoto the more fond one becomes of the green Higashiyama hills, those hanging woods that lie all along one side of the town from Mount Hiei in the north down as far in the other direction as Uji and Sambôin. No other great city of more than a million inhabitants has the green woods so near to it. The window of our hotel room looked out onto them and woodland sounds came morning and night into our bedroom. Temples beyond number stretch for several miles along their wooded shade and share their winter snows, while the pleasure quarter of Gion or Giom-machi lies towards their early slopes and feels something of their evening cool.

Into the very middle of these woods Kiyomizu is built out on giant timber substructures or scaffoldings like a huge bridge or causeway above the trees. But the delights of this most fascinating of temples start much before that in the long narrow street that climbs the hill, though one must be careful because there is a right street and a wrong street leading to the temple, and the street that runs parallel has only a few shops along it and is disappointing. But the real rows of shops leading to Kiyomizu will be one of the most fascinating sights seen in one's life, and not only if one knows no more of the Far Orient than Chinatown in San Francisco or New York City. For certainly there is nothing in Japan quite like it though as a race they have an exceptional, if altogether excessive understanding for souvenir stalls. Having seen Kiyomizu one expects great things of the stalls at Nikkô and Miyajima, and is disillusioned.

Perhaps the majority of the pottery kilns of Kyoto are at Kiyomizu. There are many pottery shops along the street and, also, the typical blue and white porcelain of Kyoto is on sale including a choice of little *sake* cups of exquisite design and quality. There are the prettiest things imaginable selling for the equivalent of twopence; pottery ducks which when filled with water are no longer penny whistles but china song birds, no two the same. Little temple bells that are marvellously sweet in tone, and during August singing grasshoppers in little wicker cages. There seem to be things in Kyoto that one can only buy at Kiyomizu so that one has to go back there for particular bits of china or pottery, or toys. In the meantime cohorts and even legions of school children are charging uphill behind their flag-leaders and colliding with companies and battalions of school children who are coming down. We surge along with them uphill having abandoned the taxi, up flight after flight, passing whole families bivouacked for the day on some stone ramp or plinth of the step or others with their *bentôs* (luncheon-boxes), eating rice or bean-curd or seaward with their chopsticks. Once beyond the vermilion gateway, and having bought our tickets which are even prettier specimens of printing than usual, we see the wooden temple buildings climbing all up the hill at different levels. At a kind of concierge's box in the main building priests are selling 'golden' charms of 'base metal' for they only cost a few yen, and texts written on little rolls of silk which they seal, importantly, by pressing the stamp on to a huge red mass of paint or sealing-wax, bigger than the Great Seal of the Three Kingdoms, and then impressing it upon the silk. You feel you have bought a Golden Bull, or the Chrysobulls of the Eastern Basileus or of the patriarchs for a few pennies.

But in front of the temple is a broad wooden platform, and coming to the edge of this we look down, down into the ravine with the human flood pouring down the steps to the tank of water at the bottom, and in the other direction to the vast wooden underpinning of the next plat-form. The wooden buildings and huge timber scaffoldings date from early in the seventeenth century; they are almost modern compared to many of the wooden temples of Kyoto, and not a single metal nail or tie was used in their construction; a temple of carpenters, and not bricklayers or stonemasons. Roofs are not of thatch, but bark shingles, and the temple hall interiors are grave and solemn for the pillars which are simple tree stems were felled from cathedral aisles in the forest.

From a further, and higher platform the view is more wonderful still down the wooded slopes to the temple roofs of Kyoto with more than one pagoda, seen either from this or the other platform, rising against the trees, or standing on the skyline. Now, at last, we know the point and purpose of pagodas, with our eyes that are used to towers or minarets.

There are more interesting temples than Kiyomizu, but the narrow street of stalls leading to it, the really wonderful view from it, and the audacity of its own mere weight together with that of the vast concourse of persons born daily upon its timbers, makes of Kiyomizu a temple apart that is unique and unforgettable. Toiling down the long steps to the water tank where the devout are drinking the holy water from a cup at the end of a long bamboo pole, or are even splashing the water over their heads and arms, one looks up in wonder at those tremendous supporting baulks of timber. They seem more appropriate to some giant pier built into the water, to some theatre or even opera house built out into the sea, they are like the underpinning or substructure of a wooden theatre; wooden equivalents of the ropes and tent poles of a circus tent. And now, walking along, and up a little in order to regain the temple gates, one notices that there are many maple trees. Kiyomizu is wonderful enough in August and up on the wooden terrace high above us I had thought of it deep in snow, but the month of November must be the time to see it at its best when the maples have turned in all their shades from fiery crimson to azalea-yellow and (smoked) salmon, colours which in the words of one writer 'much enhance its mediaeval charm'. But whoever thought to see a mediaeval temple against a falling foreground of reddening maples? Some new word for it must become current; and after seeing Kiyomizu in the August heat and thinking of it in deep snow and like a balcony or a bridge above the fiery maples, I remembered that 'pagoda' in its origins is a word in Portuguese, inferring not only what we mean now by a 'pagoda' but any and every form of Oriental temple and, as well, the idols in it. For in Kyoto, even now, there are a number of more temples to see, and in order to avoid monotony and paint the picture of them along the woods of Higashiyama, in the tassell'd shade, till we must come to an end at Sambôin, most beautiful of them all, and at Uji the village of green tea, we call them from now on not temples, but pagodas.

A term we put to use immediately for nothing could be more like the old meaning of 'pagoda' than the group of temples at Nanzenji. It is on the wooded hill slopes, standing indeed in its own pine grove a very short distance behind the Miyako Hotel, and seen by ourselves for that very reason late during our stay on the principle that it is best to go first to the farthest things away. Nanzenji is to be compared in the amount that is to be seen there to some famous old monastery in Italy or Spain, a Certosa, or Cartuja, shall we say, and it takes up a whole morning or an afternoon. Nanzenji must cover a large number of acres, more particularly because one cannot find one's way in it and has continually to retrace one's steps. As always many of the wooden structures have been burnt down and rebuilt again, but it makes little difference for the new wood weathers in a few years. The pagodas of Nanzenji are spaced widely apart in a park-like compound with the broken arches of some sort of aqueduct towards the right as you come in giving an unexpected Hubert-Robert air to the higher ground.

There are a number of good paintings at Nanzenji, inclusive of a 'crane' room but, in particular, there are three rooms with sliding screens painted with tigers by Kanô Tan-yû. I could not decide in my mind whether I liked best these at Nanzenji, or the 'tiger-rooms' by Kanô Sanraku in another monastery, the point being that in neither instance had the painter seen the living animal. The 'imaginary tigers' of Japanese art can be put in a little compartment of their own beside the heraldic lions of Gothic lands. Lions collected in this manner off banners and tombs and coats-of-arms would form a curious assembly but, at least, somewhere, in some land or other, the artist had seen a living lion. It could even be argued that the choice of lion instead of tiger was typical of the Gothic craftsman, and that it was equally typical of the Japanese to prefer a tiger, if only because lions and 'lion-dogs' play so large a part in Chinese iconography. It is very like the Japanese that an 'imaginary tiger' should be their king of beasts, but in every 'tiger-room' in the monasteries and palaces of Kyoto the painter is in difficulties to distinguish a tiger from a leopard. No doubt the painters had seen leopard skins and tiger skins brought probably from Korea for there were tigers and snow leopards, at least, in Manchuria. But the living animal they knew not and had to invent its walk and spring. At Nanzenji the tigers drinking water are famous, though an unkind critic has said of them that 'they stalk all over the screens, some of them almost as big as horses, with bleary, saucer-like eyes'. Yet here, and in that other monastery, the true comparison is with 'Douanier' Rousseau's jungle paintings; the exaggerated, sinuous movements of the grown animals are delightful; the tiger-cubs and their mothers are cartoons drawn after long contemplation of Japanese cats and their families; and if one of the cubs, or even the mother, is spotted like a leopard instead of tiger-striped, no one thinks the worse of it. On many of the screens a young bamboo plant springs, and really leaps out of the ground; or sometimes it looks more like a palm tree, perhaps a cycad or sago palm. But, ever and always, like a tethered rocket, making one long for the painter to have seen the cactus desert in South Africa or New Mexico. The 'Valley of the Tiger' garden at Nishi Honganji goes with the 'tiger-rooms' to prove what the Japanese painters had in mind when their equivalents, and nearly their contemporaries in Italy, were putting the cypresses and stone pines and Tuscan hill towns into their frescoes.

But at Nanzenji there are gardens as well as paintings. The names of three great garden architects, Musô Kokushi who passed a whole year here, Sô-ami and Kobori Enshû are all connected with it. The main garden in front of the abbot's apartments so much resembles the main garden (not the Daisen-in) of Daitokuji that it must be by the same hand. It is a rectangle of rocks and plain raked sand, and since the trees and bushes which are now so much a feature of it cannot be more than a hundred or a hundred and fifty years old it is assumed that they are a fortuitous accession and that the garden was there, at first, without them. But this could apply, too, to the picturesque jumble of roofs with tilted eaves at the back, roofs which are now half the point of the garden but do not look as though they could possibly be three hundred years old, for Kobori Enshû died in 1647. Nevertheless, this garden is perhaps even more beautiful than Daitokuji though not the same loving care has gone to the trimming and clipping of the trees which at Daitokuji amount to celestial topiary, and look as though executed with the help of an expert hair-cutter and stage designer.

After seeing the main temple garden we wandered about, lost and unable to explain our predicament, and then began to climb up under the arches of the Hubert-Robert aqueduct on top of which some adventurous children were walking, until we turned higher still, up more steps, to the left and came to a little separate pagoda-kiosk or pavilion into which I ventured, having respectfully taken off my shoes, only to be met with what must have been rebukes and reproaches from a nasty-tempered old gentleman who appeared out of nowhere as I was crossing the matting in one small room in order to look out on the garden. It was the only time in many weeks in Japan that I met with anything approaching rudeness. But the intrusion of a large and unwanted foreigner of 'red devil' conformity had upset him, and I had to turn at once and go without explanation. This garden of which I could only catch sight from the middle of the room, I take to have been the Kiun-in.

This small temple or pagoda of Nanzenji with a garden behind it on the hill slope had, I surmise, become a private dwelling. But, in general, it becomes a fascination in itself to walk on one's stockinged feet about these monasteries looking for the signs of human habitation. The needs of the Japanese are so few and small; a bedroom is no more than sheets and a thin mattress neatly piled up on a cupboard. But we were hopelessly lost, and it was now that having succeeded with the 'imaginary tigers' we enquired of a big, tall, genial-looking monk who was walking along under the resin-dropping pine boughs on one of the paved paths, fan in hand, and were directed by him to a sub-garden which is famous for its pink lotuses. This is Chosôin, and beautiful it looked on that booming, hot morning with the leaves of the lotuses almost as big as rhubarb leaves; having a childish memory, myself, of picking blackcurrants in a kitchen garden at my old home on August mornings of heat mist that seemed almost as hot as this, and carrying them away in a huge rhubarb leaf. But the lotus leaves are bluish, and veined but unwrinkled, as though smoother, and coloured by some sort of moonlight treatment. How long ago those misty August mornings at my old home before two wars! I can still hear the pantings of the colliery-engine through Foxton Wood while we were picking the blackcurrants! How wonderful to have lived long, when so many of my school friends and contemporaries were killed at eighteen or nineteen years old, long enough to be here on this hot morning looking at the pink lotuses! To be walking here among the pagodas and kiosks, put on the right path to it by a monk pointing with his fan! Lotuses that are Indian, that bring the taste and breath of India! 'The red walls of the abbey rise in front, and its towers climb into the air as though they were the tops of little hills. There is even an observatory from which to watch the clouds and make calculations from the stars. There is a water clock, and deep translucent ponds for lilies. The cloisters

Painting of imaginary tigers by Kâno Sanrakû (1559–1635), at the Tenyu Monastery, Kyoto

are endless. The storeys have dragon projections, and coloured eaves, and the pearl-red pillars and the roofs covered with tiles that reflect the light—these things make the beauty of the scene. All round lies the park or pleasure ground, with little streams and the voices of the birds.' This is Hsiouen-Thsang, a monk from China, writing of the Himalayan abbey of Nâlanda in the seventh century, having come to it through the winds of the Koko-Nor and over the high Tibetan passes. I had come to the pagodas and abbeys of Kyoto out of another direction and from another world, but my sensations were the same and I could have written his description.

Even now there was a garden, Nanzen-in of Nanzenji, that we missed seeing for no amount of running about looking for the monk with a fan had the result of finding him. But we did see Konchi-in, which is scarcely less important than the main garden or Nanzenji-hôjo, having stumbled into it by accident and by the mere persistence of walking in wherever there was an open door. Except for its being to one side of the compound it would be easy to mistake this for the main buildings. It is a typical abbot's garden of the type made familiar from Daitokuji, a flat sand garden with rocks and trained trees at one end of it, ascribed once again to Kobori Enshû, and with other bits of garden in front of smaller rooms in the same temple building. How would one ever forget wandering round looking in the gardens of Nanzenji!

These slopes of Higashiyama are one mass of temples or pagodas and their gardens. An exception being Sanjû-sangen-dô which for some reason unconnected with there being anything particularly beautiful in it is very famous. It is a long barrack-like structure, nearly four hundred feet in length, with tier after tier of statues of Kwannon, hundreds or even thousands of them, arranged on shelves or stages, all of them alike, but it becomes worse still when we find they are indeed all slightly different. At the back, behind scenes as it were, are more statues with one fine wooden, life-size figure of a hermit or ascetic. And after this we set out to find Nishi-Otani, near Kiyomizu, where the hereditary abbots of Hishi-Honganji are buried, but were beaten for once by the tropical heat which made it impossible to contemplate climbing a long narrow lane where road menders were at work and we would have had to leap from stone to stone. Nishi-Otani is said to have much shining brass or gilded metal on its gateway and sheathing its wooden columns; its main hall is reputed to have been the 'apricot chamber' of an

L

Empress; and we had been hopeful of seeing a kind of wooden cage covered with chrysanthemums in low relief where recalcitrant monks are, or were kept as in a day-prison and made to beat a drum.

The evenings we spent, by now, dining at Hamamura, a Chinese restaurant rather far away in the town. This is a place of rare beauty, conducted in Japanese fashion so that you sit upon the floor, with a lovely inner garden that the dining-rooms give onto, and the noise of laughter and singing coming from every direction. On leaving we were led down the long passages, looking in at other rooms as we passed, and accompanied by what must have been the entire personnel of the establishment, all of them uttering injunctions to us not to bump our heads, and so to the door where they helped us on with our shoes, all of them coming out into the street to wave goodbye. Or else we dined at Hyo-tei, an old and famous eating-house on the hill above the Gion quarter. From its windows, sitting there waiting for the exquisite dinner to be carried in, there was a view into the nearby houses where, as in woodcuts by Utamaro, and it is a favourite device with him, we could see figures or silhouettes outlined against the paper partitions or sliding screens, a woman filling a guest's cup with *sake*, and on a top floor some of the laborious processes of a Japanese laundry.

We were a long time at the window, varying our watching with exploring the empty rooms for that night there seemed to be no one else at Hyo-tei. But all the time there was a big party downstairs, which was why we were kept waiting, and looking down into a court we saw the arrival of two young girls walking, or almost tottering on their high chioppines or pattens. Their *kimonos* and their gilded, drooping *obis* flashed with colours, and they had high towering, bee-black 'hairdos'. For a moment they could have been Venetian courtesans come to dine in one of the vineyards of Murano in the century of Titian and Veronese, and rowed here by gondola. But look again! They are walking on high pattens; but their hair is not bleached pale, or tinted vermilion, and they have not breeches cut like a man's and gold-clocked stockings, which was the Venetian fashion. They are, of course, *maikos* of the Gion quarter of Kyoto. All that pleasure district was just below the windows. Alas! now there is no chance of going there, that we did not attempt a terrapin restaurant. There are two or three eating-houses only serving terrapin, but we had been told stories of how you begin dinner with a cup of hot terrapin blood, and end by eating everything but its shell, and did not relish the experience. Sadder still, if one thinks of these places which should be called 'enemies of the terrapin', to know that the best terrapins or 'snapping' turtles are caught in Lake Biwa, the large lake near Kyoto, that they should be between three and six years old, and have attained their age of knowledge and discretion.

Now that we are spending most of our time in this part of the town we had often to go through Maruyama Park which is just above the Gion, and of inseparable association with those spring festivals of Kyoto which cannot but remind one of the Feria of Seville. Hundreds of cherry trees (*sakuras*) are planted in this public park which is on the site of former temples ravaged by fire, and at night in the blossoming season the cherry trees are hung with lanterns. But in August and September, too, Maruyama is gay and delightful, and there are eating-houses such as Hiranoya, of reed-thatch 'South Sea' aspect, where the famous dish is *himobo*, or fish boiled with red *taro* roots, whatever those may be! On the way one often sees one of the true pagodas of Kyoto, using that old word in its particular and not its general sense. This is the five-storeyed pagoda of Yasaka but, in fact, in Kyoto pagodas are not such a feature of the landscape as at Nara where, the proportion being smaller, they are more in scale. And it was probably upon the same day that we continued beyond Yasaka, through Maruyama Park, in order to go to Tôfukuji.

In the long narrow street leading there, we found a basket-maker who by our return the next afternoon had plaited for us for four shillings a magnificent basket to carry our surplus things, and we brought his masterpiece safely back with us to England. Tôfukuji is a group of temples that entails walking along even more endless covered corridors than usual, up hill and down dale for it bridges, purposefully, a ravine full of maple trees. That day, all the paintings and works of art were locked away in the storehouse because of the hot damp weather, and there was no one about in this extreme of heat to lead us to its gardens. Of which there are several; including a small garden only laid out as setting for a single rock which is a dwarfed mountain landscape in itself, and for many centuries was the treasured possession of one *daimyô* family. Now, meaning perhaps two hundred years ago, it has been mounted on a stone base and pedestal, this earliest example of a *bonseki* or tray-garden. It would have been interesting to see it, but we only

succeeding in finding the Haizandô, or garden in front of the main hall
of the temple, and this was a feat more difficult than it may sound in the
telling for we had to exhaust all other possibilities along those miles of
covered passages. Here at Tôfukuji they have a particular use, neither for
shade, nor as a protection in the snow, but as a platform for looking
down on to the maples which the monks, we were told, have in some
places grafted onto other trees in these pagoda grounds. The calm of the
Haizandô was enlivened by the antics of a young man intent on photo-
graphing his fiancée but, in fact, they both had a sense of humour and
saw the absurdity of it, waving gratefully when we left them to themselves.

It is a remarkably pretty garden—a sand garden raked daily with a
comb or just a pointed stick, a practice which made me wonder if
anyone young has ever seen the sand artists of the seaside who scratched
out huge cartoons upon the sands of Brighton or Scarborough, portraits
of Lord Roberts or other popular idol of the time, leaving a cap in one
corner for pennies, and content that the incoming tide should obliterate
their handiwork. I am afraid it is one of the dead arts. It is certainly an
art which would have had appeal for the Japanese, and one can conceive
of Hokusai excelling in it. The raked sand in this garden of Tôfukuji
surrounds a pair of islands, moss grown, and planted with rocks and
clipped azaleas, with a cycad palm on one of them, a 'tiger island'
was perhaps the intention.

However tired we were, I was determined to see another garden that
afternoon, and so went to Kôdaiji, a temple built by the widow of
Hideyoshi. Parts of the building are supposed to have been brought
from his castle of Momoyama but the garden is, genuinely, by Kobori
Enshû, masterly in its sparing use of water and rocks, with a probably
later 'palanquin' bridge. I call it that because it is like two or three open
litters set down end to end, and gives the sensation of being carried
above the lotuses. Another group of temples nearby is Kenninji, where
we went on purpose *because* of the lotuses, the most beautiful white
lotuses I have ever seen. And always, coming back from these temples
on the Higashiyama slopes, we would pass the vermilion *torii* of the
Inari Shrine, a Shintô shrine, something that having seen the Kasuga
Shrine at Nara was becoming a new interest, and that roused expectation of the Shrines of Ise. But in fact these last few days were touched
with sadness for we were leaving Kyoto, a town which I enjoyed as

much as I have loved Rome or Venice. At the time it did not seem likely that we could go back there. But we were able to do so for a day or two a month later, and therefore we can defer the sorrow of departing, and of saying good-bye at the railway station to the one or two friends we had made, in order to give expression to all the pleasure and excitement of our return.

When we arrived back at Kyoto late at night, after ten hours in the train coming from the Inland Sea, the same Japanese friend whom we had never thought to see again was at the station to meet us. But the season had changed and it was no longer summer. No more was there the careless and glorious heat—I call it that because it banishes and drives care away—when one came out of the station. But the streets were still full, and at nearly eleven o'clock we went to buy a camera, and looked into the Kabukiya doll-shop for a moment before it let down its shutters for the night. How wonderful to be back in Kyoto! Now began a drive which I shall always remember to the Japanese hotel where we were to stay. We dropped our friend near to a tram that would take him home, passing familiar streets to begin with, and the corner shop with the bales or tubs of *sake* that we so much admired, then crossing the river near the street of restaurants, and going into a part of Kyoto that we did not know at all. Into narrow lanes, past wooden houses where everyone was asleep, round sharp corners and up steep little hills, with a last haul and a wrench and a change of gear, round one more corner up a slight precipice, and in at a gate past the large rocks of a garden, and we were at our Japanese inn, the Yoshida Sansô. Not really more than about twenty minutes by car from the railway station, but we enjoyed ourselves so much staying there, and it was so lovely an impression of Japan to take away with us at the last moment before going home, that while we were there I never looked for it in the plan of Kyoto and have not liked to do since. There was the usual welcome with everyone in the place running out to meet us although it was late at night, and within a few minutes mattresses and purple coverlets were laid out on the floor. By this time after a little experience one had learned to sleep, though it is always more comfortable to drag your mattress away from the middle of the room so that you have your head against the wall. So one fell asleep, tired after the long journey but happy to be back in Kyoto. An enchantment of the Yoshida Sansô being the marvellous bronze booming of a temple bell in some abbey, not far away, that sounds a deep note at dawn to remind you where you are.

We had little time on our second visit to Kyoto, and so went again next morning to the 'Silver Pavilion' and then to Chishakuin. For the first is perhaps the most beautiful of all the gardens, while at Chishakuin there are the best paintings in Kyoto. It is not easy to find this temple to which the safest indication is that it is near to the Museum. It is one of the less imposing shrines of Kyoto, and with so much else to see one might pass it by without bothering to go in. This time, the charming lame priest Nishizaki was at the door of the main building as we arrived, and took us at once to see the painted room. There was a most disastrous fire at Chishakuin in 1947 and many sliding screens were destroyed, some by Sanraku and by Eitoku, both painters of the Kanô school, but the losses do not seem to have been properly ascertained. For the screens that are left are by one of the greatest decorative painters of Japan. Little is known of him, and he has so recently emerged to fame that he could be called a new addition to the great artists of the world. His name was Hasegawa Tôhaku (1539–1610), if, indeed the screens are by him for that is far from certain.[1] They are only ascribed to him by long tradition. However, we are spoiling the sudden shock of being taken first to see some indifferent paintings which make it seem unlikely there should be anything sensational at Chishakuin.

But it is only a matter of walking round one set of sliding partitions into another for these spaces without solid walls are scarcely rooms. You are in an emptiness blazing with snow on gold, and that gives the sensation of looking up through blossoming boughs into the sky. This is because we are standing a few feet away from a pair of double screens painted with white cherry blossom. The left-hand screen has the huge old trunk of a cherry tree with some of the blossom shooting, as it can do on little stalks out of the main trunk, and all the rest is a glorious spreading and trembling of the flowering boughs. The background is gold, the gold of a spring day, and coming to within a few inches of the individual flowers we see they are so thickly painted in Chinese white as to be practically modelled on the golden ground. Another pair of

[1] For what little the opinion of someone who is no expert can count at all, the painted screens (*fusuma*) of Chishakuin could scarcely be by the same hand that painted the screen of 'Pine trees in a mist', or the 'Monkey screen', two masterpieces of black and white painting, or ink on paper, portions of which were shown at the Exhibition of Japanese Art at the Victoria and Albert Museum in the summer of 1958. If there is documentary proof that these are by Tôhaku, then the *fusuma* of Chishakuin must be by someone else.

screens is of a slanting pine tree with patches of lichen on its trunk, green cloud-like boughs for they echo the shape of the golden clouds, a great background excitement of long tall grasses bending and crossing their sword-like blades, a few plants of white chrysanthemum, and what I mistook at first for white paeonies, but on a later visit I knew from their leaves that they were white hibiscus. And yet another pair of autumn screens is of maple trees in all their colours. The far end of the compartment, or in fact, a smaller compartment next to it, like an oratory, has flower paintings that are not by the same hand, but are ascribed to Eitoku.

The history of these paintings is that they came from another temple built by Hideyoshi when a favourite son died, which gives the fixed date of 1591. They must be the most beautiful and perfect of existing paintings of their kind, and we are left to surmise for ourselves what other treasures of decorative painting must have perished, here and elsewhere, in Japan. For the quantity of painted screens must have been enormous. There is the historical instance of one of the early Tokugawa Shogûns confiscating fifty pairs of golden screens belonging to a rich merchant who was in trouble. But this is the finest of all surviving painted rooms in Japan, and glorious as are the screens at Nijô Castle, the *fusuma* here at Chishakuin make those others seem, not decorative painting, but mere decoration. To anyone of eclectic tastes these screens have their parallel in Persian miniature painting where there is the same blossoming of peach and apricot. Behzad of Herat, the greatest of Persian miniature painters, is about a hundred years earlier in date than Hasegawa Tôhaku, but the spirit is the same. It is the blossoming earth in all its seasons. In front of the room is a garden which one can hardly take in so dazzling is this interior flowering, but it is by the great tea-master and friend of Tôhaku, Sen-no Rikyû (1521-1591). I am afraid I remember little about it.

Our perambulations round the Gion quarter took us to another pair of temples, this little section of Kyoto becoming in imagination a fusion of the Albaicín of Granada and Triana of Seville. It is the part of Kyoto where one would want to live, and I have to say in honesty that the Gion is very much more interesting than the marriage of those two names. But, sadly, it is only after about five o'clock in the evening that one is likely to see a *maiko* in her dress of brilliant design, flashing with gold, and going with stilted walk on her high pattens. That is a sight to put matador and flamenco dancer to shame. The beautiful old lanes of Gion are a delight to walk along, and almost opposite the door of Yamanaka, the art dealer, in one of them, with the boles of enormous old trees, gingkôs I am presuming, though their dappled trunks were more like plane trees,[1] going down with their roots elephant-fashion into the green bank, is the old temple of Shôren-in which always had an Imperial prince for abbot so that it is known also as Awata Palace. In a moment we are in a monastic setting of painted screens of tigers and bamboos, and in a bewildering maze of little rooms nearly all of them with paintings, all of doll's house or dwarf apartments' dimension. It would be redundant to go into particulars of all the painted screens at Shôren-in, and for those that are visible probably a greater number still are put away, but we saw scenes of cormorant-fishing, in foretaste of Gifu, and being in the heart of Gion, there were a number of screens showing the two-wheeled *matsuri* flower-carts of the Gion festival. Some of the most delightful painted screens in Kyoto are in this temple, and as well there is a lovely landscape garden, in fact an almost perfect example of classical Japanese garden, if it lacks the more sensational features of the rocks and sand of Ryuanji, the 'moon sand-heaps' of the 'Silver Pavilion', or Katsura's premeditated calm. No large area is covered but there is a winding lake, camellias and clipped azaleas must be lovely in their seasons, and there are views out of the garden into the hills. A monolith bridge inviting one to cross it, but leading nowhere, is a subtle device for enlarging the scale of the garden in one's mind. Both Sô-ami and Kobori Enshû, two of the great names in Japanese landscape gardening, are supposed to have had a hand in this garden of Shôren-in, but expert opinion seems to allow it a later date than that. One takes away a charming mental picture of this temple and its garden looking out onto Mount Hiei and the wooded hills of Higashiyama.

There are so many places where, circumstances being propitious, one would like to spend a few days of every year in one's life, and the Gion quarter of Kyoto is certainly among them. It has its association with flowers and music and the dance, and one cannot exaggerate the feeling of these little masterpieces of landscape gardening hidden behind the temple walls. One could, ideally, want to be always, but really only a part of the time, in Venice and in Marrakesh and in Taxco, which is

[1] The old trees outside Shôren-in are camphor trees. The prince-abbot of Shôren-in was also abbot of Enryakuji monastery on Mount Hiei, and Shôren-in was his Kyoto home.

surely the pearl of Mexico and one of the beautiful little towns of the world, but for the excitement of flowers and music I had thought there was nothing to equal the Barrio de Santa Cruz in Seville. Perhaps more in the promise than in the fulfilment, but nothing could be more natural to those whitewashed courts than the tinkling of a guitar, and it is the thought of the characters so near at hand in the city of Seville and its suburb of Triana, dancers, matadors and their like, who flourish here but are so alien to the modern world. At Gion every expectation of the kind is fulfilled, and after only walking a few times in its shady lanes one finds oneself remembering at least the tag-ends of one or two tunes, though not knowing how, or why, or where one heard them, and when it is time to leave Kyoto they have become an obsession.

Meanwhile, we have come only a few moments' walk to the temple next door, which is Chion-in. Shôren-in was small and secluded, this is on a large scale, as big as Kiyomizu. As at Shôren-in there was always an Imperial prince for abbot at Chion-in. The *hondô* of the main temple had rows of big drums ranged upon the floor which gives the touch of lamaism, and one waits for the human thigh-bone trumpets of the Tibetan hermits. Somewhere up in the porch is the 'ghost-umbrella' which a fox-god held over the abbot's head when he was dedicating the temple in a shower of rain. The fox-god then vanished leaving his umbrella, but we looked in vain for it, as too, for rice-cakes sold at the entrance and stamped with the umbrella and with the character for the name of the hill on which the temple stands. That, too, I thought, had the Tibetan touch to it, as had the founder's feat in hoping to get into heaven by repeating the name of Amida sixty thousand times a day.

And forthwith we set off by covered corridor for the Amida-dô or Buddha's hall. But its interior was a little unpromising, and we started off again shuffling down what seemed like miles of 'nightingale floors', all laid according to tradition by the exuberant left-handed woodcarver Hidari Jingorô, but it must have been dull work for him. All sorts of things were going on behind the temple, lectures and Bible classes and conferences, in a vast number of rooms; among them, to remind us we are in Japan, a Plum Room with sliding screens of blossoming plum trees and, of course, a Stork Room with white storks, and then still more rooms with bamboos and pink and white chrysanthemums, but coming from the marvellous painted room of Chishakuin the paintings at Chion-in were trite and ordinary, though they would have been beautiful had one not seen something of the same kind that was so much better. At the back of these buildings is the temple garden, not easily come upon, but beautiful when found. It is a lake garden, and one is beginning by now to wonder at the sources of water for all the gardens in Kyoto, for a town with fifteen or twenty famous gardens all with lakes in them leaves a picture in the mind of a city as aqueous as Bruges with its canals. An inordinate number of springs must lie beneath the soil because of the wooded hills so near the town. This is a curving lake that narrows in the middle like an ant's waist, where a bridge crosses it, and leads up to the grave and hermitage of the priest who founded this Buddhist sect, the same who with echolalic persistence reiterated the same name over and over again. What would not rich owners of landscape gardens in eighteenth century England, patrons of Kent, or 'Capability' Brown, or Repton, have given for a Celestial hermit's hut, complete with bones or ashes, in their gardens! And here these lakes and green hills, in miniature, are in the middle of a town. They may be only the size of large pools, but they are so skilfully designed that they look like lakes. And it only remains to add that this garden of Chion-in with its water and rock arrangements is according to leading authorities, like Kôdaiji, and the two gardens at Nanzenji, and the main temple garden at Daitokuji, the work of Kobori Enshû.

Here we are on the edges of Maruyama Park, famous for its cherry trees, and where as has been said, there are many restaurants and eating-houses this being the old pleasure centre of Kyoto. Many of them have been converted from old temples, and not a few have little gardens, among them Saami, a pretty place where we spent an idiotic evening on a bus-tour from our hotel to see the 'night-life' of Kyoto. But it seemed the only method of seeing the *maikos* though two telephone numbers are given in the local guide book—with the telephone numbers of the six principal tea-ceremony schools in Kyoto: 'You should not take the tea with a gulp. Quietly making your bowl round in your palms, you have to drink the tea with three and a half sips'—two numbers for the *maikos*, one in Gion and one in Ponto-chô another pleasure district, 'if you want to see *maiko* dancing and to have them taken in your camera'. We 'assembled' outside the Station Hotel, and were conveyed by char-a-banc with a guide who 'came on the air' and chattered all the way like a magpie, asking us silly little riddles, and on arrival were put in a room looking onto the pretty garden, joined soon by the compère or master of the revels, a university graduate who, of course, had 'taken' English and read T. S. Eliot, if not, one surmised, with much understanding. A charmingly pretty *maiko* appeared, and after she had sung and danced with never changing expression, but at sad moments of the dance with real tears in her eyes, idiotically stupid games began of 'blind man's buff', 'musical chairs', 'hunt the slipper' brand, in which we resolutely refused to take part, though rousing no resentment.

Then there was a lull, and the little *maiko* came and sat in front of us, and we admired her elaborate coiffure which was as though every separate strand of her black, black hair was lacquered and combed in place, and the beautiful *maquillage* of her face and neck, and the little creature took from her sash a card-case about large enough to hold single postage stamps, and handed us her visiting card. This was a little oblong with her name and address written in a childish hand in European letters on the back, and on the front of it an exquisite design, for in fact there is no other word for it, of flowering pinks in two colours and their green leaves, and of course her name in cursive lettering in black, black lacquer going down the page. I may add that these visiting cards of the *maikos* of Kyoto are collectors' items in themselves, and worth the attention of some collector of trifles. All of them are of the same type, and could be by the same hand; and incidentally, what a delicate nuance in the sub-dividing of professions to be designer of visiting cards to the *maikos* of the Gion. Two more of their cards with which I was presented on another evening—and I only wish that many more of them were in my possession—have respectively, a leaf in golden outline with the *maiko*'s name that descends the Japanese rice paper in scarlet, as though in scarlet lacquer; and an exquisite bamboo shoot with crimson pinks in flower that trail down from it, and a pale blue rather indefinite design that could be a little bridge over a garden stream, with the same scarlet lacquer lettering. All three of the cards, of course, and one imagines the whole gamut of visiting cards of the *maikos* of Kyoto, being elegant and perfect specimens of colour printing.

The *maikos* all belong to a guild or corporation; there are some scores, or maybe a hundred or two of them in all, and they are between fourteen and eighteen years old, at which age they cease to be *maikos* and become *geishas*, and no longer wear the beautiful dresses and gilded *obis*, or have the elaborate coiffures. The occasion on which we collected more of their visiting cards was when we went to a house up a steep lane in the Gion quarter, belonging to a retired *geisha* and her mother. In fact, an acquaintance had stayed there, and described it as having *maikos* running in and out of it all day long for it was a kind of school where they learned dancing and singing. On this second evening two *maikos* were present having been 'ordered' on the telephone from the hotel, and they sang and danced, but they were round-faced peasant girls, too round faced to be pretty, though they had brocade *kimonos*—one of them with a great carp leaping up a waterfall—they wore the complicated 'hairdo', and gave us their cards.

Some little space has already been given here to the Ox-Festival at Kôryûji Temple when a man dressed in white and mounted on a bull rides into the temple yard, and to the Aoi or Hollyhock Festival at the Kamigamo and Shimagomo Shrines. The third great festival of Kyoto is the Gion Festival in the middle of July. Previous to this, the Gion quarter has been *en fête* for the Miyako Odori or 'Cherry Dance' of the *geishas* which now takes place in the theatre. But the Gion Festival must be of more fascinating character, and to be compared to the Feria of Seville to the disadvantage of the latter. It dates back at least a thousand years in origin, and begins with the ceremonial washing of the shrine-cars or floats which are of two kinds: the *yama* which is a litter carried on long poles on the shoulders of the bearers, and the *hoko* which is a tower on four wheels with a mast shooting up to a height of well over a hundred feet from its middle. On one evening in July 'a boy attired in beautiful costume, goes on horseback to the shrine to be given the rank of sacred page or *chigo*'. He has to dance a few days later on a *hoko*, and must be treated throughout the festival as an honoured person, a rôle which is familiar from Western folklore. The great procession of shrine-cars or floats must be a marvellous spectacle, with horsemen in ancient armour, and hundreds of men on foot, many of them carrying the halberds with long curved blades designed by a famous swordsmith for the original festival which had been organized by the Court astrologers of a millenium ago to drive or sweep away a plague. At night thousands of paper lanterns are lit; there is general rejoicing, and to quote from an account in the vernacular, 'there are so many varieties of dances that even the native people sometimes find it difficult to tell the one from the other'. It must indeed be a wonderful spectacle, probably the most exciting and beautiful thing of its kind in the living world. In those paradisial weeks of peach and apricot and cherry blossom, of the falling fire of wistaria, and for this land of sword fanciers the blades and lily-towers of iris.

Here this account of Kyoto and its temples and gardens must perforce end. But there remains what I think was the most beautiful drive into the country I have ever had in my life, and I must attempt a description of it. Our objective was Sambôin and Uji, the village of green tea, in a south-westerly direction from Kyoto and on the road, more or less, to Nara. The wooden houses with fences of bamboo in varying pattern dwindle into open country, but in continuous and busy habitation. Soon there came a pond with rose-pink lotuses which we were never able to identify that evening on the road home so that it was as the touch of magic and the breath of an even more exotic land. We were to see a temple garden on the way, and stopped at what seemed to be the enclosing wall of a large country house, and following that round came in at the gate and in front of the white temple building of Kanjuji, but it was about two o'clock in the afternoon and not a sign of life. It reminded me of trying to see inside some Georgian country house in Ireland, and yet Kanjuji with its tilted eaves must more resemble, I thought, a country retreat of the Grand Lama in a green valley near Lhasa, only it could not be the green of barley fields or poplar trees. How hot it was! We looked everywhere, and sent the driver round to the back but no one could be found, while every moment it was becoming more like a country house and less of a temple. In the end a monk came tumbling, heavy-eyed, out of a concealed porter's lodge behind what seemed to be a garage and unlocked the door into the garden. We were on a winding path leading down to a very big lake with tall trees on its far side, and a little tea-house or summer-house on a knoll beyond the water. So like was it to a lake in some demesne in County Kildare or County Tipperary that one could hardly believe it was a lake of the Heian period, probably a thousand years old, and dug for moon viewing and pleasure boating parties. It had begun as some *daimyô*'s country villa, and then become a temple. Coming away, the monk walked behind us on the winding path among the shrubs of a mid-Victorian 'wilderness', there seemed to be pampas grass growing in a bed beyond the azaleas, and though the eaves of the temple building curved upwards like a dragon's tail, we looked for the ghosts of the governess or of Peter Quint, the butler, at the glass-less windows and down again at the lake shore.

After which the landscape, once we left that Irish-Tibetan hamlet of white cabins, became more real, and yet more of an hallucination. Soon, but it could have been hundreds of years earlier or later, we caught sight of a five-storeyed pagoda on the left among the trees. This was the pagoda of Daigoji, one of the most famous in Japan, but we came no nearer than that, divided from it by a high wall, because we were on our way to its sub-temple of Samboin. This is one of those places in the world that have a physical beauty of their own. Such are Villa Lante, the Generalife of Granada, and the isle of Capri, in their different ways. Sambôin is of undying association with blossoming, particularly with cherry blossoming, and is the home of some exceptional paintings. Formerly it was richer in works of art than any temple of Kyoto. Even under the Ashigawa Shoguns as far back as the year 1400 Sambôin had been famous for cherry viewing, but the heyday of blossoming was in the time of Hideyoshi who planted hundreds of young cherry trees in the two years 1596 and 1598, and in the latter year (the year of his death) held his great cherry viewing party of the already centenarian trees. It is told how he took much trouble with the preparations for this, 'on the 20th March himself stretching out ropes to mark the lots', and so forth, and the Cherry-viewing at Daigo, as it was called, must be looked upon as pendant and companion piece to that other fête held by Hideyoshi in the dry river bed of the Kamo river, when he invited the tea-masters and their adepts to bring their choicest bowls and utensils to a great outdoor tea-ceremony, and Hideyoshi went round from group to group talking to them, and admiring and comparing the treasures they had brought with them.

I think that Sambôin must have the most beautiful garden in Japan. There is a huge old cherry tree by the doorway which cannot be much younger than the time of Hideyoshi. It is famous all over Japan, and large crowds come to see it when it is in flower. Its limbs, so to speak, are on crutches from old age, espaliered on bamboo trellises, and sustained and supported in every conceivable way. To see it, as we did, not in blossom, I can only compare to being given a dish of ripe strawberries without cream. Even in the coloured postcards sold at the gate one gets the poetry of its cascading blooms; held still on their twigs, just as the tumbling rills and waters of a weir that flash steadily, repetitively, in the same falling pattern that is yet quite still. And there are the blossoms thrown up on their boughs into, and against the sky, and shaking, trembling in the wind, like a carillon of rosy-ringing, creamy bells, with other cherry trees in the distance of the garden that are like rosy spurts or jets of rose-flame.

Even in high summer never has one seen such greens or yellows in a garden. And now we began walking round the outer boards, 'nightingale' floors some of them, of little rooms with sliding screens, on tiptoe, because a conference was being held in one of them, and a bald or shaven-headed monk who must be the abbot, and looked like a schoolmaster, made it plain from his glances that he disapproved of visitors. This had the result that we had to pass by without time properly to examine the paintings. There were some screens of peacocks with spread tails, and others of lovely and delicate decoration in the acme of taste, but we saw no sign of the pair of fan-screens by Sôtatsu (they were in any case on show at the Victoria and Albert Museum in London at the time), nor of his great pair of screens of a Court Dance or *Bugaku*, one of his masterpieces, which will be discussed later. These paintings are too precious to be always on view and are kept most of the time in the temple storehouse. Kanô Eitoku (1543-1590) was the favourite painter with Hideyoshi, and many of the painted screens at Sambôin, if not actually from his hand, are in his style. We must have seen several verging on his authorship, but disappointed at missing the great screens by Sôtatsu we gave all our attention to the garden.

At Sambôin there is another kind of bridge. There are the monolith bridges but, also, island is joined to shore by earthen bridges made of wood covered with soil, and with moss and grasses, and standing on four wooden legs. Hideyoshi, the conqueror of Korea, was a great amateur of garden stones. He caused some hundreds of collectors' pieces of the kind to be brought here, and after his death the work was still carried on. Many of them came from other gardens famous in their day for Hideyoshi accepted them from the *daimyôs* as forced gifts.[1] Sambôin is, therefore, probably the best place in Japan, and better than anywhere in existing China, to study this, to Western tastes, rather esoteric form of garden art. And with it the clipped and rounded shapes

[1] One famous stone is described as having been in at least four gardens and was brought here, as though on instructions from Wilde, or another aesthete of the 'nineties, 'wrapped in silk and to the sound of flutes'.

of the azalea bushes which are intended in imitation of stones. There are, as well, the tiered or layered trees, trees in several storeys or pagoda floors, a little resembling the floors or tiers of a coachman's cape; and then again, other tree forms, bare of stem in places, growing on islets that are a conglomerate of stones.

There are several of these islets that as you walk in the garden seem to, themselves, move and change place, so skilfully has every foot of space been thought out to give movement and variety. Here at Sambôin it is easy to believe that the garden is three hundred and fifty years old and unaltered, and one finds oneself thinking what has happened in the world since the stones were put down, trees planted, and the water let in precisely to cut off the little islands from the world. They are so small there is hardly room to stand or move about upon them; and one thinks of them first of all as prison islands in deep water, with prisoners who cannot swim, and then, looking more closely at their moraines and glaciers and Himalayan masses, of a new race of beings living on un-discovered islands larger than Borneo or New Guinea. The earthen bridges and monolith bridges leading from island to island, and never intended to be walked upon, have grown to be grander than Vanbrugh's bridge over the lake at Blenheim. But then, catching a reflection of the islands in the lake, all is little again and this is the 'pagoda' garden of Sambôin. Here and now, and not only on this afternoon, one would sooner have seen the garden party given by Hideyoshi for viewing the cherry blossom than have attended a fête of the Sun King's in the gardens of Versailles. It is impossible not to turn back for another and last look before it is gone for ever at this other end of the world. But only for ourselves for Sambôin has been here for three centuries and more, and is in blossom every year.

Upon this afternoon of growing enchantment we drove on past another temple pointed out to us in the distance as being in Chinese style. Or it may even have been before we got to Sambôin. This must have been Manpukuji, headquarters of a particular Buddhist sect, and built 'after the style of his own country' by a famous priest who was a Chinaman of the Ming Dynasty. We could see it again on the way home, and its tilted roofs seemed to float about like a mirage, which is why I cannot remember whether it came before or after Sambôin. Now there was an increasing liveliness as though approaching some rural centre or metropolis, and we noticed the number of tea plantations in all

'Chinese' Bridge at Shûgakuin (1820)

Nako-no-Chaya (tea ceremony room)
at Shûgakuin Palace (early 17th century)

Ryûanji garden (*c.* 1500)

directions. Within a mile or two we were in Uji, the village of green tea, for the best green tea in Japan comes from here. I call it a 'village' though it has forty thousand inhabitants, but it gives the effect of a village with its long street bordered on both sides with the most intriguing and attractive shops that one has ever seen, all selling green tea. One wanted to stop the car and get out and go into every one of them, but we resisted the temptation and went on through the village across the river to the Phoenix Hall or Byôdôin. This, which is accounted one of the three most beautiful bits of architecture in Japan (the 'Golden Pavilion' and the temple of Hôryûji are its companions), is the only surviving piece of Heian palace building, part of a villa or country palace of a Fujiwara prince, that is to say, of the middle of the eleventh century, the time of Lady Murasaki and *The Tale of Genji*. It is an open vermilion-painted pavilion, now part of a temple, consisting of a head or main body and, phoenix-like, a pair of wings, standing at the edge of a big pond. It looked to me to have been rather recently and heavily restored, though this does not detract much in a wooden building. We walked round the lake which is a thousand years old, nearly, and looked at the vermilion reflection in it of the Phoenix Hall, the ghost of a Chinese palace, the ghost of a hundred early palaces in China, now all dead and gone. Then we climbed a mound up to an old bronze bell of huge size, brought from India in India's golden age, and hanging under a wooden canopy, and came down and round into the Phoenix Hall, and looked at its echo in the water from its head and its two wings.

The green tea stalls were only a minute's walk away. Every shop sells it, and there are innumerable sorts and qualities of green tea, which means as many different shades and colours of the green powder. Certainly some part of the taste for it must come from its interesting appearance. By this time we must have drunk green tea some hundreds of times, and never liked it. In the hotel in Kyoto—the 'Western style' one, not the Japanese—there was always green tea ice on the menu, and it tasted of nothing at all, like an ice without flavouring. Green tea, itself, has a pronounced fishy taste as though sea-gulls would appreciate it. But the green powders, particularly if there were sacks or great bins of it, were of most inspiring and appetizing appearance. The different grades of packets and tins in which it was sold whetted the appetite, or the thirst, still further. In Japan they know how to make a tin, which

M

is plain black with a maroon-red or green cover fitting onto it, look as expensive and attractive as a piece of lacquer. And they were selling boiled sweets made of the green tea which did have a taste, and for which a mild future could be predicted even in London and New York.

Something of the mystique attached by the Japanese to green tea, and that they keep to themselves for it is drunk in no other country in the world, pervades and clings to Uji. It has been grown here for hundreds of years, probably since the thirteenth or fourteenth century, 'in some very choice varieties', and its tea-planters have been celebrated for 'intimate knowledge of its cultivation and extreme care bestowed upon the preparation of the leaf'. The dyed colouring is wholly artificial, and 'its only purpose is to heighten the pronounced green of the leaves'. Because of all this, at Uji you feel you are in the capital of some curious cult. That something is for sale which is a necessity, and yet a luxury. What can it be? Has the caterpillar chewed the green leaf, and put itself into an ecstasy? Or the ants been milking their herds of *aphidae*? Is the highest quality tea the dark green or the light green? The green powders are as smooth as new green cloth. Green tea has some affinity of idea of fragrance to tobacco, and its powdery substance is that of snuff. What legends there must be of certain tea-fields! The fine Havana cigar-leaf of the *vuelta abajo* must have its parallel where the camellia grows well, for the tea-plant is *Camellia theifera* or *Thea Sinensis*, and certain corners must have grown fine teas for centuries. Then, again, the mythology of China teas with all their broken and flowery pekoes and boheas is different and altogether alien to this village of green tea. I have seldom, if ever, in my life seen shops or stalls more fascinating than those of Uji.

We came back over the bridge and in a kind of ecstasy drove along the river bank—the banks of Uji, for the river has the same name. The Phoenix Hall or Byôdôin was opposite, across the water. This drive was an entire enchantment because of gilded roofs, dragon eaves and pagodas, it seemed, in all directions, on our side of the river and over the water. No wonder it has been a theme for painters.[1] But, also, cormorant fishing by night is practised on the Uji river, which is almost too good to be true, although we reserve a personal account of that

[1] A beautiful ink-painting *Sunny Morning at Uji*, by Aoki Mokubei (1767-1833), poet, calligrapher, and potter, and one of the last good Japanese painters, is illustrated in *An Introduction to the Arts of Japan* by Peter C. Swann, Bruno Cassirer Ltd., Oxford, 1958, page 138.

until we reach Gifu. For there is something still stranger and more exciting—if it still goes on, which I was unable to determine. This is the Battle of Fireflies 'which usually takes place about 10th June of each year near midnight'. Special trains are, or were run from nearby cities for the purpose. The battlefield is about an hour and a half's row upstream from Uji, and the scene is made brilliant with singing and dancing in lantern-lit boats, and *geishas* present. When the fireflies have collected their forces, 'they dart from either bank and meet and cling above the water. They are so many that they look like a luminous cloud, or a great ball of sparks. Eventually, the ball drops and breaks upon the surface of the current, and the fallen fireflies drift glittering', or we could say, vainly signalling away, and 'the river is covered with the still sparkling bodies of the insects'. For it is surely not a battle, but the nuptials or mating of the fireflies.[1] It must be the unsuccessful swains who float down with the current, their lanterns failing.

There was a little farther for us to go. Just a few moments more along the banks of Uji, and then up a narrow road where I would never have thought the car could take us, to the whitewashed gate of Koshoji, a gate 'in Korean style' though the subtlety was a little lost on me. But the garden is delightful, with clipped bushes of azalea left taller than usual, growing directly from the sand. Here, they have the formality of box, or ilex, or even of bay trees, and one wonders why they are not, more simply, bushes of green tea. At one side is another and smaller garden with a stone bridge and 'dry' stone valley. One remembers Koshoji, coming at the end of the day, for its clipped azalea bushes in white sand, and its umbrageous, even incense-dropping pine trees.

Next morning we were to leave Kyoto. We dined in the town for the last time; and I remember falling sorrowfully asleep, and waking about dawn, and hearing the great booming bell of the temple somewhere nearby, for I got up and looked out of the window, and all was pale fog. I had thought by now to have seen nearly everything in Kyoto but, as has been told already, never even looked on the map to find this Japanese hotel where we were staying. And I know no more of the

---

[1] The best account, as of so much else in Japan, is in *Terry's Guide to the Japanese Empire*, New York, Houghton Mifflin & Co., 1920 edition, pages 552-554; and the account goes on to describe the cult for fireflies and the manner of their catching; how at the firefly shops (a fascinating thought in itself!) the captured insects are sorted as soon as possible according to the brilliancy of their light; how they are sold in cages, great numbers are ordered for display at evening parties, and how at good restaurants customers are let in to the enclosure where the fireflies are kept and allowed to catch a number of fireflies to take home with them.

temple than that we could see it clearly next morning, on a hill not far away, among tall cryptomerias. This must be Kurodani temple with a view all over the city from its terrace. It was something we had missed; and now we will never visit another temple in Kyoto with *fusuma* of bamboos and blossoming plum trees, and sliding screens of 'imaginary' tigers. They are gone for ever, after four weeks in Kyoto of illusion turned reality.

Chapter Nine

❖·—·—·—·—·—·—·—·—·—·—·—·—·—❖

PAINTINGS

ONE OF OUR OBJECTS IN coming to Japan had been to see paintings by Sôtatsu, and it was exciting therefore when permission was given to see the Seikadô Foundation on one of our last days in Tokyo. The Seikadô is in a somewhat remote corner of the town and we arrived, as arranged, at midday in downpouring rain. The building in which it is housed is not only Western, but demonstrably English in style, and it was like arriving at a copy of a Cotswold manor house set down in Wimbledon or Sunningdale on the usual rainy day. There should have been apple trees at its mullion windows, and probably beaten copper and William de Morgan plates within. But, in fact, this art trust or private museum contains one of the greatest works of art in all Japan. I must here explain that my interest in Sôtatsu goes back a very long time indeed, to my schooldays when, in the summer term of 1914 at Eton, just before the First World War, an enormous bright pink telephone book arrived, for that is what it looked like, and this was the first number of *Blast*, the Vorticist paper edited by Wyndham Lewis. But 'paper' is the wrong word for *Blast*. It did have somewhat of the explosive character of a bomb bursting among artistic and literary dovecotes, and was by far the most sensational of all Lewis's rain of bulletins and pamphlets. Beside much else of controversial nature it had long lists of names in two groups, headed 'Blast' and 'Bless', and among the blessed I saw the names of Kôetsu, Kôrin, and Sôtatsu, and was constrained at once to find out who they were. Wyndham Lewis, a powerful and wonderful catalyst, and a genius *manqué* if ever there was one, had put his hand, unerringly, on something important. Kôrin I knew of already, having read *Epochs of Chinese and Japanese Art*, and it did not take long to look at Fenollosa again in the School Library and find Kôetsu and Sôtatsu. In those days one had to do such things for oneself for there was no one to ask. Now it is different. But I still think it is more inspiring to find out for oneself, and not be told. Anyway, I knew of Sôtatsu in 1914 when I was sixteen, and now I was going to see a pair of magnificent painted screens by him, in 1959.

At the Seikadô that morning, in the Japanese fashion we were shown five things only, and the two last of them were the Sôtatsu screens. We went in through the 'Sunningdale' hall, and upstairs into what could be a first floor sitting-room or library. Not that there were many books in it, but it had some bookshelves, and there the Director of the Seikadô was waiting and we sat and talked, and smoked, and were given cups of tea. Sitting in a bow window which had leaded panes and window catches like those in a copy of some old Cotswold manor house. The tablecloth was English, the carpet and the chairs looked English: all that was not of England was that we were drinking green tea. Presently, attention was drawn to a table in another corner on which a tall vase was standing. This was one of the most famous and valuable specimens of Kakiemon ware. A tall porcelain vase of pure white body, in what the Japanese call the 'brocade' style of Kakiemon, with an overglaze design on it of what one could take at first, perhaps with a distorted memory of Minoan pottery, for an octopus or cuttlefish because of its streaming tentacles. But it is a phoenix or 'ho-ho' bird with fluttering feathers, and looking nearer one saw its beak and cockscomb. The shape of the vase was what one associates with Isfahan or Rhodian ware, but the technique of the design upon it has the look of being incised in the paste and held in place by metallic edgings raised on its surface, which you can feel with your finger like the engraved names on a visiting card. It was interesting indeed that this should be one of the most prized specimens of porcelain. Kakiemon, whose dates are uncertain, or rather, the 'first' Kakiemon for his descendants went on into the sixth or even eighth generation, was the first Japanese to produce overglaze, and later underglaze porcelain in the Chinese manner at the kilns at Arita in the Southern Island of Kyûshû. But, a few moments later at the Seikadô, we were to be shown a still more controversial piece of ceramics, and one sensational enough to act as starting point for a whole discussion of Japanese art.

However, the next object shown was of another description altogether. This was a screen by some unknown painter of the late seventeenth century, of popular scenes in the riverbed at Kyoto, a setting, as it were, for a Japanese *Petrouchka*, with every kind of actor and mountebank, and booths of dancers and actors. Not by any means from the hand of a great painter, but of extraordinary popular interest because genre paintings of the kind are rare in Japan, a hundred years before the woodcuts of the *Ukiyo-e* masters. There is endless fascination in the patterns of the dresses and in the strange goings on, and although it is no considerable work of art one could examine it happily for the greater part of a morning. This screen in the Seikadô has the historical more than aesthetic interest attaching to paintings of religious processions ('*Ommeganck*' in the Flemish), festivals of guilds of archers, and the like, by D. van Alsloot, J. Wildens, P. Snayers, obscure but good fourth-rate painters in the picture gallery at Brussels. It does not compare either in interest or fantasy with the *Namban Byôbu*, screens of 'Southern Barbarians', or they are in fact the first Portuguese arriving in Japan, paintings that are on another level altogether as works of art, and which we hope to look at later on.

But now an object of extreme interest was produced. This was a famous, perhaps the most famous of all pottery jars, by Ninsei, a thing which in the saleroom in Japan would probably fetch as much as thirty thousand pounds, to regard it in this first moment from that vulgar standard. The bowl is a curious and most disconcerting problem. To a Japanese collector it is worth more than twice the sum ever paid in the open markets of the West for a piece of Meissen, Sèvres, or Chelsea. No Greek vase has ever at any time fetched anything approaching this sum of money; nor has a set of *famille noir* jars, at the time when those were most admired, ever been sold for such a price. It is one of the most valuable specimens of the art of ceramics in the world, and this in the considered opinion of aesthetes in the land where aesthetics, almost, were invented, and where they led the aesthetic life in the time of William the Conqueror, nearly a thousand years ago. Compare, for instance, *The Tale of Genji* of Lady Murasaki, and the contemporary Bayeux Tapestry! But the truth must be that ceramics in Japan have an exaggerated, an almost drugged value because of the tea-ceremony. Cups and bowls connected with that ritual, but always of pottery, not porcelain, lead the van of these enormous prices. Certain of them which are acclaimed as masterpieces, the 'Great Black' tea-bowl by Tôjirô, once the 'cherished possession' of the great tea-master Sen-no-Rikyû (1521-1591) (also a great garden architect, for he designed the garden of Chishakuin at Kyoto), and various other tea-bowls in black pottery by Kôho, or by Dônyû, take rank with those objects that are worth precisely nothing at all, say, a few pence, or every penny you have in the world if you have a craze for them. And the great Kôetsu, one of the undoubted artistic geniuses of Japan, comes directly out of Dônyû for he was his pupil.

Now let us look at the jar by Ninsei. It is on a clay base which is left unglazed for the bottom inch or two of its surface, with curious result as though Ninsei had forgotten about it, or not bothered, but it must really have been to give an effect of artlessness before his display of pyrotechnics and virtuosity above it. The glaze of the rest of the jar has an intense black ground, as black as lacquer, and as thick as that, perhaps intended for night time, but you can take it, or leave it, that seems to have been the intention. This blackness only covers the surface of the upper part of the jar, of its shoulders, and the waist and flanks of it are painted with hundreds of cherry trees in full bloom, for, in fact, this jar is called 'Mount Yoshino' after the famous cherry-viewing resort, near Nara, mentioned on another page. The mist upon the flank of Mount Yoshino is shown in gold, the attaching of gold and silver to the pottery surface being one of Ninsei's inventions. Some of the blossoms, accordingly, are in red glaze outlined in gold, while others that are outlined in red are painted with silver, though the silver has oxidized with age and looks, now, more blue than silver. There are, as well, little, hardly perceptible touches of green and of a lighter blue. The dates of Ninsei are uncertain, but this jar was thrown probably around 1730 in the kilns at Kyoto. Looking long at it one begins to realize that it is subtly beautiful, and that this is an extraordinary flight of imagination off the potter's wheel. For looking at it again, those are not cherry trees at all. There are no stems or boughs, and yet it is an impression of a blossoming mountain side.

Part of the value attached to Ninsei's pottery is, of course, its extreme rarity. A connoisseur will tell you that it is doubtful whether there are as many as half a dozen genuine pieces by him. But he was equally renowned as well for his work in porcelain, being described, indeed, as 'the originator of truly Japanese colour-glaze porcelain'. A pottery jar in the National Museum at Tokyo with the moon and cherry blossoms upon it; a porcelain jar in a private collection with a design of young pine trees in overglaze, though in the photograph it is difficult to make this out in detail, but it appears to have the same 'black lacquer' ground as the 'Mount Yoshino' jar, the identical unglazed base giving it the look of pottery more than porcelain, and a hint of hills in the background behind the pine trees, with their tasselled shapes climbing high on the curvature of the jar's sides in order to give distance and perspective. These few pieces, and another which has been described to me, a pottery jar with a design of wistaria upon it, must be nearly all there are of them. Pottery by Ninsei is as rare as that by Kenzan—of whom more in our next chapter. But this one 'Mount Yoshino' jar by Ninsei is enough to prove his aesthetic stature, and that every one of his existing pieces has the importance of a statement or pronouncement.

After this novel experience, and harbinger of new sensations, we moved into another and smaller room, next door. Here, without a word of warning about it beforehand, were the pair of screens by Sôtatsu that we had come to see. They are probably the greatest paintings in Japan. Or, at least, they are the best paintings by one of the two greatest painters, Sesshû (1421-1507) being the other—though it has to be admitted that Sesshû is no greater artist than many Chinese masters. It is even in this sense, never being at any time other than a painter of Japan, that Sôtatsu is the more unique, and therefore the more interesting of the two. Each of the screens is in six panels, quite simply, as always, in colours and gold foil on paper, obviously more tenuous and fragile material than wood or canvas, and explaining how it is that there are so few surviving screens in Japan that can be attributed with certainty to the great painters. There appears, though, to be no reasonable doubt that this pair of screens is directly from Sôtatsu's hand. The subjects are '*Sekiya*' and '*Miotsukushi*' which are, both of them, episodes from *The Tale of Genji*, but although both subjects are taken from the same narrative they are individual compositions and they are not, as is more generally the case with pairs of screens, part of one overlapping and general design.

On the '*Sekiya*' screen the theme is a chance meeting of Prince Genji with his former love, Lady Utsusemi, who is now married to a provincial governor, and living in a distant province. Genji had been in disgrace, himself, and banished, and away from Court. Their encounter takes place at the barrier station of Sekiyama, one of those *douanes* or *doganas* on the high road as described by the German physician Engelbrecht Kaempfer (see page 152), with the only difference that the protagonists in Lady Murasaki's novel are too important to be made to get down from their ox-carriages and present themselves for search. Utsusemi and her husband are on their way to Kyoto; Prince Genji and his entourage are on pilgrimage to Ishiyama temple on Lake Biwa, which is, incidentally, where Lady Murasaki (975-1031) composed *Genji Monogatari*. The 'Sekiya' episode is a scene which would be recognized at once by an educated Japanese lady or gentleman of Sôtatsu's time, and it was not even necessary for him to portray the *dramatis personae*. Indeed the leading characters, properly speaking, do not appear at all so that the effect is almost that of an abstract charade in which you are to guess the scene or keyword from the mere placing of objects; hills, or cottage, a gate or barrier, and an ox-carriage to either side of it, and they spell the '*Sekiya*' chapter from *The Tale of Genji*.

The exact moment of the narrative is when Utsusemi's husband has had to halt his ox-carriage to let Genji's retinue through the barrier. The bullock has been taken out of the shafts and led away, and in order to keep the two-wheeled carriage upright for Lady Utsusemi to sit there, invisible, the shafts are resting on a shaft-stand—there would seem to be no word for this in our language. Genji has been looking out from the window of his ox-carriage to see what is happening, and he recognizes Utsusemi's brother, and at once lets down his blind. In the next moment—at which we never arrive in the painting—he will call him over and say to him: 'I hope your sister noticed how attentive I am to her. It is not often I go all the way to the Barrier to meet her.' But we see neither Prince Genji, nor Lady Utsusemi. The only indication of him is a bit of his red sleeve coming out of the front of his carriage. This is a delightful passage in itself; black body and wheels to the carriage, painted all over with a kind of *mille feuille* pattern. His retainers are bustling around. One of them holds the bullock's red leading rein; another stands idle, doing nothing at all; two more, one of them in green, seem to have tucked up their pantaloons for greater convenience in walking; and another man in white holds a huge white, furled parasol or umbrella; all of them exactly as in the half-caricature scrolls of the Heian and Kamakuran periods of the twelfth and thirteenth centuries, it being the express intention of Kôetsu and Sôtatsu and their school of painters to return to what already seemed to them to be the historic past of Japan, the period when it had the least of foreign influence and was most Japanese. The ox-carriage of Lady Utsusemi, the other side of the barrier, seems to be a good distance, forty, or even fifty yards away, such is the feeling of dimension given by the painting. But the most typical and skilful passage of brushwork on the whole screen is the thatched cabin at the barrier, immediately recalling his

famous fan-painting of thatched farmhouses with blossoming plum
trees, which are so skilfully adapted to the shape of a fan, from his fan-
screen at the beautiful Sambôin temple of Kyoto. This fragment from
it is indeed the most well known of all Sôtatsu's paintings in Japan,[1]
but the thatched farmhouse of the Genji screen in the Seikadô Foundation at Tokyo is more beautiful still. But it is a winter month, or a
month very early in spring; the branches are bare, and the plum tree
against the thatch is not yet in blossom.

'*Miotsukushi*', the companion screen, is even bolder in composition.
It is the episode from *The Tale of Genji* where Genji meets another of
his former loves at the Shintô shrine of Sumiyoshi, which is on the
seashore. The tremendous curve of the shore line is what is memorable
in this screen, with the tethered ox-cart in the middle of it as though
standing out in the full moonlight. That, and the 'Japanese' shapes of
the pine trees which could be in no other country, and the huge,
arching, wooden bridge, starting out of nowhere and leading nowhere.
Again, the figures are unimportant and as in the early scroll-paintings,
almost caricatured. The gold foil of the paper marvellously suggests the
sand. There is a *torii* at foot of the wooden bridge; and the bridge is now
blue in colour, whatever it may have been three centuries and more
ago, but this blueness of the bridge much enhances its magical effect,
constructed on those high stilts because of the danger of spring or
autumn floods, but leading from nowhere to nowhere across the swirl
of waters. This shrine of Sumiyoshi, which is on the seashore between
Kobe and Osaka, is still famous for its giant pine and camphor trees and
is described as having an 'arched bridge' built at the expense of the wife
of Hideyoshi (died 1598)[2]. Another account of it mentions 'a pond over
which passes a semi-circular bridge'. It would seem there is a bridge at
Sumiyoshi of the same fantastic kind of construction as the Kintai-
bashi, surely one of the most beautiful and typical things of Japan, of
which I have attempted my own description much later in this book,
and on the far bank of which I would have this book to end. The
bridge at Sumiyoshi, a much simpler affair for it is in but one hop or
flight, was probably quite new at the time Sôtatsu painted it. But, if

[1] Shown at the *Art Treasures from Japan* exhibition, in the Victoria and Albert Museum, London,
in 1958.

[2] Terry's *Guide* (1920) remarks of this shrine, 'held in veneration by the lower classes of Osaka'
and especially revered by mariners and fishermen, that 'the grounds contain almost as many tanks
as an aquarium'. In the tanks are tortoises with their backs covered with seaweed and called
minogame after the straw raincoats worn by the peasants.

there at all, it climbs at such an angle that none but acrobats could have crossed on it. Perhaps no one was intended to, and that is why in fantasy it was painted blue. More probably, there was to be a bridge and this is how Sôtatsu saw it in his painter's eye. The simple way in which he gets his effects is astonishing. The strange forms of the pine trees growing out of the sand, and there are really so few of them scattered over the six panels of the screen, are as though inevitable, as if they could be growing in no other way. And when you come up close to the screen with your eyes but an inch or two away, just as true to this improbable truth are the stains of lichen on the tree trunks and the shelves or trays of the pine boughs, the flat and spiky cushions of the pine needles with the bits or ends of black twig sticking out of them. The bullock out of the yoke of the two-wheeled carriage, a black and white beast of curious markings, has been led down to wade in the sea-water under a pine tree, led there by the 'ox-groom' who holds it on a scarlet rein and he, in scroll-style, is half-caricatured. Sôtatsu, who had not to bother himself with horses which hardly occur in his paintings, was obviously interested in the muscular forms and thwarted strength of the draught bullocks. The bullock drawing the carriage of Prince Genji in the companion screen is a fawn and white beast wonderfully observed in its four-footed hauling and pulling of the heavy cart behind it. But his convention for the waves is not convincing, and in the middle of it a heavy barge is 'standing' for in no sense is it floating or riding on the water.

A brief discussion of the two Sôtatsu screens in the Seikadô must be excuse and introduction to further remarks on this great painter. He is perhaps the greatest painter of Japan just because he consciously founded himself upon what was specifically Japanese, and not Chinese, in their tradition.[1] Very little seems to be known about him; and as for the legendary Hon-ami Kôetsu (1558-1637), his master and inspirer, there is more information, but little or nothing left of his handiwork to judge him by. This extraordinary personality was a judge of sword blades, professionally—as important in his time as being an authority on aeroplane construction and design, with strong aesthetic and functional aptitudes added to it—and, also, a famous calligrapher and potter and lacquerer, as well. A tea-bowl by him, belonging to a private collector, of white 'Raku' ware for, of course, he was a confirmed

[1] *Yamato-e* is Japanese painting, as opposed to *Kara-e* or painting in the Chinese style.

adept of the tea-ceremony, is so famous that it is known as Fujisan or Mount Fuji, and must be among the most valued art objects in Japan. This, again, like the jar by Ninsei in the Seikadô, and it may be added, like the rock and sand garden of Ryûanji at Kyoto, is one of the specialized cases in a category to themselves that mean nothing at all to some tastes. But, to others, they are the dawning of new sensations hitherto the exclusive property of the aesthetes of Japan. I have tried my hardest to understand and write an account of Ryûanji, and of the jar by Ninsei, but have to admit myself defeated by the 'Raku' ware, anxious as I am to appreciate Kôetsu's genius. But it is certainly true that in the words of one critic 'they create a feeling of sombre, brooding strength which in the West would never be associated with a tea-cup'.[1] A lacquer box by Kôetsu is another thing altogether. This box to hold brushes and inkstone shows a famous bridge, but a flat pontoon not an arched bridge, at Sano in the east of Japan. The bridge is rendered in lead on a gold ground, while the poem about the bridge is in inlaid silver characters, and under it are the outlines of the boats on which the pontoon is laid; while the whole shape of the box is lumpy and suggests a flattish mountain, perhaps to indicate the hilly background of the bridge. The whole conception of this curious object is one which in the Occident only the Catalan architect Gaudí could have designed. Another inkstone box by Kôetsu has the jutting prow of a boat inlaid in sheet-lead into the lacquer, just such a boat prow as can be seen in many a *surimono* print by Hokusai—with his printer delighting in the sepias and ivories of its woodwork—and reeds and a flight of plovers form the rest of the design. If these lacquer boxes, unlike his tea-bowls, are not entirely of his own handiwork they at least represent his theories for it is evident that Kôetsu, as well as being a considerable painter himself, was in the manner of a William Morris, still more, a Daighilev, a marvellous cross-fertilizer of ideas. Eventually, Kôetsu was established by Ieyasu in a village outside Kyoto where artists of all kinds settled to be near him, and wonderful theories and ideas will have originated for he must have been, we surmise, even better as a talker than in action with his own hands.

Kôetsu and Sôtatsu may have married two sisters, and Tawaraya Sôtatsu may have been son of a fan-maker at Kyoto, for there is

---

[1] *The Arts of Japan*, by Hugo Munsterburg, Thames & Hudson, London, 1957, page 140. The lacquer boxes by Kôetsu referred to in the next sentences are in the National Museum at Tokyo.

evidence that there was a fan-maker of that name. It is not therefore so peculiar that there are fan-screens by him; the pair from Sambôin temple with only eleven fans upon it, including the famous farmhouse composition (see page 110), and another pair belonging to the Imperial Household Collection with the big total of forty-eight fans upon it. There is a particular, and an especially Japanese talent in the way the fans 'occur' upon the screens, in their placing, that is to say, though whether this is due to Sôtatsu himself, or to the fan-mounter, there is no means of knowing but, more probably, it was the latter.

It is a fact that the only contact art-lovers from the West are likely to have with the works of this great painter is from the pair of screens in the Seikadô at Tokyo, and even this is not too easily accomplished and entails a good deal of trouble. The only other access to him is in the Sambôin temple at Kyoto where there are the fan-screens, and also another pair of screens to be noticed in a moment, but there is never certainty of seeing them. Sôtatsu seems to have had some special link of association with Sambôin. One of the only letters preserved from him is thanking the abbot for sending him new bamboo shoots from the garden. It is interesting to note that even the great pair of *Genji* screens at the Seikadô came originally from Sambôin which must have been the chief repository of Sôtatsu's paintings. But the screens we are now to look at have an extreme interest attaching to them because they have for theme a Court Dance, which is nothing other than a performance of *Bugaku* such as we were privileged to be invited to watch at the Emperor's Palace at Tokyo (see page 67). They are two-panel screens, and at the lower right-hand corner—the action always going from right to left as in Japanese handwriting—there are the symbolical flame-crests of the *taikôs* or huge drums, just as we saw and heard them only this last October in the Concert Hall of the Imperial Palace, a mere two or three years after the emergence of this long hidden and semi-secret music out of the distant past into recognition as one of the most interesting and extraordinary survivals into the modern world.

Upon the golden ground of the scene the masked dance is proceeding, but with no sign of the strange instruments or their players. Four dancers, two to a panel at this present, are performing just precisely the solo dance that was put on for us at Tokyo and which we saw again at Itsukushima Shrine (Miyajima), in confirmation of how exactly these ancient dances have been preserved, untouched, in their

entirety. The masks are not the same, for what we saw in both instances
was a cat-mask, but the movements are unmistakable and it could be
either dancer we saw in action. They are red dresses and it is, therefore,
a Dance of the Left, meaning that it is of T'ang Dynasty Chinese, or
even ancient Indian origin, as against Dances of the Right which came
from Korea and Manchuria and in which green dresses are worn.
Sôtatsu's dancers make great play of their swirling tails, and the pair
with their backs to us on one panel have the silhouette of dancing bears
or dancing frogs. But the other pair of dancers facing us have so closely
the movements of the *Bugaku* dance that they could have been copied
from an instantaneous photograph. One of them dances with a drum,
and the other holds as at Tokyo and at Itsukushima a gilded stick or
baton in his hand. Sôtatsu must have, himself, seen a very large number
of performances of *Bugaku* in order to portray their movements with
such exactitude. There are gnarled old pine trees at the top of the left-
hand panel as though this was a performance of *Bugaku*, not on the
stage but in the open air; while, below, is something most strange and
peculiar, a group of four dancers 'treading' a round dance with their
hands on each other's shoulders. But their movements, or, at least, the
manner in which they are portrayed, and also their cloaks with wide
sleeves and masks and head-dresses are of utmost strangeness, and might
make one think the painter had access to some Aztec codex, or was
familiar with such Occidental folk-lore 'throwbacks' as the Abbot's
Bromley dance and the Câlusari dances from Rumania.

Now one of the secrets of Sôtatsu's style, in which he must have been
encouraged by Kôetsu his friend and mentor, is the extent to which he
based himself upon the early Japanese scroll paintings of the Heian
period, that is, of the eleventh to thirteenth centuries, choosing by
predilection the time when there was least influence from China and
painting and literature were more purely Japanese. One of the few
facts that are known for certain about his career is his visit with Kôetsu
to Itsukushima Shrine on the sacred island of Miyajima for the purpose
of restoring the *sutra* scrolls given to the shrine by the Taira family in
1164.[1] The visit of the two painters to Itsukushima was in 1602. It
would appear that many of the subjects painted on Sôtatsu's fan-

---

[1] There are thirty-three of these scrolls at Itsukushima, and three of the rolls have 'new designs'
of 'waves and hills with trees' and 'a deer standing in a sparse growth of grass'. These three designs
are attributed to Sôtatsu: cf. *Japanese Scroll Painting*, by Kenji Toda, The University of Chicago
Press, 1935, page 129 and 130.

screens are taken directly from the old scrolls of the Heian or Yamato periods, particularly in battle scenes which, practically speaking, are 'action stills' put into drawing with armoured figures on the rush, caricature horses, and so forth; and in domestic scenes on certain fans such as a lover watching his mistress in another house filling a rice bowl, where the action is put down in the merest rudiments and the painter in his haste has not even bothered to give the lover the right number of fingers on his hand. But it is precisely at Itsukushima Shrine, on Miyajima island, that Sôtatsu will have seen performances of *Bugaku* during the time, probably extending into months, that he was working there on restoring and copying the scrolls. He will have seen, as we did, masked dances on the stage that stands at high tide in the blue waters of the Inland Sea.

All important paintings by Sôtatsu have now been described, except for his 'Matsushima' screen in the Freer Gallery at Washington, one of the only Japanese paintings of the first order to find a home out of its own country, a wonderful affair of waves and rocks and fantastic pine trees, a theme of which Kôrin was to make his own more sensational version, now in the Gallery at Boston. That the rocky islets and pines of Matsushima should have been painted by both Kôrin and Sôtatsu proves the extent to which these painters travelled in their own country, for Matsushima, one of the three famous places for scenery in Japan, is near Sendai, more than two hundred miles north of Tokyo, and more than five hundred miles from Kyoto where both painters had their homes. But travel had become a fashion among painters after the example of the great Sesshû's journey to China, and as though to prove this there is a careful and detailed ink drawing of Ama-no-hashidate, far away on the north coast of the main island, third of the 'scenic trio', Matsushima and Miyajima being the others, drawn by Sesshû in some year after 1500 when he was more than eighty-two years old.

That Japan has great painters, as have Occidental countries, Italy, Spain, Holland, Flanders, France, Germany, England, is something too little appreciated owing to the extreme difficulty in seeing their works. It is due, also, to the form taken by the paintings, or, rather, to the exigencies imposed upon them by the Japanese style of living. Illuminated scrolls, or ink paintings upon silk or paper, are not so easy to put on view as panel pictures in oils on wood or canvas, or even altar paintings in churches upon which at any rate it is possible to train the

Katsura Palace pavilion, Kyoto (early 17th century)

Processional car at the Gion Festival,
Kyoto, held yearly from 10th-20th July

light. But also, the national idiosyncrasy of only showing one thing at a time, which we may call the eupeptic method of appreciating works of art, is as ingrained in the Japanese temperament as its Occidental opposite of exhibiting anything and everything on the walls at the same time, and hanging pictures one above the other as in the albums of a stamp collection. There are few, if any frescoes in Japanese temples, now the wall paintings at Hôryûji have been destroyed, while the pairs of six-leaved screens upon which many of the greatest painters displayed their talents are as fragile in their textures of gold and colours upon paper as their serpentine folds are difficult to marshal and deploy. Or, in simpler words, it is difficult to put a number of pairs of six-leaved screens on view.

As to the early scroll-paintings, it is a case of the works of great painters being confined to the dimensions of an illuminated manuscript, but one which unfolds in length, and of which you do not turn the pages. Certain of these scrolls are in as high a repute in Japan, and as familiar from reproduction, as in a comparable instance is the Wilton dyptych. The famous Chôjû Giga, for example, or 'animal scroll' of monkeys and frogs and rabbits, which is preserved in Kôzanji temple at Kyoto, on the road past the 'Moss' temple, (but in all probability rarely to be seen there because it is so often away on exhibition), drawings of *Alice in Wonderland* charm and humour, attributed with much uncertainty to the monk Toba Sôjô and dating, incredibly, from the twelfth century. This unlikely contemporary to our Bayeux tapestry has already the attributes or earmarks of one of the faces of Japan in respect of their gift for fantasy-mimicry or demi-caricature. It has been interpreted as portraying the monks of neighbouring monasteries who belonged to rival Buddhist sects, but this seems to attach too ponderous a meaning to its affectionate lightness and deftness of touch, and Professor Yukio Yashiro is surely nearer the truth in saying that in his opinion 'a master priest-painter is here simply amusing himself by depicting his favourite animals disporting themselves as his fertile humour directed the brush'.[1]

Another scroll of altogether different character, but as nationally

[1] *Two Thousand Years of Japanese Art*, pages 161, 174 and 175. The 'animal scroll' and the *Handbook of Hungry Ghosts* were on view at *The Art Treasures from Japan* exhibition at the Victoria and Albert Museum, London, in 1958. Two sentences in the description of the latter scroll are quoted from the handbook to the exhibition, which was translated by Mr William Watson of the British Museum. The scrolls could, of course, only be open at certain pages, so all their contents were not seen.

N

famous, is the *Gaki Zôshi*, given the dramatic title of *Handbook of Hungry Ghosts*, sinners, and unhappy beings condemned after death to wander the world, invisible to living persons, and always hungry. This is a theme on the major scale, and the unknown draughtsman of genius is worthy of it, resulting in a masterpiece of the morbid imagination. The 'hungry ghosts' are spectrally thin except for their swollen bellies, and in after-death they have grown great shocks of hair. Also, they are drawn darker than the living as having undergone morbid changes. In one scene, three of the thirsty ghosts with their repulsive backs turned to us are grovelling on the earth 'licking the runlets that fall from a funerary tablet on which pilgrims have sprinkled water as an offering to the gods', in another they have tried to drink at a river but are driven away and 'reduced to drinking the few drops of water falling from the feet of travellers who cross the river'. Another scene shows the ghosts 'screaming and laughing' among a group of persons, an old man, two women, and a child, who are quietly relieving themselves, and wearing high wooden clogs or pattens to avoid the filth and ordure of the open street. All round them are six of the hungry ghosts, staring at them and nearly touching them, all with huge bellies, but excepting for the ghost of one old man with white hair it is impossible to know their sex, and the ghosts could be men or women. It is a pity one can see no more of this scroll than these few scenes for it outdoes in its particular vein anything by Hieronymus Bosch or Pieter Brueghel.

Yet another scroll in a private collection can be but little below the *Hungry Ghosts* in morbid fantasy. It is the *Scroll of Diseases*, and the drawings have a strong vein of sadism running in them. A man sitting with chopsticks and a tray of food in front of him—not otherwise, though the date is about AD 1200, than it would be in any poorer home in Japan today—there he sits, grimacing, and pointing with his hand into his gaping mouth. A placid, happy-looking woman with nothing whatever wrong with her sits, pointing at him. He can eat nothing, and looks at us out of the drawing, his face furrowed and lined with pain, with throbbing stumps of teeth and aching gums. Others of the drawings are not less cruel; a soldier, as we know from his bow and quiver of arrows against the wall, sits, fan in hand, with his family. His wife, again, is the onlooker who cannot, or will not, do anything to help. Her husband has an unusual deformity in the shape of a black nose which is inherited by their two children playing on the floor, and even by the babe feeding at its mother's breast. Only the mother is, irritatingly, free from it but has conveyed it to all her offspring. Has such a phenomenon as this hereditary black nose ever occurred in medical history? Or is it the mere fantasy of an unpleasant mind? It would be interesting to know, but it looks more like an ugly fairy story. Another drawing is of a man ill in bed with a tight bandage round his head and the coverlet drawn up to his chin. The text says that he is tormented by an army of 'pygmy priests about five inches tall dressed in white paper robes and carrying long sticks', and there they all are coming towards his pillow, except for one of them who is the bear-leader and turns to urge them on.[1] Clinically, this could be one of the last episodes in a case of *delirium tremens*. Nowhere, in any of the drawings, is there a hint of remedy, or any suggestion of pity for the sufferer. Again it is impossible to avoid comparison between these scroll drawings which are done with the short hand rapidity and swift statement of a Charles Keene or a Phil May and the drawings in French or English illuminated manuscripts about 'AD 1200'; and yet these were exactly the years in which the great cathedrals were beginning to be built, but the Japanese of the time were no more capable of raising such giant structures than were our monkish scribes of making, alternatively, such fanciful, or so barbed and cruel drawings.

The other source of origin for the specifically Japanese School of painting represented by artists like Tôhaku and Sôtatsu is in the other sort of 'action' scrolls, such as the *Heiji Monogatari*, a battle of clans, now in three portions, of which one is at the Seikadô, another is in the National Museum at Tokyo, and the third roll is in the Museum of Fine Arts at Boston. This has the famous scene of the *Burning of the Palace*, with a frenzy of running and galloping forms in 'lobster' armour, twanging their bows and brandishing their swords at the edge of raging flames. Other scenes show the two-wheeled Imperial bullock carts— exactly as on Sôtatsu's *Genji* screens of four hundred years later —advancing with an escort of bowmen who are on the alert and pointing their arrows in all directions. In the Tokugawa Museum at Nagoya we were fortunate enough to see some portions of the *Genji* scrolls which were prototype for so much of *Yamato* painting. This scroll dates from the first half of the twelfth century, and is a document

---

[1] The first of the drawings described from the *Scroll of Diseases* is illustrated in *An Introduction to the Arts of Japan*, by Peter C. Swann, Bruno Cassirer, Oxford, 1958, plate 82; the other two are reproduced in Yukio Yoshiro, *op. cit.* plates 93 and 94.

of fantastic sophistication beyond parallel, unless with a touch of sympathetic exaggeration we would like to pretend to ourselves that something of the kind existed with the poets and troubadours of twelfth- and thirteenth-century Provence, at that time when there seemed to be emerging a third land of the Latins, the missing sister to Italy and Spain. The Heian civilization which is the background of *The Tale of Genji* is now familiar to many persons from the translation of Lady Murasaki's novel by Mr Arthur Waley, and this scroll in the Tokugawa Museum at Nagoya painted probably only about a hundred years after the novel was written gives the visual assurance that those scenes of verbal poetry are true. Here are the ladies with their long black flowing hair, their whitened faces and their twelve *kimonos* worn one over the other. The painter has invented a technique of his own by which the roofs of houses are lifted off in order that the spectator should see both inside and outside; and the heavy 'court' eyebrows of the faces according to Heian fashion, and the simplicity of outline of their features as though the artist could draw a closer likeness to the person were it not impolite to do so, are all typical of the mannerisms of *Yamato* painting.

It has to be conceded that the scrolls mentioned here as ancestral origins for the Yamato school can have been seen by very few persons at any time in their span of centuries. Their primal circulation was only among court circles, and when they were studied four hundred and fifty years later by Kôetsu and his disciples it was with the definite aim of trying to revive what they conceived to be the national and aboriginal style of painting which had no Chinese influence in it. This could be compared in its archaeologizing principles with William Morris's attempts at his Kelmscott press to print his edition of Chaucer in the fifteenth-century manner, only that court life in Kyoto had not altered in many of its visual aspects and was, and remained for eight centuries, almost a hermetic kingdom. Now in our day, with a lesser time separating ourselves from Kôetsu and his circle than divided them from the Heian style they were trying to revive in their mood of xenophobic nationalism, the scrolls in question can be seen illustrated in art books but have been accessible to little more than a handful of persons. But that Sôtatsu had handled them, and even copied them, is known in evidence and were it not established as fact there would be every assumption of it from the witness of our own eyes.

But interposing in these arguments is Sesshû who is the great painter, and perhaps in a global sense the only great painter of Japan. That is to say, he is to be compared to the greatest Chinese painters, and to his exact contemporaries in the West, Giovanni Bellini, Holbein, and Albrecht Dürer, more especially to the two latter because it is difficult to make a comparison between a draughtsman, however great an artist, and a painter of large canvases and huge altar pieces. His dates are 1420 to 1506, and at an early age he found himself a novice at a Zen temple in Kyoto. He stayed there for twenty years, learning Chinese and copying the Chinese paintings in the Shogun's collection, and then removed to a temple at Yamaguchi which is a town almost at the southern extremity of the main island, and therefore in the best geographical situation for a reconnaissance into China. After eight years at Yamaguchi, aged forty-eight, he at last achieved his ambition and sailed for the mainland, disembarking at Ningpo, 'in the veritable holy land of Zen', round the great monastery of Mount T'ien-t'ung.[1] Here he remained for several months, and was given the first seat in the meditation hall next to the abbot, but this was in respect of his Zen studies, not his painting. Eventually the journey to Peking was resumed, and no one thinking of it can but envy him. For the object of it was to see China and to steep himself in Chinese painting. They went by slow stages along the Grand Canal; past Soochow where there were great Buddhist monasteries and famous landscape gardens with, in place of statuary, cloud-shaped and lacustrine stones; and then up the Yangtze river past the Golden Mountain with its convents and pagodas, and so at last to Peking. But, sadly, hoping to find great painters he was disappointed, and his journey in this respect compares unfavourably with Dürer's visits to Giovanni Bellini while he was in Venice. Sesshû spent the years 1468 to 1469 in China, and on his return to Japan settled once again in a pavilion he built for himself near Yamaguchi. This was his headquarters for the rest of his long life, and it is in the Môri collection at Yamaguchi that his most famous painting is still preserved. This is the *Long Scroll*, and when unwound it is sixty feet in length; a huge landscape panorama rendered in different techniques in emulation of the Chinese masters, and drawn many years after he had come back from China, in the Chinese manner. Liang K'ai, active about AD 1200,

[1] Phrase quoted from *Sesshû*, in the *Kodansha Library of Japanese Art*, English text by Elise Grilli, Charles E. Tuttle Company, Tokyo and Vermont, USA, 1957. In this little book the *Long Scroll* of Sesshû is reproduced in entirety.

was one of the masters he most admired;[1] and yet in the universality of all great artists there are drawings in the scroll which could be by Rembrandt, while others, especially his rendering of low banks of reeds or rushes are reminiscent of van Gogh.

Sesshû's other, or ink-splash (*haboku*) manner is to be seen—if it *can* be seen—in a landscape in the Museum at Tokyo which has often been reproduced. This ink-splash style of Sesshû and other masters, like the rock and sand garden at Ryûanji, and like certain features of the Katsura Detached Palace at Kyoto, would seem to be one of those realms of art in which Japan has a decided message for the future. 'Splashed in' with apparent carelessness, though really the tension and not the relaxation of a lifetime spent in drawing, it is calculated to give both a good and a bad example to abstract painters. Personally, I have to admit to not admiring it. There are, as well, a number of painted screens attributed to Sesshû; a very pretty pair of screens with flowers and pheasants in the Freer Gallery at Washington (I would say of doubtful attribution); flowers and pine trees with a pair of splendid red-capped storks, towering on tall legs with black edges to their tail feathers among the pine needles, this in a private collection in Tokyo; and monkeys, on a pair of six-leaved screens in the Museum at Boston, monkeys with white faces swinging with one, or both long furry arms, and engaged in every activity of a monkey colony. It will be seen from this that, his *Long Scroll* apart, Sesshû is largely accessible to the public, and his is the one name likely to remain in the public mind, beside that of Kôrin.

There now comes the long dynasty of Kanô painters, beginning with Kanô Masanobu in the lifetime of Sesshû, and continuing with his son Motonobu (1476-1559) who was a better painter, but too much of an eclectic and under the influence of different Chinese painters. But a great period of Japanese painting was coming and it is personified in Kanô Eitoku (1543-1590), grandson of Motonobu, and the greatest master of the Momoyama school which once again is something entirely and characteristically Japanese. Kanô Eitoku was, indeed, a little early for it since it is considered to have lasted from 1570 until 1630. It was the period when great castles were being built and sliding screens in quantity were needed for their decoration. The Nijô Palace at Kyoto

[1] Paintings by Liang K'ai are reproduced in *Chinese Painting*, by William Cohn, Phaidon Press, London, 1948, plates 100-106. His ink-portrait of Li T'ai-Po, the Chinese poet, has certainly points of affinity with Sesshû's painting of the Zen sage Daruma sitting in meditation (and being disturbed by an unwelcome disciple who has cut off his own left arm in order to break in on the master's attention). This painting by Sesshû is in Sainenji temple, in Aichi prefecture.

gives some idea of these interior apartments, except that it is a palace and not a castle. Nobunaga had employed Eitoku to decorate five of the seven storeys of his huge castle at Azuchi on Lake Biwa, and later Hideyoshi employed him at the castle in Osaka. In only one of these castles, that of Momoyama (Peach Hill) which is outside Kyoto, beyond Sambôin, there were no fewer than a hundred pairs of screens—not all, of course, by Eitoku, but it serves to show the scale of these vast decorative schemes. There is a superlative example of Eitoku in the Museum at Tokyo which the authorities seem to suggest as genuine, a screen of *hinoki* cypress trees with intricate counterplay of coloured mosses and lichens on their chocolaty trunks, and a stream of lapis blue flowing between bold shapes of rocks, all against a billowing background of golden clouds. Like Tintoretto, his contemporary, Eitoku found the ordinary paint brushes too flimsy and slow in action, and is said to have used special brushes made of straws. *Four Wise Hermits*, *Eight Scenic Views*, and *Seven Sages in the Bamboo Grove*, were some of the themes treated by Eitoku in the castle at Azuchi, with other Chinese-sounding subjects, but his screens of birds and flowering trees were in pure *Yamato* style like the screen of *hinoki* trees just mentioned.

There is a poetic stimulus in only stating the themes of these *Momoyama* screens. A wonderful pair of them has lately become famous in Japan from coloured reproductions in the newspapers, and it will come into private possession of all knowledgeable lovers of Florentine painting if we say that it is as though a 'little master', Alessio Baldovinetti,[1] master of the cypress and stone pine, had 'influenced' the painter for the right-hand screen has tall conical hills like green sugar-loaves covered up to their summits with fir trees, and a marvellous valley of cypresses where, if I know the Tuscan landscape, the older nightingales will have their schools of song, but here in Japan it will be humming and whirring with 'singing' grasshoppers or cicadas in the early summer heat. Here and there on the hills are trees with white blossoms which will be wild plums or gean trees. The sister screen is of an earlier season for it has snow-covered hills with a few fir trees against them, beyond a sandy promontory covered with fir trees, and a strait of foam-flecked sea. And in this pair of screens the background is more silvery than gold which, also, by some process of alchemy is suggestive

[1] Fresco of *The Adoration of the Shepherds* (1460) in the court of the Santissima Annunziata at Florence.

of Alessio Baldovinetti. Another pair of screens is so thick with plum blossom that I pass over it in silence for there is nothing more to say of it. Screens from a temple on the slopes of Mount Hiei have no more than flowers and domestic cocks and hens for theme, but what plumage! and as past amateur of 'fancy poultry' I recognize a 'duckwing' stretching his neck to peck at a corncob under a spray of chrysanthemums, and his pair of hens 'discussing' a fallen corncob at foot of the giant stems of 'Indian' corn. On the other panel, for there is ever the excuse of the four seasons of the year, a white cockerel with splendidly tangled tail-feathers disports himself near to a bush of peonies, and not far from a clump of irises over which a pair of swallows or swifts are skimming, or rather, tossing themselves into the air in nuptial flight, while a rooster of breed unknown to me prepares to take up his perch upon a blossoming plum tree. Next, we have a pair of screens from Kôfukuji temple at Nara, a dazzling and intoxicating snowstorm of white cherry blossom; and a creaming waterfall and a lake of pure lapis, and a tree-peony or two and tall iris *sibirica* at the water's edge. The cherry trees must be more than a hundred years old to judge from the dimensions of their trunks, famous old cherry trees, but we do not see the tops of them which are lost in a kind of glory or ecstasy of golden clouds. What blossoms must this painter have seen with the cherry groves of Mount Yoshino blooming one after another so nearby! This pair of screens should stay for ever in its temple at Nara, for so long as there is spring in the year!

Screens with golden pheasants and mandarin ducks and white cranes are a commonplace. But there is another of cryptomérias on a hillside which is almost, if not quite, by that 'Baldovinetti' hand. And we come to a painting of solitary fir trees above the thatched roof of a peasant's cabin, and gourds, nothing but gourds, but in the right-hand panel they proliferate and tumble over one another down a wattle fence, and are more vigorous than any vine. Screens from Daitokuji temple—the temple of the hanging wood across the lake which I wanted to see by full moon—are simplicity itself, a cherry tree above a hedge, and a trellis of wistaria like falling fireworks over the same wattles bound and roped in with bamboo, and much play made of their fern-cut leaves and the lacing together of the bamboo palisading. Next, it is a screen of six horses in their loose boxes, where the peculiarly Japanese talent of the painter has delighted in the clean wooden planking, new sawn, and in the ropes tying the curvetting horses. These are of red and blue and white strands plaited together to make neat diagonals where they are tied from the corners of each box, with a heavier rope in the same colours coming down from above like a belt under each horse's soft belly, all with giant green bamboo stems at the back and trailing and waving bamboo leaves lifting and dangling above the stables. A pair of screens of towel-horses with garments of all kinds thrown upon them, one of them a *kimono* with a bold design of open fans of every colour, contrast with a pair that have two-wheeled ceremonial waggons painted on them, one sepia-black, one coral-red, but painted in *mille feuille* pattern, with 'nightingale' wheels that sing or creak, and spokes painted to look like the quills of a porcupine, bearing huge baskets in which there are flower arrangements by a masterhand, one of chrysanthemums, and the other of white wistaria and great tree-peonies, among them an undoubted blue peony which will be a mystery to every botanist. And at foot of this, a little four-wheeled child's go-cart of *mille-feuille* fashion, and carrying a square box or nest of irises.[1] But the repertory need not, and does not end here, for it includes all sorts of genre scenes, such as various professions and occupations, and crowd pictures such as that one we were admiring, not long ago in the Seikadô, of popular scenes in the river bed at Kyoto.

There is one, most particularized and fascinating branch of screen painting that must have special mention. They are the *Namban Byobû*, screens of 'Southern Barbarians'; or, in fact, they are the Portuguese voyagers. These mariners and free-lances first arrived at Nagasaki, under the command of Fernão Mendes Pinto in 1543, coming in the first place by way of Goa which already belonged to them, but out of so vast a distance that it takes one's breath away to think of it. They would sail up to Japan from the direction of the Philippines which is why they got the name of 'Southern Barbarians' for the Japanese would of course have no idea whatever where they came from. There are said to be some twenty pairs of these screens in existence, all showing the Portuguese, but obviously by various hands, and dating from rather later when the Japanese had some experience of the Portuguese, if not fully recovered from the first shock of seeing them. It must have been as strange a contact as that of the Spaniards only a few years earlier with the 'Indian'

---

[1] The screens described in this and the preceding paragraph are illustrated in *Screen Paintings of the Momoyama Period*, by H. Minamoto, Meiki-Shobo, Tokyo, 1935.

civilizations of Mexico and Peru. Saint Francis Xavier landed in Japan in 1549, and by 1600 two hundred thousand Japanese had become Christian,[1] though this was followed by fearful persecution, the expulsion of the Portuguese, and the massacre of Shimabara in 1637, 'when the persecutors were not content with the ordinary modes of hanging, crucifying, drowning, beheading, but flung the victims down from high precipices, buried them alive, had them torn asunder by oxen, tied them up in rice-sacks of plaited straw, which were then heaped up and set on fire, or put them in cages with provisions before their eyes, where they were allowed to perish of hunger'. At least forty thousand Japanese Christians were slain, but in spite of these draconian measures there were still traces of Christian belief when the ban was lifted after the Meiji restoration, near Nagasaki, and in a few other villages in the southern island of Kyushu.

The *Namban Byobû* were probably all painted in or near Nagasaki and it is pleasant to turn from these horrors to the comical view of the mariners of Portugal that prevailed in Japan. Everything to do with them was thought to be absurdly funny, though tinged with a note of warning for they brought firearms to Japan for the first time, and many, if not all of them, were cut-throat swashbucklers. A single six-leaf screen in the collection of the Royal family of Bavaria gives an intriguing and typical panorama of the 'Southern Barbarians'. The missing screen of the pair may have depicted their arrival in Japan for here they are slowly moving down as though in procession to the shore where their caravel or galleon rides at anchor—with all sail set which is the artist's fantasy, for this would not be so with the ship in port. The grand circus turn is an elephant, the first of its race to arrive in Japan, with a 'Portingale' of great importance riding it and a pair of 'mahouts' in attendance, one of whom is 'salaaming'. Further on, someone of even greater moment is being carried in a litter under an umbrella-of-state which could only have come from India. There are one or two priests or friars in funereal black; but it is the enormous width and variety of

[1] Three important *daimyos* from the island of Kyushu sent an embassy to Rome, where they were given audience by the Pope. But Christianity penetrated further into Japan than the southern island of Kyushu for there was a Christian church in Yedo (Tokyo), and further north at Sendai. The Christians were protected by Date Masamune, the *daimyô* of that province, who despatched an embassy to Spain led by Hasekura and accompanied by Padre Luis Sotelo, a Spanish Franciscan, who had settled at Sendai. They sailed across the Pacific to Acapulco, and thence in a Spanish ship to Seville, visiting Pope Paul V in Rome, and returning by way of Mexico to Japan in 1620 after an absence of seven years. Hasekura, whose portrait was painted in Rome, died in peace; but Sotelo who stayed in Manila on the way back, and tried to enter Japan in disguise, was caught and burnt alive at Nagasaki.

breeches, galligaskins, codpieces, and what not, that has caught the painter's fancy; black breeches down to the heels, and worked up all their length with criss-cross cording; a bareheaded young man in elegantly cut jodhpurs, for they could be nothing else than that; and others wearing white linen 'plus-fours' that must be the work of Goan tailors. Some of the 'Portingales' are loitering about with Indian parrots on their wrists; and what was probably true to nature, at least two flurries of quarrelling have broken out among them.

Another of the *Namban* screens was shown in London at the Royal Academy Exhibition of Portuguese Art, and comes from the Museum at Lisbon. In this the interest centres on the huge black galleon or carrack of the Portuguese, with high, castle-like poop and stern. Trading is in progress on deck, and the factor or chief merchant sits importantly with an umbrella held over him, smoking a cheroot, with men carrying down bales or boxes into the hold. But the painter has been fascinated by the rigging which has mariners aloft and crawling along the ropes, ten of them in all, in the best winter circus at Olympia tradition. A screen in the Imperial collection shows a chapel of the Christians, but built in Buddhist style, with a tremendously breeched or trousered 'Portingale' standing in its porch, and groups of others, not less peculiar of aspect, for all have long thin moustachios and long noses, tottering as though drunk, or overcome and dizzy with affectation in the direction of the church door. But the pair of screens shown in London last summer at the Japanese Art Exhibition concentrate with more emphasis upon the priests or monks who are rendered emaciate, and even taller than in the canon of El Greco; while it is worthy of notice that in all these *Namban Byobû* screens that we have examined there is nowhere a fair person, and that all are male as though a female had never set foot in Japan. All are dark 'Diegos' from the banks of the Tagus.[1]

Already, in an account of the paintings at Chishahuin temple at Kyoto, it has been argued that Hasegawa Tôhaku is one of the great painters of Japan, perhaps in company with Sesshû and Sôtatsu. That is after having seen his *fusuma* there which are climax and epitome of all Japanese screen painting. In an entirely different vein are his ink-paintings which put him in the same rank as Sesshû. In particular, the

[1] There is a single screen of 'Southern Barbarians' in the Musée Guimet at Paris, and a pair of screens at Boston. The screen from Schloss Berchtesgaden is illustrated in *Japanese Screen Painting*, in the Faber Gallery of Oriental Art, by Basil Gray, London, 1956.

pair of folding screens from Tokyo which have for subject pine trees in a mist. Seldom can there have been a more evanescent touch in painting, four of the twelve panels of which it is composed having nothing upon them but the morning or evening mist. A Chinese technique in painting, but Japanese in the result, and only possible from the hand of an artist who had enjoyed the aesthetic experience of living in Kyoto.

Two *Monkey Screens* by him, coming delightfully from different temples in that city, for to Western eyes nurtured on Italy and Spain it is pleasingly incongruous to find monkey paintings in a monastery, have, too, that lightness of touch. On the left-hand screen of one of the pairs there is nothing but a bamboo glade, but rendered in the know-ledge that in China whole generations of 'literary' painters had devoted themselves to painting nothing but bamboos, and as if to hint that bamboos grew in Japan as well as China.

With Ogata Kôrin (1658-1743) the other famous name in Japanese painting beside Sesshû and Sôtatsu and the lately resuscitated Tôhaku, there is the disappointment of wanting to admire him, for he had unique qualities as a decorative artist, and not altogether succeeding. He belongs certainly to the school of Kôetsu and Sôtatsu as, it could be said, that in Venetian painting Tiepolo follows on Veronese. Neither was living within the lifetime of the other, but Kôrin could no more have painted as he did without the example of Sôtatsu, than could Tiepolo have done without Veronese. Kôrin, moreover, had some sort of relationship with Kôetsu. He may have been his great-nephew which would mean that, likeness of temperament apart, he was close to his tradition. But, in spite of the attraction of the idea that he is one of the greatest of Japanese painters, it is not easy to find anything from his hand that will pass the solemn test. His *Great Wave Screen* at Boston is perhaps the one exception, but it is only his version of Sôtatsu's theme (in the Freer Gallery at Washington), both paintings being in the USA by the happy chance of Fenollosa's choosing. His pair of *Iris Screens* in the Museum at Tokyo, I find, personally, to be ugly and distasteful, the more regretfully because it is pleasant to think of them as having come from Nishi Honganji temple at Kyoto—the monastery with the pair of *Noh* stages and the 'Valley of the Tiger' Garden. It is not enough to paint clumps of irises in two tones of blue, and their leaves, upon a gold background. I cannot think of these *Iris Screens* as other than ugly. His painting of *The Thirty-Six Poets* (there are really about forty of them, including two women poets to be known by the long hair down their backs) which I so much admired when I 'discovered' Kôrin for myself at twenty years old, is, I am informed, now thought to be a copy, but I still consider this the best of Kôrin's paintings. An unexpectedly good portrait by him has lately come to light (and is illustrated by Professor Yashiro. It is of a rich banker who was Kôrin's patron). But the other famous pair of screens by Kôrin (in the Atami Museum at Shizuoka, on the Inland Sea between Yokohama and Nagoya), I think is decorative in a tiresome manner. It is of red and white blossoming plum trees above a perfectly impossible stream, irritatingly meandering. There are screens by him of red and white hollyhocks, with a peacock with spread tail and peahen on the companion screen; panels of almost comic noblemen admiring irises; and fans with plank bridges over march irises (*Sibirica*), or with comic characters running around and shouting.

Then there are jokes drawn by him in a few seconds with a sweep of the brush; and perhaps the weakest of all his contributions are the one or two *kimonos* that he painted with flowers, which look feeble indeed beside the gorgeous fabrics of the *Genroku* period. But Kôrin was as well a lacquerer, and probably the most worthy object left by his hands is the ink-stone box in the Museum at Tokyo, companion to Kôetsu's ink-stone box, and to be preferred to that for perfection of form and ingenuity of design. Such pieces, we must remember, are the culmination of five or six centuries of 'aesthetic' living and in a sense more deserving of that phrase than any other civilization of which we have knowledge. It is only necessary to instance a lacquer cosmetic box of the Heian period with the absorbingly curious and far-fetched design of wheels floating in a river, and 'probably suggested by the practice of putting wheels in a stream of water to prevent them from drying out', and to read that it is the oldest 'make up' box known in Japan and was intended for sticks of incense, 'dishes of rouge, and boxes of tooth-black'.[1] Powder used for blackening the teeth of the Heian court ladies tells us we are on the other shore of the world from our own; and as though to prove it, the previous illustration in the book referred to in our footnote is of a lacquer chest of Heian period carrying a design of plovers in a marsh. In thinking of these objects of a hyper-aesthetic sensitivity we have to remind ourselves over and over again of what our own ancestors were doing at the time.

[1] *Textiles and Lacquer*, Charles E. Tuttle & Co, Vermont, USA, 1958; the Heian box is illustrated in colour on plate 29, and the box by Kôrin on plate 50.

The lacquer ink-stone box by Kôrin is in a sense as much removed from the realities of its component materials as the most far-fetched dishes on a French menu. *Délices de Sole à la Walewska*, for instance, or even *Poulet Marengo*, convey mental images and create illusions that have nothing whatever to do with either sole or chicken. Kôetsu's ink-stone box, described a little way back, was the synthesis of a famous pontoon bridge with the boats moored underneath it, and the poem written across inlaid in characters of silver in the master's calligraphic hand. Kôrin's ink-stone box, and this cannot be by mere coincidence, is also 'about' a bridge, the eightfold bridge of Yatsuhashi, so called for that reason, which comes in the *Ise Monogatari* or *Tales of Ise*. So his bridge goes up the side of his box, straddles across it, and comes down the other side; its planks inlaid in lead, and the whole of the box itself being an iris garden with the flowers in mother-of-pearl, and the leaves and stalks in golden lacquer. As a piece of poetic invention and illusion it is extraordinarily successful; but other lacquer boxes by him, to be known only from illustrations, have all the irritating hall-marks of his talent. There is, of course, a box with a design of plum blossom, and others with quasi-comical figures in Yamato style, but betraying no deep study or copying of the early scrolls. Kôrin painted a few dishes by his brother Kenzan, of whom more later, but they are quick and rapid as though patented as 'Kôrin specials'. He had an adept and pupil in a later generation (as our William Kent to Inigo Jones) in the person of Kôitsu (1760-1828), an 'amateur', for he was the second son of the *daimyô* of Himeji Castle, called the 'Egret' from its white-plastered walls, and with its five storeys and innumerable turrets the largest and most complete castle now standing in Japan. Hôitsu had, of course, to paint an Iris Screen in emulation of his master; and his best painting is of *Summer and Autumn Grasses*, on a silver ground, which is on the back of Kôrin's *Wind God and Thunder God*, themselves copied from famous, but not pre-eminent, screens by Sôtatsu which are preserved in Kenninji temple in Kyoto.[1]

Maruyama Okyo (1733-1795), another famous name in Japanese painting, though quintessentially of his race, seems to fail as a painter just through lack of the finest qualities of the Japanese. His vaunted

[1] Kôrin's double screen of the Wind God and Thunder God, with Hôitsu's paintings on their backs, was shown in London at the Japanese Art Exhibition in 1958. Hôitsu published in 1810 the *Kôrin Hyakuzu*, a book with a hundred coloured woodcuts after Kôrin's paintings and designs, but I have not seen this.

realism is that of the worst designs in the *kimono* store, and he shows no reserve or reticence, his fault being precisely what is said to be his particular quality, that 'he knew how to depict objects as they really looked'. His best known work, the double screen of *Pine Trees in Snow*, has the sort of stereophonic realism coupled with the Japanese urge towards decorative effect that defeats its own ends by being as unreal as a colour slide. There are numerous paintings by Okyo in the Konchi-in and Kongôji temples at Kyoto, but his most satisfying works, artistically, are his coloured drawings of flowers and birds and animals, from nature, in various albums.

But there was to be one more school of good painters in Japan, the Nanga or Bunjin-ga, poet-painters or literati, following the precepts, or indeed, the lack of those, that had prevailed many years before in Southern China. Ike-no Taiga (1723-1776) is the most famous of this school, a most original and dauntless experimenter, albeit on a small scale, who painted just exactly as he felt without caring for tradition or convention. His imaginary ink landscapes of China are curious, indeed, and built up with little touches and recessions reminiscent of unfinished Cézannes, or even of Picasso's Spanish landscapes when he had begun to paint in cubes. Gyokudô, a still later painter, was even more in revolt against convention and intent on leading the Bohemian life. He gave up his career of *samurai* when forty-nine years old, and without any training began to paint, wandering up and down the country and leaving behind him a reputation for playing the *koto* and enjoying convivial company. His mountain landscapes show great diversity of style and mood and he gives the impression of having set out to enjoy himself in the half-conscious knowledge that the days of the old Japan were numbered and that the wonderful spectacle of its life was coming to an end. And a last painter of the school was Mokubei (1767-1833), also, in approved fashion, poet, calligrapher, and famous potter. Or is it only that Uji was his favourite subject? For when I saw Uji I thought it must be the most beautiful village in the world, with that opiate view along the river, the 'Chinese' tilt of Byôdôin and other 'dragon' roofs of temples among the trees, and magical booths selling all the different tastes and colours of green tea. Mokubei was evidently of this opinion, too, for he was continually painting its landscape with the bridge over the river and the water curling away into the hills of Bohea.

Chapter Ten

THE MASTERS OF UKIYÔ-E

WE COME NOW TO THE school of Ukiyô-e, beloved of Europeans and
despised by the Japanese, and open not with the woodcuts but with the
marvellous *Matsuura Byobû*,[1] than which there could be no more apt
introduction to the popular art of Japan. It is a pair of screens coming
originally from the Matsuura family who lived in the southern island
of Kyushu. There are the usual twelve panels, and eighteen women are
painted upon them, by an unknown artist who must have had a particular, or even a professional interest in costume and textiles. The
date is the first half of the seventeenth century. It is possible that this
exceptional masterpiece is a freak work by a designer of textiles so
strong is the emphasis upon the patterns of the dresses. They are
indeed no less than marvellous. No popular scene in mediaeval Venice
or Florence, no groups of persons painted by Carpaccio or by Benozzo
Gozzoli could better this, and for gorgeousness of costume upon this
scale of variety we have to think of tenth-century Byzantium, or of
Isfahan, or Samarcand. The point arises as to whether the singularity of
the painting does not make it probable that it was painted locally in
Kyushu, in either Fukuoka or Nagasaki, the two big towns of the
southern island. Starting from right to left, there is a woman in a
kimono of light blue, wonderfully patterned with fans and flowers and
ho-ho birds (phoenixes), holding a long Japanese tobacco pipe, the
bowl of which a young girl is holding in order to fill it from a heap of
tobacco on a paper beside her where she sits upon the floor. Impossible
to describe all eighteen figures, but there is a woman wearing a green-
flowered *obi* over a dress of pink and brown; and some way along the
first screen another, sitting, playing cards,[2] her long hair trailing to her
shoulders, and her dress covered in gyroscopic whorls or circles in

---

[1] It is illustrated in no fewer than four colour plates in *Two Thousand Years of Japanese Art*, by
Yukio Yashiro, edited by Peter C. Swann, Thames & Hudson, London, 1958, plates 135-138.
The *Matsuura Byobû* are in the Yamato Bunkakan Museum in Nara.

[2] According to Professor Yashiro, *op. cit.* page 220, she, and another woman, are playing a
card-game called 'Un-sun Karuta', a Japanese rendering of the Portuguese 'um sum carta'. This
fact, too, suggests Nagasaki as the place of origin for this painting.

A *Maiko* from Kyoto

many colours on a white ground. Upon the companion screen, the figures begin with a woman in a light blue-barred over-*kimono* having her hair done by a maid, continuing to a woman playing a three-stringed lute, to end with a dazzling quartet of women, all with long hair down to their shoulders—it is perhaps their fashion of hair more than anything else that gives so early a date to this painting—and wearing a diversity of patterned dresses that can only have come from a professional designer's mind. In some curious manner, although it may be the work of a hand unused to screen-painting, this is a most impressive picture. Another, and even better known screen, long attributed to Matabei, with the figure of a young *samurai* in sinuous and affected pose leaning on his sword hilt, is of inferior order beside the *Matsuura Byobû* which is a prophecy of the *Ukiyô-e* on a single pair of screens. The renown of Matabei as the earliest painter of the popular school is difficult to sustain in the absence of genuine paintings by him, and credit must go instead to the forgotten painter of this transcendental frieze of women.

It is probably only after having had the opportunity of seeing Japan with one's own eyes that some points concerning the *Ukiyô-e* and the art of Japanese woodcuts occur to mind. They are the truth to life of the woodcuts, and the reason why they annoy and irritate learned opinion in Japan. As to this latter point of view, which concerns the 'discovery' of Japanese woodcuts by Western painters and collectors in the middle of last century, it is very much as though 'serious' music lovers from Europe neglected concerts conducted by Toscanini and performances at the Metropolitan Opera House in New York and went, instead, to night haunts, there, and in Chicago and New Orleans, in order to study 'local music' on the spot. We hope to prove that there are even greater resemblances of fact in this suggested parallel. While, as to the first point raised, it is only necessary to sleep in a Japanese inn, or dine in a Japanese restaurant, in order to see the accuracy of fact in the woodcuts, and this in spite of the factual improbability which is their outstanding charm to Western eyes.

Names of the masters of *Ukiyô-e* which were once familiar to every art lover in Europe are unknown to the younger generation, most of whom cannot distinguish between Hokusai and Hiroshige, and have heard neither of Utamaro, nor Sharaku. This is because of a change in taste, and increasing appreciation of the earlier arts of the Far East.

o

Ambitions fixed on seeing the temples of Angkor are not to be satisfied with the popular woodcuts of little more than a century ago. But if they are viewed from a new angle and as a popular art of curious and unlikely affinities, with a possible parallel in another medium altogether that this is flourishing in our own time, they may be looked upon with new interest. Here, then, are notes on the seven masters of *Ukiyô-e*, in this order: Harunobu, Kiyonaga, Toyokuni, Utamaro, Sharaku, Hokusai, and Hiroshige, with some remarks on their best known woodcuts.

It was Harunobu (1725?-1770), it seems, who first perfected the system of printing in colours from woodblocks. His is an exceedingly graceful and pretty art, free from grimacing or dramatic implications, and fond of young mothers playing with their children, and so forth. His women are small and slight, and full of curves. Presently he showed interest in a famous beauty, Osen, a young girl who served at a tea-house attached to a shrine in Yedo (Tokyo), and many of his prints are idealized portraits of her, though it would be idle to pretend they can have been close likenesses. Entire identity to the person portrayed was probably not achieved until the ferocious skits of Sharaku, for some word must be used for describing them that is stronger than caricature. The makers of effigies upon tombs in mediaeval England were ordered to make a reclining figure of a king, a knight armed *cap-à-pie*, or a lady in caul or wimple, and such mere adaptations towards the truth, beautiful as they may have been in themselves, had to do duty until at last, perhaps about the reign of Edward III, true portraits were produced. In the same way the beauties of Harunobu were probably more easily recognized as being by Harunobu because of his known mannerisms than from any instantly recognizable likeness to their original. A beautiful and typical print by him shows a young woman, obviously a courtesan and inmate of the Yoshiwara, standing on a wooden balcony while on the paper panes of the sliding partition behind her can be seen the shadows of two persons pledging each other in *sake* cups, and of a woman playing a long-necked *samisen*. I have seen with my own eyes just such shadows in silhouette in the beautiful restaurants upon the river at Kyoto, or staying in the inn at Miyajima when the serving maids left us at night moving along the verandah the other side of the partition, or came in to wake us in the early morning. The device of *gauffrage* begins to make its appearance in Harunobu's prints, a system of stamping bits of the paper in order to leave portions of it in relief, such as the curves of waves, or the patterns or folds of the *kimonos*, and an effect obtained according to tradition by pressing the incised woodblock on the paper with the elbow. It is indeed a beautiful device. Another of Harunobu's more poetic inventions was the drawing of his women's figures under a green mosquito net, or behind a curtain of matting, an idea which had much appeal to Utamaro who produced several most beautiful prints in this convention.

Torii Kiyonaga, in the succeeding generation, is a stronger artist altogether, and in him the full potentialities of the print become apparent. His range is wider for he is a theatrical draughtsman, becoming by adoption a member of the Torii family, who were (and are still) a dynasty of painters specializing in posters and playbills for the *Kabuki* actors. This gives him a very particular and special character, and his prints are of the most complete technical assurance in the sense that his interpretation at the hands of woodblock engraver and printer are perfect. Two great areas of expression lay open to him, the *Kabuki* theatre and the 'gay' life, so often predominantly sad, of the *geishas* and courtesans. And to these there are, in supplement, his *shunga* or prints on erotic subjects, of which with Utamaro he was an exponent of exceptional talents. It would be true to say that no one can form an estimate of either artist who is ignorant of the 'secret' or 'hidden' phases of their work. In the more orthodox and accessible body of his work Kiyonaga shows an attention to the details of women's dress only to be matched in the French handcoloured fashion plates of the mid-nineteenth century—fashion plates from *Le Moniteur de la Mode*, or *Les Modes Parisiennes*, signed by Jules David, Anais Toudouze, or Compte Calix—and it is to be remembered that with astringent judgment learned opinion in Japan would be inclined to rate them at about that level.

And with this verdict at the back of our minds we look at a diptych (two-leaved print) of five women of the Yoshiwara, relieved by the early hour from male attentions, and looking out upon the snowy morning. Two of them step down bravely from the wooden verandah; one to pick some snow-covered plum blossoms of which we can feel the cold in our fingers, the other holding a long pipe in her hand to play with the icicles hanging from the eaves. Another of the women stands watching them, keeping her hands in her long sleeves for warmth; while the other two sit on the floor, in the cold coming in from outside, holding, each, one hand under the tablecloth which as in Spanish households has a *brasero* below the table to warm it. But the effect of this is to heighten our opinion of Jules David and Compte Calix, and lower our estimate of Kiyonaga. We wonder if, in another world, fashion plates by the two Frenchmen would be changing hands for hundreds of pounds.

A woodcut of another quintet of ladies—but they could equally well be the same persons—airing themselves under the wistaria trellis (which is still famous) of a shrine in Tokyo, now becomes under our scrutiny only a fashion plate, and nothing more. We only note how beautiful are the flowing lines of the *kimonos* and the gay patterns of their *obis*. Also, and this is prophetic, we note that in many of Kiyonaga's woodcuts it is raining. Before one goes in person to Japan one is apt to think it is sunshades they are so often holding over their heads in Japanese prints. But they are not parasols, as one soon learns. They are umbrellas of oiled paper. One of the finest of Kiyonaga's 'rainy subjects' is the *Sudden Shower* (at a shrine near the Sumida river), where, in improvement from a mere fashion plate, two girls are running along on their *getas* holding up their *kimonos* out of the splashing rain; in the left-hand panel a maidservant holds an umbrella over her head and two spare umbrellas under her arm, and the name of the hotel she works at is printed on her umbrella; while, on the centre leaf, four persons have run for shelter under the main gate of the shrine, two men and two women, all alike in green, and they are wringing out their wet clothes, shaking the rain out of their hats, and mopping their shoulders and wet foreheads. It is a convincing if depressing picture of a sudden shower.

Kiyonaga's interiors give a very close and accurate idea of Japanese life, even as the foreigner may see the relics of that in the meals and paper-walled rooms at his inn. I am thinking of the diptych of scenes at a pleasure house at Shinagawa, a sea-resort which used to be first staging-stage from Tokyo along the Tôkaidô highway to Kyoto. The interior is still exactly that of inns or restaurants at Ise and at Nagoya—which latter must have been a marvellous old city before it was largely 'blitzed'. In this print a maid or *neisan* walks along beside the paper walls; while another, larger and nearer, throws her shadow upon the paper-thin partition. And ranged upon the floor, right out on to the verandah which looks over the sea, are all the little trays and dishes of a Japanese meal, with a gentleman and four *geishas* or the less respectable *bijin* grouped around him. Again, the patterns of the dresses are most clearly worked as though this was the painter's chief interest in his picture, and he had promised some owner of a *kimono* store to draw all his new models and never put any two of his women into remotely the same clothes. But Kiyonaga's theatrical prints are a little tame compared with what was to come after him. There are numerous portraits of *Kabuki* actors; and in the scenes from plays it is noticeable how in a moment one can identify the *onnagata* actors and know they are men playing women's rôles. Some inner sense tells one there is something peculiar about them, and by mysterious means this message is conveyed to us by the artist's pencil.

In Toyokuni the very qualities begin to be carried to excess. His actors sometimes are hardly to be known as human beings. They have begun to grimace ferociously and curl their lips. Their hair, or, rather, their wigs are like a poodle's hair, only stiffer than that; each side of the face their hair is more like a brush made of coco-nut matting, with a waist or handle in the middle of it to hold it by. But there are all types and kinds of hair for actors; ferocious, like a mop of fur over the forehead; 'mickey-mouse' fur; close-shaved by the ears as though pressed out of a tin or mould; wind-blown like a horse's tail, or even a couple of horse tails, hung on each side of the face, near the ears. Actor's hair becomes a dramatic property; and there is the red paint on their faces as well; zigzag furrows like lightning down the forehead; Red Indian war-paint turned clown and pantaloon; underlined nostrils to make the noses fierce and aquiline; daemonic, blood-dabbled chins, with one face frowning and leering only an inch or two from another, but above it as though by mere force of ferocity to bear it down; and often, as if by the torchlight of the theatre, a pale blue line for chin and jaw.

It is obvious that Toyokuni would have made the greatest poster artist there has ever been. In fact, he is that already, for in his woodcuts there is the ferocious comicality of 'all-in' wrestling contests combined with all that there was of violence and melodrama in the early films. One *Kabuki* actor has lifted his opponent off his feet, and is about to hurl the older man in a towering passion off his back and on to the boards. One can almost hear the banging and stamping of their bare feet. His *onnagata* have all their false femininity in their sloe-black eyes and a single line of nose and chin. But his young girls have gentle, youthful faces and sleek and lovely heads of hair. His larger prints show of what he was capable, shouting and violence, and leering and frowning, apart. There is the famous woodcut of a 'gallant', all in black, holding his tobacco pipe in one hand and looking in at a window where one girl sits and talks to him, and another in the middle of the room is shown having her bath. Two more girls sit waiting, and there are clothes hung up on lines to dry. Or there is the larger and fuller composition with thirteen figures in it, which shows a party in progress on a balcony hung with paper lanterns looking on to the sea. There is only one man in the picture, and all the women are serving or waiting on him, or playing *samisens*, or carrying in a tray of pebbles that have irises growing in them. A *thai* fish (bream) lies on a dish with chopsticks beside it, and we hope it is not still alive. We notice that for once about seven of the *geishas* are wearing the same pattern of *kimono*, more or less, which must be a sort of uniform to distinguish this particular tea-house.

A last and final print by Toyokuni shows a whole group of *geishas*—or are there *bijin* among them?—embarking for a night river party? But are they embarking? Or have they just arrived? Because there is really no more room in the boat beside the two men who are sitting there already, and the boatman with his long pole. A maid or attendant carries two of the long, black lacquered cases, coffin-shaped, but light in weight, with crests painted upon them. But what do they contain? They could be music-cases for holding *samisens*. So now, with a pair of *neisans* holding lanterns to light them ashore, and the pair of men in the boat never making a move, we conceive of them as coming back from the water party to drop the *geishas* who have been entertaining them. And we see more women looking out through barred windows under the light of paper lanterns, and think our version of the story must be true.

With Utamaro (1753-1806) the tastes of the Orient and Occident more nearly coincide for Japanese opinion is willing to admit that he was a considerable artist. In the day of Fenollosa and de Goncourt both Kiyonaga and Utamaro were freely mentioned in the same breath as Raphael and Botticelli, and their drawing was compared to Tanagra figures and to Greek sculpture of the age of Pericles. Such are the enthusiasms of first discovery, whereas it is indisputable that Utamaro has some of the *fin de siècle* qualities of a painter like Toulouse-Lautrec, another noctambulist and frequenter of night haunts. This is more particularly in respect of Utamaro's *Annals of the Green Houses*. But he had preluded in a vein of delicacy beyond the attainment of most Occidental draughtsmen in his *Insect Book* of 1788, an evocation of a grasshopper or cricket's music, and of the wonder of some little six-legged creature crawling on a pumpkin, near to the pumpkin flower. His *Shell Book, Treasures of the Ebb Tide*, opens with a frontispiece of women gathering sea-shells on a sandy shore, and continues with exquisite drawings of the individual shells. My own copy of *Annals of the Green Houses*, in order to indicate to the reader some of the niceties of printing in Japanese woodcut books, has its blue paper covers printed with a design of checker boards in *gauffrage* taken from the lanterns used in the Yoshiwara processions, while the border of the index represents the main gate of the Yoshiwara. Utamaro, we remind ourselves, lived and worked in the house of his publisher which was just opposite this main entrance. Alas! that it is impossible for reasons of space to accompany him on his tour, as we can do turning the pages of his book. There is only time to notice the garish colours, as though the art of colour printing was already in decline, the elaborate hairdos and unbelievable variety in the patterned dresses. Parenthetically, it is the *kimonos* and the men's clothes in tones of blue and mauve and violet that make the beauty of the book.

It is possible while not overmuch admiring Utamaro to come across something by him of transcendental quality. Such is the print of a girl with a *sake* kettle on her lap seated on the steps of a house—or it is sometimes called *Women of the Nakata House*—the point of it being the silhouette or shadow of another girl behind her on the far side of the paper wall, with towering, huge head-dress, delicate neck and youthful line of face. There is a curious and haunting immediacy about this woodcut. It is as though a moment in time has been made permanent. The slightest movement of either head or neck would break the spell. It has been said too often that Utamaro's women are exaggerated in height. They are certainly tall compared to the average Japanese, but the distortion of stature is as nothing to that shown in paintings and drawings of Primaticcio and the School of Fontainebleau, or the Florentine Mannerists whom Fuseli took for models. But it is true that Utamaro affected and made great use of the technical *tour de force*, which must have taxed every effort of his printers and engravers. His funambu-list wanderings in the precincts of the Green Mansions inspired him to such themes as the triptych of girls, alternately, at one side or other of a green mosquito net, three of them within, and three outside it. The netting is shaped like a green tent; the three girls outside it are, it is true, taller than nature, and as elaborately dressed as ever, while the girls inside are already settling themselves on their mattresses and preparing to sleep. Or there is the single print of a girl crouching to read a love letter by lantern light under a green netting. Another, and curious background said to be derived from stamped Cordovan leather, is behind—and only an inch or two behind—the head of a girl who holds a singing cricket in an 'insect-box'. But his large single heads of girls become monotonous even when they have a bright yellow (originally) or a mica background, and there are too many of them.

Utamaro's most delicate powers are to be appreciated in the *Insect* and *Shell Books* which have only been seen by a mere handful of persons, while the notorious *Pillow Book* which effectually no one has seen at all owing to its extreme rarity, contains the most extraordinary pictorial compositions ever put between the covers of a book. As well, many of the finest woodcuts after Utamaro only exist in one or two copies in museums and private collections all over the world, so that he is an artist of whom it is extremely difficult to form a true estimate. The famous triptych of *Women Diving*, probably his best known work, is by no means among his masterpieces. A magnificent specimen of Utamaro in his full powers is his six-panel woodcut of Ryôgoku bridge at Tokyo, of the greatest and most glittering sartorial splendour for the dresses are of unbelievable elaboration. There is 'double action' in the print, from persons crossing the bridge, or passing in the boats below. And in fact the drama of the crowd of girls upon the bridge is nothing but their dresses, interrupted this time, not by green mosquito netting but by the wooden rail of the bridge which twice breaks the patterns and must have given headaches to both block-engraver and printer. The boats below have the prows, as of ebony and ivory, that are a delight in so many Japanese woodcuts. There are boatfuls of *geishas*, just as you may see them now at Arashiyama, or Gifu, and as they surely appear upon the river at Uji. One boat has a wooden roof over it, and at least five girls inside it; while another of the boats has an elegant oarsman in a male *kimono* of most ethereal and airy pattern,

looking down in admiration at his boatload of two girls sitting together under an umbrella. What a lovely spring afternoon that must
have been upon the Sumida river! And how interesting for ourselves
to think we had in our own lives spent an evening in an eating-house on
that same river, and watched the dancing, and had sitting beside us, a
little being, certainly not less pretty and graceful than any in Utamaro's
woodcuts! At the exhibition in Paris a year or two ago where I caught a
glimpse of the *Pillow Book*—the copy which had belonged to de
Goncourt and later to Toulouse-Lautrec—for it was of course hidden
away in a glass vitrine and not exposed to view, there was also an
original painting by Utamaro of a crowd scene under blossoming
cherries or plums, every bit as rich in colour and in composition as his
scene on the Ryôgoku bridge on the Sumida river.

Utamaro did not show any particular interest in the *Kabuki* theatre
but, already, in his time the stage was set for fireworks. They appeared
in the person of Sharaku, one of the most phenomenal geniuses in the
history of art. The theatrical print had by now developed on sensational
lines, and into most of its dramatic possibilities, at the hands of Kiyonaga
and Toyokuni. But there were other considerable draughtsmen who
devoted their talents to making prints of actors—among them Shunshô,
who belonged to the Katsukawa family of theatrical artists, rivals of the
Torii clan for bill-boards, posters, and so forth—and Shunshô's pupil
Shunyei who made many prints of Sumô wrestlers. There was, as well,
and most confusingly, Bunchô, who was famous for his actor-prints,
and although none of these develop quite enough personality to become
generally known to any but Japanese woodcut addicts, it is certainly true
that sometimes they excelled themselves, and produced an actor-print
to make one wonder at their unknown names. Bunchô, the last named,
in his portraits of the *onnagata* actors, conveys more than any other
draughtsman something of what the Japanese, themselves, find
admirable in the female impersonators in *Kabuki*. We see their grace,
and do not hear their pleading, whining voices.

It was the print-publisher Jûsaburô, in whose house Utamaro lived
and worked near to the Yoshiwara, who launched Sharaku. Nothing
whatever is known about him; neither his correct name, nor the exact
dates of his birth or death. On internal evidence, he was a *Noh* actor in
the suite of a *daimyô* but his patron's identity is in dispute too. All that is
known for certain is that he produced some hundred and forty portraits

of *Kabuki* actors in the ten months between May 1794 and February 1759; debuting, if that is the word for so violent an onslaught, with twenty-eight actor-portraits in that month of May only, and reaching his full flight of creation in sixty portraits from performances of November, with a few portraits of Sumô wrestlers for good measure. Then his work tailed off, becoming less inspired as he met with no success, stopping altogether after January. From that time onward no more is heard of him. He disappears entirely. Except, that is to say, that he is variously reported as 'dying in 1801'; or 'known to have been still alive in the period of Bunsei' (1819-29); or even dying as late as 1844. But his true name was probably Saito Jurobei, he was certainly a *Noh* actor, and he also seems to have been alive in 1825. He remains a mystery, and one may presume in order to satisfy one's own curiosity that he probably died young in 1801. That, at least, makes it easier to explain why no more is heard of him.

Jûsaburô, the print-publisher, must have been a person of rare discernment as may be inferred from his support of Utamaro. But he gave Sharaku his opportunity and then dropped him. No doubt the prints had a poor sale. But how much they breathe of the *Kabuki* theatre! They had the advantage of being presented with the entire technical perfection, woodblocks cut by the finest engravers, and all the resources of printing and fine paper. We may think it more than probable that the craftsmen complained at the work they were asked to do; that they felt their skill was thrown away. So, in our own day, many orchestral players complain when confronted with a 'modern' score. But the draughtsman in these woodcuts did not have to supply a completely finished drawing. As with the French fashion plates of last century where the clouds, if the setting was in the open air, were put in by a roller, and the faces and hands left more or less to the engraver's discretion, so the draughtsman in the woodcuts need only draw in enough of the pattern of a dress and let the woodblock cutter do the rest. So, in fact, we are arriving at a situation when some of the credit must go to the engraver and the printer. Then a point is reached at which the craftsmen may be judged by something they have not enjoyed doing. This would seem to be just what happened in the case of Sharaku. They worked splendidly but could not have liked the work themselves. It was as a marvellous performance of music which they hated playing. This must be a familiar sensation at times in most concert halls. The technical skill of the craftsmen made it impossible for them to do their work badly. Surviving drawings by Sharaku are much less remarkable than the finished woodcuts. On the other hand his best drawings will have perished when they were cut to pieces on the key-block. So what really happened was that engraver and printer carried out his wishes even better than he had intended. And the finished woodcut with all the resources of the art lavished on it, ten or even more blocks to be cut, one for each colour, mica backgrounds, and hand-made papers, all added up, inevitably, into an improvement upon his original drawing.

It seems to me that the only true parallel to the Japanese woodcuts is with another popular art that is flourishing in our own time. However unlikely this may seem to be, American jazz or ragtime or whatever term will cover it in all its ramifications, does present several analogies with the situation that is under discussion. It has had its great talents amounting nearly to genius in their sort. Jerome Kern, George Gershwin, Irving Berlin, are names that occur at once to mind. But how many of them are responsible for the orchestration of their scores? A friend, now a famous composer, took Gershwin to a performance of *Tristan* at Covent Garden, and his enthusiastic reaction to Wagner's music, as they left the theatre, took the form of saying: 'And to think that man did all his own orchestration!' In the instance of Irving Berlin, probably the most remarkable of such talents for he is still composing and, in a sense, initiated the whole movement with his first tunes written some half-century ago, it is to be remarked that there could be no more original genius for it is said that he cannot write down his tunes. Professional orchestrators and arrangers of the highest talents are set to work, and the finished Irving Berlin or Gershwin is heard all over the world. They are, so to speak, the engravers who cut the wood-blocks; while the printers who were not the least important of the craftsmen concerned, and were responsible indeed for the final presenta-tion of the woodcut, are the famous band-leaders and dance orchestras that play the music. Through all these processes, and despite them, the individual style and personality of the composer persists and, in general, is instantly recognizable.

This is very near to the state of affairs in the Japanese woodcuts. Technical skill had progressed apace, and by the time such extremes in nuance as Utamaro's delicate *Shell Book*, or his, and Kiyonaga's, crowded diptychs and triptychs were being printed and sold, there were no effects of which engraver and printer—or we could say orchestrator and orchestral player—were not capable. But the personality persists, and the finished work is personal and not anonymous. Kiyonaga is to be known immediately from Utamaro, and Utamaro from Sharaku. With Sharaku it could be said that Jûsaburô, his publisher, gave him over the ten months the most expert presentation that was possible, but the attempt failed and no more is heard of him. If the personality is persistent right through from the sketch for the woodcut to the finished article, then that is a translation and an enhancement, but not an alteration of the original. Or, in simpler words, Sharaku cannot have been less interesting, in fact, than in the woodcuts made after him. He achieved likenesses that must have been within a hairline of the truth for in a single second one knows it is the same *onnagata* (man playing a female rôle) in two of the woodcuts. Something in the line of the jaw gives the silliness, and if that is not enough there are the silly little eyes and eyebrows. The mica grounds produce a lurid light, and make one wonder what was the degree of lighting in the *Kabuki* theatre. A portrait of another of the *onnagata* in the rôle of a courtesan, just in the little area of the eyes and eyebrows contrives to present an entirely different personality.

There are heads of actors with mouse-furred, 'Mickey-mouse', furred bat-ears, or, rather, ear-flaps round the ears, and top-knots, more set in convention than the 'make-up' of any circus clown, and all their expression in the curve of their mouths, for by now one has grown used to staring, or even squinting eyes. Mouths like the loop in a bootlace; or dragged down to one side; or lipless, just in one down-curving line. There are different colours of mica; dark and leaden, perhaps silvery, once; black, black; or light red. One of the prints with a leaden ground has the actor, yellow-skinned, with the white of his eyes showing and the pupils contracted and squinting in the corners, unshaven, with mauvish patches on his chin and upper lip and, menacingly, with one hand upon his sword. Another print, on a black mica background, showing a youthful *Kabuki* player in the act of drawing his sword, is remarkable for his deep black collar and brick-red coat, and for having no drawn lines in it for his arms and hand. Yet another, of an actor performing a dance, but only showing his head and the upper part of his body, is in pale colours and has a marked facial resemblance to

Deburau, the famous pierrot. Probably the best known of Sharaku's prints is that of two actors, the one fat and the other thin, both with elaborate hair curls as though still in curling pins, and with contrasting mouths; the thin one, aquiline, with looped bootlace lips, snarling into the other's ear, who listens, grimly and impassively. Both have curious, pale blue areas upon their shaven pates. The most uncompromising and extreme of all Sharaku's theatrical portraits is of an actor, surely playing the rôle of the villain, and all in ominous blacks on the leaden bed of mica, except for his green sword hilt, a part of his green sleeve and the blood-red of his under eyelid, but curling up like paint toward his eyebrows.

A print of Danjuro V, the greatest *Kabuki* actor of the time, conveys that his black-lacquered hair is very nearly that of the Elizabethan-descended clown of Grimaldi's day; tragically high-bridged nose; mouth like a pair of loops of red string; lines of face precisely matching the lines in the white, muffler-like undergarment he is wearing; and canary-yellow overcloak with nothing but some white squares on it for pattern, leaving it a yellow woodcut upon a bluish mica ground. The interest of the actor-prints is of course immeasurably increased if we only know the names of the actors and the action of the play. Their identity is now largely established, before which they were as much of a mystery as the figures upon Mayan bas-reliefs. We are to conceive of this strange genius as a *Noh* actor who would of nature despise the more sensational *Kabuki* dramas while admiring the enormous range of which they were capable. It is the simplicity of means by which he expresses that gamut of emotion that makes Sharaku so great an innovator and leaves his competitors in the actor-print so far behind him. What would it not be, were there portraits of a comparable greatness of the actors (and the *onnagata*) of the Elizabethan stage! Woodcuts of the first Hamlet, of Caliban, of Falstaff, Lady Macbeth, Portia, Will Hughes, of the Dark Lady of the Sonnets!

After Sharaku one may well pause for breath, thinking that in him the whole movement must have its end. There are innumerable, even countless minor masters until we reach Kunisada who died in 1864; masters as good as Yeishi, who is not far behind Utamaro in his beauties of the Green Mansions, and by whom when twenty years old I had a set of four beautiful woodcuts of tall, elongated women in patterned *kimonos*, all in shades of blue. Probably in their time in the enormous,

sprawling city of Yedo of a million people, these were no more thought
of than are coloured postcards. But another, and extraordinary talent of
all embracing character now makes his appearance, of talents so
omnivorous in their directions that, despite his low caste as artist, he is
generally accepted even in his own country. There is scarcely a branch
of his art that he did not attempt with success and, as well, he widened
its scope and made it an art of landscape and not only of figures. It is
certainly true that Hokusai in his person sums up the whole art of
Ukiyô-e, lifts it to new heights, and carries it still further. An instance,
it may be, of talents which become extraordinary and transcendental
only through hard work.

Hokusai, who was born in 1760, gives few if any signs of his genius
until 1798 or 1800 when he was forty years old. Words may be applied
to him which are in fact descriptive of Donizetti, one of the most fecund
of Italian composers who wrote some sixty-five operas. With trans-
position of names the passage reads: 'Hokusai is remarkable as an
instance of freshness of fancy, brought on by incessant manufacture.
. . . The "craft" belonging to incessant production has been too much
despised. It learns and grows, while creating. His instrumentation,
always correct, becomes richer and more fanciful with each successive
effort. The scholar can retire for a quarter of a century to elaborate
works for scholars to come, and has his just and high reward, accordingly. Those (on the other hand) who wish to speak less learnedly to the
public, can hardly present themselves to the public too often.'[1] These
strictures are entirely applicable to Hokusai, whose output begins with
portraits of *Kabuki* actors and of famous beauties of the Green Mansions
and enlarges into incessant production of book illustrations and of
surimonos—the latter being a form of woodcut, invitation card, New
Year card, wedding announcement, and so on, printed with particular
care, and often enriched with gold and silver and metallic colours, of
which Hokusai is undisputed master. A chronological list of books
illustrated by him (in the Phaidon *Hokusai*, by J. Hillier, 1955) gives no
fewer than 207 opus numbers, many of them in several volumes with
innumerable prints from his woodcuts. It was only after 1800, with all
but a half-century of full production ahead of him, for he died in 1849
and was working to the end, that he began to produce landscapes. It was

[1] Quoted from *Thirty Years' Musical Recollections*, by Henry F. Chorley, London, 1862, Volume
I, pages 154-156. The subsequent quotation comes from page 17-21 of the same volume, though
Chorley does not in fact mention Lablache's famous 'party turn' when he imitated a thunderstorm.

at about this time, too, that he painted a *Daruma* fifty feet high—as though to emulate the, now extinct, 'sand artists' of the Victorian seaside—and would, doubtless, on request, have painted a landscape with Mount Fuji, or a crowd scene, on a grain of rice. There is the well-worn story of his putting red paint on a cockerel's feet and composing drawings from its claw marks on the paper.[1] He is something of an illusionist and conjurer. This is the side of him predominant in the *Hokusai Manga*; books of his sketches that came out over an interval of years (and eventually in fifteen volumes). To some opinions these are the epitome and crux of all his work; drawings of wrestlers, contortionists, funny faces, long noses, blind leading the blind, and a thousand and one, even ten thousand and one, different themes. But there is an over-fecundity and over-cleverness in the *Manga* which in the end reduce Hokusai, himself, in scale and bring him down to the level of a Daniel Vierge or a Gustave Doré. He makes himself into the universal illustrator and Marathon or non-stop draughtsman.

It was only in 1825 that Hokusai began work on his *Thirty-Six Views of Fuji*. He was sixty-five years old and the set was not completed until he was over seventy. Decidedly, these amount to some kind of masterpiece but it is difficult to know to what category they belong. Again, when about seventy-five years old he published *A Hundred Views of Fuji* but these are in black and white; prospects of Mount Fuji seen through waves, through a bamboo grove, in pouring rain, above a group of storks, in between the paper umbrellas in an umbrella-maker's yard, indeed through or between everything except a keyhole; but in these he is the illustrator, a great illustrator, and nothing more. The *Thirty-Six Views* are another matter altogether for they include such masterpieces as *Fuji in clear weather*, *Fuji above the lightning*, and *Fuji seen in the hollow of the deep sea wave* or it is sometimes called *The breaking wave off Kanagawa*. But these three woodcuts which are the greatest in the series present curious problems because they are really caricatures or imitations of Mount Fuji. Perhaps they can explain what has always been a minor mystery in another sphere altogether, the contemporary accounts in memoirs of the great basso singer Lablache's imitation or impersonation of a thunderstorm; Lablache, 'who was one of the greatest musicians and artists ever seen or heard on the stage, or in the

[1] Hokusai first drew a blue curve on a paper screen, like a winding river, and when the cock had run over the paper turned it into a painting of red maple leaves floating down a stream in autumn. His big figure of Daruma could only be seen properly from the roof-tops.

orchestra, with a voice that could make itself heard above any orchestral thunders or in the midst of any chorus, however gigantic either might be.' Of French and Irish origin, though born in Naples, equally great as serious or comic actor, 'of perfect acquaintance with the great Roman style, but who would give way to the wildest Neapolitan *lazzi* when the artist chose to be comical', all adapted from Henry Chorley's words. But, however interesting and original the idea of it, no writer ever tells how Lablache's impersonation of a thunderstorm was done. It is left to our imagination to think it out for ourselves. So we look at *Fuji in clear weather* which consists of nothing more than the russet or reddish-brown cone of the mountain with a few white streaks of snow high upon it, a dense dotting of greenish hue for the 'ferny forest' on its lower slopes 'where spring flowers and wild strawberries are found in August', and the white and blue rillings of a mackerel sky. Yet this *is* Fuji with an importance that is omitted from a hundred or a thousand other pictures of it. *Fuji above the lightning* is even simpler, nothing but the volcano with the forest rising higher on it, but now at a distance it looks less like vegetation and more like the lava torrents that have flowed from the crater and are lying about upon the slopes in huge and inchoate blocks, and a vast flash and hieroglyph of lightning stabbing into the black storm upon its lower flanks. *The breaking wave off Kanagawa* with the long boats riding the great waves coming in from the Pacific and the far-away white cone of the volcano in the trough between the waves must owe something to Kôrin's screen of the *Great Waves at Matsushima* (in the Boston Museum), only Hokusai has made more of the huge blue curling of the wave under its foam crest and is less intent upon the claws of foam and cloud that resemble dragons' claws. If he never saw the screen we may wonder if it, or portions of it, are reproduced in Hôitsu's publication of *Kôrin Hyakuzu*, a hundred of Kôrin's paintings in colour, which came out in 1810. For this is a book that Hokusai is certain to have seen.

After the *Thirty-Six Views* comes something more masterly still which is his *Waterfalls*, a set of eight prints, with the title *Travelling around the waterfall country*. These astonishing imitations and impersonations of falling water date from somewhere around his seventy-fifth year. It is hard to choose between them, but the *Kirifuri Falls* (not the waterfall of the same name near the red lacquer bridge at Nikko) may be the most ingenious and telling of them all. It has a most forceful,

Byôdoin Palace (1053)

Daisen-in garden (1510)

Silver Pavilion or Ginkakuji Temple, Kyoto (*c.* 1840)

humped falling movement of the water pouring in and out through rocks. In others of the series, the water pours down like a sword blade and raises sparks of foam.[1] The companion series of *Famous Bridges*, the idea of which coming from the hand of Hokusai much stimulates the imagination, has an exciting picture of a rope suspension-bridge, but the series as a whole is disappointing. Having seen with my own eyes, as the objective of a long journey undertaken mainly for that purpose, the famous *Bridge of the Brocade Sash* or *Kintai-bashi* which is one of the most striking and beautiful sights of Japan, far down in the main island, south of Hiroshima, I would hazard the opinion that Hokusai never went there in person for he misses the whole point of it. He gives its arches as being all of the same height, and makes nothing of the picturesque village on both river banks.

Hokusai is one of those artists in all the arts whom it is better for one's own pleasure to know in part rather than in the whole. This, however disparate their stature or their proportion in regard to each other, is true more particularly of Bach and Mozart who should be left *in toto* to the scholars and pedants and enjoyed piecemeal by the public. Then, there is ever the chance of hearing something unknown and unexpected, and the more often because one has not enquired too closely. But in any case to hear all of the music of either composer is out of the question because of its quantity. There is a parallel case in the instance of Renoir, the most prolific of the Impressionists, and it is most decidedly true of Hokusai. There is always something new by him. He has the Gustave Doré side to him when one may grow impatient of his unwearying pencil. At that level he is of the sort to illustrate the telephone book or railway timetable. Then, without warning and for no reason, he turns into a great artist and, as with Albrecht Dürer in his prints or Goya in his etchings, becomes a national embodiment of the race to which he belongs. But, and this is typical of his stature and of his category, there is another region in his art in which he is neither the one thing nor the other, not the mere illustrator, nor the national figure, but something intermediate and in between. In this, as with the smaller works of Bach, *little preludes* and *fughettas*, and pieces from *Anna-Magdalena's Music Book*, or Mozart's chamber music with wind instruments, his *wind quintet* and *clarinet trio*, the greatest and most varied pleasure of all is to

[1] As in another woodcut of a waterfall in *The Imagery of the Poets of China and Japan*, where the water drops absolutely straight, but foamless, and down, down, as into an underworld. Reproduced in colour in the *Phaidon Hokusai*, plate xvi.

be had, and there is the sensation of being alone with a great artist who
is doing this and taking all this trouble for yourself alone. It is impossible
for the greatest artists, who are nearly always prolific in their works, to
be great all the time. They are bound to have their bad moments, but
also the times when they seem to be working for their own pleasure as in
the works just mentioned. With Hokusai there is an almost inordinate
amount of work of this particular quality in addition to the gold and
dross of his output. It is to be found in his illustrated books, if one is
lucky enough to come across them, and in his *surimonos*. To some
extent, also, in his *Bird* and *Flower* prints, two sets of them, the *Large*
and *Small*; the cuckoo and azaleas (this must be before the first azaleas
came to Europe); the bullfinch and the cherry bough; his poppies
blowing in the wind; or the irises at Houkiri, in the still existing iris
gardens; prints which were done in direct rivalry with the *Kwachô*
(bird and flower) prints of Hiroshige. A typical book by Hokusai which
is scarce enough for one never to come across it, but for the rare
chance that one or two of its illustrations have been reproduced,[1] is his
Views along the banks of the Sumida River, in three volumes; satirical
poems, with a scene on a bridge in a rain shower, and an even higher
arched wooden bridge across the water; or a boatload of passengers
crossing the river and a live scene on the bank opposite in this city of
a million souls a hundred and fifty years ago. As for the *surimonos* of
Hokusai, they are past counting, though only printed individually in
very small numbers, and raise the point as to how great can an artist be
on the strength of a multitude of little coloured woodcuts, no bigger,
and some of them smaller, than a postcard? How important can he be
in ratio of minuscule delicacy and lilliputian smallness? For in respect of
all those qualities Hokusai is without rival in his *surimonos*, though two
of his pupils, Hokkei and Gakutei, did beautiful work in the same
medium. There could be a special line in collecting only Hokusai's
surimonos of still lives. He had the power to make something vital and
memorable out of a lacquer bowl and a box of chopsticks. Or another.
It is only a scarlet mattress upon the floor, in *gauffrage*, some rolls of
paper, their tubed ends rendered in *gauffrage*, too, a pair of paper fans,

[1] In the volume on *Hokusai* in the *Kodansha Library of Japanese Art*, plates 11, 12, 13, 1955,
Charles E. Tuttle & Co, Rutland, Vermont, USA and Tokyo. In *Truffle Hunt*, Robert Hall Ltd,
London, 1953, pages 174-179, I have attempted a description of a book of thirty-six *surimonos* by
Hokusai, printed in colours, metal, and *gauffrage*, which I think I have identified as his *Genroku
Kasen Kai Choice Collection of Poems on Seashells*, 1822. It was bought at the sale of the Ricketts and
Shannon collection in London.

one of them with Mount Fuji in snowy white on the white paper, an ink-well, and some feather pens. Or yet another?

It is a different temperament altogether from that of Hiroshige (1797-1858) who was an artist of extreme aesthetic sensibilities, but neither pictorial acrobat, nor virtuoso. His economies of effect, in order to make the effect greater, are never the tricks of the conjurer or the illusionist. He was more purely the artist, and too much of that to interest himself in the grotesque, or come down to caricature. He suggests and does not imitate, eludes and never impersonates. It is easy enough to understand the excitement roused by his landscapes when they first came out of Japan to Europe. For it was something entirely unknown and new, though not of Hiroshige's invention for he did not create the landscape of Japan. That was there already, but the formula for rendering it came to his hand. He was the translator and not the inventor. Also, because he is less based upon the past than Hokusai, and betrays few signs of any study of his predecessors, he gets closer to his subject. There are no intermediate phases of cleverness and display. He has not to show how clever he can be. He was not, as Hokusai was always boasting of himself, an eccentric and monomaniac, 'mad about drawing'. Drawing was not an end in itself for him. He did not want to get at the truth of things, but only to suggest them. His desire in his woodcuts was more to leave things out than put them in. Their effect is eupeptic and does not lead to indigestion. There is no individual print by him that is in surfeit upon itself. It is true that there are too many woodcuts by Hiroshige, but their effect is to make one content with one at a time and not ask for more. If Hokusai portrays one face of the genius of Japan, this is the other and it is not less Japanese.

Probably the most famous woodcut after Hiroshige is the *Sudden Shower* from the *Hundred Views of Yedo*. It is the print of pouring rain with a few persons crossing a wooden bridge. Nothing but that, and the far bank and the river, and the lines of rain. It makes you feel wet to look at it, and having experienced two typhoons in Tokyo I know rain comes down like that. But in the woodcut the rain does not splash upon the bridge. It falls on the near side of it, between ourselves and the timber baulking, and in a torrent on the far side of the bridge into the river, and beyond upon the far bank. But not upon the bridge, itself, which is a pure instance of elimination. For it gives the effect of total wetness, while the people crossing the bridge on foot who should be wet through are, in fact, completely dry. Another woodcut from the *Eight Views of Lake Biwa* consists of what? A leafless tree or two on the lake bank, the expanse of water with the sails of fishing boats, a line of blue hills, a mountain in mist behind that, and more sails diminishing in height into the distance, with not even the hulls of the boats showing but only the squared oblongs of the sails dwindling over the horizon. Or another, from *Eight Views of the neighbourhood of Yedo;* a fishing net hanging up in the foreground, then an extent of marshland rendered just by criss-crossing lines in green on blue, a wooded island a little way away with a *torii* in front of it, geese flying, and the same sails, this time with not even an attempt at the body of the boats, just their sails and nothing more.

The two great sets of woodcuts by Hiroshige are the *Tôkaidô* and the *Kisokaidô,* these being the two principal of the roads radiating from Tokyo (Yedo) into the provinces of Japan. The first of them is the famous road starting, like the others, from the Nihombashi bridge over the Sumida river, in the middle of the town, and leading along the coast route to Kyoto. It was along this road that the *daimyôs* made their solemn progresses from the old capital to the new, there and back, once every year. The *Kisokaidô* was the inland route to Kyoto; and the two sets are known by the number of halts or staging-posts along them as *The Fifty-three Stages of the Tôkaidô* and the *Sixty-nine Stages of the Kisokaidô.* It is inevitable in such large sets of prints that Hiroshige should, himself, at times, faint and fall by the roadside. It is mist and rain effects that he excels in. Even a majority of the rest of the prints are too plain and simple, as though in the attempt to leave out everything unnecessary Hiroshige had left in only his mannerisms, and nothing else. It is his tragedy that an artist of his reticence and sensibility should have had to produce too much and work too hard. He was of another fibre from Hokusai who improved from that. But, as with Hokusai, there are many delights among his lesser things. For instance, his fan-prints, and among those, in particular, the *aizuri* which are printed entirely in blues. They include an almost absurdly typical theme, a procession of women of the *Yoshiwara* viewing the cherry-blossom, a cortège all carrying fans and walking, decorously, under umbrellas. But the colour harmonies are new and strange; one had never thought to see the white cherry-blossom against any other blue background but that of sky, and by transvestiment of image one wishes for a Hiroshige of white-clad women walking under blue jacaranda trees. There are beautiful things too, among his *Kwachô*, bird and flower prints; a long-tailed blue bird on the branch of a plum tree. But to what species does it belong, this bird with the head of a pheasant and a racket-tail? It is not a 'Mikado' pheasant from Formosa which I have kept, myself, in an aviary; nor is it a Swinhoe, a pheasant of which I have had experience, also. It seems to be a hybrid of both birds, though they were only known to ornithologists long after Hiroshige's death. There are, as well, delicate and lovely flower prints; such as some stems of pinks with snails upon them until one remembers to have seen much the same design, and thought it pretty, on a paper-napkin.

The forte with Hiroshige is with his snow scenes. But they are also his most popular works and could have been drawn, prophetically, as Christmas cards. One of them, *The Head of the Pass at Wada*, comes in the *Kisokaidô*. Nothing could be simpler. A snowy hill ahead of one, and a scooped out passage through the snow. There is really nothing else but that, and a few stunted fir trees. Another one, *A Mountain Stream in Snow* from the *Chinese and Japanese Poems*, has the blue stream winding through it with wads of floating snow like tufts of cotton-wool, a bridge over it which is only just snow, to remind one of the turf bridges in the Sambôin at Kyoto, a bare tree or two, contours of snow for the foreground, and two tall hills which are no more than shapes in the mist with four jagged fir trees growing up the side of one of them. There is another, tall oblong snow scene that much resembles this, with the blue stream, snowflecked, but with two boats upon it, coming straight down towards one and flowing out of the picture. There is a bridge, of course, but far away in the distance, and high hills of snow in front and to either hand. A snow scene from the *Fifty-three stages of the Tôkaidô* gives a steep hill leading up to a castle-like building with cyclopean walls, and touches of yellow that are the hats and saddle-cloths of a party or procession toiling up the road.

It is satisfying that there should be a view of the bridge of Nihombashi under snow, but the woodcut is almost too simple. Cubical houses like bathing-huts, a red winter sunset smeared along the top of the page, and some straight lines of pink in front of, and behind, the white triangle of Fuji, to suggest the evening cold. The crowd crossing the bridge is interesting but figures were never successful with Hiroshige. He lacked the humour and the human observation of Hokusai, beside which it did not amuse him to draw human beings in action. There is a triptych of snow along the *Kisokaidô*, but too 'Chinese' of effect, too unreal and fanciful, as though it was something imagined, and not seen. A grand triptych of snow on the Sumida river has snow everywhere, and the snow is falling fast. But there are three huge figures of women getting in or out of a boat, and they are entirely lacking in the grace of ten or twenty other Ukiyô-e masters. By this time other artists had begun to copy his snow scenes, and there are snowscapes by Kuniyoshi that could be mistaken for Hiroshige. Perhaps the best of all his snow scenes is the *Timber Yard at Fukagawa* from the *Hundred Views of Yedo*, which it is interesting to compare with the *Timber Yard* by Hokusai in his *Thirty-six views of Fuji*. Hokusai contrives his view of Fuji which has to come into every woodcut in the series in a corner above a bamboo fence, and for the rest, his woodmen are busy piling up, throwing down, catching, or sawing away. In the Hiroshige no one is in sight at all except two men standing on rafts hundreds of yards away. There are a couple of dogs in the foreground that more resemble small bears. And the rest of the woodcut is a few planks jutting out, the river that is bluer than ice, and snow, snow everywhere. He gets his effects with much less trouble than Hokusai, and leaves out and eliminates. Probably he is better when he omits human beings altogether. Yet we know that Hiroshige sought human company, and Hokusai avoided it. By the same token, we of the West admire Hokusai and Hiroshige, but in Japan they are mainly interested in order to know what we can see in them. What is an old bead or a corner of cracked mirror in one continent is as a pearl or diamond in another; but such are truths that are reciprocal, that have two meanings and that work both ways.

Chapter Eleven

• •

APPLIED ARTS

THE APPLIED ARTS OF JAPAN are a vast field to enter, over large areas of
which one is forewarned to bring a microscope, or at very least, a
magnifying-glass. I am meaning *inrôs* and *netsukes*, and rather inferring
than naming carved ivories and *cloisonné* and also, bronzes, regions
whence taste and sensibility are long since fled. *Netsukes* and *inrôs* are
another matter. Marvels of skill and patience have gone into the making
of them, but they are knick-knacks of a land which produced great
painters like Sesshû and Sôtatsu. They are for the collector who derives
pleasure from them, but not the writer. For him there are other and
wider fields of enjoyment and opportunity, in lacquer and pottery,
but, most of all, in textiles. Historic robes and *kimonos*—if one can
contrive to see them—are wonderfully beautiful and inspiring. Vigorous
and slashing in design, or in utmost delicacy and vividness, they are an
entire revelation and form one of the most beautiful and fertile bodies
of design that the world has ever known. The dragon-writhing, ugly
robes of the Manchu Emperors of China have obtruded themselves into
any view of Far Eastern textiles, and blinded one as to how beautiful
dress must have been under earlier Chinese Dynasties. But it is more
than possible that Japan always excelled over China in this respect, and
that they had an especial genius for textile design. Their imagery and
repertory of motifs is both more far-fetched and more clear cut, so that
in effect it is more practical and concise. They seem to have embarked
happily upon projects of design which one would never think could be
carried out in textiles.

Of some few of these we now attempt a description though it is easier
to see them between the pages of a book than on show in a glass vitrine.
There must be a considerable number of old robes belonging to temples
but they are seldom, if ever on view, and one of the only opportunities
of seeing old dresses of the highest quality is in the Fujiwara museum at
Nagoya where some eight *kimonos* of great beauty are on permanent
exhibition among the treasures of the Shogunal family. These apart,

231

they are easier studied in book illustrations than in actuality. If we browse among them for a few moments this is what we find. A *kimono* of a pattern that is mottled with large cloud areas which are red-violet in colour and outlined in white, but the clouds are as islands upon which a few red flowers are formalized. The rest of the ground is green, with white sedge and reeds upon it. But this is broken by lines, which are formed by an edging of little blue squares, with a mesh of white lines dividing them, and which could be the border or edging of a mat, the ground of that being part-white, part-pink, two of these mats, if they are that, stretching diagonally from top to bottom of the garment in two parallel, but slanting bands, breaking the green ground, with the white grass and rushes waving above them as though growing from a border, and with the red-violet cloud areas looming out towards them, but not touching them. The pink parts of the ground have white flowers; the white ground has formal bouquets of many coloured flowers, with mysterious and richly coloured lengths of patterned stuffs like presents of silks, tied or knotted to them. The natural folds into which the garment falls further enrich and diversify the design, by juxtaposition of its motifs, cutting short one run of its complicated ornament and breaking all the fields together, one into another; so that it is the whole pattern all over again from its beginnings, and it is too rich and complicated to seize in detail.

Another *kimono* is a rosy haze from the neck downwards, like the mist that hangs above a snowy landscape at sunset or sunrise, which becomes whiter, as it would do, when the snow begins, which is where the pattern comes. There is an edge of shadow thrown into this, like shadowed branches, and then, on a darker ground, come drooping boughs of willow trees, outlined by the snow upon them, with purple cloud masses caught, in their other element, among the branches, flying swallows with forked tails, and at the foot, Imperial, two-wheeled, hooded coaches embedded up to their axles in the snowdrifts. Yet another is of rushing waterfalls in blue and white, tumbling this way and that among flowers and birds, upon a field of spray that merges into the sky. Or, upon a plum-coloured dress there are lattice fences, and many flowers; and, upon another, on a ground of black, are board fences, with the graining of the new wood shown, the fences running zigzag, like the leaves of screens, as though they were so many bridges or stepping-stones in a water garden.

But perhaps the boldest and simplest is the best, that of the swirling red water and the irises growing upon the banks. This, or its kind, has been seen nowhere else in history. It is the whole of a civilization in the pattern upon a dress. Just a dress with long sleeves like the others; but the design is a double curve like the half of a figure eight, or the bends of the Grand Canal at Venice; only the pattern is of swirling red waters, or rather, they are cinnamon in colour, with white bands of foam, while the banks, which are white as snow and bare as that, have clumps of blue iris growing on them. This design of the cinnamon waters, here described, with white bands of foam, was carried out in the workshops of Yuzen, the greatest Japanese craftsman of his time, according to his secret processes, and with an ingenuity of technique, never equalled, or certainly never surpassed in the history of textiles. This is of the *Genroku* period, and the particular design is by Kôrin; and how much better, one exclaims in astonishment, than his *Iris Screens*! For in this *kimono* he appears as one of the greatest and most forceful of designers ever known.

But let us continue with our perambulation in the mood of someone wandering in spring time in the flowering fields. Here is a *Kosode*, a women's short-sleeved garment, with a pattern of young pine trees, like the shoots one sees growing in the ground only a few inches high, pushing out of a sloping line that must be intended for a hillside, and young bamboo shoots just sprouting their leaves, all on a spotted ground to represent snow. Another *Kosode* is on a dove-grey ground, with a meandering stream and bamboo rafts, special grasses, and some of the rafts, but not all, have bamboo gabions filled with stones to make an embankment, lashed to them. Then, a green *Kosode*, of dark olive-green, with a pattern of weeping willows, but the leaves are in reds and whites and yellows. A scarlet *Kosode* with very tall green bamboos, just shooting their leaves, and white chrysanthemums. Or another of pea-pod green, once worn by a princess of the Imperial family 'and now owned by a Lord Abbot', with two motifs on it, a camellia tree of pink and white camellias—with Japanese sparrows perching and flying among them, while the other theme is yellow chrysanthemums and the black straw covers that are put over growing plants to protect them.

What flowering contrasts, as we might find in England between a fritillary field and a wood of lilies-of-the-valley—both of which are found in nature in our island, but I have seen neither—for here is a *furisodo* (woman's long sleeved garment) of one huge bamboo glade, light and feathery on a greeny-yellow ground, with duckwing, white-breasted cocks and hens and baby chickens busy at foot of it; while the next, on pink, strawberry-cream ice ground, has tiger-lilies and auratums and three shades of morning-glories. Designs of plank-bridges meandering away into the cherry blossom; or arbours and trailing wild vines; or fans, in variety, and of course all with different designs upon them, become a commonplace. Or there are white cherry trees in full blossom upon a light green ground, and above them, blue and white swallows dipping and darting among barred white clouds.

More unusual, are pine boughs with cloth screens tied to the branches upon a scarlet ground; or a landscape with winding rivulets and young vine shoots growing upon the banks, and lattice fences at the foot of plum trees, with birds which it is said are robins but they are not our redbreasts, perched upon the branches. Or another on a violet-purple ground, of wandering rivulets and thistle heads, but the thistles are in white and green, light blue and yellow. Here is a *Kosode*, with an all-landscape design of the Tatsuta river, which was famous for its maples; and a *furisode* of dark blue satin, with a most fascinating design of cloth curtains of the sort set up for flower-viewing, but now pitched like tents of an encampment, with maple trees in their changing colours displayed in triple fugue, as it were, against, first, the cloth screens and then the patternings upon them, some of which are of maple leaves, and for the third 'entrance' of the fugue, upon the dark blue ground that for present purposes could be the sky of autumn.

There are other *kimonos* which have designs of snow-covered camellia trees and weeping-willows upon light blue; a *Katabira* (short-sleeved garment) of peonies and chrysanthemums and lattice fences of a particular pattern upon dark brown; of a snow-covered bamboo forest and flying cranes upon dark olive green; of sprays of white and purple wistaria upon a scarlet ground, and the caption reads, romantically, 'probably worn by a courtesan'; for we have opened the second volume of fifty dresses but can go no further than a *Kosode* of splendid blue and white waterfalls, splashing, zigzag to right and left down the middle, but beginning higher under each shoulder, with trails of wistaria dangling over the falls, and swallows with forked tails flying among the flowers and in and out of the spray, until we have to come to a stop at plate 100 and end with a *Kosode* of scarlet fancy satin with waterfalls of another kind altogether for they are conventionalized into bows or hoops criss-crossing upon one another, not like rainbows but more like a whale's spoutings, and the water is only white, there is no blue in it, and the rest of the pattern is of maple trees and prettily painted fans.[1]

A verdant and flowering world, endless in diversity and imagination, but among the most marvellous of all the dresses were those worn by the *Noh* actors. There is a fine example of these in the Fujiwara museum at Nagoya for such dresses were given by the great *daimyôs* to their private companies of players. A *Kosode* from a different source, and in curious taste, probably worn by the wife of a rich merchant, has a whole landscape of the Yoshiwara of Tokyo with the pale blue walls and the painted latticed houses. A *Noh* costume from this same book is a marvellous affair, nearly indescribable, but in chequer-book squares with designs of cloth-screens, and sprays and falling cascades and waterfalls of wistaria in all colours, on a dazzling scarlet ground. I can only say that it reminds me of the distant, but approaching music in Debussy's *Fêtes*. I cannot think there is anything quite to approach this among Japanese textiles unless it is the *Noh* dress in alternating panels or strips of small clematis flowers in arabesque on black, changing place with dew-laden grasses in gold-leaf on crimson, and all this part of it 'scattered with large fans'. A *Kosode*, believed to have been given by the *Shogûn* Ieyasu to *Noh* actor for it has his three circular crests or *Mon* upon it, has its shoulder parts dyed purple and the rest of it white, while from the lower part of it a huge and bold green bamboo stalk rises, and splashes the whole garment with its pale blue shoots.

Another *Kosode* has crimson shoulders, and crimson down to the waist, where the skirt of it has a most elaborate landscape dyed in many colours on a white ground. A *Noh* play costume belonging to the Kasuga shrine, near Gifu, where *Kagura* dances have been performed for centuries, is of red silk with swallow-tail butterflies and snow-covered willows upon it, or, at least, the leaves are alternately yellow and green, or covered with snow. A lady's court dress has cherry blossom and palace appurtenances—bamboo curtains of state and and hanging scent-balls. Yet another *Noh* dress has a kind of basket-work ground in gold-leaf upon squares of different colours which are

[1] *Kimonos, a hundred masterpieces of Japanese costume*, by Tsutouro Ema, Tokyo, 1935 in two volumes, with plates in colour, deals chiefly with dresses of the *Genroku* period (1688-1703). One or two of the *Kimonos* have already been written of in my book, *Splendours and Miseries*, Faber & Faber Ltd, 1943, pages 88, 89.

left, once or twice, quite empty, but for the most part filled with clumps of irises. But now I am wondering if the most splendid and fanciful of all is not the *kimono*[1] with the *noshi* design, but this needs further description for it is in fact of crimson silk-damask which has faded into orange, a kind of Niger leather orange, and *noshi* are the ceremonial wrappings used on presents and gift parcels. A great handful or bundle of these ceremonial ribbons has been, so to speak, thrown upon the crimson silk *kimono* and they are held in place at the neck by a golden clasp so that their lengths trail down over the entire dress down to the ground, ribbons of every colour and all worked with different patterns, so that their loose ends curl and flutter, together and apart, upon the crimson. Into the multiplicity of techniques employed in these textiles it would be tedious to enter, but such a robe as this last uses embroidery, gold-leaf appliqué, and every nicety of 'tie and dye' and Yuzen dyeing. Briefly, the Yuzen technique, discovered in the seventeenth century, consists in fixing a hand-painted dyed design with the use of rice paste and the juice of a certain flower (*commelina communis*). With its help stuffs were produced which can only have been rivalled in Isfahan during the reign of Shah Abbas, and in eleventh century Byzantium.

I have been at some pains to try and describe these dresses because so little has been written about them compared with the mass of literature dealing with lacquer and *netsukes* and *inrôs*, much of it technical and difficult to read. If the effect of my descriptions dazzles and bewilders, so much the better, for that is the intention. Even at the moment of writing, a new book has reached me, arriving this morning, a volume to celebrate the recent exhibition of the works of Kôrin, and opening with a colour plate of a gold lacquer box never before illustrated to my knowledge. On the lid of it there are two circular paintings of red and white chrysanthemums, and the two sides of it visible in the colour-plate have white cherry blossoms on the smaller part, and a composition of six figures of men under a tree, all in different coloured trousers and *kimonos* and wearing the Court head-dress of black gauze. One has the longing to turn the box round and see what is painted upon its other

[1] Reproduced in colour in *The Arts of Japan*, by Hugo Munsterberg, Thames & Hudson, London 1957, plate 9. The *kimonos* described in this and the preceding paragraph are reproduced in the volume on Textiles, text by T. Yamanobe, English adaptation by Lynn Katoh, in *Arts and Crafts of Japan* series, published by Charles E. Tuttle & Co, Rutland, Vermont, USA and Tokyo, 1957. This book with numerous and excellent coloured plates, and selling at 3 US $, is one of the most effective pieces of book production of our day, and as well, the technical notes are of the greatest interest. The volume on Kôrin mentioned in the next paragraph is *The Art of Kôrin*, edited by I. Taraka, published by the Nihon Keizai, Shimbun, Tokyo, 1959.

sides. The designs by Kôrin upon his brother Kenzan's pottery in the form of freehand brush drawings are one of those particularities of Japanese taste in which it is difficult for an Occidental to participate. But this is not the case with pots by Kenzan, himself, though they are so excessively scarce that there is little or no chance of seeing one. They are as rare, or rarer, than pottery by Ninsei, which again is the reason why considerable importance has been given in this book to the jar by Ninsei which we saw in the Seikadô Foundation in Tokyo. For it is one of the most famous and valued works of art in Japan.

If Kenzan is to be appreciated only in illustration, for I have never yet seen a genuine piece by him, there is a famous tea-bowl—and almost unnecessary to add that it has a design of cherry blossom on it. But Kenzan is the perfect example of that art of packaging and presentation which is almost the leading characteristic in Japanese art. In the instance of this tea-bowl it is cherry blossom, but 'patented' cherry blossom, as though to Kenzan's exclusive design, delivered in an unbroken, sealed package bearing his signature and guarantee. We may have the same feeling about his well-known painting, so often reproduced, of *Flowers in Baskets*. One of the baskets has upset, and fallen on its side. It is the calligraphy of the poem inscribed with brush strokes on the paper, and Kenzan's signature, that the Japanese admire as much as the rapid improvisation and the spacing of the actual picture. Is it the power of personality expressed in a few seconds that they are searching for? Because, if so, to take a musical instance, they would admire the *saetas*, the strident, wavering cries of the impromptu 'arrows of song', of Gitano or Flamenco inspiration, uttered by Gypsy singers from balconies as the statues of saints and virgins are carried past during the Semana Santa of Seville—they would, or should admire an impromptu *saeta* more than a symphony by Beethoven.

What a pity, in parenthesis, that the festivals of Seville and Kyoto cannot be interchanged! That there should not be for the space of a few days *matadors* swaggering in their *trajes de luce* ('suits of light') of bright green or of damson netted with black lace, and pink silk stockings, along the Gion hill, swirling their cloaks of cyclamen, fluttering their capes embroidered with roses and carnations! *Sevillanas* danced on the *Noh* stages at Nishi Honganji and *siguiriyas gitanas* on the platforms of Kiyomizu! All in the fortissimo of the fruit blossom: and by the same token, the *maikos* in their marvellous robes and butterfly *obis* driving in open carriages down the Paseo de las Delicias under the acacias and magnolias to the plaudits of the crowd!

But, in respect of that, and by way of consolation for what could never happen, here is a porcelain bowl by Dôhachi, in an anonymous collection.[1] This is late in date, about 1820 or even after, and a product of the kilns of Kiyomizu. Painted, inside and out, with cherry trees in full bloom and maple trees with scarlet leaves. There is a certain amount of green for the young leaves of the maples, the tree trunks are in dark brown, the whole bowl has a faint bluish glaze on it, and there are little touches of gold here and there. But the bowl, to judge from the illustration, is a wonderful and ingenious synthesis of cherry and maple, and therefore of the colourings of spring and autumn. It belongs to, and derives from, the school of Kôrin and his brother Kenzan. I would favour, myself, this bowl by Dôhachi more than the black pottery tea-bowls by Chôjirô, or pottery of the 'black' or the 'white' Raku type to which connoisseurs in Japan attach such store. But it is all, of course, a matter of taste. We cannot expect without initiation to gather up all the sensations of the tea-ceremony to which painters, poets, philosophers, garden architects, gave so many hours of contemplation. The bowl by Dôhachi, just described, is free of those purposeful simplicities, and of dogmas which make of a domestic ceremony something between a philosophy and a religion.

The German traveller Engelbert Kaempfer writing of Kyoto (which he calls 'Miako'), in 1690, says of it: 'Miako is the great magazine of all Japanese manufactures and commodities, and the chief mercantile town in the Empire. There is scarce a house in this large capital where there is not something made or sold. Here they refine copper, coin money, print books, weave the richest stuffs with gold and silver flowers. The best and scarcest dyes, the most artful carvings, all sorts of musical instruments, pictures, japanned cabinets, all sorts of things wrought in gold and other metals, particularly in steel (as the best tempered blades and other arms) are made here in the utmost perfection, as also are the richest dresses. In short there is nothing can be thought of but what may be found at Miako, and *nothing, though never so neatly wrought, can be imported from abroad but what some artist or other in this capital will undertake to imitate it!*' The italics are my own, and are put there for emphasis.

[1] Illustrated in colour in the volume on *Ceramics and Metalwork*, in the *Pageant of Japanese Art* series, Charles E. Tuttle & Co, Rutland, Vermont, USA and Tokyo, 1958, plate 27.

The ingenuity of the Japanese inspired the German traveller to remark on it, and they have had the name of imitators ever since, though
this was no invention on the part of the German physician. It is a truism
or cliché that is in constant repetition, and certainly imitation is a part,
and no inconsiderable part of the native ingenuity. But they are
innovators as well as imitators, and have produced some of the most
original geniuses in all the arts. It has been said that Sesshû is the only
painter whom the Japanese themselves feel worthy of a place beside the
great Chinese masters, and that when Sesshû himself went to China in
the fifteenth century he saw buildings of stone 'far exceeding the
humbler dreams of the Japanese builders in wood'.[1] But this is to take a
depressed view of the wooden 'cathedrals' of Nara and Kyoto which are
in fact the largest wooden structures in the world. And it is arguable
that Japanese painting is at its best when it turns its back on the Chinese
influence in order to proceed upon its own. There are certain phases in
their history when this is demonstrably true. After the decline of the
early Buddhist painters in a time of isolation from the mainland of
China, when the Yamato painters of the Heian period evolved styles
and methods of their own. Again, when Sôtatsu and his followers in the
seventeenth century reverted to the Yamato style as though trying,
purposefully, to found themselves upon that. And lastly, with the
Ukiyô-e, for masters such as Utamaro, Sharaku, Hokusai, Hiroshige,
for better or worse, could be nothing other than Japanese. They could
have lived and worked nowhere else but in Tokyo, a city which had a
population of a million and a half in 1790, and was bigger than any
contemporary city in Europe.

Probably the most Japanese expression of Japan—when Japan was
most 'Japanese'—was in the Zen temples and gardens of Kyoto. And
the Zen philosophy came to Japan from China just as, in like case,
Christianity was brought to Britain from Gaul, though little is known
of that phase of it, and later still from Ireland. In no country of Europe
was Christianity indigenous. It was brought there from Asia Minor,
just as Buddhism came to Japan from India and from China. There is
no more foreign influence in the early temples of Kyoto and Nara than
there is of influence from France in our Norman or Gothic cathedrals,
and to continue with the analogy, every later building in Europe owes

[1] Quoted from the volume on *Sesshû* in the *Library of Japanese Art*, English text by Elise Grilli,
1957.

something, and often a great deal, to Italian example. To a like degree was Japan dependent, but also independent of China, and it is at its most interesting and most characteristic when it is least Chinese.

In its purest state when it was really a hermetic kingdom enclosed and cut off from the outside world for three centuries—and this is a condition which has only obtained in the Occident, and then only for a short period, in Russia in the reign of the Tsar Nicholas I—Japan must have been more 'unlike' and more 'different' than any civilization there has ever been. China, as visited by the Embassies of Macartney and Amherst, presents the spectacle of the identical things to which we are accustomed in our own lives done 'the other way round', and therefore with the appearance of naïveté and eccentricity. But, in Japan, the 'things' are not the same. The 'things', themselves, are different. The true *chinoiserie* would be, not Chinese, but Japanese.

One of the works of genius in Japan is the rock and sand garden of Ryûanji, at Kyoto. But is it a triumph of genius; or is it accident? Because it could be both, or it could be either. Has the sand really been raked that same way for some four centuries? And are the rocks in their original situations, just where they were placed? Or have they sunk deeper into the sand, heeled over, changed their position and by that given themselves another meaning? What is the answer? Ryûanji is everything, and more, than it sets out to be; or it is nothing. But the garden of Ryûanji we must look upon as a bold stroke of genius; so, too, in their different ways are the best among Sharaku's actor-prints, and such woodcuts as Hokusai's *Fuji on a clear day* and *Fuji above the lightning*. Another instance of it is Ninsei's pottery jar of Mount Yoshino which we lingered over in the Seikadô at Tokyo; while yet others are the lacquer boxes also described in these pages, by Kôetsu and Kôrin. All these show that the Japanese in the grandest sense are capable of invention; that they are a race to produce artists, scientists, and inventors. One is willing to believe that they had actors of genius in the *Kabuki* theatre. That they can produce works of the calibre to make one think, besides others of which the only destiny is pleasure.

Unless disaster comes to the Japanese from internal upheaval or war with China their future would appear to lie in assimilation of the arts and sciences of the West which they seem to have reached for with both hands, but not yet digested. India is but a remote influence, and China a warning to them. America has damaged, but not destroyed them,

The tea house at the Silver Pavilion

Pagoda at Nara (8th century)

and it may be that in the rough school of occupation they have learned their lesson. In view of what has just been said about their capacity for bold invention in the arts, though now, in long abeyance, it is re-markable and typical that the modern painter they most admire should be van Gogh. The picture of his bedroom at Arles, even the painting of his pair of boots, and especially his landscape drawings, are in the gamut of Ryûanji, that is to say, they possess absolute quality and meaning, and over and above that as much, or as little, as you care to read into them. As well, the Japanese esteem van Gogh for his furious self-dedication. van Gogh, too, could produce under extreme pressure of mind and circumstance an image which fixes itself on the visual memory as though it is patented. He has concentrated until by force of inspiration he has found the formula. This is characteristic of one phase of the Japanese as artists, from Sôtatsu in a descending scale to Kôrin, to Sharaku and to Hokusai. The discovery is from the original recipe and remains unaltered. Their great masters of this school are masters of improvisation who demand as much admiration for works performed in a few moments as for the labours of a lifetime. Therefore, there are painters who are amateur and not professional. Force of personality becomes, itself, accomplishment.

In their other vein they are more attentive than any other race to little details. This may be due in equal parts to their own physical attributes and to historical isolation. Their genius for tying up parcels and giving little presents is something only and entirely Japanese. It does not exist at all in China, a thing which, in diminuendo into the wholly trivial, makes a shopping expedition in Hong Kong different indeed from buying anything from a shop in any town in Japan. There you can see them choosing the prettiest paper to wrap the parcel, and tying the knots in the string with care. These are the surviving traces of an aesthetical golden age, just as the tenor voice singing in the street in an Italian town is relic of a golden age of singing and of song. But, also, it has to do with soil and climate. There has to be the predisposition. One would not expect a race of operatic tenors from the Orkneys and Shetlands, or the Aleutians; not from northern winds and sea-fogs, but from the sun and air of Italy. So with the Japanese their extreme aesthetic sensibility must have to do with the land of Japan, the woods and hills, the volcanoes and the hot springs, the blossom, and the teeming sea. As to what will happen in the not distant future when

Q

Tokyo becomes a city of twenty or twenty-five million inhabitants, who can tell? It is probable that even then they will keep their taste for near perfection in certain little things; in flower arrangement, and in what I have called 'soup arrangement', and this chapter ends, not with an account of *inrôs* and *netsukes* or sword guards, but with a pattern book of match-box labels sent me by one of the directors of the Japanese Shell Oil Company when I admired a match-box in a restaurant at Nagoya where we were having dinner, and it transpired that this was one of his side-interests. The pattern book was sent to me a few days later. It should be added that in every good restaurant in Japan there is always a plate of match-boxes near the door for you to help yourself to on arriving or leaving, and the labels are always different and made to look as attractive as possible with colours and fine printing.

It is a little oblong book, ink-stained on the back, and bound in card-board, with a hundred and sixty labels pasted in it, thirty-five of which are of a larger format. The first thing we notice is that they are all printed on fine thick rice-paper which 'takes' gold and silver and makes clear impressions. The whole book is as enriched with 'metal' as any collection of *surimonos*, and of course a great deal of its beauty comes from the calligraphy and the exquisite spacing of the lettering. It opens a little boringly for the first two pages as though the designer was not yet interested. And then it begins—with a frog under a golden willow branch; and a little kiosk in the distance in green and gold, and an orange bridge overshadowed by green leaves. And as the designer warms to his task, a *thai* fish in sealing-wax, red, openwork lacquer, but as though contrived into a hieroglyph; and three leaves of *paulownia* in chocolate colour with gold lettering across them. On the next page, a yellow pale lobster—why should they be red? they are lobsters from the Pacific Ocean—with gold lettering down it, and a few pale green leaves, as if for dressing. The gold is wonderfully pressed or embossed into the paper, and glitters when you hold it sideways.

Turning the page, a little man poling a raft in three or four faint strokes, and the crests of far off golden mountains. And a label which is nothing but four pairs of dark green leaves a little way from the corners of the label, and the name of the restaurant in gold letters in between. Then, a swirling stream in the manner of Kôrin, in dark blue with five strokes of the brush, and some blue reeds; and a label which is plain except for three or four dice—or are they aces?—but they remind me of the playing cards sewn on the sleeves and legs of Meissen harlequins. On another page, three fishes like an inn-sign in grey, and the name in a scarlet cartouche, and again in gold; and a label of a green bamboo stem—how thick and beautiful the green! with one white bamboo shoot upon it, and the white jointing of the bamboo stem.

Then, another of the yellow lobsters, for a fish restaurant, but in a different attitude, with black letters; a white 'pussy-cat' on a scarlet cushion, with scarlet ears and collar, and raised paw against a dark blue curtain; and a covey of seven cranes, a pair of them all red, and the others just in red outline, but all with beaks facing in one way. This is a most satisfying label with the gold lettering down, and in and between, the necks of the cranes. A label which is just white in the centre, with a bar of scarlet and a bar of olive-brown, one to either side, but the white itself, is given substance and material importance, and all three panels scarlet, white and olive brown are as one brush stroke to each. The labels become more and more delightful as the book goes on; a pot of scarlet lacquer, and that is all, and it is half the size of a postage-stamp, but how satisfying on the white paper; and now, white paper at top and bottom and a horizontal band of pea-green in the middle, with a few gold dots as though to the dottings of a golden pencil.

And, opposite, a 'ghost' fish in white outline, backed with gold and a wash of pale green on the grey panel, and the rest is white with black lettering. The interest deepens. Here is a bridge, or but one rail of it, in scarlet lacquer with the green of leaves and gilded letters; and another bridge, a little difficult to fathom, with black, black rocks below, and a golden inscription. Number sixty-five is some object in a delightful impasto blue hanging or dangling against paper-window panes, but impossible to determine what it can be. And there is a chequer-board, like a shield in squares of bright red and gold, slanting at an angle out of grey shadow, and this also I am undecided about, but it suggests some form of game or tournament.

We come now to the most ingenious of all, but they are the most difficult to describe; a label with two fans 'occurring' on it, one vermilion and one orange, with golden slats and lovely writing; another, with a scarlet tray or open box, with letters in gold and letters in white, printed as in a *surimono* into the red lacquer; and a label which is a golden fish, of goldfish form, with lapis-blue markings, of the sort I have seen swimming, or rather ogling, in aquariums but I do not know its name.

One of the prettiest has just a pea-green band at the top of it, and under on the white ground a single spray of green leaves and pink cherries (?). Another, two wavering golden lines for a river, and two leaves of vermilion-scarlet veined with gold. Yet another, the corner of a red lacquer bridge, or just its scarlet railing. We are still among restaurants and bars, and here is an exceptionally charming label of a tree-trunk looking as if it must be of sandalwood, with two labels pasted on it at different angles, one outlined in red with black letters, the other marked in grey like the graining in the wood, and golden letters. Now, a label or match-box cover of a dish of blue and white porcelain, faintly outlined, and a pair of fish lying in it, and gold stamped upon them; or wholly and entirely leaf-green, and broken up like mosaic, with a green space in middle of it for the name. And a pair of cranes, neck by neck, golden beaks and bodies in a line, and the necks are all vermilion.

And now the larger labels, beginning with an exquisite spray of maple leaves in red and yellow; and next, in three colours and gold, a grey wooden bridge, figure with parasol crossing it, green weeping willow, distant hills drawn in a single line, and crest of a golden *paulownia* leaf. A lapis-blue tank of water and green willow leaves; or, more simple, a thin white bamboo stem, jointed like the joints of a skeleton, and a formal arrangement of bamboo leaves left white in the paper, three at the top and three at the bottom, on a ground of cinnamon. Then, some green dock leaves and yellow dandelions—or are they daisies, but we are in Japan?—and on the next page a plant of violets, decidedly they are violets, and two green hills, one behind the other, each drawn with just one line. Now the violet comes into use for dark purple wistaria, just a few sprays of it, and a trailing vine. After it, a whole label in dark violet-purple with *paulownia* leaf in the top corner, stamped in gold, and golden lettering as upon a codex of purple vellum, or slab of purple. And it becomes more and more a matter of calligraphy, with grasses in but three or four lines, and a pair of blue objects that could be croquet-hoops. More bamboos, green bamboos; and a golden peony; and last a boat under a bridge and a weeping willow, all in golds and greys, and we have come to the end of it and close the pages.

Such is this little collection of match-box labels. They would appear to be all by the same designer who has used all the resources that were to hand. Some of them are just as beautiful as *surimonos*, and I have tried to write of them as I would were I describing those little woodcuts enriched with golden and mica and various metals. True, the mica is missing in them, but nothing else is lacking, and they show the perfection to which lilliputian objects of utility can be brought with love and patience. This is a characteristic of Japan, and it obtains in so many of their smaller arts and crafts. It is one phase of their national genius, and the other and bolder side of that should by now be apparent in these pages. It is in homage to the one and the other that I have written of the match-box labels.

Chapter Twelve

━━━━━━━━━━━━━━━━━━━━━━━━━━━━━━━━━━━

NIKKO

IT IS TRUE TO SAY that our only uncomfortable journey in Japan was that to Nikko. In a train that for this area was reminiscent of British Railways in one of their more Bohemian moods of careless dirtiness, and preluded by an immensely long drive through the suburbs of Tokyo to the Ueno station. No observation car, nor trail of 'air hostesses' coming round with iced coffee or baskets of fish or seaweed, and we were constrained instead to buy food on the platform and carry into the train on that boiling morning a bottle of *sake* in mistake for mineral water. It was a slow train which took some three hours to cover the ninety miles, only enlivened by talking in no language at all to a charming young woman of slight tapering form, with oval face and slanting eyes, like a Marie Laurencin painting, and her little daughter. In this direction, out north-east from Tokyo into the middle of the island, the country is very much less beautiful, and for some time all there was to notice were the poster hoardings by the side of the railway line twisted and thrown down by the typhoon. Then, after a couple of hours or so, and as we began to climb into hilly country, the beginnings to one side or other of the long avenue of cryptomerias leading to Nikko. Once there was forty miles of this, but in the not distant past the peasants cut down much of it for firewood, and in any event most of the surviving trees are dying of old age. They must be approximately three hundred years old which is just the age of the tallest and oldest cypresses in Tuscany. Even so, they are a poor foretaste of the marvellous old cryptomerias of Nikko.

When, at last, we get there it is to find ourselves in the long straggling street of an overgrown village. Never in one's life have there been so many souvenir shops lining both sides of the road as though for a crowd of hundreds of thousands to go by. And it has begun to rain gently. Then, up a steep corner at an angle, and the taxi lands us at the comfortable hotel which we were to know well after a stay of nearly a week. Our room was in an annexe building looking down on to the river, whence came a continual noise of rushing water. One has never seen so many trees, and felt their presence, or known so much rainy mist, or heard so much water, as at Nikko. The humidity of its climate, and its rainfall, must be something quite exceptional, or put into other words, its 'almost unexampled wetness', this latter aspect of it being enough to raise anticipatory fears of damp sheets which happily in this well-run hotel are quite unfounded. But Nikko is certainly the dampest and wettest, and most 'ferny' place, to create its own special adjective for it, imaginable, and it was with a little foreboding that one looked forward to the next six days. Also, it was very much colder, particularly in the early morning, and we could scarcely believe this was on the same island as the sweltering heats of Kyoto and Tokyo. Out of which we had emerged, though one could not credit it, this same morning; and we crossed a little disconsolately into the main building of the hotel which was full of Australians off a 'cruise', come for the day's excursion from Tokyo and eating a late tea.

What was the hurry? We were to be a week here, and had time to see everything. In fact after all the sightseeing in Kyoto we wanted a rest; and looking out at the rain over a table of old newspapers and magazines, most of them impossible to read because they were technical and engineering journals, we edged our way through our compatriots to the souvenir shop where we bought postcards and enquired the price of lacquer boxes and *kimonos*. At vantage points, particularly in the dining-room, were painted and carved decorations in facsimile of those in the shrines; the famous panel of three monkeys, the 'simian trinity' of 'hear no evil, speak no evil, see no evil' with one monkey covering his ears, another his mouth, and the third his eyes, and another panel carving of peonies, highly coloured, but their effect was only to lower the temperature and damp one's spirits. And at length after a heartening drink of whisky in our bedroom, into the dining-room where after the first evening we prevailed on the management to let us dine at half-past seven—always the same dinner every night, by our own choice, of trout from Lake Chuzenji—and down again to the old newspapers and magazines. In fact there could be no finer place than Nikko for a rest cure for 'they' begin turning out the lights soon after half-past eight, and whether you like it or not you are in your bedroom and nearly asleep by nine. One sleeps, as though drugged, though probably it has to do with being surrounded in all directions by so many tall old trees.

There is, perhaps, a particular soporific effect in hotels which are crowded in the daytime and almost empty at night. But, in any case, as I have said, we were entirely exhausted by the great heats and all the sightseeing, and welcomed this opportunity of sleeping, to be awakened next morning and every morning, by a bevy of *neisans* bowing at the door and bringing in breakfast, who were quite the smallest fully-grown beings, apart from pygmies, ever seen.

The view from the windows was up into the wooded hills, and down to the rushing stream, but the early morning mists were clinging to the hills as only in Japan, and nowhere else. Looking down through the other window, though it was only eight o'clock, bus after bus was crawling along the road beside the river, hooting its horn, and there were already long crocodiles of disembarked children all in line behind their flag-leader. And there were files of men and women as well; every day this happened, and it explained the souvenir stalls. But one thing was curious, that there was not a sign of the temples. I had in fact taken a walk in their direction the previous evening, had climbed a multitude of stone steps and returned drenched with sweat in spite of the cold mists and drizzling rain. But on purpose I had not gone far or looked at anything for I wanted to keep it for this morning.

Starting from the hotel down the steep hill, where you have to go quite carefully because of the motors coming up it at a rush, in a moment you are on an iron bridge carrying a tram line, with the sacred red lacquer bridge beside you only a few feet away. It is one of the most famous sights of Japan, and as much or more fuss is made of it as over the 'Bridge of Sighs' at Venice, the notion of a bridge in scarlet lacquer being a pretty one, but in the result it is nothing at all and after a day or two in Nikko one passes by and forgets to look at it. Much more impressive is the rushing mountain torrent many feet below, but again you have to walk over the iron bridge looking in both directions because of the char-à-bancs and buses. And from the other bank of the river one can walk to the shrines up a steep path and many flights of steps, arriving exhausted, so that it is better to take a taxi from the hotel and drive to the chief shrine, saying, boldly, Tôshôgû to the driver, with or without all three of its accents for all the difference that they make.

One is given the advice to come first to Nikko and see Kyoto later so as not to be disappointed, and we had reversed the process. Certainly the Shrines of Nikko are in bad taste but that should never present difficulties to a writer. Kyoto is one of the greatest cities of the world, to a degree one cannot apprehend until one has been to it, and seen temples and gardens every day for a month without tiring of them. Nikko in comparison is but a group of shrines or mausolea hidden in a wood, and if you are there long enough and look carefully at the plan you discover there is another group of shrines you might never have heard of, equally well hidden. But, above all, the architectural style of the shrines at Nikko is quite different from that of the temples at Kyoto; and it is this style with its baroque elements, its hints of Italian *Bruto seicento*, and its conscious *chinoiserie* which is the trouble. Basically, there is this difference that the temples of Kyoto are of plain wood, or cryptomeria or of *hinoki*, while those of Nikko are painted and gilded and aswarm with dragons, tigers, lions, phoenixes and peonies; they are in fact profuse and rioting with ornament. Nevertheless, they have a strong and pronounced fascination, and after the refinements and the aestheticism of Kyoto one would not have missed seeing them under any consideration. 'The glory of Nikko is that it possesses the finest handiwork of man'; these words are but mild praise compared to the paeans lavished upon the shrines of Nikko by critics in Europe and USA,[1] up to only two decades ago, at just exactly the same time when these same critics, if asked, would have been most severe and unanimous in their condemnation of Rococo churches in Bavaria, and a number of other architectural caprices ranging from Nymphenburg to Brighton Pavilion, but all of a like nature in different countries of Europe. Also, making the situation still more anomalous, the exact period of the shrines of Nikko was that, also, of Katsura and Sambôin, the most beautiful of all the architectural complexes and gardens of Kyoto, and of some of Japan's greatest painters, notably Sôtatsu. So that the Japanese during the very same years were, aesthetically, at their best, and at their worst. If, indeed, it is their worst, and this is what we have come to Nikko to investigate.

We find ourselves therefore in the avenue of huge cryptomerias that slopes uphill to the Shrines. It is a broad gravelled walk under the trees with water running down stone gutters at its sides. Everywhere in that wood there is the noise of water; the other sensations being the cryptomerias and the huge crowds. One has never seen anything quite like

[1] 'the finest religious architectural expressions east of Agra', Terry's *Japan*, 1920.

this wood of cryptomerias. Among them there must be trees a hundred and twenty feet high. Some, indeed, are straggling towards the top and obviously dying, but it is calculated that more than half of the trees originally planted in the seventeenth century are still standing. Magnificent as they look now in late September, they must be more impressive still standing in the snow; and the shrines once seen make a winter picture in one's mind with their golden roofs and scarlet timbers under the snow-laden trees. Later we were to see the sacred wood of Ise which was to my mind even more impressive and wonderful perhaps because the cryptomeria there are younger trees and therefore thinner and straighter, and are all on level ground and not on a mountain side which gives them in themselves a formal and processional air. Nikko is a collection of shrines and mausolea hidden deep in a forest. The cryptomeria woods of Japan are a feature unique in the world. I could only wish we had seen the sacred forests of Kôyasan which are the other most wonderful thing of their kind in Japan.

By now, coming slowly up the hill among the crowd we pass another tall avenue leading off to the left to other temples. And we come to the foot of a flight of stone steps, and to a kiosk where we buy tickets. At about this point there is a vermilion, five-storey pagoda to the left, not quite so tall as the tallest of the trees, and we are aware of a number of shed-like, brightly painted buildings which are the approaches to the shrine or mausoleum of Ieyasu. On the many occasions I went to look at it, at all times of day down to the evening, there was always such a crowd that it was difficult to climb the steps. Assault groups of children making the attack, and other parties in retreat, but all moving with painful slowness, and often halted. In the heat of Kyoto which we had experienced until a day or two before this would have been intolerable, and the more occasion to be grateful to the cryptomeria shade. By now we have come to another flight of steps, and are at the first gate which has a pair of red-painted demon (pantomime) kings in niches to either side, grimacing and threatening, with futile gestures, with the lichened, stone balustrading at the top of the walls forming a terrace, and a pair of enormous cryptomerias one to either side.

This first gate or *Niômon* is disappointing but now the fun begins. We turn leftwards, and are among a complex of shed-like Maori wooden huts or lean-tos for that is what they look like at the first glance. And there is an over-multiplicity of stone lanterns which get in everyone's way, and since they are never lighted serve no useful purpose. On the other hand they are part of the furniture, and the Shrines of Nikko would be nothing without their junk and bric-à-brac. To the right there is a wooden storehouse which must contain a whole theatrical wardrobe of old dresses and armour for the great processions of 2nd June (Ieyasu's birthday) and 17th September. In so many Japanese temples one is reminded of childhood friends who had cupboards full of old clothes for dressing up. The wardrobe-rooms of Nikko must have old dresses sufficient for many hundreds of persons to judge from photographs of the processions. This particular storehouse is a comparatively simple affair, but a second storehouse beyond it is another matter altogether with its wooden railing painted, or rather lacquered vermilion-red, and its multi-coloured prismatic sides, painted in most of the colours of the rainbow, with much gilding upon the roof. Gold, in fact, is beginning to predominate, and the *Official Guide* (1958) steps forward with the information that 2,489,900 sheets of gold were used in the shrines of Nikko, each of 3·84 square inches, an amount which laid out flat would cover nearly six acres. Adding that the timber used would extend for 330 miles, or nearly the distance from Tokyo to Kyoto, and we are evidently approaching an area of superlatives. The lower part of this storehouse which also contains 'valuable outfits used for the customary festivals' has its lower part gilded and vermilioned like the vanes of a radiator, and above that the welter of ornament under the gilded and bronze-tiled roof has below its eaves a remarkable and comic carving of a pair of elephants, said to be from drawings by Kâno Tan-yû, but quite evidently the artist had never seen a living elephant, thereby adding greatly to the *chinoiserie* effect.

It is interesting to think that this strange collection of 'South Sea' huts, worked up, and carved and gilded into a frenzy of *chinoiserie*, was *terra incognita* until only a couple of generations ago. The lower classes, it is satisfactory to learn, 'were not allowed inside the temple, and were only permitted to assemble on the steps'—the stone staircase we have just climbed—and certainly no European had set foot where we are standing until less than a century ago. And now to the left of us is the stable for the Sacred White Pony, now without an inmate, a plain wooden building with no lacquering but a much gilded roof, and a frieze of coloured carvings of monkeys, all in high relief, among them the famous 'monkey trinity'. At about which point one may walk back in order to look at a huge bronze, hanging candelabrum or many-branched candlestick reputed to have been brought from Holland and given to the shrine by the Dutch Governor of the Dejima factory at Nagasaki, and enclosed in a sort of bronze or copper well-cover, under an immense cryptomeria; and walking no further for the moment reflect upon this peculiar environment. There are more than one of the lanterns hereabouts; the one we first looked at is said to revolve when lit, and there is another under a still more elaborate bronze canopy like a font-cover, 'dedicated by the Korean Dynasty, and mis-designed by a Dutchess, its hollyhocks atop are set upside down', the guide says, disarmingly,[1] with yet another standing in the open, uncanopied, and 'donated by the Ryûkû sovereign', which intends the king of the Loochoo islands.

We are in a sacred wood of huge trees, standing in a compound of Maori-looking huts, painted and gilded all over and more often than not lacquered vermilion, all except for this hut with the monkey-panels which we have been told is the stable for the Sacred White Pony, carvings carried out with the degree of realism that Japanese craftsmen put into a *netsuke*, and most curious to find upon a sacred building of whatever purpose, while in addition to the pair of storehouses already described, there are odd-looking structures, one to each side of the steps, like drum-towers or belfries made of timber but metal-studded, with narrowing bases to them, and standing in the shade of the huge trees. A small red building next to the Sacred Stable is the Red Watch-House where the guardian of the terrace lives, or was living, until not long ago. Farther away on the left is the Library, but we come out of the Shrine that way, and so will see it later.

In the meantime we are at the foot of another flight of steps, always ascending, and with a gateway at top of it of which we can only for the moment see the gilded crest, for like all the buildings of the shrine it is of small dimensions, and not much taller than the stairs below it. This is no less than the famous *Yômeimon* or second gateway, the 'Gate of Sunlight', the most extreme instance of *chinoiserie* imaginable, except for one other gateway that is still to come. It gives an effect, first, of white and gold; and its whiteness could be carved out of meerschaum,

---

[1] The meaning of this is that the crests of the Tokugawa family, to which Ieyasu belonged, are cast upside down with the leaves in the wrong order. The enormous tree above it, which is not a cryptomeria but a conifer of another species, is supposed to be the very tree which Ieyasu carried about with him when it was still small enough to be held in a flower pot.

that substance of solidified foam out of which elaborately carved pipe-bowls are made. As one approaches nearer, it is more peculiar still; a gabled roof of copper and gold tiles with golden wind-bells hanging from the corners, and the whole of its cornice under the eaves, where one might think of swallows or martins nesting, a writhing mass or nursery of gilded Dogs of Fo, or Pekinese dogs, no less, with pygmy lion in their ancestry, three or four of them, one above the other. Below this, another and larger race of white dragons with gilded wires stuck into their jaws for whiskers, writhing up there under the eaves of the gateway as though in anticipation of the chandeliers of Brighton Pavilion; and, below, carved panels too intricate to describe, followed downwards by another cornice under the balcony which has carved figures of Chinese sages and 'famous children'—whatever that may mean—which carvings have but one other affinity or home in the 'Chinese' bedroom at Claydon House in Buckinghamshire, or maybe the vanished 'Managarith' or Chinese bedroom of Bubb Dodington at Eastbury in Dorset. The figures are of lilliputian 'mandarins' in coloured robes with nodding heads; and if they have not whiskers growing like moustachios from the sides of their faces, as at Claydon, it is only because this peculiarity has been left to the dragons with those gilded wires protruding from their cheeks. When we come down at last to the pillars of the porch, it is to find they are no less curious for they have designs of tigers, their stripes formed by the natural veining of the wood.

It is a relief and a pause for rest to come through the *Yômeimon* and emerge safely on its inner side, with a moment to examine its side walls which have those large coloured carvings of peonies, already familiar to us from the copies in the hotel dining-room, but looking better here *in situ* where they have a slightly Moghul air. The whole of this fantastic-ally elaborate gateway being no bigger than the bizarre structure a multi-millionaire of eccentric tastes might put up in his garden as a pigeon or even bantam house, an effect much enhanced by the knowledge that it has a balcony, and therefore must contain a little room entered at stated times, we surmise, by the guardian of the terrace who lives in the Red Watch-House in order to sweep out the nests and set things aright. And coming out to examine the *Yômeimon* once more from the front, those little extraordinary coloured figures of Chinamen, sages and children, are like the minuscule figures in some kind of peepshow or 'raree' clock. We have to come out through the *Yômeimon* and down the steps again in order to look at the long walls with coloured panels of carving to either hand extending the whole length of this second terrace. They are protected from the weather by an overhanging cornice but appear to have been repainted every few years, and are wearying to look at in detail because of their repetitive motifs, and no less so because of the hard but slippery pebbles one must walk on in the drizzling rain. Panels carved with an unusually big hand we may think as we walk to look at them between that pair of metal-studded drum-towers and in and out between the stone lanterns, but they are monotonous with their perpetual storks and phoenixes, and their only pleasing feature is the sculptor's convention for carving cherry or plum blossom to which he gives the appearance of cracked ice.

Climbing, once again, the stone steps up to the *Yômeimon* it looks, if anything, still more dwarfed and bantamish, with the curious pair of seated figures, bow in hand and quiver on back, unless my memory deceives me over that detail, in niches like porters' lodges to either side. And now we are in the most holy precincts of the shrine, with those side panels of peonies behind us, now becoming pleasanter to examine with the crimson flushing of their petals; and above them the white dragons with gold moustachios, Dogs of Fo for brackets, and more 'raree' Chinamen, with a few feet in front of us on the right-hand side the *Kaguraden* or sacred dance stage with a 'comely virgin priestess, who looks the part', in attendance, 'wand in hand', but in fact for the moment selling postcards. And now in front of us is the *Karamon* or Chinese Gate, 'made of rare wood imported from China', and decorated with 'low reliefs of bamboo, Japanese apricots, peonies and chrysanthemums', but this low gateway is of mottled, piebald texture and no less proliferant of tiny, automaton-looking figures of Chinamen. It is difficult to look at it in detail as one shuffles past in stockinged feet, and the back of it is altogether masked and hidden by the building behind it. It is of bantam-dimensions, that is certain, with figures of long-tailed dragons writhing up its pillars, and top-heavy gabled roof flashing with gold. And we go off to the right to slide our feet along the polished floor boards, lacquered a bright vermilion, and with not a speck of dust upon them. Down long corridors, and past lockers and boot-stands where the tourists leave their shoes, all in diminutive sizes, and so round the back of the *Karamon* which one can only see by holding to a pillar and leaning out beyond the vermilion planking.

We are now about to enter the *Haiden* or Oratory which only a generation or two ago was looked upon as the consummation of human taste and skill and freely compared for its wonders with the interior of the Alhambra of Granada and the Taj Mahal. Priests are sitting there at a table, prepared for a small fee to stamp our guide books with the shrine's vermilion seal; Shintô priests in black gauze hats and transparent capes of turquoise blue, and through an open door we see more of their capes hanging like the surplices in a vestry or sacristy, and catch sight of a virgin priestess in her scarlet divided skirt—a skirt which makes it look as if she is wearing trousers. The abbots of the Tôshôgû shrine until the disestablishment of Buddhism were always Imperial Princes who lived in Tokyo and came to Nikko three times a year. But although upon nearly every occasion that we saw it some sort of religious service was in progress, the shrine is shorn of much of the religious paraphernalia once attaching to it, now that Shintô in its turn has been disestablished. There was never a sign of the red and gold lacquer cups from which the holy *sake* was drunk, which were sold afterwards as souvenirs, with more dangerous-sounding cups of antimony at a cheaper rate, nor of 'the specially prepared vegetables and rice cakes with the Tokugawa crest stamped upon them, carried in by white-clad acolytes with shields tied across their mouth to prevent the breath from defiling them', which feast was later consumed after the guest had been handed a lighted paper lantern also bearing the family crest, and led into an outer room where they ate to the sound of flutes and drums, after which the inspection of the shrine was begun.

And we follow in their footsteps, but in fact it is next to impossible to describe what we see from the matting upwards in this not very large room which is one seething riot of phoenixes and pheasants, pine and paulownia and bamboo and apricots, 'angels surrounded by chrys-anthemums', and portraits, also, of the thirty-six poets. Walls, too, are hung with fine matting which has enormous tassels, there are sliding screens (*fusuma*) of huge lion-dogs and bamboos, while 'a hundred phases of dragons', 'all different', which inevitably means all the same in effect, are painted on the ceiling. Against the wall stands the Shintô altar with its *gohei* or ritual sheaves of gold paper;[1] and there is a fascinating

---

[1] These strips of paper are symbolic offerings of lengths of cloth and they are wrapped round a wand or twig of the evergreen *sakaki*, the sacred Shintô tree.

(unseen) giraffe by Kanô Tan-yû, a very curious animal indeed, quadruped, certainly, but in other respects speculative and unreal. The Shôgun's 'sitting-room' has lacquered panels of phoenixes and paulownia which could have been designed by automatic thought-transference for Brighton Pavilion; and we go from this into another room behind it with a flight of steps at one end, but I attempt no description of it beyond mention of the gold-lacquered doors of exquisite workmanship, once more of Pavilion standard.

Behind this again is the inner holy shrine or *Honden*, but the best part of that is the approach to it, which takes you for a moment outside the building so that you see the glittering and, it would seem, solid gold of its exterior ornamentation, the two chambers one behind the other with almost identical roof lines, and some wonderful carved and open-work panels to either end of the exterior passages, in fact blocking their ends. This inner, and most holy of all the rooms in the shrine, has silken hangings and lacquer chests which belonged to the Shogun Ieyasu. The locally printed guide by now in an ecstasy, proclaims that this inner holy shrine 'needed an aggregate man power of 337,000 carpenters', a computation it seeks to explain no further; and recovering we find ourselves in the open air again and heading for a building where the three sacred palanquins are kept, palanquins which are so large and heavy that they have to be carried by a multitude of bearers in the great processions. There is one more building to be seen—the Yakushidô, which is one mass of gilding and lacquering, where the pilgrims clap their hands under a painted dragon on the ceiling for the sake of the echo which makes the roar of the dragon; and then emerge, buying perchance on the way out a little golden bell or an amulet from the stall, having seen the shrine of Ieyasu, but not his tomb which is higher on the hillside and not particularly interesting. We come out, and walk down the long hill in the rain under the huge and wonderful cryptomerias.

It is a curious and somewhat exhausting experience to see the Tôshôgû Shrine. Such prodigies of technical skill and execution have been lavished upon these little, hut-like wooden structures. In spite of the laboured and inartistic nature of a good deal of the ornamentation, the technical skill, alone and in itself, is something entirely beyond the capabilities of temple craftsmen in such other centres of Buddhism as Ceylon, Burma, or Siam. The technique is superb, but the taste bad.

Shôsôin, Nara (8th century)

Kasuga Shrine, Nara: view of the roofs (8th century, but constantly rebuilt)

Kasuga Shrine: *Bugaku* dancing

Bugaku mask

Bugaku dancing at Itsukushima Shrine, Miyajima, 'Prince of Lang Ling' dance.

More curious still is it to think of the Tôshôgû shrine in retrospect, not thousands of miles away, when back at home on the other side of the globe, but as I did that night in the hotel at Nikko with the golden shrines only a few hundred yards away hidden in the deep woods. 'Maori' huts upon which a quantity of ant-like artificers have arrived to work their will. Often since in imagination one has come up the avenue of cryptomerias, and caught the glitter of those golden roofs, climbed the steps and found oneself between the drum-towers, or in front of the Stable of the White Pony, with only a flight of stone steps before the *Yômeimon*, that extraordinary gateway which exceeds in wilful *chinoiserie* any building one has ever seen. Often since has one thought of it, but that night, after the first 'live' sensation and experience its remembered reality became merged into a dream.

I had read that the *Yômeimon* had an upper storey reached only by a ladder. Indeed, so much is evident from its having a balcony, and there being no doorway into it, or other means of access. So it must have some little interior room, however small, and one can only get to that by climbing a ladder. By putting up a ladder against the balcony by stealth when no one is looking, although there are hundreds of pilgrims to the shrine, all day and every day. So it would have to be at night, or early in the morning. Then, the little painted figures of Chinamen, the 'raree' Chinamen of the peepshow, like automatons that move in front of a clock-face at the hour, put me in mind of the mechanical figures in the workshop of Doctor Coppelius, surely such another room of mystery as this, and I heard 'the little tinkling air' which regulates Coppelias's movements, but confused in memory with that little geisha song, the *Gion Kouta*, which now in my last days in Japan was beginning to be an obsession.

Frantz, or some other youth, brings a ladder. He leans it against that balcony, above the painted Chinamen and the golden Dogs of Fo, and just below the white dragons with whiskers of gilded wire. The moment has come of going into the hidden room. And what will we find there? This strange gateway with roof out of all proportion to its size, of copper and bronze tiling laid, as always in Japanese temples, like the half or bisection of an early gun or cannon, the halves of gun-barrels laid, side by side but, of course, tilting upward at their ends, and much gilding on the eaves of the roof, and upon its cresting. This top-heavy

R

golden gateway with its secret room and balcony; the *Karamon* or
Chinese gate behind that, smaller in size and almost more peculiar still,
with the stage for sacred dances to one side, and the double roofs of the
Haiden and the *Honden*, one behind the other against the tall trees, all in
the middle of the cryptomeria wood. What will we find? At four or
five o'clock in the morning, which was the time when I looked at my
watch only a few moments ago? And in my half-dream the *Yômeimon*
becomes confused with the purpose I suggested for it, that it was
intended as a pigeon or even bantam house.

We have found a little door leading into it from the balcony, and
while the 'raree' Chinamen below it nod their heads and move their
hands, and we hear again 'the little tinkling air', the one or other of
them, for in my dream I know not which is which, we crawl in
through a low door. What do we find? Bantam Shoguns and Princesses,
roosting upon their perches. A red-yellow, black-tail cock; 'everything
one could wish for in a Japanese bantam; in one word, it is a jewel'.
Large, broad set up, regular and very deep cut comb, a broad head,
wonderful neck feathers, short in the leg (creeper), and a splendid
widely carried fan-tail with much down between the tail-feathers, and
a sabre-like chief sickle. The wings trail deep on the ground when it
walks. The bird is of a beautiful red-yellow colour, and has a black tail
with brown edged sickles. The black-blue cock is still broader and more
cobby. It also has beautiful abundant side sickles, the chief sickle being
sabre-like. One of the two yellow, more tea-coloured hens is a beauty,
its feet being invisible, giving it the appearance as if sitting. And there
are almonds which look very grotesque owing to their spangled
plumage, a *butschi* (spangled) cock, and cuckoo-coloured (speckled)
hens.

But more peculiar things are to happen. The dawn comes in with
trumpeting or crowing. These are the voices of the *Nanagako-dori* or
long crowers; 'very few in number and preserved for many centuries
in Japan for the purpose of announcing the dawn'. Of three breeds;
Totenko, brown in colour, with a shrill plaintive tone, the length of the
crow being generally seven to eight seconds, and the longest crow
taking sometimes as long as twenty seconds; *Tomaru*, black in colour,
the highest and clearest, the length of the crow extending from five
to ten seconds, and the longest being from twelve to thirteen seconds
by the stop-watch; and *Koeyoshi*, brown in colour, a deep solemn bass,

five to ten seconds.[1] These birds lift their voices for an hour before the rising sun, and we may think the living figures of those early dawns can have not been less curious than the ghosts that they dispelled. We hear their crowing voices and wonder at them, till they flutter down like clockwork figures and go back into the little room. The dream concludes with one of the long-tailed *nago-o-odori*, from Oshino village on Shikoku island in the Inland sea; a pure white cockerel, white all over, with tail twelve or thirteen feet long. So long that as it stands on the balcony of the *Yômeimon*, its tail sweeps on the ground and is held up like a train by a woman who has had the care of it almost since it tapped its way out of the eggshell. And with that vision of the white cock perched on the balcony with tail reaching to the ground the dream ends.

When the little *neisans* came in, bowing, the three of them, with our hebdomidal breakfast of green tea and salmon fish cakes, the dream was still remembered and did not seem out of place. But the Japanese have their individual and nationalistic ideas about breakfast, preferring a cup of 'instant' soup or even seaweed, and everything has to be ordered separately from the menu card. They do not understand for instance that we eat bread or toast for breakfast. Rice is instead of that, and a simple breakfast of coffee and toast has to be ordered carefully beforehand. But this was always a beautiful hour of the day at Nikko, rain or fine, because of the wooded hills in front of the windows, and one had begun like the Japanese to admire a misty morning as much or more than a sunny day. It is now that one learns to understand and appreciate their ink paintings, of which this view of misty hills, that altered almost momentarily, was a perfect example. Not one new painting, but several new paintings, every morning and every evening, by the Nanga school of painters with personal choice as to whether they should be by Gyokudô or by Mokubei, both of them *literati* and what we would call Bohemian or convivial characters, but with a slight preference for the latter because of his paintings of Uji, the green tea village. And after it had settled down to rain gently for the morning we would make our way under the dripping trees to the Shrine Museum where there are a few interesting things to see; litters and lacquer chests, and a suit of armour belonging to Ieyasu which from shape of helm and breastplate

[1] Quoted from a little book on Japanese Poultry Breeds, by V. Kinogawa of the Agricultural Faculty, Tokyo University.

was closely copied from the Spaniards or Portuguese. Not a fine or important suit of armour, but just such as would be worn by Cortez's or Pizarro's men, and aboard the *Namban Byobû* galleons in the screen paintings worn by Southern Barbarians. For the rest, the Shrine Museum especially on this wet day is a little dark and creepy, and there is a tableau *à la Madame Tussaud* of a *daimyô* eating his huge, compulsory bowl of rice at the shrine, with a priest standing over him. It was a gift from the god of the shrine, and therefore an insult not to finish it. How it had rained as in a Hiroshige woodcut, on the way back to the hotel!

There being two continual rows of souvenir shops for some half-mile or more as far as the railway station, we spent the afternoon going from one to the next, and now and again splashing across the road. But Nikko is a poor village depending on pilgrims and tourists, and there is little to buy. Interest centred more on the use of the abacus for calculating even the smallest sums of money, but the workings of which remain a mystery to an Occidental mind—on the abacus, and upon a beautiful blue and yellow swallow-tail butterfly which as soon as we were seen admiring it, the shopkeeper tried to grab with his hand as it fluttered bravely through the rain. The neatest shops of all are the sweet shops, but here in Nikko given something of the musty confidential air of the old established wine merchant, not open stalls, that is to say, like oyster stalls, but enclosed, with discreet, and of course tastefully wrapped parcels with beautiful printing in the window. Selling Nikko peppermints which are gently nasty, and a kind of sweet made of chestnuts and bean-paste. The occasional bear-skin of the guide book was not visible in any shop window, but there was a plentitude of hideous objects made out of turned wood or treen including a veritable arsenal of salad bowls. Misguided ingenuity finds ever new fields, and there are plates and other things fashioned from a tree-fungus which the Japanese call, prophetically, 'ape-stool', together with others made from a black fossil wood, from camphor-laurel, magnolia, or even rhododendron wood, and then hideously lacquered. Walking-sticks of wistaria wood we enquired for in every shop, liking the idea of them, but there were none. Instead, there were walking-sticks of wild vine; and I remembered one of the guides of the hotel with whom I talked telling me that the autumn, which came about a week or two after we left, was the most beautiful season in Nikko, because of the processions and the maple trees. And 'sometimes', he added, 'we make wine from grapes of the wild vines on the way up to Lake Chûzenji.'

On another morning of only intermittent rain we went to Rinnôji temple which has a fine old winding garden, and a lake now undergoing puddle-trenching. Rinnôji which had abbots of Royal blood, has choreographic traditions and on 2nd June every year a Longevity Dance is performed in front of its main hall by two priests wearing short swords and carrying fans, described as an old *dengaku* dance of the Kamakura period (twelfth century); while one of the screens in the abbot's apartments shows figures taking part in a sacred dance that is only performed in Nikko twice in every hundred years. This main hall of the temple is a building higher up the hill, and called the Sambutsu-dô, which was one mass of scaffolding when we saw it and climbed a succession of ladders into its roof.[1] Nothing of its interior could be seen. But in front of the temple is the famous old cherry tree which has yellow blossoms of a rare sort, not presumably the yellowish-green variety known as *Yukon*, but according to report a double cherry more like a yellow *Banksian* rose. As stated earlier in this book, I enquired in vain for the pine-needle garden, if indeed it ever existed, but doubtless there are other small gardens at Nikko, and we would have accepted the guide's offer to take us to them had there been more time.

There are a great many damp walks round Nikko, to the Back-viewing Waterfall, the Vermicelli Cascade, and so forth, but clambering round the shrines is more than enough exercise; up the slippery stone steps which are a short cut, past an odd modern statue of Ieyasu (?), and down again by a range of new buildings that are offices of the Shrine. But there are other half-secret places hidden in the trees and which need a little finding. The long avenue of cryptomerias leading off to the left from the main one takes you, rather deviously, to the Futaarasan shrine, standing with a marvellous amphitheatre of huge cryptomerias behind it, their tall bare trunks appearing almost like pillars above and at the back of it. This is a simple and unpretentious Shintô temple but I enjoyed it almost as much as anything at Nikko. There is another temple belonging to this same shrine on Lake Chûzenji; and another, or, in fact, two more on Mount Nantai to which pilgrimages are made.

---

[1] The Sambutsu-dô, astonishingly, for it is a large and heavy wooden structure, was moved to its position about seventy years ago. Before that, it stood near the Futaarasan shrine. Wooden buildings put together without nails, can be taken apart and moved more easily than one might imagine.

But the attraction of the Futaarasan shrine is the sacred dancing. Coming out of the oratory or *Honden*, as we approached, we heard the sound of some kind of flute or flageolet and the booming of a drum. The dance had just ended, and the pair of virgin dancers in their white tunics and scarlet Kimono-shaped skirts were walking back across the temple courtyard. It was then that we made friends with a young priest, who, smilingly, took up the telephone in his box-office, and with one of the dancers prompting him, gave us the address and telephone number of the Shintô shop in Tokyo where the scarlet skirts could be bought and, also, a virgin priestess's fan.

The dance which was performed more than once afterwards for our benefit is a *Miko-Kagura* dance to the music of a flute and two drums, and is undoubtedly of great antiquity. There are several tunes in the Kagura music, we were told. A leaflet describing the dancing says: 'The long hair on the neck of the maidens is bundled with a sheet of clean white paper. The effect is very tidy and pious'—and this it certainly is, while 'in some dances particular head-gears are used', and what are beautiful in imagery are the objects held by the virgin priestesses in their hands, an evergreen branch of the *sakaki* (eurya ochnacea), the sacred Shintô tree. But, also, they have a form of head-dress like a little coral tree, dance with a bell in their right hand, and as well perform a ceremonial sword dance. And at other times hold a paper fan with much gilding upon it, which has a design of cherry trees on one side of it and pine boughs on the other. At the time of hearing this *Kagura* music I had not yet heard the *Bugaku* music of the Emperor's private band in Tokyo, nor been to the shrine of Ise, nor yet to Miyajima, and the dancing and music seemed therefore most beautiful and entrancing. That we were not alone in thinking so emerged one evening in talking to an old Australian, a rugged old man of much instinct but little education, who had been sitting by my side, watching. He told me he had been to Japan once before as a young man, forty years ago, when he walked all over the country, and was always determined to come back. And had in the meantime been to Bali. He spoke of that marvellous island and its *gamelan* music and dancing, and of what Japan had been like when he remembered it, finding it almost impossible to believe that something so old and simple as this should still be danced in this shrine at Nikko.

Next morning we set off up the hairpin bends to Lake Chûzenji.

There are some twenty to thirty of them, the drivers taking a childish delight in the notices to test their brakes, and in waiting at the corners for the down-going traffic. The road is in fact like a staircase, in flights to right and left, and it is with some relief that one reaches the top. Here, the vegetation changes, and soon we see the wild vines growing by the roadside, though with some doubt as to the wine made from them. The wild flowers must be a wonderful sight in the spring and early summer; and there are white birch trees, wild wistaria, and when we reach the lake, enormous numbers of azaleas and maples. But there is a rude interruption in the form of a rash of souvenir stalls, selling nothing of any interest whatever, and then we resume our drive along the lake bank to an inn where we have luncheon. Mount Nantai is just to the back of us through the lovely and romantic forest, so different in all its mythology and associations from the woods at home, using that term in its larger sense to embrace all woods from Sweden to the Mediterranean. We come back along the lake bank in order to see the Futaarasan shrine and another temple beyond it, both of them picturesque, but neither of them particularly interesting; and a little sated with lakes which are the same all over the world, and down the hairpin bends again and back at Nikko, quicker, at any rate, than the driver had bargained for.

The Shrine of Ieyasu, seen once, and sometimes even twice a day for nearly a week, and the surrounding avenues explored, lead sooner or later to the Shrine of Iemitsu. But the grandson's Shrine and Mausoleum are not a paler, but if anything a more golden imitation of his grandfather's. Yet for some reason they fail to hold the attention, and one never finds oneself thinking of them except as something lost and forgotten on a rainy day. It is a pity not to have seen them in the snow when their bright and barbaric colours would have their chance against the ivies and the ferns. The way to the shrine of Iemitsu is down that long walk of cryptomerias leading from the main avenue, and past the Futaarasan shrine, where probably we stay for a last dance of the virgin priestesses, and then walk on.

That there should be a second group of shrines, lying almost at right angles to the first, and hidden in the wood, we discovered to our advantage on our last day in Nikko. The way to them is through a wilderness of stone lanterns, more depressing than any cemetery, through a wet underworld of ferns and mosses that may riot with wild

flowers, but was only rampant with ivy in October. Of a sudden, there
are gateways and flights of stone steps climbing steeply up the hill under
the tall cryptomerias, but all of it only reminded me of some neglected
old municipal garden of the Second Empire in Paris; the garden of the
Place de la Trinité, past the Gare St Lazare, or a dozen others, and the
shrines once reached seemed to be buildings brought over for an
international exhibition a hundred years ago, now deserted but kept
polished and in a high state of repair. They are, in fact, in the charge of
Buddhist, and not Shintô priests, and one or two of them are about
with shaven heads, in their brown habits which it is intriguing to be
told are of *mokuran* or magnolia fibre. But this is after climbing the
steps and passing three gateways of 'Indian-red' lacquer, covered with
golden Tokugawa crests and Dogs of Fo and peonies, and guarded by
demon-kings ready at a moment, to go down the trap-door with a
puff of smoke and a Bengal flare in the dusty pantomime. The last of
these gates is the *Karamon* or Chinese gate, with nothing particularly
Chinese about it, and now we are in a pebbled court where we take off
our shoes and shuffle into the *Honden* or oratory, which stands with the
holy of holies or *Haiden* immediately behind it, like a pair of huts,
back to back, but overladen with gold and glittering with precious
metal. The interior is as that of the Shrine of Ieyasu, only more so, and
in paradox, less so, as well, being the copy and not the original. All the
usual dragons, phoenixes, giraffes and peonies; tigers with *hôwô* (what-
every they may be) and bamboo on one panel, and *shishi* flowers and
birds on the other. The holy of holies behind it is not shown but must
be still more glittering and golden, though, as always, these are but
small, hut-size buildings. And coming out again we had to be content
with walking to the sides of this forbidden secret and guessing at what
it must be hiding from us. To the right of it, a gateway in the wall
called the Kôkamon, a curious affair with stooping rounded shoulders,
whitewashed and much dilapidated, and said to be in 'Chinese Ming
style', leads up more steps to Iemitsu's tomb. But the 'Chinese' gate was
shut and locked, and there was no climbing through more trees to see
another tomb. And we came down the long stairways just as it began
to really pour with rain.

Chapter Thirteen

·•·•·•·•·•·•·•·•·•·•·•·•·•·•·•·

THE INLAND SEA

THERE MUST COME THE MOMENT of satiety in Japan, though I never felt the faintest hint of that, just as there are limits imposed by time and by physical factors on the amount that one can see. It is of no use to attempt everything—a term which even in achievement would only mean a little more than nothing—and to try and do in a few weeks what might occupy a lifetime. Better to pick and choose, and to eliminate. The grand object in coming to Japan had been to see the temples and gardens and the works of art. This ideal had by now reached to some response in respect to temples and gardens though owing to the season the flowers were lacking, but perhaps in years in Japan one would never see all the works of art but only about half of them, with sad failures and considerable disappointments. So one had best be content with realities and grateful for a month in Kyoto with new wonders every morning and afternoon for nearly thirty days on end.

We were not able to visit the northern island of Hokkaido which is about the size of Ireland, and in consequence never saw the Ainu of whom there are only about sixteen thousand still surviving, Stone Age, *Sacre du Printemps* Aryans, or pre-historic Russians, almost, notorious for their abundant black hair, men and women alike, long beards, and luxuriant walrus-style whiskers or moustaches. They are not yellow-skinned but have blue eyes, wear dresses of beautiful bold pattern, breed yellow dogs of Spitz type which they use for bear-hunting, and show no resemblance whatever to the Lapps of Northern Europe who are decidedly Mongolian in type and to whom they are obviously not related. But neither do they in the least resemble other northern peoples, Eskimos or Samoyedes. Outside the towns such as the island's capital, Sapporo, 'laid out in 1871 on the American plan, with wide tree-lined boulevards intersecting each other at right-angles', Hokkaido is an island with crater lakes and active volcanoes, coal mines and skiing resorts. It has immense forests; and returning travellers, who are more often not tourists but business men, will tell you of huge magnolias seventy or eighty feet high and giant snow-laden cryptomerias standing on the hillsides; while if they cannot claim in the words of the old guide book that the bleaching bones of the cachalot are often to be seen along the coast, so teeming are those cold seas, it is at least true that there are inland lakes which in spring are one mass of edible water-lilies and that in May and June the sandy shores of some parts of the island are thick with lilies-of-the-valley. There are no temples and no works of art in Hokkaido[1] but the woods and flowers and hills are lovely, and without having been there one can understand the motives of at least one Japanese family of art lovers who have houses both in the northern island and in Kyushu, the southern island, in order to enjoy its bamboo glades and semi-tropical flowers and trees.

About half-way (two hundred miles) from Tokyo, on the main island going north towards Hokkaido, is the large town of Sendai with a temple which we should perhaps have visited. This is the Osaki Hachiman shrine built soon after 1600 by Date Masamune, the *daimyô* who at one phase in his career leaned towards Christianity and even sent an embassy to Rome. The *Honden* of this temple is a much lacquered and gilded affair in Nikko style, more restrained than its fellows, but still on the cricket or golf-pavilion scale of size, and lying as is so often the case in Japan among beautiful cryptomeria groves. But this one temple, more or less, could be little compared to what we had seen in Kyoto, and we even felt more interested in the Sendai chests which are a local industry and have a character of their own, particularly the older ones, though these do not compare with the Korean cabinets with their brass trimmings and great hinges. And owing to not seeing Sendai we never went to Matsushima, which is only a few miles away, the famous bay with hundreds of pine-clad isles and islets, and a temple or two upon them, the inspiration of Kôrin for his great *Wave Screen*, his best, or only good painting, now in the museum at Boston. But there is no loneliness like that of famous beauty spots at night, and fresh from the lilies and languor of Nikko where it had never stopped raining, night or day, and one's mind was confused with dragons and peonies, chrysanthemums and phoenixes, we decided to give Matsushima a miss and go instead to Miyajima which is on the Inland Sea, a project with the additional attraction that it meant

---

[1] Also, there are no monkeys in Hokkaido, as on the main island, but, instead, the woods of the northern island have grizzly bears which enter largely into the Ainu mythology.

adventuring again into the warm south, some two hundred and fifty miles farther than we had been before, in late September or the first days of October.

On the way south we were to visit the Shrines of Ise and made a stop, therefore, at Nagoya which with well over a million inhabitants is one of the three or four largest cities in Japan. Our cousin who was taking round a colleague in the Shell Oil Company was to arrive with other high officials of the Japanese sister company in the evening, and in the meantime we spent a most interesting afternoon. I had long wanted to come to Nagoya to see 'a flourishing provincial town', in the same way that one is curious about provincial towns in any other country including one's own, for I never went to Coventry which is at no great distance from my home until only a year or two before it was destroyed in the 'blitz', and was then surprised at the number of its red sandstone, mediaeval churches. Nagoya is, in fact, in some ways a counterpart to Coventry but with ten times its population, and like Coventry it suffered terribly during the last war. I did not care to ask what was the death roll but it must have been appalling and due to American bombers based on Okinawa. The entire centre of Nagoya has been entirely rebuilt, and on the whole in good modern style. When the plans are completed it will be a fine modern town.

That one would prefer the old with the new goes without saying from a sybarite who like the writer is ever in search of both worlds. For Nagoya from what little is left of it which is chiefly restaurants must have been strangely, even perversely picturesque. From our hotel which was more modern and efficient than in any provincial town in England we set forth, shepherded by officials of the Japanese Shell Oil Company, for Nagoya Castle, or, at least, the enclosure where it once stood and is rebuilding. This huge structure of five storeys a hundred and fifty feet high in Japanese castle-style was built soon after 1600 by one of the sons of the Shogun Ieyasu, and was the seat of the Owari branch of the Tokugawas, one of the 'Three August Families' who could provide a successor to the Shogunate in default of a direct heir. But little or nothing remains of its former magnificence. One would have liked to see the room on the top floor where, 'at each of the four corners there were sliding windows with seats where sentinels kept watch, night and day, over the plain, and there was a table in the centre with scores of lines radiating in all directions, like sunbeams, with the names of towns, roads, and passes whence enemies might come' (Terry's Japan, 1920), in prophecy, one might think, of dispositions in the Pentagon, or at Fort Alamo. In a temporary building there was, however, the pair of golden dolphins which used to be seen glittering all over the city from the top of the Donjon, and also a number of paintings from the castle though these fell far short of expectation. A slinking tiger or two with heavy pads and bleary eyes, but no more than that of the *Toranoma* or tiger rooms, with sliding panels of tigers and bamboos; and walking on slippered feet over 'nightingale floors', of the doors painted with pines and brightly coloured leaves, the Civet-Cat Room with the cat-eyes looking straight at one from whatever angle, peach and apple-blossom panels, owl and oak tree paintings (that read like Lear's *Nonsense Rhymes*) upon cedar doors, willow trees and white storks upon a golden ground, waterfalls beneath arching trees, to the climax of snow-laden trees with blue magpies, and a painting of a giant plum tree which was forty feet long. There only remained of this splendour that must have rivalled the Nijô Castle at Kyoto, the tigers and a few other damaged paintings, and the rest must have been either destroyed in the fire, or removed elsewhere.

There are marvellous relics of that past however, in the Tokugawa museum which displays the treasures put on view by 'Mr' Tokugawa, as he is now known since the abolition of titles, the head of the Owari branch of the family. They are shown to advantage in a big museum hall, the most immediately impressive of the exhibits being a series of magnificent *kimonos*, some eight or ten in number, so glorious in design that they nearly take one's breath away. But enough, or even too much has been written in this book already about patterned dresses, and I will only mention one greenish-yellow *kimono* of exquisite colour, and another like a chequer-board of flowering squares. They were the most splendid that we saw in Japan and my descriptions on earlier pages are from illustrations. The huge size of the *kimonos* is very impressive. They do not seem to have been intended for a race that are small in stature. Other works of art on view include wonderful early scroll paintings of the *Genji Monogatari* with a page open at a group of Court ladies with their long straight hair flowing over their shoulders, peculiar moustache-like eyebrows, and twelve-layered, 'dodecaphonic' *kimonos*. There are, as well, lacquer objects, and in particular a curious con-trivance rather resembling a lacquered clothes-stand or towel-horse but of exemplary finish, and used to scent the clothes with incense that burned inside it; and two superlative suits of armour, of *Oyoroi*, or great harness, one laced with purple or violet but I would prefer it wistaria lacing, and the other with white lacing but I am wondering whether it could be the deutzia scabra blossom which is white lacing. All in all, the Tokugawa museum in Nagoya contains wonderful and satisfying memorials of one of the historic families of Japan.

Our next quest was of another nature altogether. I had long known that Nagoya was the house of the *chin* dogs or Japanese spaniels. The guide book says that the dog shows held from time to time 'attract certain travellers', a category to which we belonged from the moment it was mentioned by virtue of having owned Cavalier spaniels which are their English cousins. While we were in the museum the chauffeur had been diligent in enquiries, ringing up the police and every pet shop in Nagoya, and had at last tracked down the only family of these remaining in the town. The others had all disappeared from Nagoya during or after the war. The only ones left belonged to a restaurant keeper to whose house we were taken, where there were anxious moments while we heard the dogs barking but no one came to answer the door, and we were afraid we would not get inside the house to see them. But at last a woman awakened from a siesta replied to our knocking, and we were in a room one half of which was partitioned off for the dogs and was a step higher than the floor. There were two fully grown dogs with black and white coats and bushy tails, with even and lovely splashes of white, spoon-shaped down their black foreheads, three or four bitches, one of them in whelp, and several puppies. Japanese spaniel puppies are probably the most delightful of all dogs, like playful and animated muffs or bounce-balls. These were larger than Pekinese, to which they are related, being descended from dogs brought from China perhaps a thousand years ago, and having become during the long interval a separate race. For some reason which is unknown Japanese spaniels bred in England or in Europe are more often red and white than black and white, but these were all of the latter colours, and one and all of the adult dogs were wearing delightful red silk frills or ruffs, which they wore already and that were not put on specially for our benefit. This tribe of spaniels was as 'Japanese' as anything we saw in Japan, as much so as Sumô wrestling, or as the doll-shops of Kyoto. They had become, we were told, extremely valuable owing to their rarity; and remembering the message of a friend who had owned a beloved Japanese spaniel which he had bought in Japan and brought back with him to England, an injunction to give his love to any of the breed if we were lucky enough to meet with them, we fulfilled the task imposed upon us and took our leave, extricating ourselves with some difficulty from their embraces.

For the remainder of that sunny evening we toured the big stores of Nagoya which were little inferior to those of Tokyo, returning to the hotel in time to meet our cousin. That night there was a grand gala dinner in honour of the Shell Oil officials, held in a restaurant some way out of the town, or, at least, in its suburbs. Probably it was in this neighbourhood that the temples stood which were destroyed during the war. Nagoya, like Kyoto, had its Higashi Honganji, though 'entirely reconstructed' early in the last century, and in any case reduced to ashes by aerial bombardment in 1945; but rebuilding in Japan means something quite different from rebuilding in Europe even if this applies more to Shintô than to Buddhist shrines and the Higashi Honganji at Nagoya must have been very picturesque, if only for its great kitchen with huge copper cauldrons wherein the pilgrims boiled their rice. The Tôshôgû shrine, another temple also burned to ashes, was, and still is, the scene of great processions held in April, with sacred cars or floats carried on men's shoulders *à la Sevillana*, escorted by robed Shintô priests on horseback which is a fresh conception for one has never thought of mounted priests apart from Tibetan lamas, followed by hundreds of men in ancient armour and 'fantastically clad youths and maidens'. Yet another temple, the Atsuta Shrine, also burned to the ground, was one of the most sacred places in Japan and contained the Sacred 'Grass-mowing' Sword which with the Mirror at Ise and the Jewels formed the Imperial Regalia and have been revered for close upon two thousand years. With all this the conclusion forms in one's mind that one would wish to have seen Nagoya before bombs rained down on it and it was destroyed. A fine modern city from municipal standards, if not the comfort and quiet of its inhabitants, is rising in its place, and Nagoya is the centre of a new religion with many adherents which in our godless century must make one careful what one says for the late Greek and Latin writers have been combed for a stray sentence, or even a phrase, in mention of a new religion that was starting in those days, not that the time was godless, but the gods were defunct or dying and, as now, some new god has to take their place.

The restaurant where we were taken to dine must have been near to those burned temples. Never had one seen such an extent of corridors with speckless floors along which one had to shuffle in slippers that were several sizes too small. There was now opportunity to put to the test what a Japanese friend had told us that this hygiene-mad people, to regard them from our sordid, smog-ridden experience and point of view, like to have the kitchens of their restaurants and eating-houses open to inspection for all to see, and therefore put in some conspicuous situation near the door. And here sure enough was the kitchen, as visible in every detail and action as an ant community put into a square box with a glass top, and with effects that were a great deal more appetizing as we watched from the passage, having to stoop and bow our heads owing to clumsy, barbarian height, and saw the lilliputian maids and scullions at work in clean linen fresh from some celestial snowdrift laundry, most of them wearing masks to spare us the contagion of their breath. After such an experience one feels one can never eat again in Soho!

But to the banquet! Which is in a large room with a steady draught, relentless as the twelve winds of the Ancients, but harmless in the results, where we dined at a table only some five or six inches from the floor, waited on and attended by *geishas* galore who to tell the truth become a little monotonous in their *idée fixe* which is to amuse and please, and who cannot compare with the *maikos* of Kyoto either in beauty of dress or manner. The customary, exquisite soups were served, as beautiful as ever in 'arrangement' with a strand of nereid weed or spray of fern; esoteric extract of prawn or mushroom, tasting, alternately, of ocean or of pine forest, but with always the hint or *soupçon* of seaweed. There was *thai* fish; and there was, or there seemed to be, octopus, which I ate recalling the polyps upon Cretan vases, and remembering that for anyone who has eaten *calamares en su tinto* in the Balearics, or in the Casa Solé that sea-temple of a restaurant down by the port in Barcelona, cuttle-fish are a commonplace and all but daily fare. One famous speciality was given us which, it seems, is expensive as caviar; a chestnut, no more or less, that has been evaporated or dehydrated in its own sugar by lengthy and secret process in some distant village in the hills. One family possessed this secret and had practised it for generations in true Japanese style. The transformed or resurrected chestnut tasted rather good. As we left, and went, stooping, of course, down the long corridors looking into the other dining-rooms and into the little courts and corners of landscape gardens in this land of the most beautiful restaurants in the world, my cousin remarked to me that the last time he was in Nagoya he had been taken to dine in a restaurant that was better and nicer still. Then, what a beautiful place that must be!

The next morning we were to go to the shrines of Ise and this was certainly an experience one will always remember. We started off early in a local train, noticing one or two pilgrims on the station platform who dressed very much as mediaeval pilgrims bound for Santiago, staff in hand. About half-way to Ise we changed trains into a two-decker pilgrim express, almost brand new, complete with 'vista-dome' on every coach, and with head-phones on the back of every seat. We disembarked from this super-train, worthy of the Roman-thermal railroad station at Chicago and the 'run' through the Rocky Mountains to the Pacific coast, at Yamada, drove a short distance, and then, as was unavoidable, got out and walked. One crosses a handsome bridge, and is immediately upon a broad gravelled path which leads directly into the sacred forest. It is a walk of half a mile or more, and the first drops of rain began to fall. Never has one seen such gigantic and straight-stemmed trees; cryptomerias, many of them eighty or a hundred feet high, with a number of sacred white cocks and hens walking sedately as though conscious of their holy immunity, and giving further point by their diminutive stature to the giant woodland scene. The avenue makes a turn to the left and the cryptomerias become taller still. It is the sacred grove *in excelsis*, such as there can be in no other land, and a place of marvellous and impressive solemnity as the rain comes down in sheets and the thunder shakes and booms. Already after a moment or two one is dripping wet, and is not half-way to the shrine. I have to confess to being in somewhat of a mental and visual haze owing to the pouring rain and the loud peals of thunder, but at last we came up some steps to the Gekû shrine, stood near to its timber structure, and could see the golden roof of the forbidden holy of holies only a few feet away. It is the most classical specimen of Shintô architecture come down unchanged for fifteen centuries or more, and entirely rebuilt in a new clearing in the forest every twenty years. Built of unvarnished cedar

Yômeimon Gate, at Nikko (early 17th century)

Hirosaki Castle (early 17th century)

Higashi Honganji Temple (early 17th century)

wood, 'selected *hinoki* and cryptomeria of the finest grain', cut from the sacred forests on the Kiso mountains, even the felling of the trees being attended with particular ceremonies, as that the carpenters must wear clean white clothes, bathe often, and if a workman cuts his finger and a drop of blood falls on the wood it is immediately thrown away. In fact, as much of care and of ritual goes into the periodical rebuilding of this shrine in all its simplicity as was put into the raising of the Temple of Solomon in all its glory. But the shrine of Geku has, comparatively speaking, no interior, and in any case one is not allowed inside.

Dripping and squelching with rain we now repaired through the downpour to the *Kaguraden* or sacred dancing hall a few hundred yards away. Here a special performance was put on for our benefit, in large part thanks to a Japanese friend accompanying us who had been at school with the prior or high priest. The dancing hall was empty as we entered and took up our places on the matted floor. But in a few moments the sacred virgins came in and began arranging things, as it were behind the scenes. Then the musicians made their appearance and sat with knees in front of them ready to begin. Immediately eight of the maidens took up their positions in front of the altar, four to each side, and with solemn step the high priest came in, making his entrance from the right. There followed a most beautiful and decorous dance of the maidens, who held rattles in one hand and a branch of the sacred *sakaki* in the other. On their heads were ornaments, little coral tiaras, shaped like trees, and their sleek hair combed into a tail touched their shoulders where it was bound into a twist of clean white paper. All the maidens were pretty, and much alike in height and feature, which with the graceful character of their dancing reminded me, I am not ashamed to say, of Mr Cochran's Young Ladies. I would think it is incontrovertible that someone, and someone with considerable taste, has 'been at' their dances within the last few years. I cannot believe their dancing has come down unaltered from ancient times. Indeed, as we shall see, there is every evidence that their dances have been reformed and purified. The dances, themselves, obviously signified some form of purification or lustration from the gestures of the virgins, while the ritual of the high priest consisted in the unsheathing and waving of a sword blade, not without, I must remark, solemn and beautiful as it was in symbolism, some little affinity to Nazi ceremonies at the Nuremberg rally.

Through the medium of coloured postcards on sale at the shrine we

s

can obtain some idea of other sacred dances performed at Ise, or, as it should be more correctly called, the Jingû shrines. The coloured folder, also a reproduction of a drawing in colour, shows one of the huge drums of the *Gagaku* stage, just as we saw that in the Imperial Palace at Tokyo and on the isle of Miyajima, thus affording a clue as to the origin of the music and the dances at Ise, and finishes in lighter vein with a hand drum and a sacred white cock and hen, exactly as those we saw under the tall cryptomeria trees.[1] The series of postcards then proceeds with a *Gagaku* dancer in gold tiger or cat mask, persimmon-coloured dress with long train, dancing, gold stick in hand, just the same dance we saw performed in the two places I have named; continuing with a kneeling priest in ant-like head-dress, a head-dress like the whole outline of an ant, in a white robe, the hilt of his sword showing, who is holding and offering a spray of leaves. I do not know what leaves. They look like maple leaves before those turn colour; and now I see that the priest has a little spray of yellow flowers tucked into the waistline of his ant-like hat. Next, we have one of the virgin priestesses kneeling in her white surplice and scarlet divided skirt, holding a bough of the same green leaves which is, of course, the sacred *sakaki* tree, and now we can see her coral tiara properly, like a little flowering tree of coral, with long green streamers falling from it to below her waist, and her neat black hair. And the last of the drawings is of a butterfly dance; that is to say, the girl wears a parrot-green gown with long sleeves which have a crimson lining, a curious kind of bib or gorget, a little reminiscent of the 'heraldic' bib of the Himalayan satyr tragopan in the courting season, and a magnificent pair of wings, putting to shame the plain gauze wings of the 'Sylphide' Taglioni. These wings in many colours, scarlet and red predominating, are the width of her wide sleeves; and we follow up her green silk head-cords and look into the dancer's face, and see that above her silver forehead band she has a spray of yellow *sakaki*(?) flowers put into her sleek hair, and holds another spray of the yellow flowers in her hand.

When we emerged from the sacred dance hall it was really pouring. It was emptying itself over one out of the clouds. It was no longer the phenomena of simply being wet through. We were, ourselves, pouring like fountains. There were cascades running from my hair and hands,

---

[1] For the description of a journey to see the white 'chickens' of Santo Domingo de la Calzada, in Northern Spain, see my *Truffle Hunt*, Robert Hale Ltd, London, 1953, pages 298, 299.

and my shoes dripped water like water-cans. The rumbling thunder now
crashed and roared, one would say, among the top boughs of the
cryptomeria trees. With that long squelching walk ahead of us till we
could pour ourselves into the waiting car we had to abandon visiting
the other shrine, the Naikû, four miles away, where the Sacred Mirror
is kept, but in any event no one is allowed to see it, and the exteriors of
both shrines are said to be so alike as to be almost indistinguishable from
each other. We had also to give up going to see the pearl fisheries, near
by, which had been the other object of the day; and it would be
invidious to remark that the women pearl divers in their special
costume, 'consisting of knickerbockers, a short skirt, and a blouse', can
have been no wetter than we were, even when reclining, wooden tubs
tied to their waists, on the ocean bed reaching for the oysters.[1] Instead,
we went off to luncheon, leaving trails of water in our footsteps as we
disembarked. It must have been at one of the restaurants at Yamada,
where the ladies of the party had their clothes dried and were given
kimonos to wear, meantime, but I remained in my sopping wet suit,
fearing the worst, which never came. I was entirely wet through for
some twelve hours that day with no ill results, and remembered reading
of the Scots shepherds who would wet their plaids with water—or was
it whisky?—before going out of their turf cabins to spend all day in the
mists and rain. The restaurant at Yamada was as beautiful as any we had
seen and we spent much of the pouring afternoon there, talking, and
warming ourselves at a charcoal brazier. It was in this town, of old, that
special dances of somewhat notorious character were performed for the
pilgrims; the famous or it is even called 'infamous' Ise-*ondo*, with
ascending stage in best pre-war Hamburg night-club tradition, but, we
may be sure, with a good deal more of outward propriety. Other
'trashy' dances were performed, including a Moorish-sounding one,
reminiscent of Fez or Marrakesh, where the spectators threw coins at
the dancers, who ducked their heads and collected the money at the
end. The Ise-*ondo* is said to be of great antiquity; and we are even told,
which is more interesting, that up till the Meiji Restoration in 1868 the
Kagura dances we saw at the shrine were only performed in private
houses, in which year private performances were prohibited and
henceforth the dances were only performed at the shrine. One is un-

[1] 'A lively woman will bring up a hundred from ten fathoms in sixty seconds. . . . They are
interesting figures when they dive and splash and thrash about in the water, uttering hoarse
whistling sounds as they go under and when they come up.' Terry's *Japan*, 1920, pages cxx, cxxi.

willing to believe that Mr Cochran's Young Ladies, as we saw them at the Gekû shrine, can ever have performed in such circumstances, and it is for this reason we conclude that the *Kagura* dances have been much altered and improved in tone.

We returned to Nagoya for the night, and the morning after the deluge was spent nearby, at Yokkaichi, inspecting the huge oil refinery with the planning of which my cousin had been much concerned. 'Inspection' is a term used advisedly in this context, and with serious reservations, because it cannot apply at all in the case of someone who has no understanding whatever of machinery. But the refinery is certainly a marvellous example of modern engineering, costing sixteen million pounds to install, we were told, and being at that moment, so to speak, at the word 'go', and ready to begin operating at the pressing of a button. The Dutch and British engineers who took us round, and tried patiently to explain the workings, obviously regarded it with much pride and affection, and it must be in their eyes as though they had planned the building of some great cathedral that was now about to charge itself and begin pumping and throbbing. They looked on it as a live thing with a purpose. Certainly it was not without beauty with its gleaming metal shafts and pylons. The principle of the catalyst was explained at length but I was only able to grasp it in its human and historical implications, as that certain persons in history, or even within one's own personal knowledge, have clearly been the catalysts in their own environment and age. We were shown the quays at which the oil tankers would soon tie up and discharge their cargoes; and engine rooms where as many screws and taps as would work an atomic submarine were in charge of one Japanese mechanic who looked to be not much more than eight years old. The work of construction and installation had been done nearly, if not just as well as it could be done in Europe, in half the time, we were told, and at about half the price. After all this, we had luncheon in a club to which the officials, Europeans and Japanese alike, belonged, and then took our cousin back to Nagoya along a road crowded with lorries, arriving only just in time for him to catch his train.

In the afternoon we went to the big stores again, finding some new ones we had not seen before, and one, in particular, with a children's playground and a garden on the top floor. It was to be noticed in the shops in Nagoya that foreigners were still a subject of curiosity and the cynosure of every eye. All the same it was impossible for any Japanese to be more surprised at seeing me than I was astonished at finding myself, so improbably, in Nagoya. Indeed, on returning to the hotel, I lay down in a state of happy exhaustion, and not for the first or last time could hardly believe I was in Japan. That evening we dined in a beautiful restaurant, Heiankaku, serving Chinese food, near the hotel, and down a narrow lane one side of which gave upon a small river. This was a part of the old town that had miraculously survived bombardment. Our restaurant did not look onto the river, and had the usual enchanting little corners of garden. The waitress who attended on us was tall for a Japanese, and imbued with a very personal and graceful melancholy of her own, as though, which was more than probable, she had had a sad and difficult life and was a prey to melancholy regrets or memories. It was a pity that it was not possible to hold more than monosyllabic conversation with her. She came from Tokyo, and we wondered why she had left the capital. Afterwards she showed us the other dining-rooms, and I remember her graceful way of walking and the gesture with which she threw open the sliding partitions and then passed on to the next. We walked the short distance back to the hotel, crossing the bridge and looking down the other half of that narrow street along the river which was one mass of lurid theatre and night-club signs and posters, made stark with neon lighting, to find that while we dined, one side of the main street had become an encampment of canvas booths where people were sitting, eating. Generally in pairs, a young man and a girl, hidden in clandestine manner by the flaps of canvas. The stall-keepers were women, and the booths seemed to be set up according to what they were selling, rice or noodles along one stretch of the street, and meat or fish on another. Such stalls, all over the world, would seem to be a theme inseparable from shell-fish, and I would think that oysters must have been their original inspiration. Despite the oriental accent one could not but be reminded of Cruikshank's London when Whitstable 'natives' were the cheap food and sold for threepence a dozen. We were tired and went to bed early, but when I looked out of the window towards midnight the booths were still there, lit by their flares, and no doubt the flirtations and the whispered conversations were still in progress. But when I looked out of the window in the morning the street was as usual and the booths were all gone.

The following afternoon was one of enchantment for we went to
Gifu. It stands out in my memory as second only to the afternoon we
spent at Uji, the village of green tea. But there was another, and still
more beautiful experience of an afternoon still before us, which I need
not mention yet for it is where this book must end. The manager of the
hotel at Nagoya already knew me for a neuropath owing to my
repeated questions which for the last day or two had centred around the
cormorant fishing at Gifu. At last all was arranged satisfactorily and he
had telephoned to a colleague in the hotel there called, simply and
engagingly, the Nagaragawa, undoubtedly asking him to look after us
on arrival as he would a harmless pair on ticket of leave from a mental
home. And look after us they did, even too carefully, as we shall see,
though it was not really their fault. Gifu is only about forty minutes
from Nagoya, but we went there, typically, by slow train, and then drove
down the immensely long street towards the river. All the way we
were looking in the shop windows for paper lanterns. Gifu is famous for
them, and at last we were in a part of the street with lantern shops on
either side. The hotel manager at Nagoya had told us we would find
just the same lanterns selling in the big stores. But he was wrong. We
had enquired in the lamp department of every one of them, and there
was not a sign of a paper lantern. This had been disappointing at the
time, but was now highly satisfactory. What could be more typical of
the legendary Orient, as that should and ought to be, than to spend a
half-hour choosing paper lanterns on our way to the cormorant fishing!

There were lanterns that were simply lanterns in a variety of shapes
and sizes, and others that opened like concertinas and had black lacquer
plinths and cornices. They were in every colour and had enchantingly
pretty designs on them. Perhaps the simplest were the prettiest of all;
but there were others that were so elaborate that they opened into
eaves and turrets that were like the castle of Nagoya. And all of them,
of course, shut up as flat as an old gibbus opera hat. Waiting about,
and becoming confused with so many shops all selling paper lanterns,
I began thinking of them as huger versions of the paper flowers that
come out of a packet and open their petals in a tumblerful of water, thus
joining them still more strictly in imagery to fishes and to cormorant
fishing. And then in any case paper lanterns carry with them an association with festivities and fireworks and lit up gardens. Near by, there
are lights and music upon the water. And we crossed the street looking

for more lanterns, but came back to where we had started which was the best shop of them all. When we left, we had enough paper lanterns to give a water party on our own.

In a very few moments we were crossing the Nagara river on a fine wide bridge. From it there is a lovely view up and down the river, and a building on the far bank down to the right must be the hotel, to which we drive along an embankment, looking up at the building that could, in fact, be a station hotel at—where shall we say? For it must be some-where in the British Isles where, exceptionally in a wet climate, there can be clear evenings. And I am settling in my mind for Parknasilla, or somewhere on Galway Bay looking towards the Aran Islands, when the loveliness of the evening comes over me and I know in my mind I shall never see anything like it again. By which time we are in the hall of the hotel, wrestling about our supper-basket and enquiring about late trains back to Nagoya. Soon it is time to be off, and with two *neisans* carrying our supper and leading the way, we stumble over the pebbles and into the boat which has an awning, and the extravagant and unnecessary complement of three boatmen. Immediately, we cast off and cross over to the other bank of the river where we join the flotilla of other boats that are all waiting. It is a lovely evening with long shadows upon the water, and high wooded banks, and the next boat to us which is so big that it has a large table amidships, has a number of *geishas* aboard who are all singing. Presently, a plaintive, monotonous fluting is heard, and it comes nearer and nearer and is only a foot or two away. Next, it sounds almost into my left ear; and a begging monk stands in the water, wastepaper basket over his head and face, and contriving somehow in spite of that to blow into his bamboo flute. We give him a few *yen* in order to get rid of him, but this only attaches him to us as though in permanence, and lamely and stutteringly he pipes a phrase from *Auld Lang Syne* over and over again, an air which the Japanese have adopted as their own because of its resemblance to their native music.

It gets darker and darker and we begin to eat our supper, a little tormented by mosquitos, and still finding it difficult to eat rice with chopsticks. It is a fish supper, and includes some *ayu*, a kind of trout which is what the cormorants are after. The begging monk will not go away although he is standing in the river up to his thighs, and the *geishas* in the next boat sing louder and merrier with their male admirers joining in. Suddenly there is a flurry and a creaking of rowlocks, and a long thin boat appears without an awning but with a brazier of flaming pitch-pine hung out on an iron pole from its bow, a decoy fire to draw the fish, and we see by the light of that in the darkness the standing figure of the master fisherman who wears a special kind of 'ceremonial' hat shaped like a priest's biretta. The master cormorant-fisher is a famous character, locally, and it being in Japan is very probably the twelfth or fifteenth of his family in hereditary succession. What are not so easily distinguished in the dark are the cormorants. However the characteristic outline of the head and neck of the bird, and its sinuous, rather snake-like black body are familiar from having seen a pair of cormorants on the lake on a demesne in Ireland. How well I remember seeing them there all those years ago, and thinking that cormorants were used for, I thought, sea-fishing in China, and were just the sort of subject for a *chinoiserie* tapestry or painting! How wonderful now to be at the start of the cormorant fishing on this lovely river after an evening spent in buying paper lanterns!

There are about a dozen of the birds standing on the gunwale or being put into the water, all with strings attached to them like marionettes. The master manipulates his twelve birds which are on strings or reins about twelve feet long, and his assistant works four more. They sweep swiftly past us going down stream, and at once all the pleasure boats in the flotilla push out from the bank and follow them. Every boat, which is most aggravating, except our own; and no amount of either cajoling or storming will induce our boatmen to join in the procession which has now floated down below the bridge and is out of sight though we still hear the sound of voices and singing. In this manner we attended the cormorant fishing without ever seeing a cormorant catch a fish. Each bird on a good night catches forty to fifty fish, which makes a catch of six to eight hundred *ayu*.[1] We missed seeing the fish caught; and we never saw the comedy of the cormorants delivering up their catch, squabbling over it and about their supper, into which questions of precedence and *placement* enter as much as with any grandee of Spain, and the final touch of their being put to bed in their separate baskets. All this we missed, although we had paid dearly for it, because of the refusal of our boatmen to lift an oar, or make even the feeblest attempt at following the other boats. Instead, we drifted about from

[1] Cormorant fishing, like most other things, is no longer what it used to be. In the 1880s a well-trained bird would catch a hundred to two hundred fish in an hour, coming up with them, two or three at a gulp.

bank to bank just in front of the hotel, never moving as much as a hundred yards from our starting point. We never found out the reason for this. The manageress of the Nagarawara, no less a person, affected not to understand, and then made a pretence that her colleague at Nagoya had told her we were too august to be mingled with the common herd. The commonsense explanation is that the boatmen were lazy and preferred talking and dallying with the two *neisans* who had moved down into the stem of the boat for greater convenience in conversation. On this idyllic evening on the river one could hardly blame them. So it was a delightful, if expensive and unsatisfactory excursion. And it was not to end without comedy of a more serious import. For on arrival at the station, having memorized the direction in which our train had come from when it landed us at Gifu, we found ourselves being put into a train on the same platform and heading the same way. Taking us, therefore, diametrically away from Nagoya, although several passengers nodded when we pointed and said 'Nagoya'—and heading for goodness knows where. For somewhere in the mountains where we should be put down late at night, hardly speaking a word of the language, and would have to spend most of tomorrow in the train coming back again. We hurriedly rushed from the carriage, brushing aside restraining hands, and boarded a train on the opposite platform, just as it began to move. Passengers were leaning out, beckoning to us to come back, just as our new trainload of companions were nodding and smiling at hearing the name 'Nagoya'. It was a mystery which never solved itself for obviously both trains were starting to go to Nagoya in different directions. But, at least, we had changed trains into the express and were safe back at Nagoya under the half-hour.

Next morning we had a journey of about two hours and a half to Osaka though, in fact, it was not the first time we had been in this city of two and three-quarter million souls. We had gone there from Kyoto about a couple of months before, but in order to make the narrative easier both visits are combined together into one. On that first occasion which was in August we had come to see over a silk factory. It was quite the hottest day in a month of continuous heat wave, and the cement paving outside the factory was little short of incandescent. Within, the water put down in order to wet the floor had been converted into steam. The floor of the factory extended over some acres, and the machinery was at work monotonously stamping out the patterns. It was a curious, and yet more heating experience to be in that gaunt building surrounded by, and all but treading on, what amounted to kilometric lengths of rosebuds, as at some Neronic banquet, and quarter-mile stretches of whatever the design might be. All in charge of one solitary female in blue overalls, with nearly as much of machinery at work as we would find in the engine room of an Atlantic liner. But this was only in a part of the factory, and as we plodded round, the four of us, including my cousin's wife and her small boy, with a kind of sergeant-major as from a prison camp in charge of us, we came into a huge hall where there must have been about a hundred young women and girls working at the bench. It was during a crescendo of the midday heat and we must undoubtedly have presented a comic spectacle. A quartet of red or white devils, it matters not which for one becomes careless of accuracy on the equatorial brink, but devils of whichever hue transformed by heat and weariness into 'eccentrics' of the old music hall at whose mere appearance the audience would go off into fits of laughter before a word was spoken. The Japanese have naturally good manners where foreigners are concerned, at any rate in peace time, but our arrival was too much for them. Our strategic situation was made worse by there being a staircase in the far corner of the hall towards which the sergeant-major was leading us, with another floor in prospect presumably covering just as large an area, and no possibility of retreat. For the first and last time in our lives we had an audience in fits of laughter and had to run the gauntlet of them as down the *hanamichi*, or, 'flower way' of the *Kabuki* theatre. It fell to me moreover, being the adult male of the party, to be the last to climb the stair, and my head was above the landing while my feet still trod that sea of mirth. Mercifully, to our astonishment, that next floor consisted of one room only where there were scale models of the factory which were brilliantly lit at the turn of a switch and showed the whole process of silk-dyeing, just the toys to absorb and interest a young boy, and we had the vista of an endless time of experiment and explanation. But the heat had been too much even for my small cousin Nigel, and he asked if he could lie down, and expressed a desire to return immediately to the hotel. This was agreed, unanimously, but we had to come down that stair again into our audience, tread the 'flowery path', women and children, first, myself in rear, laughing helplessly, ourselves, for it was in fact extremely funny, and so through the scorching empty halls, backstage, and to the hotel.

Perhaps one had never realized before the full beauty of air-conditioning as on that afternoon when we came through the swing doors on to the deck of the iceberg, as it were, and sat down and ordered iced lemonade. So we were in Osaka. But it is a little worse than presumptuous to write of a city of almost three million inhabitants upon an acquaintance of hardly as many days. Later that afternoon being somewhat recovered we went to the *Kabuki* theatre, but it was an inferior company not nearly so good as either of those we saw in Tokyo. Even so the scenery was beautiful, and the *onnagata* with their strained voices were as tearful and pleading as ever. One had been in bigger towns than Osaka but none that *seemed* to have so huge a population. It was really and truly swarming with young men, all appearing to belong to the same age group, and all in white shirt sleeves. Orientals, certainly, but not inscrutable for they were all smiling, which with the Japanese means little more than a nervous habit. How could one understand them except that, basically, we all have the same problems! In Osaka, as in Tokyo, the worst of these are overcrowding, though even in the poorer quarters it is doubtful if there are more persons sleeping in one room than in the slums of Glasgow. The long journeys to work by train or tram must be another bane, and there are no open spaces or recreation parks. Formerly there were many temples but all of them are destroyed. Osaka lost more than half of its houses in the war, and nearly half of its population suffered war damage. Walking one evening, with a little Japanese friend of ours who commuted from Kyoto, which is only three-quarters of an hour away, we were spectators of the evening rush hour. He had obtained leave of absence from his office in order to look after us, and when we commented on this struggle which is as violent as a wrestling match, twice every day, in the morning and the evening, he replied 'And to think I am one of them!', and I felt a sudden pang of pity and of sadness. What is it all for, they may well ask themselves, and the only answer is in order to get enough to eat.

The memory of Osaka is of a pallid white city with tall mock skyscraper buildings rising into a pale sky. Of the 'Venice of Japan' with its canals and its eight hundred bridges there is little evidence since the rebuilding. The Yodo, its main river, apart, there is perhaps no more sign of water than there is at Sheffield which is on the river Don. Yet, even now, boat-restaurants are spoken of which make a speciality of oysters in their season. There are, of course, quantities of other Japanese and Chinese restaurants some of them no doubt as pretty as any in this land; and it is of Osaka in particular that the guide book says: 'In the yards of some of its tea-houses are huge cages filled in summer with fireflies, which are liberated for the pleasure of the guests, or put into tiny bamboo cages for them to take home', (*Terry's Japan*, 1920). Even though the temples and shrines are destroyed the festivals continue, as, for instance, at the Temmangû shrine where there is an all night river procession, but not upon the Yodo river, with dancing upon boats and side shows upon the river banks; and the portable shrine reaches a certain place about midnight, and the return journey lasts till dawn. But for knowing this, one might think no city of nearly three million inhabitants was so ill-provided for in respect of places of worship but, much worse still, in works of art. Osaka Castle, which was the castle of Hideyoshi and the biggest thing of its kind, 'has now been re-constructed in reinforced concrete and provided with elevators', but of a purpose we only viewed its five-storeyed donjon from afar.

It is another matter altogether where theatres and music are con-cerned, for Osaka is the scene of music festivals and concerts and many of the great virtuosi of the world have performed here. But Osaka has a feature that is absolutely and entirely unique, and that is the *Bunraku*. We came over from Kyoto especially in order to see it. For the *Bunrakuza* of Osaka is the only puppet repertory theatre in the world, and all who only know of marionettes from a Punch and Judy show are heading for a new experience.[1] There also are, or were, the Sicilian marionettes that performed in Palermo and in Catania, and this was a genuine art form. Their repertory was largely taken from Tasso's *Gerusalemme Liberata*, and the forced voices and clanking armour of the paladins remains long in the mind. But *Bunraku* has an older and fuller history than either Punch and Judy or the marionettes of Sicily, and it was with high expectations that we found ourselves at the door of the almost brand new *Bunrakuza*. It was in fact opened on 1st January, 1955 and, let it be said at once, is handsomer than any London theatre. A curious sensation to find this great new puppet theatre in a huge new sprawling town! We came early and went down to the

---

[1] There are German and Russian and Swedish puppet companies, and the Teatro dei Piccoli which performs operas, but none of these have a tradition and all are spoiled by 'artiness'.

restaurant for a cool drink, emerging just as the audience was going to its seats and buying paper fans. The drop had white peacocks painted on it, large as miniature aeroplanes, and after premonitory clacking of wooden clappers the *Jôruri* reciter and the *Samisen* players swung into place and the curtain rose.[1] The play, needless to say, involved a ghost-fox that was manipulated 'on' and 'off' with odd, unconvincing gait. But the whole performance is peculiar indeed, to begin with the *Jôruri* reciter who to a Western ear makes noises like a person of deepest and most inherent affectation explaining matters to an infant Bible class; using, too, the technique of the 'action story'. It is all in the tradition of the famous *Jôruri* reciter Takemoto Gidayû (1651-1714) who was a native of Osaka.

Oddest of all is not so much the narrative as the conversation between the characters. The reciter must change his voice according to the environment of the story; or to quote the leaflet sold with the pro-gramme: 'If it is in a town house, he has to begin his recitation lively: if it is in the woods, then ghastly; if it is in a *Geisha* quarter, then fascinatingly.' A great majority of the plays performed are by the great Chikamatsu Monzaemon (1653-1724) known, with little meaning, as the Shakespeare of Japan; but it seems to be the truth that the *Bunraku* puppets became so popular during the *Genroku* period more for the excellence of the plays than of the puppets, which explains how it was that the same dramas were later taken over by the *Kabuki* theatre and given 'live' performances that have persisted till today. The Japanese derive great pleasure from the *samisen* accompaniment which also, largely speaking, would be lost upon a Western audience. The puppets are two-thirds life size, by Nipponese standards, and are manipulated by the puppeteer who walks along a sort of trench below the footlights, and wears high clogs in order to be tall enough to hold the doll. The marionettes, therefore, are not worked from above by strings; but the chief puppeteer holds it as if it were a child, working its right arm and head, while his two assistants work its left arm and feet. It is the presence of the two assistants who wear black hoods and robes, and are not allowed to show their faces, that makes the *Bunraku* stilted and unreal. Creepy, also, because puppets like waxworks 'give one the creeps' in any case, but, also, the hooded pair who have to crawl and crouch low

---

[1] The *Samisen* is said to have been brought to Japan about four hundred years ago from the Ryuku islands (Okinawa), whence, also, come many of the best 'weaves' and folk arts of Japan.

and run 'on' and 'off' keeping their heads bowed low seem like servitors of the Inquisition or assistant hangmen.

The dolls look so clumsy and heavy; they are less like marionettes and more like ventriloquists' dummies. They are hoisted and held up with considerable strain, and it is peculiar indeed when the trio move the doll along with much effort, and you see the puppeteer in his rich silk robe and his Misericordia attendants in funereal black. During that afternoon performance we saw the veteran puppeteer, Bungoro Yoshida, who is ninety years old, and deaf and blind, but still famous for his manipulation of female dolls, especially the 'three princesses' of Bunraku. His mask-like countenance was most curious to watch, with hairless head and sightless eyes. His performance seemed mechanical, but sent the audience into raptures. It is an art said to be dying out owing to the difficult and tedious apprenticeship for the children begin by only being allowed to work the puppets' feet, and it may be as long as twenty years before they graduate into being allowed to work its head and hands. There are now thirty doll manipulators in the *Bunrakuza*, and the fact that this theatre now sometimes amalgamates and gives joint performances with its rival company, which was an offshoot from it, gives perhaps some promise that the *Bunraku* will continue. The dolls are gorgeously dressed and can move their lips and eyebrows, but it is even a little frightening to see them kicking and struggling, held up in mid-air. One cannot rid one's mind of the idea that there is something evil about them. Quite a number of persons might not like being left alone with the puppets. That they grow upon one and begin to assume human personality may be true enough, though that would always be dwarfed and stunted, and perhaps vindictive. Stories are told of puppeteers who have become, as it were, infatuated with their charges, lived with them and never allowed them out of their sight.

It is perhaps the strangest anomaly of all that there should be this puppet theatre in midst of a town larger than Manchester and Liverpool combined. One would have thought the public to be too sophisticated and that, if at all, *Bunraku* would have survived in some remote country town. For the rest, Osaka is unremarkable except for its sky signs. These attain to a pitch of imaginative fantasy that makes poor work of Piccadilly Circus or Times Square. I had meant while I was in Osaka to make a list of them. It would be fantastic reading, and should have a special vocabulary of its own as in a sales list of fireworks or the dictionary of hawking. The sky signs are perhaps best seen if you come through Osaka on a train by night, as we did more than once, but even in the middle of the morning there are all the advertisements flown from little tethered captive balloons, floating at about the height of the upper storeys of a skyscraper, a device unknown, or forbidden by police regulation, both in the West and in the USA. In the sky signs there is real fantasy, as though originating in a child's mind that is still at the stage of playing with electricity.

But the special draw of Osaka, and also its drawback, was as the starting point for other places. We went backwards and forwards through Kobe several times. It is only twenty miles away, but we had little longing to get out at this seaport with a million inhabitants. There is nothing whatever to see in Kobe, and its only possible attraction must be found among the astonishing list of restaurants; four Chinese in Peking style, two Cantonese, and twelve Japanese, together with four others serving *sukiyaki* (of beef, for which Kobe is celebrated), four more famous for broiled eels, *Kabayaki*, one or two for globe-fish, a great delicacy but sometimes deadly poisonous, and therefore the more thrilling, and yet four others for *sushi* which are slices of raw fish wrapped up in rice balls. But, for ourselves, Osaka had the sad attraction that it was our last chance of going to Kôyasan, a very different objective from Kobe, and all other considerations apart, a centre of austerity compared to the deleterious delights, just mentioned. In fact, for a short visit, a thaumaturgic and, withal, vegetarian paradise. For Kôyasan is the holy mountain, and we had to decide there was no time to see it if we were to go down the Inland Sea. It is a series of Buddhist temples and monasteries on a mountain side, about three hours from Osaka. But, in order to enjoy the shade and fragrance of its mighty forests one should stay a couple of nights in the monasteries, and we were leaving Tokyo next week. There was not time. Of the things we missed seeing in Japan, which must be many although we did in fact see nearly everything that was on our programme, the Shôsôin at Nara with its incomparable treasures of the eighth century and Kôyasan are most to be regretted.

There are still more than a hundred temples on the mountain, but the works of art they contain are shown with reluctance because of the dampness, and it is difficult to arrive at any decided opinion as to how much, even with the necessary permits, is still to be seen at Kôyasan.

There are Buddhist scriptures written on blue paper in alternate lines of gold and silver as in the *musée imaginaire* one installs for oneself upon Mount Athos, and there must be early sculptures and paintings. Many, if not most of the temples have been ravaged by fire, as always in Japan, and the great pagoda was burned to the ground and never rebuilt. But in the opinion of all who have been to Kôyosan it is the place itself which is wonderful. It is the sensation of waking at dawn and going to one of the temples to hear early mass. But, more still, the marvellous old cryptomerias and *hinoki*, and the way in which one temple leads on to another till, eventually, you reach the cemetery which is the great sight of Kôyasan. This was described to me as one of the beautiful places of the Orient, if not of the world; more beautiful, and this is to say much, than the Turkish cemetery at the mosque of Eyoub, on the Golden Horn. There, it is the turbanned headstones and the cypresses, and Europe and Asia on each bank of the narrowing waters. Here, and one is willing to believe it is more beautiful still because of remoteness and seclusion upon the holy mountain, the cemetery takes the form of an avenue a mile and a quarter long through the giant trees. Having seen the avenues at Ise and the woods of Nikko, one may have some conception of the huge old trees of Kôyasan. They are cryptomerias and Japanese cedars but, also, and in diminishing number as though growing rarer from their own antiquity, *Koyomaki*, the species to which Kôyasan has given its name, the umbrella pine (*Sciadopytis verticillata*), a survivor from before the Ice Age, and a tree which has the habit of growth that its bracts open, not as umbrellas performing their normal function, but like umbrellas or parachutes blown inside out, progressing, thus, not as branches, but by protected leaps and jumps.[1] There are, it seems, a few enormous specimens of umbrella pine at Kôyasan, and I would have dearly loved to see the sacred forest, the holy mountain, and the long avenue of the dead among its ancient trees.

Instead, in this age of railways in decadence in most countries of the world, we were to have the most enchanting railway journey. At the time, and now in retrospect, it seems a long day of enchantment, starting from Osaka at about ten in the morning and continuing for ten hours. In fact, a slow train for it covered not much more than two

[1] An umbrella pine known to me personally for it was planted in my own garden grew only three inches in ten years. From this, making allowance for their native soil, the age may be deduced of the older trees at Kôyasan. It is easy to believe, too, that the umbrella pines must make their own landscape, as araucarias, another primitive survival (but, also, they are the 'monkey puzzles' of Victorian gardens), must do when they grow to great stature in their native Chile.

Long tailed cockerel from Oshino, Shikoku

Kite fighting at Hamamatsu, Shikoku

hundred miles. But heading due south which always takes the mind to
Italy or Spain, and made agreeable from the start by the way in which
you can move about in the nearly empty saloon car and switch about
your arm-chairs. In this manner it is not necessary to spend all day in the
same seats, and you get the sensation of being mobile yourself while you
are moved along. The day opened unpromisingly with the run of
twenty miles of factories as far as Kobe, reminiscent of that from Leeds
to Bradford, or Halifax to Huddersfield. To this point one might have
felt misgiving as to what lay ahead for in fact this part of the journey is
only redeemed by being near the sea. But there is also the interest of
looking into the backyards of any Oriental town. At Kobe, too, the
train passes over some of the main streets; and in Kobe station the
'golden voice' of the loudspeaker after preluding fiercely and rapidly,
almost as though in parody of itself which we determined was only a
cynical reiteration of its own name, then softened into elegiac renderings
of *moshi-moshi* and *arrimasu*.

The journey down the Inland Sea has begun. Soon we are out of the
town, and near to the shore where there are huge old pine trees. The
morning mists are lifting like the transparent 'drops' in a transformation
scene and we are going to have a fine day. Those shapes rising behind
one another over the water must be Awaji island, which after long study
of the map I still confuse with Oshima or Vries island (called after the
Dutch navigator) lying off Tokyo, of which I have read and re-read the
description telling of the *anko* or island girls who wear *kimono* 'splashed
over with a white pattern', 'speak with a nasal twang', and have fair
skins and reddish hair, the result of rubbing it with camellia oil, the
chief product of the island. But this is Awaji and not Oshima; and
once we are past the tip of it we are really upon the Inland Sea, and
trying to find out more about Awaji I can only quote appetizing news
of it given in an old edition of *Murray*, to the effect that the production
for which it is chiefly noted is 'a sort of marmalade made out of an
excellent variety of orange resembling the Seville orange, and sold in
boxes with another pleasant sweatmeat made of acorns, cinnamon, and
sugar, the two sweetmeats together being known by the name of
"floating bridge", while a third preserve, made of plums, is known as
"sound of the lute",' information to remind one, here and now, that the
luncheon hour is approaching, and that we are depending for the day
upon the *bentô* or luncheon boxes sold along the line.

T

In about an hour, or it could be longer or shorter for one has lost all count of time, we are nearing Himeji and get a view from the window of its 'Egret' or 'Snowy Heron' Castle, now that the castles of Osaka and Nagoya are gone the grandest left standing in Japan, and it does in fact look strange and imposing from this distance and utterly unlike any western castle with its base or bastion of cyclopean stonework (from a photograph), and the whitewashed walls and tilted eaves of all the turrets in its three main donjons and the three minor donjons; more like a flight of 'snowy herons' with black heads, primaries and wing tips, than a single heron or egret as it hovers on patrol above the town. Certainly Himeji castle looks Japanese, no doubt of that, and it is only to be expected that it should stand in a park that is famous for wistaria. To this point, the castle and the backyards of the town apart, the scenery to tell the truth is a little disappointing. But there is a fascination in every village and small town we go through, the sun is shining and at every mile it becomes more interesting.

Now we are ninety miles from Kobe, right out 'in the blue', somewhere one has never been before and will never come again; and in fact if not in the blue on the glorious and brilliant edges of it as we go along the shore of the blue sea. Moreover, there is an unexpected and supernumerary enchantment of haunting sort, which puts all kinds of strange and fantastic ideas and comparisons into one's mind. It is this. The conductor of the train makes periodical announcements upon the loudspeaker for no determined reason that one can see, generally in mid-air between stations, and it would seem for his own pleasure. One cannot follow a word of what he says except for the familiar *dôzô* (please) and *arrimasu*, which comes in at nearly every other word and means almost anything, but, particularly, 'is there?', or, even, 'isn't it?' And every time he makes an announcement it is preceded by a little tune played upon a *glockenspiel*, and this is nothing more nor less than Schumann's *Traümerei* which will now for ever mean for me our day along the Inland Sea. When I was young a little piece like *Traümerei* meant much for me, and now it had new meaning. Each time the *glockenspiel* played those few and simple phrases in our carriage I experienced that tightening of all the receptive senses which is one of the sacred powers of music. It is indeed a trance, a *trauma* in which one must keep perfectly still, not moving or stirring. For I have no technical knowledge or understanding of music, and its effect on me is exactly that of the

Antarctic explorer playing the gramophone to a penguin. All I want is to listen again and for the music to go on. And is not Schumann in the *Fantasiestücke*, or in the *Kinderscenen* (from which *Traümerei* comes) the most traumatic of composers, to say nothing of *Carnaval*? Thanks to the little tune I was at a temperature of receptivity that was almost painful as we wound along the Inland Sea. How could it be otherwise, recalling early memories, and now spending the whole daylight of a beautiful and sunny morning looking out onto the changing landscape in this land of little and small things!

Now we are coming into Okayama and stopping at the station. This is another of the towns we have practically never heard of before with a population of about a couple of hundred thousand. With expressive gestures we had asked the guard to get us something to eat, having read that the *bentô* at Okayama were better than anywhere else along the line. He returned in a moment with two little plywood packing cases elaborately tied with string, but the knots slipped easily, and inside were chopsticks wrapped in tissue paper, rice, and some gelatinous sheets of seaweed. At which moment a woman passed the window hawking the most appetizing-looking baskets, bucket-shaped, of large size, as big as a lampshade, and with ferns protruding from them. We had positively to buy one of these, and haul it in just in time through the window. We hardly liked to open it, and wanted to take it home with us next week all the way to Honolulu, over the Pacific again and back to England, for it was one of the most attractive objects of its sort one had ever seen. But we had to open it for there were signs of premature melting and running, and under the ferns we found a clutch or nestful of the most delicious peaches. We would have liked to get out at Okayama, as almost everywhere else along the line, but particularly in order to see the Kôrakuen garden laid out by the local *daimyô* towards the end of the eighteenth century, with bridges, hills and waterfalls, and wistarias, cherry, apricot and maple trees—and a crane said to be over two hundred years old, but one fears it must be dead by now.[1]

It must be explained that the line does not run entirely along the sea

---

[1] Kyoto apart, the Kôrakuen is one of the three most famous landscape gardens in Japan. The others being the Kenrokuen at Karazawa, on the west coast, north-west of Kyoto and Lake Biwa, with among curiosities a famed cherry tree of which the flowers have two or three hundred petals; and the Kairakuen at Mito, about two hours from Tokyo, once belonging to the Mito branch of the Tokugawa family, who were Vice-Shoguns. Of its former ten thousand apricot trees, two thousand still remain. To a foreigner, the names Kôrakuen, Kenrokuen, and Kairakuen are confusing. Perhaps they are landscape parks more than gardens.

coast as, idiotically, it does whenever possible along the Mediterranean shores of Italy and Spain. But it runs inland as though to give one a taste of orange groves or persimmon, or the tea gardens, from time to time. The *glockenspiel* would play, and the voice of the diminutive guard make some announcement of which we would not understand a single word. It must mean something, and must be telling passengers the name of the next stop, and where to change trains. But for ourselves it was beginning to have magical connotation as though but to lead one the deeper and deeper into this enchantment of distance where we had not been before and would never come again.

Is the Inland Sea at all like lake scenery? For a little moment, now and then, it is like Lake Maggiore when you come out of the tunnels and the mountains, and are in Italy. But only for a moment, and then you see hills and islands rising behind one another, and many absurd little islets with nothing more than a fir tree or two growing upon them. Only to look at one of those islets, and you know immediately where you are. If it is not Matsushima which inspired Sôtatsu and Kôrin with its hundreds of islands, it must be the Inland Sea. And it is not Matsu-shima because there are other and bigger islands at the back. We are now right in the middle of the most beautiful stretches of the Inland Sea, where are many islets, and the mountains at the back which look like another mainland must be Shikoku, the fourth in area of the Japanese islands, which has a population of four to five millions and is about the size of Wales. This is the point at which we are nearest to Shikoku; then it recedes so that the Inland Sea is some thirty miles across and we are only near to it once again.

There are reasons for wanting to go to Shikoku, and one could reach it from several of the ports along the Inland Sea. As, once again, that tune played nostalgically upon the *glockenspiel*, I wished I were in the orange groves of Matsuyama; but, more so still, climbing the street of shops to Kompira or Kotohira shrine; small shops where one liked to think (but could be disillusioned) all sorts of little fascinating objects, sea-shells and pilgrims' staffs and rosaries would be for sale. As always at the shrines and temples there are camphor and *hinoki* trees of hoar antiquity; and there are, or were, tiger and stork rooms painted by Okyo, and 'an inner room with bunches of flowers' by Jakuchin. He is the fowl-painter by whom, when I was younger, I remember a painting of a hundred spangled cocks and hens, as bright and gay as the hundred and one harlequins. Once Buddhist, now Shintô, Kompira is among the most famous shrines in Japan. But, also, provincial journeys in Shikoku would be remarkable if not thrilling; to Naruto where there were kite-flying festivals (now no longer) and a thousand kites could be seen in the air at once 'on windy days in July and August'; kites fifty feet in diameter, and requiring two hundred men to hold them down (*Japan: Official Guide*). No doubt the kites had beautiful designs painted upon them in prophecy of sky signs, and one wishes to have seen them.

Nor is this all. If you continue a few miles further on to Tokushima it could be in time to see (in August) the *Awa-Odori*, a local puppet show of much fame with *Jôruri* chanting, which has to be performed between harvests because most of the puppeteers are farmers. Hereabouts, too, are the Tosa fighting dogs which in the small towns and villages are almost as much a centre of attention as fighting bulls. One sees photographs of champion dogs wearing their belts of office and rich collars. A breed that has been known for at least six centuries, though a canine authority says no pure breds have ever existed, the term being loosely applied to a cross-bred mastiff type.[1] Yet the only Tosa dog I have seen belonged most distinctly to a race of its own. It was the house dog of an acquaintance in Tokyo; a friendly black animal with the coat of a retriever, but smaller and more cobby in build. This is a breed that it seems has not been brought to England. But, most of all, I wanted to go to Kochi on the southern coast of Shikoku, another town with the incredible population of nearly two hundred thousand, with many new buildings, and a comfortable hotel, newly opened on the top two floors of a big department store. For it is near Kochi that there is the village of Oshino where are bred the *naga-o-dori* or long tailed fowls, some of them with tail feathers fifteen, or even eighteen feet long. They are produced by selection and inbreeding over many generations; and by the transvestiment that is the practise among birds it is the cock bird that is the princess and has to have its train borne and lifted out of the dust by a human train-bearer for most of its valued life. While that little tune is still playing how I would have loved to visit Oshino and its single-minded inhabitants intent on their snow-white birds with the long

[1] *The Observer's Book of Dogs* by Clifford L. B. Hubbard, Fredrick Warne & Co, London, 1945, page 191. 'Today, dog fighting is run on organized lines on almost all conceivably festive occasions, superintended by the police who award prizes to successful combatants.' Colours are black, tan or brindle.

trains! Shikoku seems to be an island where one should stay to forget
one's cares and worries, let time stand still for those few days and not
think ahead to the inevitable separation and to growing old.

But let us pay more attention to the present and forget the future! It
begins to press more heavily upon one than the past. We are going by
many little seaports, and there are modern shipyards opposite on the
island of Shikoku. The sun is shining from a cloudless sky. Today the
Inland Sea is another and remote Mediterranean which is all one's own.
It does not even belong to the millions who are living along it, but is our
personal property seen from the train window. We arrive at a town
called Fukuyama, and are brought down to earth by seeing something
new and interesting that we want to buy. But it is such a long train that
there is hardly time for the vendor to come past a second time. We step
out on to the platform wondering if we will ever get back on to the train
again. Not only into the compartment but into ordinary quotidian life,
and yet not wanting over much to be left behind. Because the illusion is
all of our own making and would be quickly shattered. Or perhaps not?
And at that moment the trolley is wheeled past, and we climb back on
board the train, each of us holding a brown pottery bowl of hot shrimp
soup with noodles. It is becoming an experience to buy *bentô* at the
different stations. We are off again and back in the enchantment.

In a moment or two more sets of islands come into view. All of them
unattainable even if there were room enough to land upon them,
impossible of access as the one set of stars which the mariner exchanges
for another as he sails into the southern hemisphere. And in fact we are
at the other side of the world. Let us not forget that. On the far shore of
our world and travelling along its Inland Sea that is now fairly scattered
with islets as far as one can look in every direction. The old guide (early
edition of *Murray's Hand-Book*) tells us we are passing a small town
which manufactures anchors for the whole of the Inland Sea, as well as
nine kinds of liqueurs—one flavoured with plum-blossom, another
tasting of chrysanthemums, and a third which is effectual in warding
off the years; and as *Traümerei* is played once more I think of Plougastel
on the far shore of our side of the world, in fact in Brittany, not far from
Finistère. Plougastel that lies on a promontory which is almost entirely
covered with strawberry gardens, where a liqueur called *Liqueur des
Quatre Saisons* is made, where till not long ago the men all wore
Phrygian caps, and the women a head-dress like that of the goddess

Isis, where other country people called them *Les Galiléens*, they only intermarried with each other, and were said to be emigrants, of all places, from the Troad. More rain falls there than in any other part of France. How far can it be from Plougastel to Fukuyama? From one end of the world to the other, but it can flash by before there is time to think of it. Which, too, is the way life must seem if one lives to be old.

We arrive at a town called Onomichi on a beautiful region of the Inland Sea near to where the best *tai* (sea-bream) are netted, and where gourmets eat them in the fishing boats, uncooked, as they come out of the sea. But, also there is a famous local brand of *sake* so that the gourmet is provided for in other respects as well. Onomichi must have been a picturesque place not long ago, with its 'shore lined with go-downs', and its fine, decaying temples up flights of steps among ancient groves of trees. It now being hot as ever and nearing five o'clock in the afternoon, which one discovers not knowing the day could go so quickly. There is only about fifty miles to go to Hiroshima, and marvellous clouds are gathering and towering in the sky. We stop at a station where some politician or local person of great importance comes on board after making a short speech from the window of his com-partment. All the crowd bow low to him; and when that is over stand in little rings and bow to each other, keeping their heads down in submission till their superior raises his.

It is the golden hour of the day, and I have an almost unbearable burden and presentiment from *Traümerei*. Already, the times the little tune has played itself seem out of touch and long ago. The four or five times it played this morning, and even this afternoon only an hour ago, are lost and gone for ever. The nostalgia becomes an agony. How could Schumann do this to me, coming back again and again to get me! And I began to think of a house, or even one room in it, with some little air by Schumann, protected, as it were by copyright, and belong-ing to it, a little air which you could hear nowhere else but here. *Traümerei* had become the embodiment of this whole day spent in the train. It was the symbol of the journey, and this little phrase out of the Romantic Movement was taking upon itself to personify an entire adventure into little and lilliputian enchantments, a land where every-thing was small and exquisite and no building was bigger than a tea-house. Every time it played it was a lifetime gone. How much, or how little had happened, now all forgotten! And it played again. I could see it would have a different connotation when all was dark outside the window, when the world was but the lighted compartment, and all the rest was but a trance or dream. For as long as it played one was young again, in youthful enjoyment of the day that was for this once and never more.

And it grew dark at last and we were coming to Hiroshima which we dreaded, where we never thought to be. By which time the sky had blackened, and it was raining hard and we were left long on the platform without a porter. The train did in fact go on to Miyajima where we were to stay the night, but we had made up our minds to go to the hotel at Hiroshima, rest a few moments, and continue the dozen miles by taxi. The hotel was a nearly new building standing on stilts in an empty part of the town a long way from the station. By the time we got there it was a downpour, and telling the driver to wait we got the hotel manager to telephone to Miyajima, and ask for the hotel jeep which was the only car on the island to meet us at the landing stage. For it was raining as it had rained at Ise, and in Tokyo at the beginning of the typhoon.

We did in fact return to Hiroshima two days later, but wanting this book to end as it should and must, I will speak of Hiroshima as we saw it by the morning light, and then resume our journey to Miyajima as we did in a few minutes, in the pouring rain. The hotel stands, as we said, in a part of the town which still shows all the signs of devastation, as from open cast mining. It does not here give the impression of some terrible disaster, and if one did not know one would only wonder why it stood alone and there were no other buildings. It is not unlike any other area where demolition squads have been at work. We did not spend a night at Hiroshima. We only saw it that evening and two mornings after. I think the hotel is near to that part of the town where there was the worst destruction. This is the area known as the 'Atomic Desert' where for a time it was supposed that no vegetation would grow and that it would be barren for seventy-five years. Why for that exact term of years I do not know except that it is a full human life span. There is a new cement bridge over a branch of the river, hereabouts, and it must have been here that there were the shadows of an old man leading an ox-cart and, I think, a woman sitting on the ground. These shadows were burned into the earth as by the glare from some frightful reflector, and we were told, whether truthfully or not I do not know, that this negative or reflection had to be dug down forty or fifty feet into the earth before it could be got rid of. The shadows seem to have been just at the foot of the bridge as though about to cross it. At any rate the shadows are now gone. Once the new bridge was built they were no longer there. Perhaps the most apt comment on the dropping of the atom bomb is that after so many aeons of human knowledge and sensibility it called into being the only human ghosts.

Another of them is yet to be seen in Hiroshima, sitting on the stone ramp outside a bank. That is to say, it is a solid stone building, one of the only such to survive the bomb burst, and still functioning as a bank. The effect of the intense heat of the bomb was to granulate the whole body of the stone and turn it into granite. All except for where this person, probably a beggar, was sitting. For there is a ramp about a foot or two from the ground running along the whole front of the building. Upon this at a certain spot you can see the dim outline of a sitting human figure. It is where the stone has remained stone and not turned to granite. Probably like most of his countrymen he was wearing white clothes. Perhaps because of that the appalling flash passed him and did not finger him. There is an iron rail round the shadow of the sitting man, and an inscription above it in English and in Japanese. I approached this dreadful object in shame and horror for it is a blot on all human beings, and did not like to look at it but found it curiously flat and unmoving. I can only say of it that like many another technical feat you do not see the point of it until it is explained to you. One could even pass it without noticing it. Yet there it is. The first, or the last human being; the only ghost in Hiroshima, sitting there, day and night, for all to see. For of the atomic explosion there is no other human sign. The bomb, which was dropped at the busiest time of the morning during the shopping hour, killed, outright, seventy-eight thousand men, women and children, and maimed nearly forty thousand more, while another fourteen thousand were never accounted for and given, therefore, laconically, as missing. Total, a hundred and twenty-nine thousand, five hundred and fifty-eight. This was rather more than a third of the population in the city just before the bomb exploded. It was the shopping hour, too, the morning we were in Hiroshima, where there are now some three hundred thousand inhabitants again, and of course there is nothing to see but modern buildings. It is a city one leaves at the earliest opportunity and never wants to see again.

So we resume our journey to Miyajima, two evenings before this in the pouring rain. It was an eerie experience driving along through dark suburbs which one presumed were all devastated areas. In fact they are not so for the destruction was only within a radius of two miles from where the bomb dropped. But we seemed to be passing endless mud flats, and I remembered that Hiroshima Bay had been famous for oysters (*kaki*), and wondered what the effect had been upon their spawning beds. But, at last, after half an hour of this, we reached the ferry station, and had the curious experience of running through the deluging rain behind a pocket-Hercules of a porter who was carrying all our luggage, running, moreover, down a long open corridor that had rails and pillars of scarlet lacquer. This was the more exciting because we knew it was the last ferry that day. However we caught it, slipping and slithering on the wet planks just as it cast off, and found it was a large and nearly empty ferry boat, obviously meant to accommodate great hoards of pilgrims. The journey takes about ten minutes or a quarter of an hour; and on arrival the same mini-Hercules who apparently belonged to the hotel, bundled us with our luggage on top of us into the jeep, and we splashed down a long narrow street of shops to the hotel. Then, we had a long walk in a perfect downpour, passing various small buildings, and arriving at last at the furthest one of all, a little self-contained pavilion that was all our own.

A detached dwelling consisting of one largish square room with a glass-enclosed verandah running round three sides of it, and 'usual offices' to quote the house agent's phraseology. That is to say, a little entrance hall with a step where you took off your shoes and put on your slippers, a larder, various cupboards, a wash-basin in a little separate compartment, and beyond that a rather curious lavatory. So, in fact, it had everything. You could stay there for weeks on end with no need to come out of it. The inner walls of the room were all sliding partitions with paper panes. On the verandah there were two metal chairs and a table and, those apart, there was no furniture at all excepting a low table and a pile or two of cushions put upon the floor. Soon there came a knocking at the outside door, one of the partitions was drawn open, and a pair of even unusually small *neisans* brought in our dinner; the usual two soups with exquisite fern arrangements, *tai* and prawns and lobster tails, rice in quantity, and good melons. But the hour was late, getting on for ten o'clock, and dinner was soon over.

The cupboards were then opened, and pillows and mattresses taken out and spread in the middle of the floor. Thereafter, with much bowing and putting of both hands to the ground we were left alone for the night.

We were in the middle of a wood with loud rushing of water as of a waterfall in spate, just under the windows, which made sleep difficult. But, in any case, why not stay awake, and even keep oneself awake, when we were so soon to leave Japan? I had enjoyed it more than any other experience except first going to Venice, and years after that when I first went to Spain. One begins to think one must lose the capacity for such enjoyment, and the feeling immediately following upon that, is will one ever enjoy oneself so much again? How I wished I could go on with this journey; only a hundred and twenty miles to Shimonoseki which is at the southern end of the mainland of Japan. There, we would be some seven hundred miles from Tokyo: and now an underwater tunnel leads from Shimonoseki to the southern island of Kyushu. How much I wanted to go to Kyushu which has Nagasaki on it; an island where are no great temples or works of art but where the climate is sub-tropical, and surely there must be villages as beautiful as Uji, rivers as lovely as at Uji and Gifu!

One of the first towns we come to would be Fukuoka with a population, a little horrifying in the aggregate, of some four hundred thousand souls. A huge manufacturing town, but at least it makes the *Hakata-ningyô*, pottery dolls which have generations of tradition behind them though they in no way equal the dolls of Kyoto, and it has fêtes with processions in fancy dress and *geishas* in theatrical make-up. Nagasaki lies only four hours further on by train; but Nagasaki was devastated by the second atom bomb, and it is only that one would have wished to see it at the time of its great festival in October. Even now booths for jugglers and strolling players are put up in the streets; and old accounts tell of 'great platforms erected in different parts of the town on which actors and singers of renown go through all manner of performances'. Another Dutch writer of the early eighteenth century describes 'the banners and embroidered ornaments, covered with skilful needlework representing some renowned man or celebrated woman, a hill covered with snow,[1] the instruments of various trades,

[1] This and the two following phrases, read like the subjects of as many *Surimono* prints by Hokusai, woodcuts sprinkled with gold and silver leaf and dusted with mica.

or scenes from ancient Japanese history. Next follow musicians playing
upon drums, cymbals, and flutes, strangely attired, and accompanied by
a number of servants. Then appears a long train of children. . . . This
part of the show is most admirable; clad and armed like the warriors of
former times the leaders march gravely along, followed by the repres-
entatives of the Imperial Court, male and female, displaying the greatest
pomp and luxury, and surpassing every conception of dainty beauty.
Each of these trains is accompanied by a number of palanquins, which
are intended for any of the children who may become fatigued. After
these come companies of actors; every now and then high benches of
equal size are ranged along the road, and on these the actors perform
with great spirit and emphatic gesticulations . . . accompanied by the
music of flutes and *samisens*.' The trains of children and of actors are
beautiful to read of and think about; and, as well, there are rowing
races of 'men from the waterfront villages', and kite-flying festivals
where the contestants, 'young and old', try to bring down each other's
kites by crossing their kite-strings which are stuck all over with ground
glass.

It is to be feared that the temples of Nagasaki with the great old
camphor trees growing in their courts must have perished in the man-
made typhoon. And with it much else will have gone for ever, Nagasaki
being the town in all Japan that was most influenced by China. Not only
that, but there is the long story of its association with the Portuguese
missionaries and mariners, and the *Kasuteira* (sponge cake) made and sold
in Nagasaki is said to be a relic of that. Then there is the island of
Deshima in Nagasaki harbour, an islet only six hundred feet long by
two hundred and forty feet broad, on which about fifteen to twenty
Dutchmen of the Dutch East India Company were confined in order
to trade with Japan, an arrangement which persisted for over two
centuries from 1641 to 1858. All objects of lacquer or porcelain, even
the little eggshell saucers in the cupboard on the stairs in my old home
here, must have come through Dejima, across the stone bridge via that
little island. Lastly, Nagasaki had a large Russian colony. I have wondered if like Biarritz and San Remo and Monte Carlo it had a Russian
church with onion domes. The Russian Asiatic fleet went there until
1905, the officers' wives wintered there, and Russian signboards hung
above the shops.

Perhaps above the town, where the villages go up on terraces into the hills, there are still 'tiny houses where lotuses bloom riotously in the yards', where there are pomegranates growing on the hill slopes, and 'the deep scarlet leaves of vegetable-wax trees'. And in imagination, forgetting the hideous persecution of the Japanese Christians, hundreds of them crucified and tortured to death in other ways, we will continue our journey through this southern island of Kyushu with its traditions of porcelain-making, Arita, Imari, Kakiemon, Satsuma, and other kilns under Chinese or Korean inspiration. To Hakata, a town famous for its sashes (*obi*), and for silk fabrics 'with a pattern imitating the shimmer of frost-crystals'; to Kumamoto, a town of three hundred thousand, with the ruins of a huge castle and the Hommyô-ji temple with its flight of stone steps and cherry trees. A journey in imagination that must finish at Kagoshima for the reason that one can go no further. It is at the southern end of Kyushu. There we would be nine hundred and fifty miles from Tokyo, on a landlocked bay with an active volcano rising from an island in the middle of it. In a semi-tropical climate where flourish every kind of orange, citrus and loquat tree. In this town with its Nishi Honganji temple, 'marked by all the splendour and luxury of temples of this sect'; or has that gone, too, gone for ever from the scene? Where the fruit trees blossom in October, *wo die zitronen blüh'n* . . . as in Mignon's song, but hearing now the little tune upon the *glockenspiel*, altered in meaning, as can happen in music, and become wholly and entirely of Japan, where the hilltops are dense with huge and graceful ferns, and at certain seasons the vegetable-wax trees are full of young women who gather the berries and place them carefully in baskets hanging from adjacent limbs, where *sake* cups of eggshell porcelain are put into our hands by kneeling maidens in golden *obis* with mimosa skins; where the waters of the bay are lapislazuli and the swallow-tail butterflies upon the water are but distant sails; where the Satsuma horses, 'a large proportion of which are milk-white'[1] . . . and so on, and so on, until the *Traümerei* has ended and the music dies.

It is only in Japan that I have woken in a wood by a waterfall, and on hearing voices looked to see groups of pilgrims and school children upon

[1] An American officer I met in Washington in 1952 had been employed during the Occupation in listing and preserving what was unique and rare in Japan. He told me of the hairless horses or ponies found on an island off Kyushu, and bred for many centuries by a *daimyô* family. I tried to verify this story, but could hear no more of this parallel to the hairless dogs (*tepeizcuintle*) of the Aztecs, now almost extinct, and only found in remote villages in Mexico, mainly in the state of Guerrero.

the forest paths. This was well and truly Miyajima, the sacred island, with a still more musical name which is Itsukushima. The sun was shining after last night's rain, and the only inconvenience the long trudge in *kimono* and slippers, many sizes too small, to the bath-house. On the way we met a long file of school children with their flag leader, and all at sight of us dissolved in helpless laughter. It may have been the high point of their holiday, and like the episode in the silk factory it was extremely funny. The return ordeal accomplished in safety we set out to see the island.

In a moment or two we were among the hundreds of souvenir shops which, sadly, have nothing particularly nice for sale. Or perhaps we were sated with souvenir shops though, as ever, the packaging of the sweets was a delight to the eyes, if not the taste. But we continued round the side of the bay in order to get a view of the shrine before we entered it, and in this way found ourselves at the stable of the sacred horse, a beautiful, if old animal, of Palomino sort, with its head out of its loose box, waiting to be fed. For a few *yen* you buy a saucerful of maize from a woman attendant, and give it to eat: but in this short interval the animal had changed its mind and gone into its paddock which was a little yard at the back. On talking to the hotel manager about the sacred horse, later in the day, I noticed some signs of reluctance to discuss it, which is in fact an absurd position to take up with an Englishman. I was not able to discover its significance in the Shintô faith.

It was high tide and the painted galleries of the shrine were therefore standing in water. We walked along the shore till we were level with the huge vermilion-painted *torii* which stand in the water about a couple of hundred yards out into the bay. From there we could look back at the shrine and its galleries standing in the sea and the high wooded island rising behind it, a beautiful sight, and one worth coming this long way to see. But the temple, itself, is more galleries than shrine. The galleries are painted vermilion, are endless and built for the pleasure of walking over the water, a sensation which of course is diminished at low tide. A service was in progress in the prayer hall with much clapping of hands to invoke the deities. More interesting were the sacred virgins in white surplices and scarlet divided skirts, selling postcards, or otherwise engaged. And stacked along the galleries were huge straw-covered bales of *sake*, brought here to be blessed as first of the year's vintage from the rice fields; bales which had the most fascinating bold designs painted upon them, presumably as trade marks; peonies, and dragons and bamboos, in fact, a perfect repertory of design. Of the treasures of the shrine, early painted scrolls, fans, lacquer chests, suits of armour, four *Oyoroi* (great harnesses), swords, masks for *Noh* plays, we saw no sign. But, best of all, in a small room built out over the water we could hear the musicians practising the *Gagaku* music, and practising it, too, with conscientious care.

The rest of the day we spent on the island, wandering in the temple, and looking in the shops. On a hill behind the shrine there is a vermilion-painted five-storey pagoda, beautifully placed, and more than once we walked to it up the hill and down again. As we got to know the temple better, going in and out of it several times a day, at high tide and at low tide, until,—can I say this?—it began a little to remind me of Brighton Pier and pierrots on the sands, but magically removed into semi-tropical seas; it was even while thinking of this that treading the planks for it seemed the hundredth time, and looking at the distant shore of the mainland put into perspective by the vermilion *torii* standing in the water, it was then I remembered seeing photographs of masked dancers posing on these boards against the peacock sea. And at that moment we found the dancing stage, which is a square platform with a wooden railing raised on the planks, on that particular platform of them all which is built furthest out into the water. In the open air with no roof over it, but with little roofed pavilions for the musicians to either side; and the huge *torii* in the water immediately in front of it, so that the backdrop is the water and the distant shore.

This was the stage for the *Bugaku* dancing; and if it be a theatre at all, it is one of the beautiful open air theatres of the world. We looked again at postcards and photographs on sale at the sacred virgin's stall. There seemed to be a large repertory of dances using the old masks and costumes which are among the temple treasures; one dancer in a peaked cap wearing a hideous mask of an old woman, the fringed apron of the *Bugaku* dancer, and an enormous train; another which must be a Dance of the Right, meaning it is of ancient Korean origin for the dancer is dressed in green; and a dance performed by four warriors in great helmets with quivers on their shoulders, brandishing drawn swords. Apart from the Imperial Palace at Tokyo, the *Gagaku* music and *Bugaku* dancing are described, officially, as being preserved 'in a few Shintô shrines and Buddhist temples'. Where are these few shrines and temples? Perhaps *Bugaku* is to be seen at the Shintô shrine of Izumo over on the other coast of Japan? The ordinary *Kagura* dances are also performed in the shrine at Miyajima but we did not see the dancing of the sacred virgins.

On one of our walks down to the shore we saw the dragon boat coming in to the landing stage full of pilgrims. There are two of these boats that make the trip round the island. Their front is the head of the dragon, and their stern the tail; and they are prettily painted throughout their length, and look charming as they come round a corner of the island and past those vermilion galleries standing in the water. But, already, we had the sensation of leaving, of departing. It caused one to walk uneasily among all the streets of souvenir stalls. There was nothing more to do. We were waiting to go away. It was late afternoon. The school children had come back by ferry from the mainland; and now as the schoolgirls still in their neat sailor suits were helping their parents in the souvenir stalls we could see that what we had been told was true and that Japanese schoolgirls are now taller than their mothers. This is the result of a better diet, and of the simple physical exercises they do at school, and if it continues the whole physique of the nation will alter in a generation. With that a great deal of their national character must change, too, and it will no longer be the traditional Japan.

It was difficult indeed on that last evening not to feel nostalgic. There is even a particular quality of evening sunlight that enhances this. And now a new tune, another little air that was somehow familiar, seemed to be heard everywhere, as if it were coming out of the houses, as though it were playing itself in the souvenir stalls, and we could not remember where we had heard it. We stopped to look at some children, particularly a dear little boy not more than two years old with his grandparents, and there the tune was again. When it stopped I tried to remember it, not knowing a note of music, and making all sorts of little mental pigeon-holes to put it in. So that I could take it out when I wanted to, and sing it to myself, but it eluded me. I could not quite get it, and always failed, and then forgot it altogether. Yet it embodied or personified a great deal that could be said no other way.

At last it grew dark, and a little cold, and we went back to the hotel. The hotel manager came to talk to us in our one-roomed house, and I asked him to tell us about the dropping of the atom bomb at Hiroshima.

17th century Kimono: design of flowers and birds of the four seasons

17th century Kimono: design of irises over a heptagonal pattern

17th century Kimono: design of arrows, paulownia crests and leaves

17th century Kimono: design of scene of spring flowers and *Bugaku* dance curtains

Modern Japanese matchbox designs

He had been here on the island which must be some ten to twelve miles from Hiroshima across the bay. They had been bombed often, and in spite of rumours that something worse than usual was coming no one was particularly disturbed for it could fall anywhere. There was no particular consternation therefore when a bomb was dropped and there was a great explosion. Perhaps the wind was carrying the sound, but the reverberation continued, rolling like thunder. Then rose the terrifying mushroom cloud. But what frightened them most was the darkness that fell about twenty minutes later, and a black and appalling rain. Was it dark for the rest of the day? He could not remember distinctly, for by that time people were trying to get in to Hiroshima to find out what had become of their friends and relations. None of those who got into the town in the first few hours survived. But no one was hurt on Miyajima, and for the first time in history ninety thousand human beings men, women and children, were dead in a few seconds from a single movement of a human hand.

We had dinner in our little house in the wood, and soon after that shut the sliding partitions, and there being nothing else to do settled down to try to sleep. We had asked the manager to telephone to the shrine—one of the charms of Japan is that the most improbable places and persons are on the telephone—and ask the 'lord-abbot' to arrange for a performance of *Bugaku* at ten o'clock tomorrow morning. There was that to look forward to, and think of. And what else? We were to catch the boat for the mainland immediately it was over, at half-past ten. A taxi would be waiting, which was to take us to the train at Hiroshima. But, first, we were to go to see the *Kintai-bashi* or Bridge of the Brocade Sash, and this meant going a little further, say, twelve or thirteen miles further south. And, in the end, I fell asleep thinking of the bridge, and wondering if it would be as beautiful as I thought that it could be. Just at the moment of going to sleep I tried to remember that little tune, and heard it perfectly.

In the morning we were up early, and seeing our luggage off on a handcart drawn by the herculean porter, we set off for the shrine. A Mediterranean morning of sunlight and blue sea with little wavelets gently rocking the moored boats and lapping at the piles. For by now we were treading the wooden platforms of the shrine. The wooded island was behind us, and in a few moments would be gone as completely as yesterday. A day or two more and the maple trees would turn
v

to flame, up in the wood all round the little house where we had stayed. We crossed the hump-backed bridge, lacquered vermilion like the rest of the shrine, and already could hear the music. And coming past the prayer hall and the ticket stall we found a couple of empty benches put in position, and the performance waiting to begin. There were three musicians in the little left-hand pavilion, and the instruments were a huge drum and two kinds of flutes. Forthwith the performance started, but in fact the hotel manager had asked for it to be as punctual as possible in order that we should not miss the ferry.

The long drawn whine of *Gagaku* and the beating of the loud drum began, to which the priest-dancer came forward walking with that curious cat-like tread all along the covered passage coming up the steps into the sunlight, until he stood on the raised stage against the vermilion *torii* and the sea and sky. There he stood with arms extended, looking bigger than lifesize, in red, persimmon—red robe, gold stick in his right hand, and wearing a golden cat or tiger mask with some kind of a bird or phoenix on its crown, a fifteenth-century mask that we had seen before in the Imperial Dancing Hall at Tokyo. It was our old friend 'Ranryôô, the Prince of Lan-ling', a character in eighth-century China who wore a terrifying mask in order to put fear into his enemies. It was performed exactly as we had seen it done in Tokyo. Not only that, but with little, if any difference at all, it was as in Sôtatsu's pair of screens of *Bugaku* in my favourite monastery of Sambôin, at Kyoto. In the left-hand panel there, the Prince of Lan-ling dances in cat mask, gold stick in hand, with swirling and sweeping of his persimmon train. Have the dances then been collated as you collate old books, comparing them as done in Tokyo and at Miyajima? The Abbot's Bromley hobby-horse dance, or the Flamborough Head Sword dance, are given with presumed accuracy if performed but once a year. There is no reason why the same old dance should not be performed perfectly in two different places. So probably the *Bugaku* dances are little tampered with and genuine. Now, of course, we wanted to see the whole repertory and hear the full orchestra. But too late. Even as we looked at the priest-dancer standing on the boards, just as in a theatre, but in exaggerated height against the sky and sea, the dance ended and with that curious cat-like tread he was gone out of the sunlight into the shadow to the beating of the drum.

A few minutes later we were in the ferry and making for the shore.

The taxi was waiting and we took the road to the left running along the coast. We passed the end of Miyajima island, and other isles that were hidden behind it came into view. There is a childish interest that persists in one as to the furthest in any direction one has been away from home, and never in all my life have I been so far away. I felt I might never get back, but wanted to go on. Presently the road left the coast and turned inland passing a small town where it was the opening day of a new shop, and outside it propped up on poles were numbers of the huge bouquets, as big as cartwheels, made of paper flowers. This was just where we turned left, and in another mile or two we had reached Iwakuni, where is the *Kintai-bashi* or *Bridge of the Brocade Sash*. We had seen pictures of it, and knowing now most of the temples and gardens, had thought it must be one of the beautiful things of Japan. We had come all the way to Miyajima largely in order to see it.

The town consists of one long street, and with impatience it is quite a long time before you reach the river. But here, at last, it is. The river; and the extraordinary and fantastic bridge across it. Built on stone piers and with five huge wooden spans or arches. The piers are of almost cyclopean stonework, and the wooden spans are all of different sizes. It is called the *Abacus Bridge* because it is like an abacus board, or the *Bridge of the Brocade* or *Damask Girdle*; and Nishiki which is the name of the river is, also, that 'of a fine leather with white figures on a purple ground, used formerly by Court Nobles' (Terry's *Japan*). This explains why it is known as the *Bridge of the Brocade Sash*. It is extraordinary to see the underneath of the wooden arches, carpenters' work all put together without metal joints or nails. This fantastic structure, more 'Japanese-looking' than anything it is possible to imagine, was built by the local *daimyô* in 1673. One of its arches was always rebuilt every five years, so that the bridge is wholly renewed four times in every hundred years. It is in fact almost entirely new at this time having been rebuilt after a disastrous flood. But the only effect of the rebuilding is that we see the *Kintai-bashi* precisely as it was when new.

The river, where fishing with cormorants is practised as at Uji and at Gifu, flows down swiftly between wooded hills, and the importance of the bridge is that it is on the main road from the rest of Japan to the southern isle of Kyushu. That must be why so bizarre a structure was built, out of local importance; and why the bed of the river between the piers has been laid with pebbles so that the water flows over them as over a pavement. In pictures of it there is often a bough of cherry blossom in the foreground, and pleasure boats upon the river, for the *Kintai-bashi* is famed from end to end of Japan.

We had to cross the bridge, of course, and began to climb its steps or ridges, for the woodwork becomes so slippery when it rains that the crossplanks are put down like little bars of steps. It is slow work to cross the five arches of the *Kintai-bashi*. No sooner have you climbed to the top of one of them than you have to go down the barred incline and begin to climb another. It gives one the impression of a series of fantastic leaps and bounds, and out in mid-stream, or on perhaps the third arch you wonder what it means and where it is leading. We had seen enough temples and gardens, and could only think of Gifu, the town of lanterns and cormorant fishing, and Uji, the village of green tea. There must be more enchantments on the other bank, at the far side of the *Bridge of the Brocade Sash*. But, also, it was like crossing a watershed, like climbing to the climacteric, and having enjoyed Japan too much, one could perhaps never enjoy anything so much again. It was getting late. But only for oneself, and there would not be enough time upon the other side. On about the third arch of the bridge there was music, not nearby, but music in the air. And we hurried over the last pair of arches to the far side where was a long line of shops and stalls, and walked a little way in order to look back at the *Kintai-bashi* from this other side. But it was like setting foot in a land where one could go no further; and like those sad and fleeting illusions of one's youth come back again. Time was passing. At which moment stopping at one of the stalls I took up a little musical-box, and held it to my ear. It played that little air the *Gion-Kouta* which I had been trying to remember, just as the same tune sounded from the radio in the next house.

The little tinkling notes with all of Japan in them sounded in the air around, taking one to the pleasure quarter of Kyoto. Again, and once again it played, aloud, and now secretly and for ourselves alone. We must go back over the *Kintai-bashi*, and the first and the last of Japan was the *Bridge of the Brocade Sash*.

INDEX

NB For separate temples and gardens in towns, see under towns in question